Sheridan®

CJK GROUP

450 Fame Avenue
Hanover, PA 17331
United States
717-632-3535

Ship To:
BARNES
UCONN
2075 HILL
STORRS
UNITED S

AF633458

Order Date		Reference Number
01/30/2025		05523309-0003

Quantity	ISBN	Title/Publisher
1		Propaganda and International Criminal Law (From Cognition to (), Ed., CPI Antony Rowe Ltd, CPI Group UK
9	9780415823982	Propaganda, war crimes and International Law (), Ed., CPI Antony Rowe Ltd, CPI Group UK

Total Quantity: 10

*** Packing List **

01/31/2025

&NOBLE BOOKSTORE #8207
OOKSTORE
IDE RD
T 06269
TATES

	Ship Method	Provider Order Number
	UPS Ground	1494855

	Collection Title/ISBN	Material #
iminality)		1
		2

Propaganda and International Criminal Law

This book addresses the conceptual and evidentiary issues relating to the treatment of propaganda in international criminal law.

Bringing together an interdisciplinary range of scholars, researchers and legal practitioners from Africa, Australia, Europe and the United States, the book provides an in-depth analysis of the nature, position and role of the concept of propaganda in mass atrocity crimes trials. A sequel to the earlier *Propaganda, War Crimes Trials and International Law: From Speakers' Corner to War Crimes* (Routledge, 2011), this book is the first to synthesize the knowledge, procedures and methods of international criminal law with the social cognitive sciences. Including a comprehensive overview of the most relevant case law, jurisprudence and scientific studies, the book also offers a series of practical insights and strategies for both academics and legal professionals.

An invaluable resource for those working in the area of international criminal law, this book will also be of interest to academics, practitioners and students with relevant interests in legal theory, politics, linguistics and psychology.

Predrag Dojčinović worked for the Office of the Prosecutor (OTP) at the International Criminal Tribunal for the Former Yugoslavia (ICTY) from 1998 to 2017. He was the Gladstein Visiting Professor of Human Rights at the University of Connecticut in 2014 and is currently a research affiliate and adjunct professor at the Human Rights Institute at the University of Connecticut.

Propaganda and International Criminal Law

From Cognition to Criminality

Edited by
Predrag Dojčinović

Routledge
Taylor & Francis Group
a GlassHouse book

First published 2020
by Routledge
2 Park Square, Milton Park, Abingdon, Oxon OX14 4RN

and by Routledge
52 Vanderbilt Avenue, New York, NY 10017

A Glasshouse book

Routledge is an imprint of the Taylor & Francis Group, an Informa business

First issued in paperback 2021

British Library Cataloguing-in-Publication Data
A catalogue record for this book is available from the British Library

Library of Congress Cataloging-in-Publication Data
Names: Dojčinović, Predrag, editor.
Title: Propaganda and international criminal law : from cognition to criminality / Edited by Predrag Dojčinović.
Description: New York: Routledge, 2020. | Includes bibliographical references and index.
Identifiers: LCCN 2019029758 (print) | LCCN 2019029759 (ebook) | ISBN 9781138335639 (hardback) | ISBN 9780429443695 (ebook)
Subjects: LCSH: International criminal law. | Propaganda. | Accomplices (International law) | War crime trials. | Sociological jurisprudence.
Classification: LCC KZ7094.P76 2020 (print) | LCC KZ7094 (ebook) | DDC 345—dc23
LC record available at https://lccn.loc.gov/2019029758
LC ebook record available at https://lccn.loc.gov/2019029759

ISBN: 978-1-138-33563-9 (hbk)
ISBN: 978-1-03-208778-8 (pbk)
ISBN: 978-0-429-44369-5 (ebk)

Typeset in Galliard
by codeMantra

To Daniël,
My Word

Contents

Figures

Tables

Contributors

Dr. Saskia Baas worked as an assistant professor at the University of Amsterdam and as an affiliated researcher with the NIOD Institute for Holocaust and Genocide Studies. She is the author of *From Civilians to Soldiers and From Soldiers to Civilians: Mobilization and Demobilization in Sudan* (2012). She has conducted extensive research on the Syrian conflict and leads a research program on forced displacement and refugee rights in Middle East.

Mohamed Elewa Badar is the Chair in Comparative and International Criminal Law at Northumbria Law School, Northumbria University. He has published on issues related to comparative criminal law and Islamic law. His work has been cited and quoted by international and national criminal courts and tribunals. He served as Senior Prosecutor and Judge in Egypt from 1997 to 2006.

Rogier Bartels is a legal officer in Chambers (Trial Division) of the ICC. He has previously worked for the Dutch National Prosecutor's Office in Chambers of the ICTY, and as a humanitarian law adviser at the Netherlands Red Cross and the Netherlands Defence Academy. Bartels is affiliated with the University of Amsterdam and the Vrije Universiteit Amsterdam.

Predrag Dojčinović worked for the Office of the Prosecutor at the ICTY from 1998 to 2017. He has authored numerous articles and has edited several volumes on the social, political and legal aspects of the 1991–99 series of armed conflicts in the former Yugoslavia, including *Propaganda, War Crimes Trials and International Law: From Speakers' Corner to War Crimes* (2012). He has lectured widely in Europe and the United States. Dojčinović was the Gladstein Visiting Professor of Human Rights at the University of Connecticut in 2014 and is currently a research affiliate and adjunct professor at the Human Rights Institute at the University of Connecticut.

Robert J. Donia is an adjunct lecturer in history at the University of Michigan and a member of the Academy of Sciences and Arts of Bosnia and Herzegovina. As an historical expert, he testified during seventeen trials at the ICTY.

He is the author of *Sarajevo: A Biography* (2006) and *Radovan Karadžić: Architect of the Bosnian Genocide* (2015).

Dr. Polona Florijančič is a research associate at Northumbria Law School. She taught Islamic law, human rights and criminal law, among other modules, at Brunel Law School and has conducted field research, most recently for the EUROMED justice project on criminal cooperation and counterterrorism in the MENA region.

Gregory S. Gordon is a professor of law at the Chinese University of Hong Kong (formerly Associate Dean, External Affairs). Having earned undergraduate and law degrees from University of California, Berkeley, he worked on the ICTR's landmark "Media" cases and then as a prosecutor with the US Department of Justice. He is the author of *Atrocity Speech Law: Foundation, Fragmentation, Fruition* (2017).

Celia Guillard is a social neuroscientist and graduate of the University of Connecticut and University College London. She was awarded the Goldstone Fellowship to join the Office of the Prosecutor at the ICTY during the trial of Ratko Mladić. Her research examines the psychology of political violence.

Rebecca J. Hamilton is an associate professor of law at American University, Washington College of Law. She worked previously at the ICC. A former journalist, she is the author of *Fighting for Darfur: Public Action and the Struggle to Stop Genocide* (2011).

Lasana T. Harris is an associate professor in experimental psychology at University College London. Prior to this, Harris was an assistant professor at Duke University and Leiden University. He is the author of *Invisible Mind: Flexible Social Cognition and Dehumanization* (2017). His research explores the social neuroscience of person perception.

Jordan Kiper is a postdoctoral fellow in the Department of Anthropology at UCLA. With expertise in cognitive science, his research centers on cooperation and conflict, with particular focus on debates in human rights and political and legal anthropology. He has conducted experimental research, long-term fieldwork in the Balkans and extensive research on Vojislav Šešelj.

Molly K. Land is a professor of law and human rights at the University of Connecticut School of Law and Associate Director of the UConn's Human Rights Institute. Her most recent book is *New Technologies for Human Rights Law and Practice* (2018), coedited with Jay D. Aronson.

Clare Lawson is the Legal Advisory Team Leader at the Kosovo Specialist Prosecutor's Office. Previously she worked as a legal officer in Chambers (Trial Division) at the ICC, in the Office of the Prosecutor at the ICTY, as a human rights adviser to the Irish Government, and in private practice with a leading Irish law firm.

Évariste Ntakirutimana is a professor of sociolinguistics at the University of Rwanda. His publications include *Le Rwanda et la politique du saumon: un retour à la source pour un développement durable intégré* (2011) and *Kinship Terminologies: Crossed Perspectives, Kinyarwanda, French, English, Swahili* (2013). From 2002 to 2015, Ntakirutimana worked as an expert in Discourse Analysis, Lexicology, Terminology and Semantics at the ICTR.

Dr. Wibke K. Timmermann is a criminal lawyer at Legal Aid Western Australia in Perth, Australia. She has previously worked as a legal officer at the Prosecutor's Office of Bosnia and Herzegovina, Special Department for War Crimes, and the ICTR. She has authored various articles and book chapters, including the book *Incitement in International Law* (2015).

Marie-Claire Uwamariya is the vice-mayor of social affairs in Musanze District, Northern Province, Rwanda. She holds a master's degree in Genocide Studies and Prevention from the University of Rwanda. In 2015, she presented her dissertation titled *Song as Incitement to the Genocide Perpetrated Against the Tutsi: The Case Study of Simon Bikindi.*

Richard Ashby Wilson is the Gladstein Distinguished Chair of Human Rights and Professor of Law and Anthropology at the University of Connecticut. He is the author or editor of 11 books on human rights, transitional justice and international criminal law, and his latest book is *Incitement on Trial: Prosecuting International Speech Crimes* (2017).

Acknowledgments

I would like to express my most profound gratitude to a number of people and academic institutions who have directly or indirectly contributed to the evolution of the ideas encapsulated in this book. I remain indebted to Nanci Adler, Camille Bibles, Robert J. Donia, Dermot Groome, Celia Guillard, Nadan Hadžić, Barbora Hola, Rachel Jackson, Ozren Jungic, Emily Kaufman, Arnaud Kurze, Molly Land, Kathryn Libal, Glenn Mitoma, Christian Axboe Nielsen, Aneta Pavlenko, Vladimir Petrović, Dan Saxon, Dragana Spencer, Jonathan Sykes, Arthur Traldi, Iva Vukušić, Bojana Vuleta, Richard A. Wilson and many other of my fellow companions in pursuit of international criminal justice.

Over the past several years, I had a unique opportunity to give a series of lectures, seminars and collaborate on special projects dealing with some of the themes included in this book. I have benefited greatly from the insights offered to me on these occasions by the scholars and students of the Human Rights Institute, Law School and Thomas J. Dodd Research Center at the University of Connecticut, Princeton Institute for International and Regional Studies at Princeton University, the School of Law at the University of Greenwich, the Faculty of Humanities at the University of Oslo, Leiden University College in The Hague, the Department of Justice Studies at Montclair State University, the *NIOD* Institute for War, Holocaust and Genocide Studies, the Department of Criminal Law and Criminology at the VU University of Amsterdam and the School of Culture and Society at Aarhus University.

But most of all, and before all, the emotional omnipresence of my family has provided warm inspiration reaching way beyond the realms of intellectual significance. In this constellation, again, my two guardian angels, Daniël and Janneke, who have watched over me day and night through the entire journey, will always be my brightest stars.

Abbreviations

AC	Appeals Chamber
AI	Artificial intelligence
AP I	Additional Protocol I (International Humanitarian Law)
AP II	Additional Protocol II (International Humanitarian Law)
APROSOMA	Association for Social Promotion of the Masses
ARBiH	Army of the Republic of Bosnia and Herzegovina (Armija Republike Bosne i Hercegovine)
ARK	Autonomous Region of Krajina
BCS	Bosnian-Croatian-Serbian
BiH	Bosnia and Herzegovina
BTA	Bar table motion
CCL	Control Council Law
CDR	Coalition pour la Défense de la République (Coalition for the Defense of the Republic)
CERD	International Convention on the Elimination of All Forms of Racial Discrimination
CIA	Central Intelligence Agency
ECCC	Extraordinary Chambers in the Courts of Cambodia
ECHR	European Court of Human Rights
FDLR	Forces Démocratiques pour la Liberation du Rwanda (The Democratic Forces for the Liberation of Rwanda)
fMRI	Functional magnetic resonance imagining
FRY	Federal Republic of Yugoslavia
HDZ	Croatian Democratic Union (Hrvatska demokratska zajednica)
IAT	Implicit association test
ICC	International Criminal Court
ICL	International Criminal Law
ICCPR	International Covenant on Civil and Political Rights
ICRC	International Committee of the Red Cross

ICTR	International Criminal Tribunal for Rwanda
ICTY	International Criminal Tribunal for the Former Yugoslavia
IFC	Inferior frontal cortex
IHL	International Humanitarian Law
IMT	International Military Tribunal
IRMCT	International Residual Mechanism for Criminal Tribunals
ISIS/ISIL/IS/Da'esh	Islamic State
JCE	joint criminal enterprise
JNA	Yugoslav People's Army
KOKV	Karlobag-Ogulin-Karlovac-Virovitica
LRT	Leadership Research Team
LTP	long-term-potentiation
MDR	Mouvement Démocratique Républicain (Democratic Republican Movement)
MICT	Mechanism for International Criminal Tribunals
mPFC	Medial prefrontal cortex
MRND	Mouvement Révolutionnaire National pour le Développement (National Revolutionary Movement for Development)
NCTA	No case to answer
NMT	Nuremberg Military Tribunal
ODM`	Orange Democratic Movement
OTP	Office of the Prosecutor
PNU	Party of National Unity
POW	Prisoner of war
PTSD	Post-traumatic stress disorder
RDC	République Démocratique du Congo (The Democratic Republic of the Congo)
RPF	Rwandan Patriotic Front, also 'RPF-Inkotanyi'
RTLM	Radio-Télévision Libre des Milles Collines
RuSHA	Rasse und Siedlungshauptampt (SS Race and Resettlement Main Office)
SANA	Syrian Arab News Agency
SCSL	Special Court for Sierra Leone
SDA	Party of Democratic Action (Stranka demokratske akcije)
SDG	Serbian Volunteer Guard
SDS	Serbian Democratic Party
SFRY	Socialist Federal Republic of Yugoslavia
SIO	Syrian Information Organization
SRS	Serbian Radical Party
STE	Syrian Telecommunications Establishment

TC	Trial Chamber
UDHR	Universal Declaration of Human Rights
UN	United Nations
UNDOC/TBP	United Nations Office on Drugs and Crime's Terrorism Prevention Branch
UNHRC	United Nations Human Rights Council
UNITAD	United Nations Investigative Team to Promote Accountability for Crimes Committed by Da'esh/ISIL
VRS	Army of Republika Srpska (Bosnian Serb Army)
WIT	Weapons identification task

Table of cases

Canada

Mugesera v. Canada (Minister of Citizenship and Immigration), [2005] 2 S.C.R. 100, 2005 SCC 40.

European Court of Human Rights

Arslan v. Turkey, Application No. 23462/94, 8 July 1999.
Incal v. Turkey, Application No. 22678/93, 9 June 1998.
Jersild Against Denmark, Application No. 15890/89, 23 September 1994.
Sürek and Özdemir v. Turkey, Applications Nos. 23927/94 and 24277/94, 8 July 1999.
Zana v. Turkey, Application No. 18954/91, 25 November 1997.

International Criminal Court

The Prosecutor v. Charles Blé Goudé, Case No. ICC-02/11-02/11.
The Prosecutor v. Germain Katanga, Case No. ICC-01/04-01/07.
The Prosecutor v. Thomas Lubanga Dyilo, Case No. ICC-01/04-01/06.
The Prosecutor v. Callixte Mbarushimana, Case No. ICC-01/04-01/10.
The Prosecutor v. Mathieu Ngudjolo Chui, Case No. ICC-01/04-02/12.
The Prosecutor v. Bosco Ntaganda, Case No. ICC-01/04-02/06.
The Prosecutor v. William Samoei Ruto and Joshua Arap Sang, Case No. ICC-01/09-01/11.

International Criminal Tribunal for the former Yugoslavia

Prosecutor v. Milan Babić, Case No. IT-03-2.
Prosecutor v. Predrag Banović, Case No. IT-02-65/1.
Prosecutor v. Vidoje Blagojević and Dragan Jokić, Case No. IT-02-60.
Prosecutor v. Tihomir Blaškić, Case No. IT-95-14.
Prosecutor v. Radoslav Brđanin, Case No. IT-99-36.

Prosecutor v. Stanislav Galić, Case No. IT-98-29.
The Prosecutor of the Tribunal Against Goran Hadžić, Case No. IT-04-75-I.
Prosecutor v. Karadžić, Case No. ICTY-IT-95-5/18.
Prosecutor v. Dario Kordić and Mario Čerkez, Case No. IT-95-14/2.
Prosecutor v. Momčilo Krajišnik, Case No. IT-00-39.
Prosecutor v. Radislav Krstić, Case No. IT-98-33.
Prosecutor v. Zoran Kupreškić, Mirjan Kupreškić, Vlatko Kupreškić, Drago Josipović, Dragan Papić, Vladimir Šantić aka "Vlado," Case No. IT-95-16.
Prosecutor v. Miroslav Kvočka, Mlađo Radić, Zoran Žigić, Dragoljub Prcać, Case No. IT-98-30/1.
The Prosecutor of the Tribunal Against Slobodan Milošević, Case No. IT-02-54.
Prosecutor v. Milan Milutinović, Nikola Šainović, Dragoljub Ojdanić, Nebojša Pavković, Vladimir Lazarević, Sreten Lukić, Case No. IT-05-87.
Prosecutor v. Ratko Mladić, Case No. IT-09-92.
Prosecutor v. Mladen Naletilić a.k.a. "Tuta" and Vinko Martinović a.k.a. "Štela," Case No. IT-98-34.
Prosecutor v. Naser Orić, Case No. IT-03-68.
Prosecutor v. Biljana Plavšić, Case No. IT-00-39.
Prosecutor v. Vujadin Popović, Ljubiša Beara, Drago Nikolić, Radivoje Miletić, Vinko Pandurević, Case No. IT-05-88.
Prosecutor v. Milomir Stakić, Case No. IT-97-24.
Prosecutor v. Vojislav Šešelj, Case No. IT-03-67.
Prosecutor v. Vojislav Šešelj, Case No. MICT-16-99.
Prosecutor v. Duško Tadić, Case No. IT-94-1.
Prosecutor v. Zdravko Tolimir, Case No. IT-05-88/2.

International Criminal Tribunal for Rwanda

The Prosecutor v. Jean-Paul Akayesu, Case No. ICTR-96-4.
The Prosecutor Versus Ignace Bagilishema, Case No. ICTR-95-1A.
The Prosecutor Against Simon Bikindi, Case No. ICTR-2001-72-I.
The Prosecutor v. Sylvestre Gacumbitsi, Case No. ICTR-2001-64.
The Prosecutor v. Juvénal Kajelijeli, Case No. ICTR-98-44.
The Prosecutor v. Jean De Dieu Kamuhanda, Case No. ICTR-99-54A.
The Prosecutor versus Clément Kayishema and Obed Ruzindana, Case No. ICTR-95-1.
The Prosecutor v. Tharcisse Muvunyi, Case No. ICTR-00-55.
The Prosecutor v. Ferdinand Nahimana, Jean-Bosco Barayagwiza, Hassan Ngeze, Case No. ICTR-99-52.
The Prosecutor v. Eliézer Niyitegeka, Case No. ICTR-96-14.
The Prosecutor v. Callixte Nzabonimana, Appeal Judgment, Case No. ICTR-98-44D.
The Prosecutor v. Georges Ruggiu, Case No. ICTR-97-32.
The Prosecutor v. Laurence Semanza, Case No. ICTR-97-20.

Israel

Ploni v. Minister of Defence, Dinim-Elyon, 1994, vol. LVI, no. 921.

Nuremberg trials

High Command Case, Judgment, XI Trials of War Criminals Before the Nuremberg Military Tribunals Under Control Council Law No. 10, 651, 1949.
Indictment of the International Military Tribunal (Count III) in 1 Trial of the Major War Criminals Before the International Military Tribunal, 1947.
Judgment of the International Military Tribunal (Göring) in 22 Trial of the Major War Criminals Before the International Military Tribunal, 1947.

UN Human Rights Committee

Robert Faurisson v. France, UN Doc. CCPR/C/58/D/550/1993.
J.R.T. and the W.G. Party v. Canada, UN Doc. CCPR/C/18/D/104/1981.
Malcolm Ross v. Canada, UN Doc. CCPR/C/70/D/736/1997.

United States of America

Brandenburg v. Ohio, 395 U.S. 444 (1969).
Elonis v. United States, Case No. 13-983 U.S. (2015).
Hess v. Indiana, 414 U.S. 105 (1973).
N.A.A.C.P. v. Claiborne Hardware Co., 485 U.S. 886 (1982).
R v. Smith [2000] 4 All ER 289 at 342-343, [2001] 1 AC 146.
Texas v. Johnson, 491 U.S. 397 (1989).
U.S. v. Lee, N.W.2d 250 (1993).
U.S. v. White, 401 U.S. 745 (2012).
Whitney v. California, Case No. 274 U.S. 357, 377 (1927).

Introduction

Predrag Dojčinović

> [...] the use of propaganda is not in itself a criminal act but [...].[1]
>
> Judge Flavia Lattanzi

Without moving into the subterranean realms of ontological obscurities and epistemological ambiguities, it can be stated with confidence that some of the most basic foundations of social reality, both mental and physical, can be found in words and phrases, symbols and meanings created by speakers as engineers of their own environments. As succinctly phrased by John Searle, "when you have a language, other social institutions will inevitably grow up out of language."[2] If recognized and defined as such, armed conflicts and their origins and offshoots are not an exception to that rule. With the pre- and post-Searlian generally accepted premise in mind that "language is constitutive of social reality,"[3] a shared reality built by and from cognitive, primarily linguistic concepts as building blocks of human cognition and action,[4] this volume addresses the relevance and impact of the basic underlying conceptual and evidentiary, intra- and extra-legal, issues implicitly present in the many manifestations of propaganda as a cognitive and legal phenomenon identified within a broader framework of international criminal law (ICL).

Propaganda between cognitive social sciences[5] and international law

The social science studies and literature on various manifestations of propaganda as an integral part of any social and psychological reality are voluminous. With the evolution of cognitive science,[6] research on propaganda has shifted into a domain of human cognition active in virtually all spheres of our lives, collective and individual. Recent empirical research strongly indicates that the seeds of false beliefs and ideas fall on the fertile grounds of our mental landscapes.[7] As neurobiologically and cognitively hardwired storytellers and myth-makers,[8] we all seem to be potential propagandists. The insights into the concept of propaganda in legal publications, both treaties and laws, including international case law and jurisprudence, have, however, lagged behind empirical studies and scientific publications. This may leave both communities with a false impression that cognitive science and law reside, or ought to reside, in two only remotely related domains.[9]

A point of convergence in propaganda studies has so far been identified in the cognitive element of *intent*, or intention.[10] As a separate area of study in the social and cognitive sciences,[11] including humanities and philosophy of law, the concept of *intent* is situated at the epicenter of all manifestations of propaganda. In most cases,[12] intent can, more often than not, be described as a cognitive, linguistically driven mental state.[13] Initially, however, as "a purely internal thing," as G.E.M. Anscombe put it, intent is a thing residing "purely in the sphere of the mind."[14] Physical manifestations of intent, such as various categories of speech acts,[15] that is, "acoustic blasts"[16] as the "minimal units of linguistic communication,"[17] are, however, generally determined by the *reasons*[18] incorporated in words as transmitters of the intent of the speaker. The role *reasons* play in the description of *intentional actions* is critical. Reasons can perhaps be described as the fuel pumps of intent and may, or may not, drive internal modes of intent toward motion and action with a specific range of conceivable and foreseeable *consequences* as the next phase in the process. As philosopher Donald Davidson succinctly phrased it, "Someone who acts with a certain intention acts for a reason; he has something in mind that he wants to promote or accomplish."[19] The key to intent as a state of mind is thus its purposeful actionability and specific consequences emerging from that process.

Numerous propaganda studies and definitions in social sciences have followed and documented a similar line of reasoning. In the mid-1960s, Jacques Ellul, a social scientist and a legal scholar, stated, "Propaganda is necessarily a declaration of one's intentions."[20] Four decades later, Garth S. Jowett and Victoria O'Donnell argued that "often, *the direction of a specific behavior* is the intent of a propaganda effort."[21] Along similar lines, Philip M. Taylor concluded that "what distinguishes propaganda from all other processes of persuasion is the question of intent."[22] Even when intent is not specifically mentioned in a definition of propaganda, the presence of intent can be identified as the driving force of virtually every description of propaganda.[23] The concept of intent, understood as a mode of intentional action initiated for a reason and with anticipated or foreseeable consequences, can thus be placed at the center of any act of propaganda as a cognitive mechanism.

Descriptions of various forms of intent as *mens rea* in legal publications, international case law and jurisprudence, however, represent a relatively diverse combination of national and international approaches to this core concept in criminal law. As Cassese observed, "depending on the legal tradition to which it belonged, each court has placed its own interpretation on the notion of intent."[24] However, apart from its key role in defining *mens rea*,[25] the international jurisprudence places different forms of intent at the center of various modes of liability and substantive crimes, such as *discriminatory intent* required for persecution as a crime against humanity,[26] *specific intent* for both crimes of persecution and genocide,[27] including a whole range of related discussions on the issues of the nature, position and role of intent in the legal doctrines such as, for example, joint criminal enterprise (JCE) and superior responsibility. All of them, treated separately or in combination, indicate,

> a cognitive fluidity of the concept that is more often than not left to the discretionary right and power of the judges to determine what the element of *intent* is and whether, when and how it can be applied in various criminal cases.[28]

All of them, however, intuitively agree that the building blocks of intent (e.g., desires, beliefs, fears, hate, pride and other forms of *intentionality*,[29] a concept which defines mental states and their direction toward both physical and abstract objects or targets), as we shall show through the analysis of selected jurisprudential records, are some of the key cognitive elements of human agency and conduct. (See Chapter 1 by Badar and Florijančič in this volume on the use of linguistically coded forms of propaganda as cognitive conditioning for the commission of the inchoate crime of direct and public incitement to commit genocide by the ISIS propagandists. See also Chapter 12 by Baas as a model of contextual expert evidence on the specific content and role of propaganda of the Syrian regime in the creation of the sectarian violence which erupted in 2011.)

Propaganda in international treaties, case law and jurisprudence

Since the International Military Tribunal (IMT) at Nuremberg in 1945–46, various forms of propaganda have formed some of the strongest underlying evidentiary currents in all international criminal trials.[30] It can be argued that, historically speaking, no inter-ethnic or inter-national armed conflict could have taken place without the systemic utilization of propaganda before, during, and sometimes after a conflict. Yet the position of propaganda in ICL has to a large extent remained underdefined. The intuitive construal of this multifaceted phenomenon, as argued elsewhere by this author,[31] seems to be taken for granted.

Drawing on customary international law, there are two legally binding international treaties that have been instrumental in introducing propaganda as a form of criminal offense: *The International Covenant on Civil and Political Rights* (ICCPR) and the *International Convention on the Elimination of All Forms of Racial Discrimination* (CERD). First, the much-cited Article 20 of ICCPR states the following: "1. Any propaganda for war shall be prohibited by law. 2. Any advocacy of national, racial or religious hatred that constitutes incitement to discrimination, hostility or violence shall be prohibited by law." Article 19 of the same treaty, however, states, "1. Everyone shall have the right to hold opinions without interference. 2. Everyone shall have the right to freedom of expression […]"[32] A degree of incoherence and tension between these two articles, and particularly the nature and position of the concept of 'propaganda for war'[33] can clearly be detected.[34] Second, following the principles embodied in the *Universal Declaration of Human Rights* (UDHR), and most particularly Article 7,[35] the CERD declares punishable "all propaganda and all organizations" promoting discriminatory theories or ideas of racial or ethnic superiority, expressed most clearly in Article 4(b), referring specifically to organized propaganda activities which promote and incite racial discrimination.[36]

Both treaties have been referenced in some of the landmark judgments issued by the International Criminal Tribunal for the Former Yugoslavia (ICTY) and International Criminal Tribunal for Rwanda (ICTR). Perhaps the best initial discussion of the binding guidelines offered by the ICCPR and CERD can be found in the ICTR's Nahimana et al. trial judgment, also known as the 'Media Case.'[37] The Trial Chamber (TC) in this case reviewed the most relevant domestic jurisprudence relating to both treaties. The general outline of the discussion, however, remains within the strains created by the seemingly conflicting principles determining the limitations of freedom of expression. In this regard, the TC offered a litany of well-known domestic cases, such as Ross v. Canada,[38] J.R.T and the W.G. Party v. Canada,[39] Robert Faurisson v. France,[40] Jersild v. Denmark,[41] Zana v. Turkey,[42] Incal v. Turkey,[43] Arslan v. Turkey[44] and Sürek and Ozdemir v. Turkey,[45] most of which were either tested by the UN's Human Rights Committee or ultimately adjudicated by the European Court of Human Rights (ECHR).[46] Given the factual and legal elements of the Nahimana et al. case, the issues discussed by the TC revolved primarily around the conceptual roles and interplay of *incitement* and *hate speech*[47] as relevant within the framework of this case. The nature, role and position of propaganda, an overarching concept in the Nahimana et al., has, however, yet again remained less than fully resolved.

The international case law and jurisprudence, as noted earlier, commonly employ the concept of propaganda to describe behavioral patterns and forms of intent in a variety of ideological, political and military, individual or collectively coordinated efforts. The ICTR judgments, for instance, use expressions such as "propaganda campaign [...] fabricating events," "anti-Tutsi propaganda," "[...] inciting genocide," "designed to [...] hate the other,"[48] or "[...] contaminated the minds," "ethnically biased propaganda,"[49] "specific intention to disseminate [...] propaganda"[50] or "propaganda instrument."[51] A similar pattern can be identified in the ICTY jurisprudence: "Propaganda offensives,"[52] "Serbian propaganda,"[53] "propaganda and misinformation"[54] and "electoral propaganda"[55] are among multiple examples. The preferred phrase used by virtually all trial and appeals chambers is 'propaganda campaign,' or only 'campaign' in its detached form, a noun which offers itself as a verb too. The word *campaign* carries an implicit reference to an organized action with a specific plan, purpose and, most importantly, *intent*. Thus, implicitly emphasizing the intentional and actionable components of the phrase, both have been repeatedly used in the cases involving aspects of propaganda. Some ICTR and ICTY examples include the Akayesu,[56]

Nahimana et al.,[57] Bikindi,[58] Brđanin,[59] Stakić[60]and Babić[61] cases. All of these examples strongly suggest that various techniques of propaganda[62] contain and carry various forms of *mens rea* in each distinct situation.

The ICTY cases of Milan Babić and Predrag Banović, on the other hand, introduced propaganda as a form of potentially mitigating evidence. In Babić, the defense argued that the appellant, a leading pro-Serbian propagandist who pleaded guilty to the crimes against humanity of persecutions on political, racial, and religious grounds, was "strongly influenced and misled by Serbian propaganda."[63] In Banović, after his guilty plea and based on the psychological expert examination of the Accused, the defense argued that "with his low education and modest intellectual capabilities, the Accused easily succumbed to the *war propaganda* which spread collective hatred and rumours about the enemy's brutality"[64] (emphasis added). The TC, however, rejected the "argument that the Accused did not have the strength of character to resist the *war propaganda*,"[65] thereby dismissing the mitigating factors in this case[66] (emphasis added). Possibly overwhelmed by the gravity of the crimes committed in both cases, the judges dismissed not only a reasonable line of defense but also an entire set of contextual cognitive factors recognized as necessary prerequisites and conditioning factors for both the collective and individual psychological mobilization and preparation of any international armed conflict, including the specific crimes committed by individuals as a result of that process. (See Chapter 9 by Guillard and Harris in this volume on the psychological impact of social context and language on dehumanization and, as a result, various types of criminal conduct.) As earlier stated, all *intentional actions*, including intentional actions within any propagandistic backdrop, have explicit *reasons* as part of its cognitive mechanism and, as a result, awareness and knowledge of foreseeable *consequences* of these actions. In both the mentioned cases, the judges acknowledged the *intentional actions* and the *consequences* of the actions but not the multifactorial scope of the *reasons* as the key link between the other two components of this tripartite cognitive mechanism.

This author would argue that the wide spectrum of approaches to propaganda, as offered by the international conventions and existing jurisprudence, falls short of determining its true nature, role and impact in international criminal trials and, most specifically, its position and status in ICL. It is more than evident that the concept of propaganda is too complex to be treated as a single type of intentional offense. A pronounced tendency within the existing case law and jurisprudence to link propaganda to a family of concepts originating from ICL testifies to this effect. The many faces of propaganda have therefore often been processed either through modes of liability, such as instigation, aiding and abetting or JCE, or through substantive crimes, such as direct and public incitement to commit genocide and persecution as a crime against humanity. As part of the same conceptual constellation, hate speech,[67] whose status remains unsettled within customary international law,[68] has been positioned as some sort of fluid go-betweener in all of the above-listed offenses.[69] (See Chapter 6 by Land and

Hamilton in this volume on the nature and impact of the newly emerging online platforms containing genocidal forms of hate speech propaganda and their unsettled status within international law as a whole.) Despite still lacking full recognition, forms of propagandistic conduct have emerged and could possibly be accorded a status of newly defined, or redefined, types of offenses in ICL. Some of the examples include a refined approach to the differences between *propaganda for war* and *war propaganda* by Michael Kearney[70]; the modes of *fear propaganda*, also related to hate, threats and terror, as argued by this author[71]; Wibke Timmermann's proposal to introduce *incitement to hatred*, a more carefully defined offshoot of *hate propaganda*, as the crime against humanity of persecution[72]; a cognitive science-based research introducing the innovative concept of *revenge speech* by Richard Wilson[73]; and a cluster of, broadly speaking, propaganda-related modes of liability and substantive crimes, such as incitement, instigation, ordering, abetting and ordering, within *a unified liability theory for atrocity speech law* proposed by Gregory Gordon,[74] including the recent proposal for a new form of liability of intentionally, directly and publicly inciting the commission of any crime under the International Criminal Court (ICC) Statute drafted by a group of legal and social sciences experts in *The Hartford Guidelines on Speech Crimes in International Criminal Law*.[75]

The inchoate and continuing nature of propaganda

In all discussions on modes of liability and substantive crimes related to the many manifestations of propaganda, the *inchoate* nature of propagandistic conduct can be described as critically important for the process of its conception and progression. (See Chapter 3 by Gordon in this volume on the inchoate nature and shifting status of 'ordering' toward a substantive offense in ICL. It should be noted that, historically speaking, the speech acts of 'ordering' have deeper contextual, cognitive[76] and also propagandistic[77] implications.) Unlike some short-lasting, momentary forms of criminal conduct, such as *crime passionnel*, propaganda is always, and under any circumstances, a *process* which takes place over a longer period of time.[78] Similar to the process underlying all mass atrocity crimes, propaganda is an intentional, premeditated, strategy-driven form of conduct. As a process, propaganda is typically initiated by one or more agents, usually networks of associates or associated groups and organizations,[79] prior to the occurrence of the physical crimes, which may then possibly be linked to the preceding actions and the emerging consequences. That is why two fundamentally different but potentially connected cognitive phases of the propagandistic process can be identified: (1) the intentional actions as distinct forms of propaganda and (2) the knowledge, awareness and foreseeability of the potential or likely consequences incorporated into the intentional actions. These two phases define propagandistic conduct as an intentional type of *inchoate* process initiated by the propagandist(s). Moreover, as a purposefully and strategically planned process toward its objectives, propaganda cannot be described as a single, one-off act but as a continuing form of conduct, or set of related actions, taking place in time.[80] All known manifestations of propaganda are designed to last longer than a single utterance or speech act. That is why some forms of propagandistic conduct could be described and defined as a *continuing* type of act or, possibly, offense. (See Chapter 2 by Wilson in this volume on the praxis and value of social science expert evidence focusing on the substantial, factual and legal but also temporal dimensions of specific speech acts introduced as types of impactful propagandistic evidence at the ICTR and ICTY.)

The most pertinent discussion on inchoate and continuing crimes in international case law and jurisprudence can again be found in the ICTR's Nahimana et al., the foremost international 'propaganda case' in both jurisprudence and related scholarship. Primarily in the context of the evidence that emerged from the articles published in *Kangura*[81] and radio broadcasts on RTLM (Radio-Télévision Libre des Milles Collines),[82] the two major anti-Tutsi media outlets from Rwanda, the *inchoate* and *continuing* offenses are placed within the framework of direct and public incitement to commit genocide as charged in Nahimana et al. The Appeals Chamber (AC) in this case drew a clear distinction between these two types of offenses by emphasizing that the inchoate offense "is consummated simply by the use of a means or process calculated to produce a harmful effect, irrespective of whether that effect is produced."[83]

As opposed to the nature of inchoate offenses, the AC stated, "A continuing crime implies an ongoing criminal activity. [...] A crime that continues after an initial illegal act has been consummated; a crime that involves ongoing elements [...] 2. A crime [...] that continues over an extended period."[84] The aspects of temporality of the evidence introduced into this trial, as well as the jurisdiction *ratione temporis* of the ICTR, are clearly placed at the center of the discussion. The AC writes that "direct and public incitement to commit genocide is completed as soon as the discourse in question is uttered or published, even though the effects of incitement may extend in time,"[85] thereby indicating that the evidence of the crime relating to the time period prior to the physical crimes committed in 1994 can be considered as causally relevant but not prosecutable *per se*, as coming from outside the temporal jurisdiction of the ICTR.[86] The AC added that

> even if it could be concluded that the totality of the articles published in Kangura and of the RTLM broadcasts constituted one *continuing incitement* to commit genocide [...], the Appellants could be convicted only for acts of direct and public incitement to commit genocide carried out in 1994.[87]
>
> (emphasis added)

It is the opinion of this author that specific forms of propagandistic conduct can realistically be charged both as *inchoate* and/or *continuing* offenses. As inchoate offenses, following the basic distinction between the three subcategories of inchoate offenses outlined by Cassese,[88] specific forms of propaganda can be charged (1) as *attempt*, a preparatory conduct to an intended but not consummated offense; (2) as *planning* and/or part of *conspiracy* to commit a crime of aggression, when the preparatory culpable phase is ultimately absorbed into the physical crime, whereby two or more agents can be charged with at least two different types of criminal conduct and (3) as *incitement* and/or *conspiracy* to commit genocide, as well as *ordering*, a "criminal conduct that is punished per se,"[89] regardless of the consummation of an offense involving at least two or more acts and culpable agents, much in line with the reasoning applied in charging the crime of direct and public incitement to commit genocide in all relevant ICTR cases.[90]

A propagandistic speech act, as part of a pattern, or the pattern itself (e.g., 'propaganda campaign'), can at the same time be separated and/or connected as part of related forms of criminal conduct. (See Chapter 5 by Lawson and Bartels in this volume for the critical role and position of speech acts as evidence assessed, construed and processed differently by different parties involved in an international criminal trial.) In other words, a speech act, within a pattern or sequence of speech acts as forms of culpable propagandistic conduct, can potentially be charged both as inchoate and continuing offense. All of them are *intentional actions* committed with a *reason*, or reasons, and with knowledge, awareness and/or foreseeability of *culpable consequences*.

Fear[91] *propaganda* as a form of culpable conduct

Various manifestations of propaganda can be identified as separate forms of culpable conduct. Apart from the earlier-mentioned examples, other culpable manifestations of propaganda may be emerging from the international trial records and jurisprudence. The concept such as 'hate propaganda,'[92] only briefly touched on in the Nahimana et al. judgments,[93] or variable forms of 'propagandistic terror' identified as some of the dominant contributing factors in the commission and perpetration of crimes,[94] and many other types of propaganda remain outside the reach of newly and clearly defined forms of culpability. Let us, however, limit our discussion to only one example: the phenomenon of *fear propaganda*, its nature, presence and impact in some of the international criminal trials.

Initially, a conceptual distinction needs to be made between *hate speech* and *fear speech*,[95] both likely components of a corresponding but distinct propagandistic conduct. As mentioned before, international case law and jurisprudence have basically approached hate speech within the framework of the following two crimes: persecution as a crime against humanity and direct and public incitement to commit genocide. While establishing hate speech as an act of discrimination in regard to the most fundamental human rights such as dignity and security of individuals as members of the targeted group, the Nahimana et al. AC stated that it is "not satisfied that hate speech alone can amount to a violation of the rights to life, freedom and physical integrity of the human being."[96] The same AC also drew a distinction between hate speech and direct and public incitement to genocide, attributing to hate speech the status of an underlying act of persecution,[97] as such potentially relevant within a broader framework of direct and public incitement to genocide. Other relevant discussions on the criminalization of hate speech can, for example, be found in the case of Rwandan singer Simon Bikindi.[98] (See Chapter 11 by Ntakirutimana and Uwamariya in this volume for an analysis of the culturally determined content of hate speech in Bikindi's lyrics and its impact through artistic expression on the cognitive, linguistic conditioning of the *génocidaires* in Rwanda in 1994.) Referring to the Nahimana et al. AC opinion, the Bikindi TC restated the question "as to whether hate speech occurring in isolation could be considered to be of equal gravity" to other crimes against humanity and reconfirmed the status of hate speech within the comparable factual and legal context.[99]

In the ICTY case of Vojislav Šešelj, while assessing only parts of the key exhibit relevant for the specific speech charged in Šešelj,[100] the AC concluded that "Šešelj's speech rises to a level of gravity amounting to the actus reus of persecution as a crime against humanity."[101] The relevant part of the exhibit absent from both TC's and AC's findings in this case, however, contained the most impactful form of hate speech, namely, the reference by Šešelj in his speech to the targeted Croat civilian population as 'Ustashas.' (See Chapter 4 by Timmermann and Chapter 10 by Kiper in this volume for an analysis of Šešelj's use of persecutory type of language and the judges' failure to assess, both legally and factually, the content and impact of this evidence on the instigation of specific crimes charged in the Šešelj case.) This derogatory speech act utilized by Šešelj was admitted and contextualized by the prosecution through *viva voce* witnesses and numerous exhibits during the course of the trial.[102] Thus, due to the incomplete and erroneous factual assessment of evidence in some of the pertinent cases, such as the Šešelj case,[103] the position of hate speech, contrary to its status as a substantive crime in various domestic legislations,[104] has been relegated below the threshold requirements for a substantive crime in ICL.

Based on its presence and impact as per the records of international criminal trials, however, as a close conceptual relative of hate propaganda, the concept of *fear propaganda*, including its more often than not related components of 'hate speech' and 'fear speech,' could potentially constitute a new applicable concept in ICL. The existing international criminal jurisprudence contains a wealth of references to the role and impact of fear in various manifestations of propaganda. For example, as one of the leading Bosnian Serb politicians during the armed conflict in Bosnia and Herzegovina (BiH) in 1992–95, Radoslav Brđanin was charged for his "role in the campaign designed to permanently remove by force, or *fear*, the non-Serb population [...] He played a leading role with respect to the *propaganda campaign*"[105] (emphasis added). In order to describe the process toward a permanent removal of non-Serbs from specific areas, the TC consistently used the phrase 'force and fear'[106] as reference to one of the intended effects of

Brđanin's propagandistic communications. Moreover, the TC also addressed the temporal aspect of propaganda by stating the following:

> *Prior to the outbreak of the armed conflict*, the SDS [Serb Democratic Party] started waging a *propaganda war* which had a disastrous impact on the people of all ethnicities, creating mutual *fear* and *hatred* and particularly inciting the Bosnian Serb population against the other ethnicities.[107]
>
> (emphasis added)

Apart from attributing value to the evidence dated prior to the physical crimes charged in this case, the TC used the phrase 'fear and hatred'[108] as another conceptual instrument in describing the process taking place over a longer period of time. The TC established the fact that "the *propaganda campaign* achieved its goals" by "preparing the Bosnian Serb population for the crimes that were committed later, it also instilled *fear* among the non-Serb population and created an atmosphere of *terror*, which contributed to the subsequent massive exodus of non-Serbs"[109] (emphasis added). The use of language by Brđanin is perhaps best illustrated in the following paragraph:

> By his public statements the Accused created *fear* and *hatred* between Bosnian Serbs on the one hand and Bosnian Muslims and Bosnian Croats on the other hand, inciting the ethnic groups against each other. The Accused repeatedly used derogatory language to refer to non-Serbs, calling them 'Balijas' (Muslims), 'Ustaša' (Croats), 'Šiptar' (Albanians), 'vermin', 'scum', 'infidel' and 'second rate people.'[110]
>
> (emphasis added)

In this case, through the distinct combination of fear, hate, derogatory and dehumanizing, and direct and indirect culture-specific references[111] and types of linguistic communication, the concept of *fear* is placed at the center of Brđanin's and other JCE[112] members' propagandistic conduct. (See Chapter 7 by Donia and Chapter 8 by Dojčinović in this volume for the use and impact of historically, politically and culturally determined type of language in the cognitive conditioning and commission of the crimes committed by the Bosnian Serb political and military leadership and their forces against the non-Serb civilians in BiH between 1992 and 1995.) As a matter of fact, the TC described in detail the trajectory of evidence showing specifically how 'fear propaganda' had a direct effect and impact on the commission and perpetration of the charged crimes committed against the targeted groups. In other words, the linkage between the speech acts and the physical crimes committed in this case was established in both time and space.

In the related trial of the Bosnian Serb leader Radovan Karadžić, *fear propaganda* again played an important role in explaining the *mens rea* and the *actus reus* of the specific charges.[113] The Karadžić trial judgment states,

"In evoking *fears* of a 'Serbian genocide,' Bosnian Serb leaders suggested that territorial claims beyond Serb-inhabited areas were justified"[114] (emphasis added). The reference in this case is to the Second World War genocidal policies of the Croatian and other Nazi allies carried out against the Serb civilian population from Croatia and BiH. The purpose of this type of fear propaganda, publicly repeated countless times before and during the armed conflict, was to revive historical collective memories and existential fears of an alleged new threat with the disappearance of the entire Serb nation in the region. As acknowledged by the TC, various forms of fear propaganda were used to create a mobilizing, both preemptive and retaliatory, in-group predisposition against the alleged, designated non-Serb enemies, that is, Croats and Muslims in general, stating *inter alia* that "Serbs were under threat as they would be killed and eliminated from BiH when an Islamic state was formed. These speeches instilled *fear* amongst the Bosnian Serb population"[115] (emphasis added). In this case, fear propaganda was intentionally directed toward its own population rather than the targeted enemy, revealing the powerful use of fear as a cognitive instrument with multiple functionality.

Similarly, the case against Vojislav Šešelj was almost entirely placed within the framework of his propagandistic statements and his participation in the JCE. Given the most voluminous evidence ever submitted in any of the so-called 'propaganda cases' since Nuremberg onward,[116] the AC in Šešelj determined that "such statements are undoubtedly capable of creating *fear* and emboldening perpetrators of crimes against the non-Serbian population"[117] (emphasis added). Šešelj was ultimately convicted only for the speech delivered on 6 May 1992 in the village of Hrtkovci. The AC *inter alia* determined that, as a result of that speech, many Croats left for Croatia "out of fear."[118] The AC also concluded that there was a link between Šešelj's speech acts and "the crimes of deportation, persecution (forcible displacement), and other inhumane acts (forcible transfer) as crimes against humanity."[119] Thus, the requisite degree of causal nexus for instigation was hereby satisfied.[120]

One of many ICTR trials worth mentioning in the context of *fear propaganda* is again Nahimana et al. Apart from the complex contextual, historical, political and ideological components of the case – as briefly illustrated by the TC through the example of "the activities of the CDR [Coalition pour la Défense de la République], a Hutu political party that demonized the Tutsi population as the enemy, generated *fear* and *hatred* that created the conditions for extermination and genocide in Rwanda"[121] (emphasis added) – the vast amount of documentary evidence in this trial emerged from the newspaper *Kangura* and the RTLM radio station broadcasts. "Through *fear-mongering* and hate propaganda, *Kangura* paved the way for genocide in Rwanda, whipping the Hutu population into a killing frenzy,"[122] determined the TC in this case (emphasis added). "Similarly, RTLM broadcast a message of *fear*, provided listeners with names and encouraged them to defend and protect themselves, incessantly telling them to 'be vigilant,' which became a coded term for aggression in the guise of self-defence,"[123] reads the conclusion of the TC in relation to the role played by the RTLM radio, adding that "radio heightened the sense of *fear*, the sense of *danger* and the sense of *urgency* giving rise to the *need for action* by listeners"[124] (emphasis added). Most references to 'fear' in Nahimana et al., as part of various forms of propagandistic conduct, constitute inferences and links between the evidence of *fear propaganda* and the commission and perpetration of a wide range of physical crimes.

Thus, given the persuasive body of evidence found in the records of international criminal trials and jurisprudence as a whole, at least three basic types of *fear propaganda* (hereinafter FPT1, FPT2 and FPT3) can be identified. All three of them can essentially be defined by the temporal and causal aspects of their manifestations. The FPT1 occurs prior to the outbreak of an armed conflict, the FPT2 manifests itself during the armed conflict, and the FPT3 describes a continuing pattern of conduct connecting in time both the FPT1 and FPT2. As theoretical as these differences may sound, they are, or can be, decisive in determining the nature of 'fear propaganda' as a distinct form of culpability. While the FPT1 can establish the *inchoate* nature of culpable act(s), the FPT2 can establish the *knowledge*, *awareness* and *foreseeability* of physical crimes as a result of the preceding act(s), the FPT3 can ultimately establish the act(s) as a *continuing* offense forming the *mens rea* linkage in time and space between the previous two types.

The main question to be posed in this case is whether 'fear propaganda,' as only one of several types of culpable propagandistic conduct, can be defined as a method of committing a mode of liability,[125] a mode of liability, or a crime *per se*. This publication does not pretend to have the final answer – its purpose is, first and foremost, to highlight the cognitive range and relevance of the particularly linguistic type of propagandistic conduct and related evidence found in the international criminal jurisprudence but equally to open a discussion on an issue vital for both the prevention and punishment of the offenses that currently fall within the overly broad ambit of the concept of 'propaganda.'

The synapses of the book, the chapters of the book

Part I: Law to science

1 The speech acts of genocide: decoding the language of ISIS

The opening chapter of the volume presents a model approach to the legal analysis of the most intricate cognitive, linguistic aspects of propaganda within the framework of ICL. As indicated by the authors, Mohamed Badar and Polona Florijančič, the chapter offers an analysis of "key concepts and labels employed by ISIS by placing them in their linguistic, historical, religious and ideological contexts." This approach presents an advanced method of investigating various manifestations of *mens rea* evidence, on the one hand, and their likely impact on the prospective perpetrators of the physical crimes, on the other hand. Two distinct, but potentially related, cognitive modes of criminal conduct emerge from this method: the intentional, propagandistic conduct and the anticipated impact on the perpetration of the physical crimes. The key lies in the historically and culturally determined meanings of the linguistic concepts employed by the ISIS propagandists, as subsequently understood and acted on by the ISIS combatants. The authors ultimately demonstrate how this type of propaganda can be prosecuted as the *inchoate* crime of direct and public incitement to commit genocide. This chapter can provide both the legal and academic contextual roadmap for the ISIS-related prosecutorial enterprises, such as the ICC investigations into the mass atrocity crimes committed by this terrorist organization in Syria and Iraq or within any national jurisdiction within which this type of propaganda may have been distributed.

2 Science in the courtroom: expert evidence in international criminal trials

In the subsequent chapter, Richard Wilson underpins the argument for a more profound scientific interpretation of the cognitive, linguistic type of propaganda evidence, most particularly through expert witnesses as conduits of specific knowledge and information the international criminal trials ought to utilize in most cases. As Wilson states,

> Adjudicating crimes where the main evidence is a speech act or acts requires a nuanced appreciation of local languages and the cultural context of their usage to establish what specific utterances mean, what the utterances encouraged the listener to do and what the consequences of the utterances were.

Apart from the methodological recommendation as to the source of expertise, Wilson offers two particularly relevant case studies in some of the landmark international trials involving various components of propaganda. The first concerns the sociolinguistic evidence provided by Mathias Ruzindana to the ICTR in the Akayesu and Nahimana et al. cases, whereas the second addresses the sociological method of content analysis of different categories of propagandistic utterances submitted by Anthony Oberschall in the ICTY's case of Vojislav Šešelj. While the former played a critical role in decoding the language used by the propagandists and the *génocidaire* in Rwanda, the latter had very little, if any, impact on the trial judges' assessment of the *mens rea* evidence originating from the Accused himself. Wilson's chapter makes a compelling case in favor of a cautious but necessary engagement of social and cognitive scientists in international criminal trials, particularly those whose forensic expertise can contribute to the critical understanding of the contextually most intricate aspects of culture and language-based evidence.

3. *The inchoate nature and status of* ordering

The status of *ordering* in ICL has customarily been defined as a mode of liability. As such, ordering has additionally been burdened with a causal nexus between the order and the actual commission of the crime. The ICTR and ICTY jurisprudence has established, as the Kamuhanda judgment indicates, that the order must have "a direct and substantial effect on the commission of the illegal act,"[126] creating thereby a situation in which the speaker, that is, the superior officer or any other person in the position of command and/or authority, could fully shift the burden of liability to the principal perpetrator of the crime. Furthermore, in the situation in which the physical crime is not executed, the superior would again not be held liable. These are only some of the problems arising from the traditional status of ordering as a mode of liability. While pursuing an immaculate historical overview and analysis of *ordering* as one of the less than adequately understood forms of potential criminal conduct, as part of his proposal for a Unified Liability Theory of atrocity speech law,[127] Gregory Gordon offers a persuasive line of argumentation that "the crime of ordering should be modified from its present restrictive form and expanded to encompass inchoate liability." What had once been assigned the status of a mode of liability by the ICTY and ICTR, the status not unambiguously advanced by the Rome Statute's Article 25(3)(b), could be elevated to the level of a substantive offense with inchoate liability. After Cassese's and Cryer's initial references to ordering as an inchoate offense,[128] Gordon's line of argumentation is the best developed thus far and falls impeccably within the grand framework of potentially culpable propagandistic, cognitive and linguistic forms of intentional actions such as *directive* and *commissive* types of speech acts.[129] Gordon's proposal to accord ordering the status of an inchoate offense lies at the heart of a cognitive process which integrates in time the intentional and the criminal components of an order on both ends of the speech act, the speaker's and the recipient's.

4 The language of instigation and the appeal judgment in Šešelj: the final word

As a result of the TC's factual and legal failure to address and infer the relevance of the linguistic type of *mens rea* evidence introduced in the case against Vojislav Šešelj, which resulted in the full acquittal of the Accused, Wibke Timmermann's chapter focuses on "the impact of the Appeals Chamber's findings on instigation and the use of language to stir up hatred or violence," which reversed the trial judgment and found Šešelj guilty of instigating persecution (forcible displacement), deportation and other inhumane acts (forcible transfer) as crimes against humanity and for committing persecution (violation of the right to security) as a crime against humanity. Timmermann's analysis of various forms of 'hate speech,' 'incitement to hatred' or 'incitement to violence,' and particularly Šešelj's utterances from his key speech delivered in the village of Hrtkovci on

6 May 1992, offers the most astute legal analysis of the impactful use of various forms of cognitively and linguistically driven propaganda as the mode of liability of instigation in the commission of the above-listed crimes against humanity.

5 The slippery slopes of prosecuting speech acts: the Ruto and Sang case

The chapter by Clare Lawson and Rogier Bartels is the first scholarly examination of the evidentiary aspects of the use of specific speech acts found in the case against William Samoei Ruto and Joshua Arap Sang tried by the ICC. The authors, who both share inside knowledge of the evidence and deliberative reasoning applied by the ICC judges in this case, address the charging decisions, the language used by the Accused and how the evidence, or its lack thereof and its specific deficiencies, impacted the trial outcome as a whole. As legal practitioners and scholars, Lawson and Bartels address the charges against Joshua Arap Sang, a radio presenter who was alleged to have contributed to the commission of crimes against humanity through his radio broadcasts, as well as some aspects of the utilization of language attributed by the prosecution to Samoei Ruto during the political rallies held prior to the Kenyan postelection violence in 2007–08. Perhaps the most important lesson from this trial, as emphasized by Lawson and Bartels, is that the "prosecution's almost exclusive reliance on witness evidence," and particularly "where the alleged speech is ambiguous, metaphorical or coded," made the evidence insufficiently supported and consistent for the judges to determine the level of culpability alleged by the prosecution in this case. Thus, standing in stark contrast to the jurisprudence from the IMT, ICTR and ICTY, the Ruto and Sang trial showed that a lack of supporting documentary, archival and expert evidence may fundamentally and conclusively affect the reliability and impact of fact witness testimonies in all the so-called 'propaganda trials.'

6 From online hate speech to genocide: problems, regulations, and recommendations

The chapter by Molly Land and Rebecca Hamilton takes the legal discussions on specific forms of propaganda straight into the most interesting arena of international criminal and human rights law debates of the present day defined by online hate speech propaganda. Land and Hamilton first outline the case study of "Facebook's role in the Rohingya genocide as an example of coordinated speech campaigns and the limitations of current social media policies," then they offer an "overview of international human rights law and the law on remedies that require proportionality in responses to harmful speech" and, finally, they introduce "innovative responses to hate speech that go beyond content takedowns or user bans." Some of the key aspects of the online forms of dangerous speech addressed in this chapter are the cognitive conditioning, that is, "coordinated speech campaigns that create the conditions in which human rights violations are easier to justify," also termed 'conditioning speech' by the authors, and the 'coded' speech or speech determined by indirect cultural references understood only by local speakers.

Part II: Science to law

7 The words of mens rea *in historical and political records*

As jurisprudence and trial records clearly show, international criminal trials regularly encounter lexical elements of cognitive provenance veiled by complex contextual, historical, sociopolitical and cultural factors. Combining a historical approach to evidence with a linguistic analysis, Robert Donia's chapter follows a hybrid methodology commonly used by historians to reveal the meanings and connotations in the language used by significant historical actors. As Donia puts it, "My purpose here is to show that tracking a movement's semantic innovations can yield valuable insights into its leaders' guiding principles, intentions and plans [...]." Donia places the Serbo-Croatian concept of the *narod*, commonly translated as 'a people' or 'a nation,' at the center of his study. His focus is on the use of *narod* mainly by the Bosnian Serb leadership, who, as Donia points out, "enhanced the everyday meaning of *Serb narod* by attributing to it semantically the qualities of elasticity, anthropocentricity, suffering and congenital impossibility of committing genocide." Along with the use of discriminatory language revolving around the lexical constellation of the lead concept, Donia's chapter reveals how Bosnian Serb propagandists intentionally employed 'semantic innovations' in order to cognitively condition the targeted groups for the armed conflict and the crimes committed in the former Yugoslavia in the 1990s.

8 The ways and means of inferring genocidal and persecutory intent

Over the course of his two-decade-long experience in investigations, research and analysis, Predrag Dojčinović has been developing and implementing analytical models addressing various categories of propaganda and speech-related evidence in international criminal trials. All of them are based on an interdisciplinary combination of cognitive and social science research in the humanities and law. In this chapter, Dojčinović focuses on the specific research and analytical project within the Office of the Prosecutor (OTP) of the ICTY in the trial of Ratko Mladić, the Commander of the Bosnian Serb Army (VRS). The analytical model designed and utilized throughout this trial is based on the specific speech acts identified in all categories of evidence indicating *genocidal* and *persecutory intent* of the Accused shared with other members of the JCE at all levels.[130] The chapter places strong emphasis on the semantic content of the speech acts, the type of intent identified in the content, the effect they may have had on the principle perpetrators as well as their relevance, probative value and modes of admissibility as a special category of evidence. Ultimately, the chapter demonstrates that international criminal proceedings have seen the emergence of a new type of key evidence: a cognitive, linguistic, contextually determined manifestation of *mens rea* within a shared historical, political and cultural referential framework. Dojčinović argues that this emerging body of evidence requires a new set of rules and methods in international criminal proceedings and a more comprehensive intellectual, scientifically minded approach to the identification and interpretation of mental elements in mass atrocity crimes.

9 *From the cognitive science of dehumanization to the courtroom*

Dehumanization is a pervasive force in society that can be observed in a range of behaviors from small interactions to large-scale, systematic violence during conflicts. Understanding the fundamental science behind our ability to dehumanize is essential in the practice of human rights law and the prosecution of mass atrocity crimes. Celia Guillard and Lasana Harris show how decades of empirical social psychology and neuroscience research has established that *all* people have the capacity to dehumanize as a consequence of social context. While emphasizing the cognitive role of language in the process of dehumanization, this chapter draws on previous research to establish how social contexts facilitate dehumanization, which neural pathways might allow atrocities to occur and how we can prevent this behavior in the future. The chapter examines the implications of these findings within the broader context of serious violations of human rights, including some of the specific cases documented through international criminal trials. Most importantly, the expert evidence offered by Guillard and Harris can assist all parties – the prosecution, the defense and the judges – engaged in fact- and truth-finding procedures as instituted through international criminal trials.

10 *A cognitive science perspective on the propaganda of Vojislav Šešelj: the posttrial expert evidence*

Jordan Kiper's chapter shifts the frequently sought cause-and-effect positions on potentially perilous forms of propaganda in international criminal trials toward a firmer contextual framework of propaganda allowing "collective intentionality to change social relations, making violence against particular groups more acceptable, on which perpetrators then act." Kiper proceeds in a three-step methodological manner. First, he explains and applies John Austin's speech act theory[131] relevant for the semantic, intentional and interpretative components of linguistic communication, second, he underscores the significance of social psychology studies for understanding the contextual and psychological positions of the influencer and the influenced and, third, through the case study of Vojislav Šešelj as the most vocal single political and military propagandist from the former Yugoslavia, Kiper offers new empirical research and original insights into the evidentiary aspect of the ICTY trial of Vojislav Šešelj, thereby refuting some of the key factual arguments of the TC in this case. Lastly and most importantly, Kiper's chapter offers itself as a model outline of an expert study on the effective forms of political and military propaganda in any similar case, such as virtually all propaganda situations investigated by the ICC.

11 The lyrics of Simon Bikindi and the genocide in Rwanda: the final analysis

When a defendant is charged with incitement to mass atrocity crimes, such as genocide, understanding the culture-specific resonances and impact of communications on the perpetrators can determine the ultimate issue in a trial. As Cassese noted, "even implicit messages or utterances may amount to incitement, as long as the addressees immediately grasp the implications of the message in light of its cultural and linguistic content."[132] In this regard, one of the most complex and controversial international criminal trials has been the case of Simon Bikindi, a Rwandan singer-songwriter whose music played a significant role in Rwandan society prior to as well as during the 1994 genocide in Rwanda. The prosecution at the ICTR has, however, failed to prove the charges relating to Bikindi's music in the conditioning and execution of the genocide. In this chapter, Évariste Ntakirutimana and Marie-Claire Uwamariya offer the final authoritative interpretation of three of Bikindi's songs in Kinyarwanda from the perspective of two expert native speakers. The particular emphasis is placed on the cognitive, linguistic but also historical, political, social and culture-determined manifestations of propaganda concealed in the messages communicated by Bikindi's lyrics to the *génocidaires*. The authors thus offer firsthand expert evidence of, and new insights into, the content and role of Bikindi's words as contributing factors to the crime of direct and public incitement to commit genocide.

12 From the Syrian state propaganda to violence: the expert evidence

The closing chapter by Saskia Baas represents an example of the manner in which a social science expert report should be compiled for the purposes of understanding the relationship between the contextual and criminal components of serious violations of international humanitarian and criminal law. Baas discusses the role of the Syrian state media during the escalation of peaceful protests to mass violence in 2011 and the transition into the sectarian type of mass violence abetted by a state-controlled Syrian media propaganda campaign. In line with the existing jurisprudence discussed in this volume, the sectarian framing of the demonstrations was not explicit but tacit and was coded into the specific language and symbols within the authorized public speech in Syria as implicitly understood by the audiences familiar with this type of public communication. The analysis of the Syrian situation is based on both documentary and live sources researched and consulted by Baas throughout the region. All of them together constitute a valuable combination of the archival open source evidence and the interviews with the "Syrian journalists who occupied key positions in state-controlled media institutions." This chapter lays out the initial, intentional phase of the Syrian government's sectarian conflict-driven propaganda and the consequences of this conduct as reflected in the mass atrocity crimes, which is where any investigation of the serious violations of international humanitarian law should begin.

A final preliminary word

This collection constitutes an attempt at bringing together two seemingly diverse but connected areas of study in the theory and practice of ICL: the legal and the scientific. In this volume, they reside under the overarching phenomenon of propaganda and its principally linguistic, cognitive building blocks. While the first part of the volume focuses on the blending of varied issues related to the modes of liability and substantive offenses with, as indicated in the subtitle, the evidentiary process linking the specific legal forms of cognition to the criminality of their manifestations, all converging at the point of the redefinition of the nature, role and status of various forms of propaganda in this area of ICL, the second part of the volume lays out some of the key cognitive background conditions for the same process emerging from the contextual or, more specifically, the historical, political, cultural, social and psychological components of international criminal trials. It should therefore become clear that the phenomenon of propaganda can neither be understood nor applied without an advanced forensic approach as a cross-disciplinary combination of law with other relevant fields of research through an amalgamation of cognitive and social science research with the humanities. Applying this method in all international criminal trials would demonstrate how and why this legally and intellectually advanced hybrid method should effectively be introduced into the process of the identification, investigation, prosecution, defense and judgment of the guilty minds of the propagandists and the networks of their associates.

Notes

1 The Prosecutor v. Vojislav Šešelj, Judgment, Case No: IT-03-67-T, 31 March 2016 [hereinafter Šešelj TJ]. Partially Dissenting Opinion of Judge Flavia Lattanzi – Amended Version, Volume 3:

> I agree that, as stated in paragraph 300 of the Judgement, the use of propaganda is not in itself a criminal act but, as the ECHR [European Court of Human Rights] found, 'it is vitally important that in their public speeches, politicians should avoid making comments likely to foster intolerance.'
>
> para 109. [hereinafter Šešelj, Lattanzi PDO]

2 J.R. Searle, *Making the Social World: The Structure of Human Civilization*, New York, NY: Oxford University Press, 2010, p. 63.

3 Searle, *Making the Social World*, p. 109.
4 Ibid., pp. 90–122.
5 R. Sun (ed.), *Grounding Social Sciences in Cognitive Sciences*, Cambridge, MA: The MIT Press, 2012.
6 J. Friedenberg and G. Silverman (eds), *Cognitive Science: An Introduction to the Study of Mind*, London: Sage Publications, 2006, p. 2.
7 A. Lynch, *Thought Contagion: How Belief Spreads through Society*, New York, NY: Basic Books, 2006, p. 8. C. O'Connor and J.O. Weatherhall, *The Misinformation Age: How False Beliefs Spread*, New Haven, CT, London: Yale University Press, 2019.
8 M. Turner, *The Literary Mind*, New York, NY, Oxford: Oxford University Press, 1996, p. 15. P. Stockwell, *Cognitive Poetics: An Introduction*, London, New York, NY: Routledge, 2002, p. 27. B. Dancygier, *The Language of Stories: A Cognitive Approach*, Cambridge: Cambridge University Press, 2012. P.C. Hogan, *Ulysses and the Poetics of Cognition*, New York, NY, London: Routledge, 2014.
9 B. Garland (ed.), *Neuroscience and the Law: Brain, Mind, and the Scales of Justice*, New York, NY, Washington, DC: Dana Press, 2004.
10 *Black's Law Dictionary*, Ninth Edition, B.A. Gamer (ed.), St. Paul: West, a Thompson Business, 2009, pp. 881–883. See also *Stroud's Judicial Dictionary of Words and Phrases*, J.S. James, Barrister-at-Law, vol. 3, I-O, London: Sweet & Maxwell Limited, 1986, pp. 1324–1326.
11 *Encyclopedia of Cognitive Science*, Wiley Online Library, 2006. Online. Available HTTP: <https://onlinelibrary.wiley.com/doi/book/10.1002/0470018860> (accessed 13 June 2019).
12 For exceptions, see P. Dojčinović, 'Word Scene Investigations,' in P. Dojčinović (ed.), *Propaganda, War Crimes Trials and International Law: From Speakers' Corner to War Crimes*, Abingdon, New York, NY: Routledge, 2012, p. 94.
13 B.J. Baars and N.M. Gage, *Cognition, Brain, and Consciousness: Introduction to Cognitive Neuroscience*, Second Edition, Amsterdam: Elsevier, 2010, pp. 371–398. J. Friedenberg and G. Silverman, *Cognitive Science: An Introduction to the Study of Mind*, London, New Delhi: Sage Publications, 2006, pp. 276–310. F.J. Varela, E. Thompson and E. Rosch, *The Embodied Mind: Cognitive Science and Human Experience*, Cambridge, MA: The MIT Press, 1993.
14 G.E.M. Anscombe, *Intention*, Cambridge, MA: Harvard University Press, 2000, p. 9.
15 J.R. Searle, *Mind, Language and Society: Philosophy in the Real World*, London: Phoenix, 1999, pp. 149–150.
16 J.R. Searle, *Speech Acts: An Essay in the Philosophy of Language*, Cambridge: Cambridge University Press, 1969, p. 3.
17 Searle, *Speech Acts*, p. 16.
18 H. Mercier and D. Sperber, *The Enigma of Reason*, Cambridge, MA: Harvard University Press, 2017.
19 D. Davidson, *Essays on Actions and Events*, New York, NY: Oxford University Press, 2001, p. 83.
20 J. Ellul, *Propaganda – The Formation of Men's Attitudes*, New York, NY: Vintage, 1973, p. 59.
21 G.S. Jowett and V. O'Donnell, *Propaganda and Persuasion*, Fourth Edition, London: Sage, 2006, p. 13.
22 P.M. Taylor, *Munitions of the Mind – A History of Propaganda from the Ancient World to the Present Day*, Manchester, New York, NY: Manchester University Press, 2003, p. 7.
23 A. Pratkanis and E. Aronson, *Age of Propaganda: The Everyday Use and Abuse of Persuasion*, Revised Edition, New York, NY: W.H. Freeman and Company, 2001,

p. 11. B. Kushner, *The Thought War: Japanese Imperial Propaganda*, Honolulu: University of Hawai'i Press, 2006, p. 4.

24 A. Cassese, *International Criminal Law*, Second Edition, Oxford, New York, NY: Oxford University Press, 2008, p. 56.

25 The Prosecutor Versus Jean-Paul Akayesu, Trial Judgment, Case No. ICTR-96-4-T, 2 September 1998, paras 477–478 [hereinafter Akayesu TJ]. The Prosecutor v. Clement Kayishema and Obed Ruzindana, Appeal Judgment, Case No. ICTR-95-1-A, 1 June 2001, paras 159, 198 [hereinafter Kayishema AJ].

26 The Prosecutor Versus Jean-Paul Akayesu, Appeal Judgment, Case No. ICTR 96-4-A, 1 June 2001, paras 464–469.

27 Kayishema AJ, para. 138. Prosecutor v. Vidoje Blagojević and Dragan Jokić, Appeal Judgment, Case No. IT-02-60-A, paras 122–123. Prosecutor v. Radovan Karadžić, Rule 98bis Judgment, Case No. IT-9S-SI18-AR98bis.l, 11 July 2013, paras 79–80.

28 P. Dojčinović, 'The Chameleon of *Mens Rea* and the Shifting Guises of Culture-Specific Genocidal Intent in International Criminal Proceedings,' *Journal of Human Rights*, vol. 15, no. 4, 2016, pp. 454–476. See also M.E. Badar, *The Concept of Mens Rea in International Criminal Law: The Case for a Unified Approach*, Oxford: Hart Publishing, 2013. Cassese, *International Criminal Law*, p. 60. R. Cryer, H. Friman, D. Robinson and E. Wilmshurst (eds), *International Criminal Law and Procedure*, Third Edition, Cambridge: Cambridge University Press, 2014, pp. 382–383.

29 Searle, *Mind, Language and Society*, pp. 64–65.

30 Apart from Julius Streicher, Hans Fritzsche and Alfred Rosenberg, virtually all IMT cases had various components of propaganda as part of the evidentiary proceedings in Nuremberg.

31 Dojčinović, *Propaganda*, p. 7.

32 Online. Available HTTP: <https://treaties.un.org/doc/publication/unts/volume%20999/volume-999-i-14668-english.pdf> (accessed 13 June 2019).

33 M.G. Kearney, *The Prohibition of Propaganda for War in International Law*, New York, NY: Oxford University Press, 2007.

34 Ibid., p. 165.

35 Online. Available HTTP: <https://www.un.org/en/udhrbook/pdf/udhr_booklet_en_web.pdf> (accessed 13 June 2019).

36 Online. Available HTTP: <https://treaties.un.org/doc/Treaties/1969/03/19690312%2008-49%20AM/Ch_IV_2p.pdf> (accessed 13 June 2019).

37 The Prosecutor v. Ferdinand Nahimana, Jean-Bosco Barayagwiza, Hassan Ngeze, Judgment and Sentence, Case No. ICTR-99-52-T, 3 December 2003 [hereinafter Nahimana et al. TJ].

38 Ibid., para. 986.

39 Ibid., para. 987.

40 Ibid., paras 988–989, 1001, 1004.

41 Ibid., paras 992–993.

42 Ibid., para. 994.

43 Ibid., para. 995.

44 Ibid., para. 996.

45 Ibid., paras 997–999, 1002–1003.

46 Ibid., paras 983–1010.

47 For more, see W. Timmermann, *Incitement in International Law*, London, New York, NY: Routledge, 2015, pp. 17–53, 144–198.

48 Akayesu TJ, paras 99, 100, 105, 127 and 353.

49 Nahimana et al. TJ, paras 1078, 5.17.

50 The Prosecutor v. Simon Bikindi, Trial Judgement, Case No. ICTR-01-72-T, 2 December 2008, para. 254 [hereinafter Bikindi TJ].

51 The Prosecutor v. Georges Ruggiu, Judgement and Sentence, Case No. ICTR-97-32-I, 1 June 2000, para. 50.
52 Prosecutor v. Dario Kordić and Mario Čerkez, Appeals Chamber Judgment, Case No. IT-95-14/2-A, 17 December 2004, fn. 179.
53 Prosecutor v. Milan Babić, Judgement on Sentencing Appeal, Case No. IT-03-2-A, 18 July 2005, paras 15, 20 and 21 [hereinafter Babić AJ].
54 Prosecutor v. Biljana Plavšić, Sentencing Judgment, Case No. IT-00-39 & 40/1-S, 27 February 2003, para. 46.
55 Šešelj, Lattanzi PDO, paras 58, 114, 116–117, 122.
56 Akayesu TJ, paras 99, 123, and 732.
57 Nahimana et al. TJ, para. 935.
58 Bikindi TJ, paras 255–256, 263–264.
59 Prosecutor v. Radoslav Brđanin, Judgement, Case No. IT-99-36-A, 3 April 2007, fn. 537, paras 270, 309, fn. 731, paras 454, 496 [hereinafter Brđanin AJ].
60 Prosecutor v. Milomir Stakić, Case No. IT-97-24-A, Judgement, 22 March 2006, paras 49, 51–53.
61 Babić AJ, para. 21.
62 Šešelj, Lattanzi PDO, para. 107.
63 Babić AJ, para. 20.
64 Prosecutor v. Predrag Banović, Sentencing Judgment, Case No. IT-02-65/1-S, 28 October 2003, para. 78.
65 Ibid., para. 81.
66 Kearney, *The Prohibition*, pp. 218–219.
67 For more, see the following two opposite approaches to the concept of hate speech: J. Waldron, *The Harm in Hate Speech*, Cambridge, MA: Harvard University Press, 2012, and N. Strossen, *Hate: Why We Should Resist It with Free Speech, Not Censorship*, New York, NY: Oxford University Press, 2018.
68 R. Cohen, 'Regulating Hate Speech: Nothing Customary about It,' *Chicago Journal of International Law*, vol. 15, no. 1, 2014.
69 Ferdinand Nahimana, Jean-Bosco Barayagwiza, Hassan Ngeze v. The Prosecutor, Judgment, Case No. ICTR-99-52-A, 28 November 2007, paras 692–693, 986–987 [hereinafter Nahimana et al. AJ]. See also Bikindi TJ, paras 381–382, 386–394.
70 Kearney, *The Prohibition*, p. 217.
71 Dojčinović, *Propaganda*, pp. 7, 12, 16, 25, 86, 89, 93.
72 Timmermann, *Incitement in International Law*, pp. 144, 175.
73 R.A. Wilson, *Incitement on Trial: Prosecuting International Speech Crimes*, Cambridge: Cambridge University Press, 2017, pp. 244–245.
74 G.S. Gordon, *Atrocity Speech Law: Foundation, Fragmentation, Fruition*, New York, NY: Oxford University Press, 2017.
75 Online. Available HTTP: <https://internationalspeechcrimes.org/> (accessed 13 June 2019).
76 Searle, *Mind, Language and Society*, pp. 149–150.
77 J.-M. Kamatali, 'Following Orders in Rwanda,' *New York Times*, 5 April 2014.
78 "Influence is a function of the processes of time." Nahimana et al. AJ, Partly Dissenting Opinion of Judge Shahabuddeen, para. 25 [hereinafter Shahabuddeen PDO].
79 M. Thompson's report *Forging War: The Media in Serbia, Croatia and Bosnia-Hercegovina*, London: Article 19, May 1994. See also A. Des Forges, 'Propaganda and Practice,' in *Leave None to Tell the Story: Genocide in Rwanda*, New York, NY: Human Rights Watch, March 1999.
80 Nahimana et al. AJ, Shahabuddeen PDO, para. 25.
81 Nahimana et al. TJ, paras 122–257.
82 Nahimana et al. TJ, paras 342–544.

83 Nahimana et al. AJ, para. 720. See also Nzabonimana Callixte, Appeal Judgment, Case No. ICTR-98-44D-A, 29 September 2014, para. 234.
84 Nahimana et al. AJ, paras 721.
85 Nahimana et al. AJ, para. 723.
86 Art. 1, Statute of the International Criminal Tribunal for Rwanda.
87 Nahimana et al. AJ, para. 724.
88 Cassese, *International Criminal Law*, p. 220.
89 Ibid., p. 220.
90 See, for example, Nahimana et al. AJ, paras 720, 722–724, and The Prosecutor v. Simon Bikindi, Appeal Judgment, Case No. ICTR-01-72-A, 18 March 2010, paras 145–146, 148.
91 For cognitive neuroscientific summary research findings on fear, see R. Sapolsky, *Behave: The Biology of Humans at Our Best and Worst*, London: Vintage, 2017, pp. 44, 34, 36–40, 42, 44, 85, 87–90, 97, 129. On fear as understood in the humanities and social sciences, see C. Robin, *Fear: The History of a Political Idea*, Oxford, New York, NY: Oxford University Press, 2004.
92 For more, see R.J. Sternberg and K. Sternberg, *The Nature of Hate*, New York, NY: Cambridge University Press, 2008. For neurobiological research on hate, see S. Zeki and J.P. Romaya, 'Neural Correlates of Hate', *PLoS One*, vol. 3, no. 10, October 2008. Online. Available HTTP: <http://www.plosone.org/article/info%3Adoi%2F10.1371%2Fjournal.pone.0003556> (accessed 1 January 2011).
93 Nahimana et al. AJ, para. 516, citing para. 950 of the Trial Judgment referring to 'hate propaganda.'
94 Prosecutor v. Radoslav Brđanin, Judgment, Case No. IT-99-36-T, 1 September 2004, para. 83 [hereinafter Brđanin TJ].
95 E. Buyse, 'Words of Violence: "Fear Speech," or How Violent Conflict Escalation Relates to the Freedom of Expression,' *Human Rights Quarterly*, vol. 36, no. 4, November 2014, pp. 779–797.
96 Nahimana et al. AJ, paras 986–987.
97 Ibid., para. 987.
98 Bikindi TJ, paras 381–382, 385–397.
99 Ibid., para. 394.
100 Šešelj TJ, para. 331, exhibit no. P00547, and Prosecutor v. Vojislav Šešelj, Appeal Judgment, Case No. MICT-16-99-A, 11 April 2018, para. 147, exhibit no. P00547 [hereinafter Šešelj AJ].
101 Šešelj AJ, paras 159, 163.
102 See, for example, the testimony of VS-004, a Serbian political leader from Croatia, who described the cognitive aspects of this key derogatory and persecutory concept used by Šešelj and other Serbs propagandists as follows: "The word 'Ustasha,' [...] it's something that exists as the worst in the world, as an executioner," trial transcript, 8 March 2011, p. 16747. Online. Available HTTP: <http://www.icty.org/x/cases/seselj/trans/en/110308IT.htm> (accessed 13 June 2019).
103 See W. Timmermann, 'Inciting Speech in the former Yugoslavia: The Šešelj Trial Chamber Judgment,' *Journal of International Criminal Justice*, vol. 15, no. 1, March 2017, pp. 133–155.
104 Nahimana et al. TJ, para. 1075. Bikindi TJ, para. 380.
105 Brđanin TJ, para. 9.
106 Ibid., paras 65, 67, 69, 72, 305–307, 349, 473, 477, 532, 575, 582, 667, 981.
107 Ibid., para. 80.
108 Ibid., paras 82, 325.
109 Ibid., para. 83.
110 Ibid., para. 325.

111 Dojčinović, 'The Chameleon of *Mens Rea*.' See also Sapolsky, 'Metaphors We Kill By,' *Behave*, pp. 553–579.
112 For detailed definition of JCE, see Brđanin AJ, paras 363, 364.
113 Prosecutor v. Radovan Karadžić, Judgment, Volume I of IV, Case No.: IT-95-5/18-T, 24 March 2016, para. 669 [hereinafter Karadžić TJ].
114 Ibid., para. 55.
115 Ibid., para. 1101.
116 See the IMT case against Julius Streicher, *Trial of the Major War Criminals before the International Military Tribunal, Nuremberg, 14 November 1945 – 1 October 1946, Volume 1*, Nuremberg, Germany, 1947, pp. 33–34. In Šešelj, see two separate annexes with over 400 excerpts from Šešelj's speeches admitted into evidence as part of A. Oberschall's expert report *Vojislav Šešelj's Nationalist Propaganda: Contents, Techniques, Aims and Impacts, 1990–1994*, Šešelj TJ, exhibit no. P00005.
117 Šešelj AJ, para. 133.
118 Ibid., para. 154.
119 Ibid., para. 154.
120 For the role of causation in Šešelj, see Wilson, *Incitement*, pp. 14, 123–133, 139–140. See also P. Dojčinović, 'The Metaphors of Causation or A Conflict of Concepts in International Criminal Justice,' a research paper and a lecture delivered to the senior legal staff of the Office of the Prosecutor at the ICTY on March 7, 2008 on the specific shortcomings and remedies in the evidentiary approach to the element of causation in the Prosecutor v. Vojislav Šešelj. Online. Available HTTP: https://papers.ssrn.com/sol3/papers.cfm?abstract_id=2850854 (accessed 15 June 2019).
121 Nahimana et al. TJ, para. 1073.
122 Ibid., para. 950.
123 Ibid., para. 1028.
124 Ibid., para. 1031.
125 M. Shahabuddeen, *International Criminal Justice at the Yugoslav Tribunal: A Judge's Recollection*, Oxford: Oxford University Press, 2012, p. 218.
126 The Prosecutor v. Jean De Dieu Kamuhanda, Appeals Chamber Judgment, Case No. ICTR-99-54A-A, 19 September 2005, para. 75.
127 Gordon, *Atrocity*.
128 Cassese, *International Criminal Law*, p. 220. Cryer, *An Introduction*, pp. 375–376.
129 Searle, *Mind, Language and Society*, pp. 149–150.
130 For the concept of 'shared intentionality,' see S. Sloman and P. Fernbach, *The Knowledge Illusion: Why We Never Think Alone*, New York, NY: Riverhead Books, pp. 115–118. For the related concept of 'intentional causation,' see Searle, *Mind, Language and Society*, p. 64. For empirical evidence on 'intentional causation,' see J.W. Moore, C. Teufel, N. Subramaniam, G. Davis and P.C. Fletcher, 'Attribution of Intentional Causation Influences the Perception of Observed Movements: Behavioral Evidence and Neural Correlates,' *Frontiers in Psychology*, vol. 4, no. 23, 2013.
131 J.L. Austin, *How to Do Things with Words*, Cambridge, MA: Harvard University Press, 1962.
132 Cassese, *International Criminal Law*, p. 229.

Part I

Law to science

Chapter 1

The cognitive and linguistic implications of ISIS propaganda

Proving the crime of direct and public incitement to commit genocide*

Mohamed Elewa Badar and Polona Florijančič

Introduction

The self-declared Islamic State (ISIS/ISIL/IS/Da'esh) spread their propaganda far and wide through radio stations, television, social media, online forums, physical distribution of writings, and so on.[1] When assessing whether this propaganda constitutes the international crime of direct and public incitement to commit genocide, one must consider utterances which directly fulfil the necessary *actus reus* and *mens rea* of said crime as well as the propaganda techniques used in the surrounding narrative which prepares the audience to become susceptible to carrying out such calls.

Dealing with the crime of incitement to genocide itself is unique in the sense that it requires the expertise of linguistics in order to determine the meaning of the words uttered in their geographical, cultural or religious contexts. For example, in determining whether incitement to genocide took place, the International Criminal Tribunal for Rwanda (ICTR) was faced with the challenging task of understanding the Kinyarwanda language.[2] None of the judges and very few lawyers in the prosecution and defense teams spoke the language.[3] Alexander Zahar argues that the tribunal was thinking in English semantics rather than Kinyarwanda semantics.[4] Essentially, thinking in different semantics and through the prism of a different culture or tradition can result in a failure to accurately determine the intent of the speaker as well as how the targeted audience perceived a certain discourse, both essential elements of establishing the crime of incitement to genocide.[5]

* This work was originally presented by Prof. Mohamed Badar at a conference on 'The role of parliamentarians in addressing the threat of foreign terrorist fighters and associated challenges' co-organized by the United Nations Office on Drugs and Crime's Terrorism Prevention Branch (UNDOC/TPB), and the House of Representatives of Egypt, the Inter-Parliamentary Union and, the United Nations Office of Counter-Terrorism, 26–28 February 2019, Luxor, Egypt. It was also presented during a workshop on 'Drafting the Bill on Digital Evidence to the benefit of Iraq' as part of UNODC/TPB's Global project on 'Strengthening the legal regime against terrorism in Iraq after the liberation of Mosul (2018–19), 24–25 February 2019, Sharm El Sheikh, Egypt.

This chapter thus analyzes the key concepts and labels employed by ISIS by placing them in their linguistic, historical, religious and ideological contexts. By doing so it will convey the intended implications of the discourse on the part of the speaker as well as its likely perception on the part of the audience. It is important to note that in order to appeal to their audiences, ISIS rely heavily on culturally and religiously well-established Islamic concepts; thus, even when writing or speaking in other languages, they refer to such concepts in their original Arabic form. A clear understanding of the meanings behind the words uttered is further essential for a finding of the requisite *mens rea* in lieu of excessive reliance on a causal link with subsequent crimes committed for this purpose.[6]

This chapter further analyzes the cognitive implications of ISIS propaganda by looking at how they employ various media, imagery, music and sound effects in order to make their polarizing messaging more effective. In ISIS Al Hayāt Media Centre's[7] own words, their aim is to "convey the message of the Islamic state in different languages with the goal of unifying the Muslims under one flag."[8] While essentially the same themes run through their various media, each one serves to achieve a different psychological effect on the audience with the main aim of creating a black-and-white picture of the world. The audience are either presented with a choice of being with the ISIS and following their strict interpretations of Islam, including the necessity of killing and terrorizing everyone who remains outside the group, or are themselves branded unbelievers and therefore a lawful target for killing. The demarcation between the in-group and out-group is thus constructed entirely on a very specifically defined religious belief and practices with absolutely no room for leniency or compromise with regard to variations in said belief or approach to the 'other.' ISIS tap into mainstream Muslim expectations and beliefs, sentiments and grievances, to structure a convincing narrative of hatred and the denial of any dignity of the out-group.

Building a case against ISIS and putting together evidences proving incitement to genocide is very timely, particularly in light of the adoption of the United Nations Security Council Res. 2379 (2017), which established an investigative team to promote accountability for Da'esh/ISIL crimes (UNITAD, i.e., United Nations Investigative Team to Promote Accountability for Da'esh/ISIL Crimes) and to ensure that perpetrators of those heinous crimes be brought to justice.[9] Since Iraq has ratified the Genocide Convention on 20 January 1959,[10] individuals sufficiently involved in ISIS media organs could be prosecuted for the crime of direct and public incitement to commit genocide before Iraqi courts.

ISIS ideology and its embeddedness in Jihādi-Salafīsm

The ISIS *jihādi* campaign is a mixture of *Salafīsm* and Qutbism.[11] The term *Salafīsm* is a form of Islamic revivalism which seeks to bring society back to the practices of the first three generations of Muslims, the *salaf*.[12] This idea as well as the rest of the core *Salafī* theological corpus was adopted from the medieval scholar Ibn Taymiyyah (d. 1328), a controversial figure of his time, who has become one of the most influential medieval writers in contemporary Islam.[13] According to Taymiyyah, the correct method of interpreting the *Qur'ān* was crucial. He attacked what was known as *'tafsīr al-Qur'ān bi-al-ra'y* (interpretation based on personal opinion) and contended that even if one arrived thus at the true divine meaning of the *Qur'ān*, such an interpretation would have to be rejected since it was done through the wrong method.[14] According to him, one is strictly bound in their interpretation of the *Qur'ān* to the *Qur'ān* itself, the *Sunnah* (the Prophet's acts and words) and the interpretations of the *salaf*, considering them more knowledgeable due to their proximity to the revelation.[15] While the medieval exegetical tradition refused to succumb to such a radical restriction on the authority of the exegete,[16] Taymiyyah's radical hermeneutics, nevertheless, resonates with a segment of the Muslim population. As is the case for all Muslims, the fundamental component running through the belief of *Salafīsm* is the doctrine of God's oneness (*tawhīd*).[17] However, *Salafīs* principally criticize other Muslims for what they see as denying *tawhīd* by corrupting the faith with beliefs and practices that are not Islamic. The idea that most Muslims despite professing *tawhīd* do not follow or even understand it was also espoused by Mohamad bin Abdel Wahhab, the founder of the Saudi, and arguably more radical, version of *Salafīsm* pejoratively called Wahhabism.[18] In this sense, Saudi *Salafīsm* presented itself as a correction to widespread *jahiliyyah* (ignorance) declaring anyone else an infidel.[19]

Salafīsm evolved in the twentieth century, with the emergence of Hassan al-Banna's Society of the Muslim Brotherhood (*al-Ikhwān al-Muslimīn*). A legendary speaker himself, Banna carefully chose other individuals with oratorical capabilities for high positions within the society, created his own press and played heavily on the emotions of people to win support.[20] Most importantly, he organized mass meetings for strengthening loyalties, proclaiming aloud the facts of unity, universality and power, and creating an atmosphere of internal strength and hostility to the outside world.[21] These propaganda techniques were highly effective, and the Brotherhood became the ideological and institutional epicenter of fundamentalism in the Arab sphere and the Islamic world.[22]

ISIS echo these divisive propaganda techniques and the *Salafīst* ideology in the aggressive assertion that their view is the only pure and authentic interpretation of the worship of God. To give legitimacy to this claim, they purport to follow the so-called prophetic methodology (*'ala minhaj al-nubuwwa*). They have produced a video on the topic,[23] and all major decisions and laws promulgated are claimed in their press pronouncements and on billboards, license plates, stationery and coins to adhere to said methodology.[24] Unsurprisingly, they also call their political creation the 'Caliphate on the prophetic methodology' and claim that all the *Shari'āh* institutions therein, training camps and even the kindergartens, are on the methodology of prophethood.[25] This propaganda technique serves to close the doors for any alternative opinions and interpretations and presents ISIS as infallible, as the only ones who follow divine as opposed to man-made laws thereby creating a polarized view of the society, whereby either you follow them or you are a *kāfir* (unbeliever, pl. *kuffār*).

When the originally peaceful *Salafīst* concepts were incorporated into the school of *jihād*, the military dimension became essential.[26] The adherents of the *jihādī-Salafīst* movement follow a stricter approach to the question of *hakimiyyah* (ruling in accordance with God's sovereignty) and believe in a duty of declaring unbelief (*takfīr*) on those who have deviated from this principle, showing an open display of enmity, disavowal and hatred toward them and waging *jihād* (holy war) against them.[27] The core aim of the *jihādī-Salafīst* movement lies in "a revolutionary program of overthrowing un-Islamic regimes in the Muslim world, as well as irredentism aiming at expelling non-Muslim military presence and influences from Muslim lands."[28] An important event in light of this was the killing of Egyptian president Anwar Sadat in 1981 when his assassin shouted, "I have killed the Pharaoh, and I do not fear death."[29] The concept of Pharaoh as a paradigm of the evil ruler and a prototype of tyranny stems from the book of Exodus for the Judeo-Christian religion.[30] For Muslims, the Pharaoh similarly appears as the ultimate example of the irreligious and oppressive ruler whom it is the believers' duty to disobey and if possible to overthrow.[31] In the words of Lewis, the choice of Pharaoh as the "prototype of tyranny conveys a religious perception of the offense, the judgment, and the punishment executed."[32] The inspiration and coordination of Sadat's assassination came from Abd al-Salam Faraj. In his work *The Neglected Duty*, Faraj called on fellow Muslims to assassinate their 'un-Islamic' leader, whom he considered 'the near enemy,' in order to establish a truly Islamic caliphate which would eventually take on the 'far enemy,' that is, the crusader Americans and the Zionist Jews, and rule the world.[33]

As many other contemporary radical Islamist movements, ISIS subscribe to the core *jihādī-Salafīst* aims and employ much of the same language when describing the enemy, for example Pharaoh for a ruler they perceive to be un-Islamic.[34] However, the extremeness of their approach to *jihād* and their widespread application of *takfīr* distinguishes them from other radical groups, such as Al-Qaeda, and has led also to the killing of thousands of civilians at their hands.[35]

A fundamental part of *jihādī-Salafī* as well as ISIS ideology is the principle of *al-walā' wa-l-barā* (loyalty and disavowal) in the sense of openly showing animosity toward what is non-Islamic. They employ it as a tool for polarizing audiences along a strict delineation between their construction of Islam and everything and everyone else.[36] In essence, *al-walā' wa-l-barā* signifies love and hate or loyalty and disavowal for the sake of God, understood as steering away from *bid'ah* (heretical innovation in religion), *kufr* (unbelief) and *shirk* (idolatry or polytheism), that is, anything that might be non-Islamic, be it thought, action, individual or institution.[37] During the first two Saudi states, the concept was politicized in the sense that it counseled tribes and rulers against seeking the help of non-Muslims. Thus, portraying the Ottomans as *mushrikūn* (idolaters or polytheists) the concept of *al-walā' wa-l-barā* was developed in an attempt to win the loyalty of wavering Hijazi tribes for al-Sa'ūd's reign instead.[38]

In his famous work *Millat Ibrahim* (The way of Abraham), Abu Muhammad al-Maqdisi, however, transformed this passive concept into a muscular and aggressive one, requiring a series of positive and affirmative acts.[39] Apart from Prophet Ibrahim's acts representing *al-walā'* to God, the example of physically destroying a number of idols surrounding the Ka'ba is given as his most important *barā* from them.[40] Maqdisi quoted Hamad ibn 'Atīq to clarify that uttering the *Shahādatayn* (the two testimonies of faith)[41] was not sufficient for a Muslim to declare his religion when among the unbelievers but in fact he "has not openly declared his religion until he opposes every assembly [of disbelief] in whatever disbelief it is famous for, while clearly declaring his enmity toward it and his disavowal (*barā*) from it."[42] *Millat Ibrahim* still enjoys a sustained readership within radical circles and by Maqdisi's own testimony has become the cornerstone of *jihādi* ideology.[43]

The radical interpretation of *al-walā' wa-l-barā* includes the practice of ***takfīr***, which is an act of religious censure depriving a Muslim of their Islamic status based on an accusation of ***kufr***, thus making them subject to lawful killing.[44] The issue with the practice of ***takfīr*** lies in its subjectivism, rendering it an extremely dangerous weapon in the hands of fanatical sectarians.[45] Historically, its use often went beyond the religiously defined 'unbelief' and served in political, social, or cultural conflicts between individuals or groups.[46]

Accusations of unbelief and the resultant trials, aimed at monitoring and repressing parties opposed to the established theological and political order, began in the second/seventh century with the emergence of the *Khawārij*, who followed a simple principle, namely, that anyone disobeying God should automatically be condemned as a ***kāfir***.[47] They saw themselves as the only real Muslims, branding everyone else as ***kuffar***[48] and considered their killing permissible.[49] Like the *Khawārij*, ISIS considers resisting a single ruling (***hukm***) of the *Shari'āh* as a reason for declaring ***takfīr*** and a justification for killing.[50] Unsurprisingly, they also reject the idea of ***irjā'*** (postponing) as "the most dangerous ***bid'ah***."[51] This concept refers to the call for postponing the question of who is a true Muslim until God's own judgment in the afterlife, as humans are not fit to evaluate the faith of another. It was brought forward by the *Murjia'ah*[52] who witnessed the bloody massacres between the proto-Sunnis, the proto-Shi'a and the *Khawārij*.[53] ISIS, on the other hand, praise those who "fight, massacre, and terrorize the ***kuffār*** while not differentiating between them under the influence of ***irjā***"[54] while accusing those practicing ***irjā'*** as the ones, who "made Islam into a mere claim having no reality."[55]

The most infamous declaration of ***takfīr*** by the *Khawārij* was on Caliph 'Ali for concluding an arbitration agreement with Mu'awiya.[56] The *Khawārij* argued that by doing so 'Ali had followed human judgment instead of divine judgment and thus his action was clearly ***kufr***.[57] It is ***hakimiyyah*** or the doctrine of absolute sovereignty of Allah which dictates that all governance is in accordance with the *Shari'āh* and not man-made laws, a principle rigorously followed by ISIS.

Regarding situations of ruling or judging in accordance with anything other than the *Shari'āh*, the general *Salafī* doctrine places importance on whether such governing is regarded as being permissible. It distinguishes between major and lesser *kufr* in this regard, whereby somebody is a *kāfir* in cases where he regards it as being permissible or denies that which Allah has revealed, and in cases of promulgating legislation that goes against the laws of Allah.[58] In instances of injustice and oppression in individual cases, this is considered to be only lesser *kufr* which does not make one a *kāfir*, provided that he believes that he is sinning and that the ruling of Allah is true.[59] While not a major disbelief, this is still a major sin and is worse than many other major sins.[60]

The *Khawārij* in comparison considered it a major *kufr*, even if it was only in a specific case, and even if the one who did it, believed that he was disobeying Allah.[61] The *Khawārij* cited a precedent for their declaration of *takfīr* on 'Ali, namely, the murder of the Third Caliph, 'Uthman. This murder had been justified by declaring that 'Uthman had "broken God's law by not inflicting a penalty prescribed in the *Qur'ān*."[62]

The unbelief is ascribed based on the logic that those who rule by legislation other than *Shari'āh* usurp the divine attribute of God as 'the legislator' (*al-Hākim*) for themselves and are categorized as tyrants who rebel against God and impose this rebellion on others *ṭawāghīt* (sing. *tāghūt*). They are also considered polytheists (*mushrikūn*) for making themselves as objects that are worshipped, followed and obeyed as partners beside God.[63] If they profess the Islamic faith, they are also hypocrites[64] and *murtaddīn* (apostates, sing. *murtadd*). Furthermore, turning away from the laws of Allah (*tabdīl shara' Allāh*) and conferring on oneself the authority to make *taḥlīl and taḥrīm* (declaring something to be either permissible or impermissible in a way that contradicts the divine legislations of God) "in and of itself, nullifies Islam."[65]

Salafī-jihādīs interpret any sign of secularization or democracy as major unbelief and subsequently rush to declarations of *takfīr* and *jihād* on such political regimes and their supporters.[66] Islamists tend to refer to Ibn Taymiyyah anti-Mongol fatwa in justifying this attitude and have used it as a call to rebellion against the rulers of governments of certain modern Muslim countries.[67] However, according to Yahya Michot, this is a betrayal of the medieval scholar's thought.[68] He rather links the fatwas to the Mongol project of invading Syria and thus sees it as a call to struggle against a foreign invader (whose newly claimed belief in Islam was suspect) and not the struggle against a Muslim ruler who ruled in a manner that could be subject to serious reserve or criticism.[69] For the latter situation, Taymiyyah rather commanded patience above all in contrast with the radicals referring to him.[70]

The hate propaganda of ISIS media machine

The above-described ideology, embedded in *Salafī-jihādism* and further radicalized by ISIS, is spread to their targeted audiences through their sophisticated media machine[71] using well-established propaganda techniques and high-quality productions.[72] ISIS create daily radio and text bulletins, photographic essays and videos alongside official audio statements from senior members of the group, including the so-called 'caliph' Abu Bakr al-Baghdadi and the then official spokesperson Abu Mohammad al-Adnani. In ISIS-held territories they are controlling several TV stations, distributing DVDs and hard copies of their writings as well as showing their videos on big screens in public parks and blasting their radio broadcasts through speakers.[73] Their media, however, also reaches beyond these territories. For example, *Dabiq* and *Rumiyah* are ISIS's English language online magazines, and until early 2018, they were freely available to anyone who had access to the World Wide Web.[74] Their radio station *Al-Bayan* broadcasts in Arabic, Kurdish, English, French and Russian, and while FM frequencies could be tuned into from neighboring territories, it was also available online through links and later even through an app.[75] They have been using a variety of social media including YouTube, WordPress, Twitter WhatsApp and Telegram, among others, to communicate with recruits and disseminate propaganda materials,[76] and their own Arabic twitter app available through Google Play, called 'The Dawn of Glad Tidings,' automatically posted ISIS material and links through the accounts of everyone who had signed up for it.[77]

In places under ISIS control, one can thus observe an environment where the marketplace of ideas has been severely diminished and replaced with a saturation of hate propaganda, thus creating a fertile ground for its calls to violent action.

Speaking in Vox Dei

In the theory of Staub, the basic sources of genocide are cultural characteristics and difficult life conditions.[78] In terms of the former, authoritarian cultures as opposed to those that celebrate individual freedom and rights are more susceptible to genocide.[79] Second, the hierarchy of motives of a particular society sets which motives are higher on the list and thus easier to 'make active' than others.[80] And third, culture dictates the identification of the enemy.[81]

It is clear that ISIS use an extreme reading of the religion for the 'identification of the enemy.' Furthermore, ISIS ideology fits important characteristics of Muslim culture, tradition and society. Unlike in Christian Europe, where religion has taken a back seat to mostly secular values, in Muslim societies across the world, religion is still the most important aspect of an individuals' life with an emphasis on avoidance of sin and the obedience to God. The name Islam in itself stands for 'submission to God.' This indicates a culture, not with an acute sense of individual freedom but rather of obedience, albeit not to any worldly figure, but God himself. Radical Islamist narratives cherry-pick excerpts from scripture, take them out of their context and burry the significance of central Islamic practices[82] to manipulate and hijack this noble sentiment (which can also be described as one of the main 'motives' of the culture), and employ it for less than noble ends.

Using a testimonial persuasion technique, that is, pretending to speak in Vox Dei,[83] ISIS heavily lace their narrative with reference to the *Qur'ān*, the teachings of the Prophet Muhammad as well as numerous Islamic scholars, some more other less known.[84] This method of persuasion relies on the selective omission of facts and the deliberate mischaracterization of events and adversaries and is what transforms hate discourse into hate propaganda.[85] In the context of ISIS, it is ultimately persuasive to a section of the population as it creates the illusion that to deny the orders of ISIS would be to deny the orders of Allah. ISIS further seek to present an aura of legitimacy by publishing and broadcasting in the name of 'caliph' Abu Bakr al-Baghdadi who claims direct descent from the Prophet.

Polarization of audiences

One could categorize ISIS articles, programs, videos and songs according to their different topics; however, the polarization of the audience and the creation of a crisis–solution dichotomy is the leitmotif that runs through nearly all of them. Thus, already the titles of the newspapers *Dabiq* and *Rumiyah* convey this message, when understood in light of their theological connotations. Dabiq is a small town in Syria, where, according to Islamic prophecy the apocalyptic battle against Rome (Christians) will take place. To reiterate the location's importance, every issue begins with a quote by Abū Mus'ab al-Zarqāwī[86]: "The spark has been lit here in Iraq, and its heart will continue to intensify – by Allah's permission – until it burns the crusader armies in Dābiq." ISIS claim they are fulfilling this prophecy by establishing a caliphate and those who join it will be saved whereas all others will "melt as salt melts in water" on facing him.[87] The same idea is hammered in with the title of the second issue of the magazine called "The Flood," whereby the story of Noah is used to portray the ISIS caliphate as the arc while anyone failing to join shall be wiped away.[88] Referencing such events may appear insignificant and merely metaphorical to secular audiences, yet a large percentage of the Muslim population believes that they will live to see the apocalypse,[89] which highlights the importance of conducting an analysis of the material thrust into the social sphere by ISIS in light of how their intended audience understands its implications.

In issue 4 of *Dābiq*, entitled "The Failed Crusade" and bearing an image of the Vatican on its cover, al-Zarqāwī is quoted as saying, "We perform *jihād* here while our eyes are on al-Quds. We fight here, while our goal is Rome."[90] He then reassures those skeptical that "Allah will grant the Muslims the conquest of Rome, just as Allah's Messenger (sallallāhu 'alayhi wa sallam) promised."[91] His successor Abū Hamzah al-Muhājir further declares that "we will not rest from our *jihād* until we are under the olive trees of Rome, after we destroy the filthy house called the White House."[92] After 15 issues and when ISIS lost control over Dābiq in a humiliating defeat to Turkish-backed rebels, they renamed the magazine to *Rumiyah* (Rome) in order to avoid reminding the readers of their loss while keeping the reference to the same apocalyptic narrative. The fight against "Rome" now represents the fight against all Western civilization as a continuation of the ancient Roman Empire, against which the early Muslims fought.[93] Thus, already the very titles of *Dābiq* and *Rumiyah* coincide with the group's genocidal intent as it highlights their aim to eradicate everyone outside the realm of their Islamic belief, a vision embodied in their establishment of their utopian caliphate.

ISIS thus present the 'Islamic State' as the *only* justified and legitimate political structure of *the Ummah* (Muslim society) and Abu Bakr al Baghdadi as the *Amīrul Mu'minīn* (the Commander of the Faithful). By doing so they present it as a religious *duty* to pledge allegiance to them and migrate to what is described as a 'glorious' new caliphate. To them, in the name of God, victory is promised which will bring the end of humiliation for the Muslims and restore the golden age of Islam.[94] With this comes a necessary rejection of one's loyalty to any other group based on tribe, nationality or citizenship.[95]

Anyone who falls outside the circle of ISIS's adherents, falls in the camp of *kufr* (unbelief). In *Dabiq* 3, al-Zarqāwī puts before the readers a clear choice: "There are only two camps: the camp of truth and its followers, and the camp of falsehood and its factions. So, choose to be from one of the two camps."[96] This out-group does not merely include the traditional targets of Islamist groups such as those of Al-Qaeda, that is, the 'far enemy' (the crusader West or the communist Russians) and the 'near enemy' (secular regimes of Muslim majority countries), but also all other religious groups, different Islamic sects, such as the Shi'a, and even other Sunni Muslims. Using derogatory language and names, these groups are described, as deviant, wicked, innately hostile to Muslims, and their killing is not only described as permissible but as an essential part of practicing the religion and 'a form of worship' in itself.[97]

In contrast with the constant denigration of 'the enemy,' the articles glorify ISIS fallen leaders and fighters, always writing *tarahhum*[98] after their names, referring to them as martyrs and their suicide missions as *istishhādi* operations, that is, heroic deaths.[99] On the other hand, active fighters are called 'knights' acting to defend Muslim honor[100] or more commonly the *mujāhidīn*, that is, those engaged in a battle against the enemies of Islam.

In *Dabiq* 4, "The Failed Crusade," the then spokesperson for ISIS, Shaykh Abū Muhammad al-'Adnānī ash-Shāmī, is quoted adoringly flattering the soldiers:

> O soldiers of the Islamic State, what a great thing you have achieved by Allah! […] Who are you? Who are you O soldiers of the Islamic State? From where have you come? What is your secret? Why is it that the hearts of the East and West are dislocated by their fear of you? Why is it that the chest muscles of America and its allies shiver out of fear of you?[101]

Dabiq interweaves rational- and identity-choice appeals using a variety of narratives. According to Ingram, similarly to Al-Qaeda's *Inspire* magazine, the architects of *Dabiq* strategically generate psychological, existential and sociopolitical anxieties in the audience which is presented with a clear choice between the out-group (tied to the image of crisis) or the in-group (tied to the image of solution).[102]

The use of sound and vision

Using sound and vision, ISIS push further their divisive narrative as well as their claim of fulfilling God's will. *Dabiq* and *Rumiyah* are thus replete with images of scripture and the *mujāhidīn* reading scripture or praying; staged or photoshopped representations of events from the *Qur'ān* or Islamic history; the *tawhīd* gesture declaring the oneness of God; the ISIS flag; actions signifying allegiance to ISIS; instances of ISIS exercising their authority by enforcing *Shari'āh* rulings and cases of ISIS engaging in social welfare activities.[103]

Furthermore, the magazines are full of images of the 'far' and 'near' enemies and the outcomes of the battles between them and ISIS. High-definition depictions of the most abhorrent brutality are not rare, with graphic images of beheadings, the dead bodies of ISIS fighters, the damage caused by Coalition-led airstrikes, and mass killings of civilians are scattered throughout the magazine. The blame for this misery, which ISIS have largely been responsible for creating, is squarely put on the shoulders of the stereotyped and generalized out-groups, further stirring up passions of resentment and desire for revenge. The wide broadcast of unvarnished violence is, furthermore, an attempt at desensitizing audiences and blunting empathy, attracting individuals to violent action and frightening victims into compliance.[104]

ISIS also use *jihādi anashīd* as one of their main propaganda techniques either stand-alone or as video soundtracks. *Anashīd* (religious hymns) have always existed in Islam. However, during the rise of Islamists movements in the 1970s and 1980s, a new form emerged, that is, *jihādi nashīd*. Islamists in Syria and Egypt used *nashīd* songbooks, records and cassettes to change the public's interpretation of Islam, while exiled Egyptian Muslim Brotherhood members set up youth camps in Saudi Arabia where attendees sung *anashīd*.[105] Some of the *anashīd* written at this time are still used in videos of terrorist organizations today.[106]

Initially, ISIS relied on existing *anashīd*; however, they gradually shifted to producing their own and founded a specialized unit for this purpose in 2013.[107] By 2017, 94 percent of their videos used IS-specific *anashīd*. Since they are less prone to being removed from the web, they have become the most popular *jihādi* content online.[108]

Sang *a cappella*, producers make the recordings sound more impressive by multitracking them with digital software, as if there were a multitude of voices singing in perfect harmony. Composed in classical Arabic, they follow the rules of classical Arabic poetry (*qasida*).[109] They tend to adhere to a monorhyme and monometer and thus usually have a strong rhythm, which suggests a great potential to "hook their listeners."[110] The poetry, repetition and engaging rhythm, coupled with the use of themes that are likely to resonate with Sunni Muslim audiences on an emotional level, make them a powerful tool for reinforcing grievances and motivating violent action. For example, *anashīd* decrying the current weakness of the *Ummah* are likely to arouse emotions in those that have traditionally viewed it as destined for world leadership. *Anashīd* focusing on a sense of humiliation are likely to resonate with younger Muslims, be it those in the Middle East, facing high levels of unemployment despite being educated,[111] or second or third generation migrants in the West experiencing feelings of double non-belonging.[112]

Staub identified difficult life conditions and the needs and motives that arise from them, as one of the main sources of genocide. He sees humiliation as such a life condition.[113] Reflecting on radical Islamism in the 1970s and 1980s, Emmanuel Sivan noted that the twentieth century had been particularly hard on Muslim self-esteem; "[a] civilization that had always viewed itself as destined for leadership suffered one setback after the other at the hands of infidels who now set the pace in all realms of human activity."[114] Several new Western foreign policy disasters since then have only added insult to injury.

Playing on these emotions, the *anashīd* present as the only solution to humiliation brutality and the waging of war against anyone and anything un-Islamic which offers great pride, victory and rewards in heaven.[115] An illustrative example is the most famous ISIS *nashīd*, "My *Ummah*, Dawn has appeared, so await the expected victory." An excerpt from another *nashīd*, "I am not pleased with the life of humiliation," reads,

> The life of humiliation, no, I am not pleased with it
> And love of death with honour is a desire
> By God, I do not fear death, for the slave has no place in the world,
> For the slave has no place in the world
> For the slave has no place in the world.[116]

Lemieux and Nill find that melody can increase the ability to convey a message, because rhythmic and tonal elements can make it very captivating and addictive, while at the same time making the listeners less critical to the message conveyed, by engaging them on an emotional level.[117] For music with aggressive lyrical themes they found that it demonstrates "the potential to increase aggressive thoughts, feelings, and potentially behaviors among listeners."[118] In the context of radicalism across different ideologies, Pieslak found abundant examples of music's pivotal function, from recruitment strategies to engendering a culture of militancy and motivating action.[119]

It is exactly the ability of music to evoke emotions that has made *anashīd* problematic in the eyes of Wahhabis. They take a suspicious stance toward *anashīd* because they see them as a distraction from studying and listening to the *Qur'ān*.[120] On the other hand, the Muslim Brotherhood is more relaxed on music. The *jihādi* movement, taking inspiration from both, uses music extensively, however only following the strict *Salafīst* conditions placed on it.[121]

The *anashīd* play an important role in creating a sense of community. ISIS videos clearly document *nashīd* sessions in which *jihādis* recite *anashīd* together as well as *da'wa* (preaching Islam) events involving considerable live recitation.[122] Behnam Said notes that they are a common cultural asset which connect people all over the globe and therefore are a valuable tool in creating a global *jihādi* community.[123] ISIS group-specific *anashīd*, furthermore, reflect its distinct political identity as a state.[124] By replacing the existing Islamic *anashīd* with their own productions, IS signaled the beginning of a new era which demands the purging of all cultural items contaminated by anything non-ISIS, reflecting the dominant Muslim imagination which projects a binary between Islam and *jahiliyyah*.[125]

Another powerful tool employed by ISIS in its propaganda efforts is the use of skillfully produced videos. The videos professionally reflect the format of modern Western action movie trailers or video games, where violence is depicted as exciting entertainment and any negative impact in terms of human suffering is left out of the picture, desensitizing viewers to the violence. Accompanying the images are typical movie trailer sound effects skillfully intertwined with *anashīd*.

A good example of this is one of the most professionally produced videos, the "Flames of War" produced by Al Hayat Media Centre.[126] Its first part depicting 'the crisis' is filled with classic cinematic tension build-up sound effects, creating anxiety in the audience, which is then soothed with the introduction of the calming sound of the *nashīd*. Finally, the built-up anxiety is released through 'the solution,' that is, depictions of ISIS violence against the enemy.

Negative stereotyping and generalization

In order to incite to genocide, ISIS employ the technique of extreme negative stereotyping in a somewhat complex fashion using religious justification. Unlike the Nazi genocide with its at least theoretically manageable target of exterminating the Jewish and other minority populations, and the Rwandan genocide focusing only on the Tutsis, ISIS make its target the vast majority of the world's population. While it is tempting to do so, it would be oversimplistic to describe ISIS narratives on the out-group as dehumanizing. Although they are certainly denying any dignity to the people belonging to these groups, they are not dehumanizing them, since in their perception humanity holds no value *per se*. People are not intrinsically worthy of respect, and nothing of human origin is of value or importance but rather characterized as *bid'ah* or *shirk*. Human emotions, apart from those in reference to God, equally hold no importance. A human only gains value by becoming a slave to God, following the rules of *Sharī'āh* and spreading the realm of Islam by *jihād*. In this sense, they also render the intrinsic morality of a human to be flawed; thus, any sympathy an ISIS follower may feel for the *kuffar* should be suppressed and replaced by the adherence of strict IS rules which dictate their killing 'wherever possible.' An example of suppressing natural instincts of humanity and compassion is clear in *Rumiyah*, issue 1, where a picture of a seemingly kind and smiling seller of flowers is accompanied with the caption "Even the blood of a merry Crusader citizen selling flowers to passers-by [is permissible for you to shed, so shed it]."[127]

The out-group, is termed by ISIS "the camp of *kufr*, *riddah* [apostasy] and hypocrisy," "the camp of the Jews, the crusaders, their allies, and with them the rest of the nations and religions of *kufr*, all being led by America and Russia"[128] or the civilization of *shirk*, the civilization of *riba* (usury) and prostitution, the civilization of humiliation and subjugation.[129] Within are different subgroups distinguished by what ISIS present as their respective lack of belief in the Islamic religion. Each holding a specific connotation, ISIS use several names for these groups, many times bearing a deeply derogatory meaning from a (Sunni) Muslim perspective, such as the *murtaddūn*, the *mushrikūn*, the crusaders, the innovators,[130] the rebellious,[131] the hypocrites,[132] the quasi-*jihādists*, mock *mujāhidīn*, the *tawāghīt* and their followers, and the *Rāfidah* (the rejectors).

There is at least in theory a hierarchy between the groups. Based on the teachings of Ibn Taymiyyah and Muhammad Ibn 'Abd-al-Wahhab, ISIS categorize disbelief and polytheism from the most to the least severe. Thus, the refusal to excommunicate Satan, or claiming to be a deity, as well as worshiping them is at the top of the list. Wrongly described as devil-worshippers,[133] the Yazidis thus fall into this category. The next category are pagans, Christians, Jews and anyone that has 'deviated' from Islam, while other categories consist of those who are simply 'immoral' or do not pray.[134] In *Dabiq* 9, a further hierarchy between the Christians and the Jews is explained: "because the *kāfir* Christians did not curse Prophet 'Īsā ('alayhis-salām) nor accuse his virtuous mother of sin, they were made to humiliate the Jews who cursed 'Īsā and slandered Maryam."[135]

Below we thus examine the meanings behind the names given to specific groups on IS's list of enemies and the main IS narratives on them in light of the relevant context which clearly convey direct incitement to genocide.

ISIS category of the devil – worshippers: Yazidi

Yazidis are considered to be one of the oldest ethnic groups in Mesopotamia.[136] They identify themselves, not merely in terms of ethnicity but also in terms of religion. Their monotheistic belief emanate from a mixture of other religions including Christianity, Shamanism and Zoroastrianism.[137] For centuries and long before the emergence of ISIS, the misinterpretation of this belief, has made the community a target of genocidal language and violence.[138] For example, the Ottomans constantly subjected them to forced conversions[139] and those who rejected such religious assimilation suffered violence or even death.[140] In the Ottoman archives and unofficial documents, one can find the characterization of Yazidis as a "pervert community," "looters and bandits who do not pay their taxes."[141] Furthermore, they are described as the "descendants of Yezid bin Muaviye"[142] (647–683 A.D.), the second caliph of the Umayyad dynasty, known as the perpetrator of Karbala Incident and thus an utterly disliked figure among Shi'a, 'Alawites and Sunni Muslims. ISIS continue to ascribe this lineage to the Yazidis, despite the name having nothing to do with Yazid, but rather deriving from the Farsi word "ized," which means angel or deity. The name Izidis simply means "worshippers of god," which is how Yazidis describe themselves.[143]

In *Dabiq* 4, ISIS brand the Yazidis an "originally *mushrik* group," that is, polytheists (*mushrikūn*) since pre-Islamic times. They describe their 'creed' as entailing,

> the worship of *Iblīs* [devil] who they [Yazidis] consider to be a fallen but forgiven angel amongst the angels who were ordered to prostrate to *Ādam*! He alone refused to prostrate to *Ādam*, and they consider this arrogant disobedience of Allah to be his noblest deed! They consider him to be misunderstood by mankind! They consider him to be good and enlightened, and claim that Allah will openly forgive him on Judgment Day after already forgiving him beforehand for crying tears of piety over a period of thousands of years! So they have made *Iblīs* – who is the biggest *tāghūt* – the symbolic head of enlightenment and piety! What arrogant *kufr* can be greater than this?[144]

Here, ISIS are taking actual elements of the Yazidi religion and distort them in order to portray the group as devil-worshippers and stir up disgust for them among the Muslim population. While in fact monotheists, Yazidis believe in the angel Melek Taus whose story resembles that of Satan, however, according to their belief he is not the devil but rather has become an intermediary between God and humanity after having reconciled with God. In the extremist ISIS view on the world however, there is only space for one interpretation and meaning of the story and Yazidis display the biggest *kufr* by understanding it in their own way. In the words of ISIS, the

> continual existence [of Yazidis] to this day is a matter that Muslims should question as they will be asked about it on Judgment Day, considering that Allah had revealed Āyat as-Sayf (the verse of the sword) over 1,400 years ago.[145]

With this ISIS makes a clear call to genocide as they present to their followers the destruction of the Yazidi group as a religious duty of utmost importance. The destruction however is not focused on the Yazidi as an ethnic group but as a religious group, thus conversion to Islam is offered as a way out of death and even the sexual enslavement of Yazidi women and children is presented as a way to the eventual conversion of the group to Islam.[146] This does not however make their aim any less genocidal as

> protecting against forced religious conversions safeguards the very existence of certain human groups and endorses elementary principles of morality. By including religious groups within the Convention's protections, the drafters reveal their intent that protecting religious beliefs is of paramount importance.[147]

ISIS category of the pagan Christians (Nassarah, Nazarene)

In *Dabiq* ISIS refers to their *fuqahā'* (scholars) to explain how each out-group should be dealt with. Thus the *fuqahā'* indicated that Jews and Christians could pay *jizyah* (religious tax) and continue their existence within the Caliphate.[148] On the contrary, for the Yazidis as 'original *mushrikūn*' there was no room for such an arrangement.[149] This official narrative of IS has lead the United Nations Human Rights Council (UNHRC) to conclude that IS do not intend to eradicate Christians, as they do the Yazidis, but instead offer to protect and respect them through the traditional Islamic option of entering a *dhimmah* covenant of security and safety and paying the *jizya* (religious tax).[150] Yet interviews with the Christian leaders directly involved with negotiations with ISIS reveal that the claims of this option are a "deception and a propaganda ploy" more akin to extortion than the seventh-century Pact of Omar according to which the community paid a progressive tax, in exchange for the protection of their families' lives and property and for their religious rights.[151] *Dabiq* 15, furthermore, makes it clear that it is not enough to pay the *jizya* but that the Christians have to live under the authority of Islam in humiliation and even so, ISIS declare "we would continue to hate you [the Christians]."[152] They, furthermore, stipulate that the hatred is a religious duty based *first and foremost* on the 'disbelief' of the Christians for rejecting the oneness of Allah by making partners for him in worship, a reference to the concept of the Holy Trinity.[153] For this, they declare the Christians to be pagans and polytheists and this *shirk* makes them a legitimate target to be killed.[154] Second, the hatred is based on Christian societies being secular, liberal and nationalistic and permitting what "Allah has prohibited while banning many of the things He has permitted."[155] Western foreign policy is only further down on the list of reasons for hatred which the article makes explicitly clear:

> What's important to understand here is that although some might argue that your foreign policies are the extent of what drives our hatred, this particular reason for hating you is secondary [...] The fact is, even if you were to stop bombing us, imprisoning us, torturing us, vilifying us, and usurping our lands, we would continue to hate you because our primary reason for hating you will not cease to exist until you embrace Islam.[156]

Dabiq explains that any halt to the IS war against Christians can only be temporary, until all Christians convert to Islam.[157] The inviolability of their blood in cases of a *dhimmah* contract would be an exceptional ruling, and whenever that ruling is terminated – either due to their violation of the covenant, or due to the expiry of the duration of the covenant – "their blood would go back to the default ruling of it being permissible to shed."[158]

The genocidal intent of ISIS propaganda is also evident from their video depicting the slaughter of Christians in Libya and Ethiopia and the destruction of churches, crosses and paintings depicting the Virgin Mary. A voice in the video says,

> To the nation of the cross, we are back again [...] Muslim blood that was shed under the hands of your religion is not cheap. We swear to Allah [...] you will not have safety even in your dreams until you embrace Islam.[159]

Despite describing Western foreign policy as a "less important" factor, IS seek to arouse hatred in their targeted audience for all Christians exactly by stereotyping them and presenting them as the coalition forces and crusaders. This way, absurdly, even Coptic Christians from Egypt get branded crusaders before being slaughtered:

> Oh people, recently you've seen us on the hills of Al-Sham [Greater Syria] and on Dabiq's Plain, chopping off the heads that had been carrying the cross delusion for a long time, filled with spite against Islam and Muslims, and today we [...] are sending another message: Oh crusaders, safety for you will be only wishes especially when you're fighting us all together, therefore we will fight you all together until the war lays down its burdens and Jesus peace be upon him will descend, breaking the cross, killing the swine. The sea you have hidden Sheikh Osama bin Laden's body in, we swear to Allah we will mix it with your blood.[160]

In *Dabiq* 9, Christians are presented as those who 'plot' against Muslims in an apparent 'accusation in a mirror,'[161] while Baghdadi dispels any possibility of a peaceful coexistence between Muslims and Christians saying,

> O Muslims! Whoever thinks that it is within his capacity to conciliate with the Jews, Christians, and other *kuffār*, and for them to conciliate with him, such that he coexists with them and they coexist with him while he is upon his religion and upon *tawhīd*, then he has belied the explicit statement of his Lord.[162]

Furthermore, *Dabiq* 7 leaves little doubt as to the instructions to their followers regarding the treatment of this group when it states, "We will argue, before Allah, against any Muslim who has the ability to shed a single drop of crusader blood but does not do so."[163] *Dabiq* 15 makes it clear that while Christians are being dragged by ISIS "further and further into a swamp" they are offered a way out by way of conversion to Islam[164] while *Rumiyah*, issue 9, sanctions the slavery of Christian women and children.[165] From the above it is clear that the future IS propagates for the Christian communities is much like that of the Yazidi, that is, their destruction.

In 2016, the European Parliament unanimously passed a resolution recognizing the rapes, murders, kidnappings, enslavement and dispossessions of Christians, Yazidi and other religious minorities by ISIS as genocide as did later the US House of Representatives and the UK Parliament.[166]

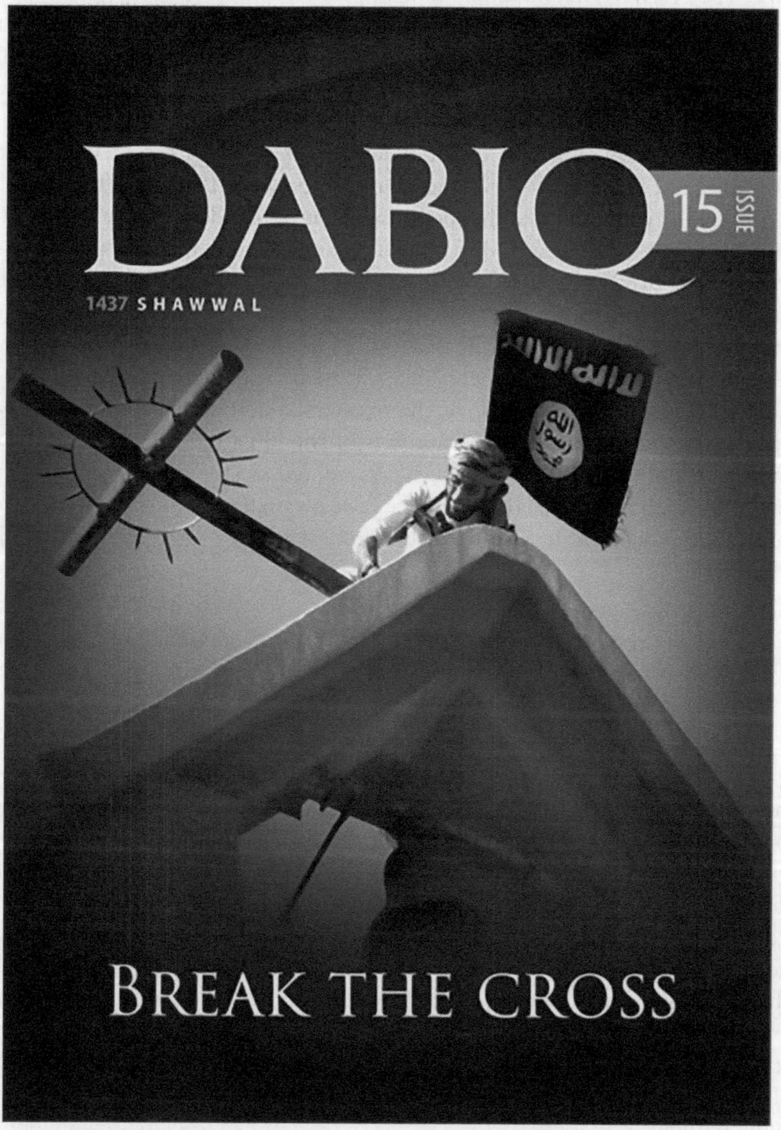

Figure 1.1 The cover of *Dabiq*, Issue 15, shows an image of the destruction of the main Christian symbol of faith. Courtesy of Aron Y. Zelin and Jihadology.net.

ISIS category of apostates: the Shi'a, 'Alawites, Durūz and Ismā'Īliyyah, the Sahwāt and the followers of the Tāghūt

The apostate group, according to ISIS, includes, among others, the *Rāfidah/ Safawi* (pejoratively referring to Shi'a Muslims), *Nusayriyyah* (pejoratively referring to 'Alawites), Durūz (Druze community), Ismā'īliyyah (branch of Shi'a Islam) and followers of the *tawāghīt*.[167] According to the ISIS *fuqahā'*, unlike the *mushrikūn*, the 'apostate' groups cannot be enslaved but "can only be given an ultimatum to repent or face the sword."[168]

The Shi'a are arguably one of the main targets of IS hatred and aggression, which does not reflect only the sectarian divide between the Sunni and Shi'a but also the hostility found across the spectrum of the *Salafī* ideology toward the Shi'a beliefs.[169] The former Grand Mufti of Saudi Arabia, 'Abd al-'Aziz bin Baz stated that every sect of Shi'a has forms of *bid'ah*[170] and contradicts the Islamic way called by the Prophet Muhammad.[171] Zarqāwī declared all Shi'a apostates and publicly announced that their "perfidy engraved in the forehead of history."[172] *Dabiq* 13, refers to more than 20 scholars who allegedly made *takfīr* of the Shi'a.[173]

ISIS refer to Shi'a as *Rāfidah*, or the rejecters, a derogatory term dating back to the Umayyad dynasty used on account of the Shi'a refusal to recognize the first three caliphs as legitimate. Shi'ism is presented as a plot by a Jew[174] and their awaited Messiah as the Dajjāl, that is, the false messiah or the great deceiver – the most dangerous figure in Islamic eschatology (theology concerning the end of the world):

> The closer the Hour approaches, the more the *Rāfidah* fall in line with the Jews in preparation for the appearance of this awaited evil leader. Upon reading the *Rāfidī* account of the 'Mahdī,' it becomes clear that he is none other than the Dajjāl.[175]

One can, furthermore, observe classic hate propaganda techniques of depicting a people in animal terms. "The *Rāfidah* are the insurmountable obstacle, the lurking snake, the scorpion of deception and malice, the prowling enemy, the deadly poison."[176] The Shi'a are also stereotyped as *Safawiyyah*, a term associated by Sunnis with any expansionist Shi'a groups acting against Sunnis or their interests.[177] In the article "Know your Enemy: Who Were the Safawiyyah?" ISIS presents them as a group started by a Sufi order "which transformed into a militant *Rāfidī* movement to become a tyrannical state that subdued Persia with ambitions to wipe out all traces of the *Sunnah* and its people."[178] Today's Shi'a are presented as the continuation of this 'cult' propagating Persianism and allying with the crusaders.[179]

Nibras Kazimi traces the current intensified Sunni hostility toward the Shi'a to a book supposedly written by a Syrian member of the Muslim Brotherhood in which he claimed that the Iranian revolution was only in part about the revival of Shi'a Islam while the rest was about restoring Zoroastrianism, which threatens Islamic and Arabic culture.[180] This is reflected in another name ISIS use for the Shi'a, that is, the *Majūs*, a pejorative term for Zoroastrians, who despite being the first monotheists were wrongfully branded by Islamists as "fire worshippers" due to their belief that fire represents God's light or wisdom.[181] *Dabiq* also features an image of a Shi'a shrine dedicated to Piruz Nahawandi, termed in Arabic Abū Lu'lu'ah al-Majūsī, a Sasasian general revered by the Shi'a but hated by the Sunni due to his assassination of Caliph Umar who was holding him captive.[182] The 'al-Majūsī' indicates that the Sunnis consider him to be a Zoroastrian. The reference to his shrine is an apparent attempt to tap into historical resentments and mainstream Sunni sentiments as many Sunni scholars have called the shrine offensive and un-Islamic and have demanded its destruction.[183] It is also important to note that the term *Majūs* was used for Iranians as part of Iraqi propaganda already in the 1980s during the Iraq-Iran war to depict Iranians as not real Muslims.

In sum, ISIS portray Shi'a as apostates that worship the dead and other forms of *kufr* and *shirk* and claim that they have "nothing to do with Islam other than to deter the people from it."[184] In another classic case of 'accusation in a mirror,' IS claim that the Shi'a have a tradition of hatred toward the *Ahlus-Sunnah* (Sunnis) and aim to eradicate them and replace them with a population of apostasy.[185] This talk can easily fall on fertile ground as within the last decade, polls have found that at least 40 percent of Sunni Muslims from five Middle Eastern and North African countries did not recognize the Shi'a as true Muslims.[186] Exploiting this collective sectarianist view allowed IS to ally themselves with other Sunni militant groups with which it had previously been fighting.[187] Thus, this demonization also serves as a unifier through hatred of the 'other'.[188]

Numerous other groups fall under the catch-all category of 'apostates' due to their beliefs such as the 'Alawites, Durūz and Ismā'īliyyah. Still other groups fall under this category due to their political orientation, despite professing a Sunni belief. As mentioned above, any ruler embracing nationalistic or even democratic ideas as opposed to pure *Shari'āh* is named a *tāghūt* and their followers *murtaddūn*. For example, in *Dabiq* 6, a picture of Egyptian soldiers holds the caption "The *murtadd* soldiers of Egypt's new Pharaoh,"[189] while a picture of Jordanian pilots meeting the king holds the caption "The *murtaddūn* meet the *tāghūt* of Jordan."[190] After IS had shot down a Jordanian plane and captured its pilot, *Dabiq* ran an interview with him. Instead of his name, Muath al-Kasasbeh, the word *murtadd* appeared before every answer he gave, a clear propaganda technique of relentless repetition of the derogatory term to achieve the desired effect on the audience.[191]

Even the modern Muslim Brotherhood get the name "The Murtadd Brotherhood" on the front cover of *Dabiq* 14.[192] Inside, readers are told the *Ikhwān* (Brotherhood) is,

> nothing but a secularist party with an 'Islamic' cloak [...] the wickedest of the secularists [...] [a] party that worships seats and parliaments [...] a party that would prostrate to *Iblīs* if it were required to achieve seats [...] a party of

> extreme apostasy and [...] it is thus obligatory upon the Muslims to declare the stance of *takfīr*, *barā'ah*, animosity, and enmity towards this group and its members.[193]

In other words, no better than devil-worshippers, the Muslim Brotherhood is at the receiving end of ISIS hatred due to the Brotherhood embracing democratic procedures and legislation as in their ideology this goes against the *hakimiyya*.[194] The Taliban are also condemned for their *murtadd* nationalism, their 'superficial application' of the *Shari'āh* their support for *kāfir* systems and embracing of *tawāghit*.[195]

Since political affiliation is not one of the categories defining protected groups under the Genocide Convention, one might conclude that the targeting of the supposed *tawāghit* and their followers could not fall under the definition of the crime of genocide. However, since ISIS themselves do not distinguish between the political and the religious and target these people as 'apostates,' their persecution, nevertheless, falls under 'religious.' As far as the framing of the protected groups is concerned, there has been a shift in international jurisprudence from an objective understanding to a combination of objective and subjective criteria. The ICTR thus considered both self-perception (self-identification by the group) and perception (identification by others) as criteria for defining a people as a protected group under the Genocide Convention.[196]

Much attention of ISIS is also dedicated to the disdain of the so-called *Sahwāt* (Awakening). A fairly modern term, *Sahwāt* has its roots in the war in Iraq where it was used for local Sunni tribes which collaborated with the US forces against al-Zarqāwī and the Al-Qaeda in Iraq, the precursor to ISIS. The term is now used by ISIS to denote all Sunni 'traitors,' who do not support ISIS and fight against them.[197] According to the black-and-white ISIS logic, this makes them also apostates.

All these categorizations of people as *kuffar* and their rejection and persecution follow from the aggressive interpretation of the concept of *al-walā' wa-l-barā*, a fundamental part of ISIS ideology, and its many implications described above. As mentioned earlier, ISIS are far more radical in their use of *takfīr* than other Islamist groups. Thus in *Dabiq*, ISIS strongly criticize Al-Qaeda, and their leader Ayman al-Zawahiri, for not making *takfīr* of the Shi'a in general, but only on account of their support of America in their aggression toward the Sunnis.[198] Likewise, they are criticized for not making *takfīr* on the supporters of the *tawāghit* except for those officers who torture Muslims and belong to some specific departments of National Security.[199] While Zawahiri refuses to declare *takfīr* on these groups of Muslims due to their 'ignorance,' ISIS strongly oppose this option.[200] ISIS also criticize Zawahiri for not issuing a blanket condemnation on anyone resisting any *Shari'āh* laws, while they make it clear that the slightest disobedience to the *Shari'āh* would be met with a declaration of apostasy and the subjugation to killings, enslavement and the taking of wealth.[201]

As with most totalitarian movements, the ISIS idea of purging the society through the practice of *takfīr* reached absurd proportions, when a fatwa was issued on 17th May 2017 with "the second most important seal" in ISIS, that is, the Delegated Committee which is directly subordinate to Baghdadi. The ruling declared "making of *takfīr* of the *mushrikin* as one of the *utmost principles of the religion*, which must be known before knowing the prayer and other obligations that are known of the religion by necessity" (emphasis added).[202] By elevating *takfīr* to a principle of the religion, they essentially declared *takfīr* on any Muslim, who failed to exercise *takfīr* on others.[203] In contrast, the Grand Mufti and one of the first *jihādist* ideologues supporting Baghdadi's caliphate, Turki Al-Bin'ali himself rejected the fatwa and said it would have led to an 'endless chain of *takfīr*' denouncing as unbelievers even adamant *takfīrists* such as al-Zarqāwī and Abu Muhammad al Adnani, who refrained from declaring *takfīr* on all Muslims who did not follow their ways.[204] After publishing it in *Rumiyah* and *Al Naba*, ISIS eventually rescinded the ruling in an effort to quell the controversy and released numerous lectures through *Al Bayan* radio, cross-promoted by *Al Naba* proclaiming that *takfīr* was in fact not a principle of the religion but merely an obligation and that 'ignorance' was a sufficient excuse for failing to excommunicate other Muslims in some cases.[205] Furthermore, he made it clear that it is permissible to refrain from *takfīr* in the lightest forms of disbelief, that is, when Muslims are merely 'immoral' or not praying.[206]

Placing ISIS rhetoric in the context of international criminal law

Incitement to hatred and hate propaganda have been dealt with in the international criminal jurisprudence since the Nazi propagandist Julius Streicher was found guilty of crimes against humanity by the International Military Tribunal at Nuremberg (IMT), while another propagandist, Hans Fritzsche, was acquitted. Since then the United Nations Convention on the Prevention and Punishment of the Crime of Genocide (1948) established the international crime of direct and public incitement to commit genocide.[207] This crime was incorporated verbatim into the statutes of the International Criminal Tribunal for the Former Yugoslavia (ICTY, 1993) and the ICTR (1994), while the International Criminal Court (ICC, 2002) statute, in respect of the crime of genocide, established individual criminal responsibility for anyone who directly and publicly incites others to commit genocide.[208]

While publicly uttered hate speech falling short of direct incitement to commit genocide did not get its own specific provision in any of the statutes, it can still be considered criminal if it amounts to instigation, aiding and abetting[209] or participation in a joint criminal enterprise[210] in relation to any of the enumerated crimes in the statutes. For the establishment of liability in these instances, a causal link is necessary between the speech and subsequent crimes committed, while such a link is not necessary in terms of incitement to genocide.[211]

In Nahimana et al. and more recently in Šešelj the ICTR and ICTY respectively established that hate speech can *per se* constitute persecution as a crime against humanity, when there is discrimination in fact and the denial of a fundamental right, such as the right to dignity or the right to security.[212]

The elements of direct and public incitement to commit genocide

In Nahimana et al. the Appeal Judgment defines the elements of direct and public incitement to commit genocide as follows:

> A person may be found guilty of the crime specified in Article 2(3)(c) of the Statute if he or she directly and publicly incited the commission of genocide (the material element or *actus reus*) and had the intent directly and publicly to incite others to commit genocide (the intentional element or *mens rea*). Such intent in itself presupposes a genocidal intent.[213]

The public element of incitement is satisfied when call for criminal action is communicated to the public at large, for example, through means of mass communication.[214] It is clear that IS more than satisfy this element by spreading their propaganda relentlessly through numerous means and channels, as explained above. The other element of the *actus reus* is whether the call for criminal action is direct. In this regard, the Akayesu Trial Judgment made it clear that

> the direct element of incitement should be viewed in the light of its cultural and linguistic content. Indeed, a particular speech may be perceived as 'direct' in one country, and not so in another, depending on the audience [...] incitement may be direct, and nonetheless implicit [...] The Chamber will [...] consider on a case-by-case basis whether, in light of the culture [...] and the specific circumstances of the instant case, acts of incitement can be viewed as direct or not, by focusing mainly on the issue of whether the persons for whom the message was intended immediately grasped the implication thereof.[215]

In Nahimana et al. the Appeals Chamber (hereinafter AC) confirmed this approach and noted that it had been adopted in several other judgments and by the Supreme Court of Canada in Mugesera.[216] The Chamber further stated that "the principal consideration is thus the meaning of the words used in the specific context: it does not matter that the message may appear ambiguous to another audience or in another context."[217]

ISIS narrative is laced with explicit calls for killing and destruction,[218] which would be clearly understood as such by any culture around the globe. For example, consider the statement in issue 13 of *Dabiq* referring to the Shi'a: "the *Rāfidah* [...] must be killed wherever they are to be found, until no *Rāfidī* walks on the face of earth."[219]

However, taking into consideration the particular context, culture and ideology, these are not the only statements which their audience 'immediately grasps' as direct calls for extermination. Every time ISIS describe an individual or group as 'apostate,' this is undisputedly understood by their followers as a call to kill. While there is some controversy in the Muslim community as to whether *Shari'*āh prescribes a worldly punishment for apostasy, there is no doubt in the *jihādi-Salafī* ideology that the punishment is death.[220] It is exactly for this reason that declarations of *takfīr* in itself, without a need for any further explanations of what this implies, are perceived for their inherent danger of inciting violence and an effort to legislate against them has been taking place in Tunisia and Iraq.[221]

On the other hand, for anyone branded an original polytheist, such as the Yazidi, for *jihādī-Salafīs* the verse of the sword will apply, undoubtedly perceived by their audience as essentially the same instruction, that is, to kill. There is some room for enslavement and forcible conversion, when it comes to so-called original polytheists; however, this falls squarely under the destruction of a community, its culture and religion, regarded by some to fall under the definition of genocide.[222]

Furthermore, several statements advocate for a 'genocidal rape' campaign against Yazidi women. Issue 4 of *Dabiq* magazine, "The Failed Crusade" asserted that

> enslaving the families of the *kuffār* and taking their women as concubines is a firmly established aspect of the *Shari'āh* that if one were to deny or mock, he would be denying or mocking the verses of the *Qur'ān* and the narrations of the Prophet and thereby apostatizing from Islam.[223]

One of the aims of these rapes is to produce Muslim children out of Yazidi women. This is clear from the justifications for the rapes given by ISIS, when they describe as a sign of the end times that "the slave girl gives birth to her master," that is, based on the father's religion the child will be a Muslim and thus the master of the non-Muslim mother.[224] These calls constitute direct and public incitement to commit genocidal rape as recognized by the ICTR in its Akayesu Judgment, which concluded that even those rapes that do not result in the death of the victim could constitute genocide where "[s]exual violence was a step in the process of destruction of the […] group – destruction of the spirit, of the will to live, and of life itself." [225] As in the Rwandan example, the rapes of Yazidi women resulted not only in their psychological destruction, but also of their families and their communities.

Furthermore, in Nahimana et al. the AC noted that

> while it is not necessary to prove that the pronouncements in question had actual effects, the fact that they did have such effects can be an indication that the receivers of the message understood them as direct incitement to commit genocide.[226]

Widespread killings, rapes and acts of genocide have been attempted and committed by followers of ISIS, which additionally indicates that their propaganda is perceived as a call for such actions.

For example, in June 2016 the Independent International Commission of Inquiry on the Syrian Arab Republic submitted their report to the UNHRC, which found a genocidal campaign orchestrated by ISIS against the Yazidis' by demonstrating that the five enumerated acts of genocide have been materialized by ISIS:

> ISIS has sought to destroy the Yazidis through killings; sexual slavery, enslavement, torture and inhuman and degrading treatment and forcible transfer causing serious bodily and mental harm; the infliction of conditions of life that bring about a slow death; the imposition of measures to prevent Yazidi children from being born, including forced conversion of adults, the separation of Yazidi men and women, and mental trauma; and the transfer of Yazidi children from their own families and placing them with ISIS fighters, thereby cutting them off from beliefs and practices of their own religious community, and erasing their identity as Yazidis. The public statements and conduct of ISIS and its fighters clearly demonstrate that ISIS intended to destroy the Yazidis of Sinjar, composing the majority of the world's Yazidi population, in whole or in part.[227]

As mentioned above, in terms of the *mens rea*, the AC in Nahimana et al. established that it requires the intent directly and publicly to incite others to commit genocide, which in itself presupposes a genocidal intent.[228]

While unveiling the intention behind the ISIS general narrative and their particular statements, one should employ much of the same considerations as for determining whether the calls for criminal action were *direct*. That is, the cultural and ideological contexts as well as the context of any criminal acts being carried out while the message was disseminated. In Nahimana et al., the AC noted that "the fact that a speech leads to acts of genocide could be an indication [...] that this was indeed the intent of the author of the speech."[229]

The religious and ideological contexts of ISIS publications and broadcasts as analyzed in this chapter clearly demonstrate the requisite *mens rea* for direct and public incitement as does the fact that these messages were disseminated while religious minorities were actively being targeted and killed on the basis of their membership in religious groups.[230] The praising and glorification of such attacks and attackers in the relevant newspapers, videos and radio stations, furthermore, indicates the necessary intent.[231]

One should, furthermore, not overlook the fact that groups such as the Yazidis, Christians and Shi'a have been subject to widespread and systematic violence in the region in the past. This likewise indicates the intent of the propagandists to incite the commission of further crimes against these groups. The promotion of the destruction of minorities' places of worship and other cultural objects of significance to their existence as distinct groups is likewise an indicator of the intent to incite to genocide.[232]

Hate discourse surrounding the direct and public incitement to commit genocide as its essential context

In Nahimana the Prosecutor sought a characterization of the crime of direct and public incitement to commit genocide as a continuing crime, since an accused embarks on a course directed toward inciting, or instigating genocide, with every discrete act which is done in the pursuit of that goal necessarily building on and renewing the preceding acts done for the same purpose.[233] In the particular case, the Prosecution thus sought a conviction based on the totality of the articles published in *Kangura* and the totality of RTLM (Radio-Télévision Libre des Milles Collines) broadcasts for forming part of a *continuous transaction calculated to incite genocide.*[234] The AC did not consider it necessary to decide whether the totality of said articles and broadcasts could constitute one continuing incitement to commit genocide; however, it emphasized that an accused cannot be convicted simply on the basis of 'programming' in general but only on the basis of clearly identified specific acts of direct and public incitement[235]:

> It appears from the *travaux préparatoires* of Genocide Convention that only specific acts of direct and public incitement to commit genocide were sought to be criminalized and not hate propaganda or propaganda tending to provoke genocide.[236]

Despite this, the AC made it clear that context is a factor to consider in deciding whether the relevant discourse constitutes direct incitement to commit genocide and that uttered speech which does not by itself amount to this crime can, nevertheless, provide such a context.[237] As other contextually important information, it could explain how the listeners perceived the relevant speech and the impact the speech may have had.[238]

The AC acknowledged that "[i]n most cases, direct and public incitement to commit genocide can be preceded or accompanied by hate speech" that is not prohibited as such under Art. 2(3)(c) of the Statute.[239] In fact, more than merely 'accompanying' or 'preceding' genocide, history shows that extensive and systematic hate rhetoric which forms part of a persuasion campaign aimed at the relevant audience, is a *sine qua non* of a successful genocidal campaign. A direct and public incitement to commit genocide uttered in a vacuum, absent of a prior hate propaganda, would fall on unfertile ground and never reach the stage of prosecution at any international criminal tribunal. In this sense, it is not merely a trigger dependent on a particular culture, but it also importantly influences and molds that culture.

Our analysis shows that ISIS narrative covers all three components found in hate discourse that motivates and justifies violence, that is, negative stereotyping; presenting the group as an extreme threat to the well-being of the in-group; and the eliminationist solution in its most radical form, that is, calls for killing and rape.[240]

ISIS rhetoric is not only embedded in the existing culture, geopolitical situation of the region in which they operate and the religious ideology of violent *jihādi* groups that preceded them, but is also an important influence on all three that will outlive the group itself to inspire the ideological framework of the next generation of mass-murderers.

Conclusion

Tapping into mainstream emotions found across different Sunni Muslim communities, ISIS use negative stereotyping and labeling of the out-group to drive existing dislikes to hatred which arouses passion for revenge and aggression and a numbness toward the killing of the victim.[241] Such hate is found at the extreme end of a scale that runs from dislike, through animosity to outright hatred and it is negative stereotyping that leads to a move on this scale from less toward more negative emotions.[242] With their elimination of the gray zone,[243] they, furthermore, seek to undermine nonviolent modes of conflict management and instead unabashedly and relentlessly openly call for killing and genocide. In genocidal rhetoric the victims are characterized as a threat to the survival and well-being of the in-group creating a public demand for a response to reduce the threat.[244] As Ervin Staub theorizes, the immediate cause of genocide is that perpetrators come to believe either that the victims have something they want or (more likely) stand in the way of something they want.[245] In the discourse of ISIS, the victims are presented as a threat to the religious purity or even the existence of the *Ummah* and stand in its way of fulfilling its religious duty of establishing a pure Islamic Caliphate which will rule the entire world. Using a classic persuasion technique, the ISIS hate narrative is, furthermore, never changing and repeated *ad nauseam* through their various media platforms.[246] It would be appropriate to consider *Dabiq* and *Rumiyah* as well as other ISIS outlets as media for incitement to genocide[247] and try and identify, apprehend and bring to justice individuals involved in the ISIS media apparatus.

Notes

1 'IS' is referred to as the Islamic State of Iraq and Syria (ISIS), the Islamic State of Iraq and the Levant (ISIL) or the Arabic acronym Da'esh. The use of "IS" in the present chapter in no way acknowledges or accepts the so-called Islamic State's claim as a legitimate 'Caliphate,' nor does it support its claims or ambitions in this respect. The acronym Da'esh comes from al-Dawlah al-Islamīyah fī al-'Irāq wa-al-Shām (i.e., the Islamic State of Iraq and the Levant (ISIL)), which was the initial title the militants gave themselves. However, since acronyms are rare in the Arabic language and have an unusual tone for the native speaker, the term Da'esh plays the role of mocking the militants.

2 The Prosecutor v. Jean-Paul Akayesu, Trial Judgment, Case No. ICTR-96-4-T, 2 September 1998, paras 146–153 [hereinafter Akayesu TJ].

3 M. Ruzindana, 'The Challenges of Understanding Kinyarwanda Key Terms Used to Instigate the 1994 Genocide in Rwanda,' in P. Dojčinović (ed.), *Propaganda, War*

Crimes Trials and International Law: From Speakers' Corner to War Crimes, Abingdon, New York, NY: Routledge, 2012, p. 145. See also R.A. Wilson, *Incitement on Trial, Prosecuting International Speech Crimes*, Cambridge: Cambridge University Press, 2017, p. 192.

4 A. Zahar, 'The ICTR's "Media" Judgement and the Reinvention of Direct and Public Incitement to Commit Genocide,' *Criminal Law Forum*, vol. 16, 2005, pp. 33–48, 40.

5 Ruzindana, 'The Challenges,' p. 147.

6 The crime of incitement to genocide does not require a causal link with an actual genocide subsequently committed. Nevertheless, the ICTR has occasionally turned to causality as a substitute for a systematic method of proving the necessary *mens rea*. W.A. Schabas, *Genocide in International Law: The Crime of Crimes*, Second Edition, Cambridge: Cambridge University Press, 2009, p. 324.

7 *Markaz al-Ḥayāt l-il-I'lām* (al-Ḥayāt Media Center): IS Media unit responsible for publishing online magazines, see endnote 71.

8 A. Al-Kinānī, 'It's Either the Islamic State or the Flood,' *Dabiq*, no. 2, 'The Flood,' 2014, p. 5.

9 S/RES/2379 (2017) adopted by UNSC at its 8052nd meeting on 21 September 2017. Pursuant to this resolution the United Nations Secretary-General António Guterres appointed Mr Karim Khan as the Special Adviser and Head of the Investigative Team to support domestic efforts to hold Islamic State in Iraq and the Levant (ISIL/Da'esh) accountable by collecting, preserving and storing evidence in Iraq of acts that may amount to war crimes, crimes against humanity and genocide committed by the terrorist group.

10 United Nations Treaty Collections. Online. Available HTTP: <https://treaties.un.org/Pages/ViewDetails.aspx?src=IND&mtdsg_no=IV-1&chapter=4&clang=_en> (accessed 4 June 2019).

11 Sayyid Qutb, a leading figure of the Muslim Brotherhood in the 1950s and 1960s, who advocated violent *jihād* to establish governance according to Islamic law. His ideas were further radicalized by Abd al-Salam Faraj in his working paper 'The Neglected Duty,' see endnote 33.

12 T. Hegghammer, 'Jihadi Salafis or Revolutionaries? On Theology and Politics in the Study of Militant Islamism,' in R. Meijer (ed.), *Global Salafism: Islam's New Religious Movement*, New York, NY: Columbia University Press, 2009, pp. 244–266.

13 C. Bunzel, *From Paper State to Caliphate: The Ideology of the Islamic State*, The Brookings Project on U.S Relations with the Islamic World. See also Y. Rapoport and S. Ahmed, *Ibn Taymiyya and His Times*, Karachi: Oxford University Press, 2010.

14 'A. Zarzūr (ed.), *Ibn Taymiyyah, Muqaddima fī uṣūl al-tafsīr*, Kuwait: Dār al-Qur'ān al-Karīm, 1971, pp. 105, 108.

15 Zarzūr, *Ibn Taymiyyah, Muqaddima fī uṣūl al-tafsīr*, pp. 93, 95, 105.

16 Rapoport and Ahmed, *Ibn Taymiyya*.

17 B. Haykel, 'On the Nature of Salafi Thought and Action,' in Meijer, *Global Salafism*, endnote 12, pp. 38–39; N. Shama, 'Al-Jama 'Al-Islamiya And The Al-Jihad Group in Egypt,' in J.L. Esposito and E. El-Din Shahin (eds), *The Oxford Handbook of Islam and Politics*, Oxford: Oxford University Press, 2013, p. 608.

18 A. Bin Qasim (ed.), *Ad'durar As'samiyah fi Al-Ajwibah An'najdiyah*, vol. 10, Alqassem Publishers, 1996, as cited in B. Al-Ibrahim, 'ISIS, Wahhabism and Takfir,' *Contemporary Arab Affairs*, vol. 8, no. 3, 2015, pp. 408, 413.

19 Al-Ibrahim, 'ISIS.'

20 R.P. Mitchell, *The Society of the Muslim Brothers*, Oxford: Oxford University Press, 1993, p. 190.

21 Ibid., p. 191.

22 R.H. Dekmejian, *Islam in Revolution: Fundamentalism in the Arab World*, Second Edition, Syracuse, NY: Syracuse University Press, 1995, p. 73.
23 Al-Furqa‾n Media Foundation, 'Ala minhaj al nubuwwa,' 2014. Online. Available HTTP: <https://jihadology.net/2014/07/28/al-furqan-media-presents-a-new-video-message-from-the-islamic-state-upon-the-prophetic-methodology/> (accessed 4 June 2019).
24 G. Wood, 'What ISIS Really Wants,' *The Atlantic*, March 2015.
25 U. Sumayyah al-Muhājirah, 'To Our Sisters: A Jihād without Fighting,' *Dabiq*, no. 11, 2015, p. 45.
26 Mitchell, *The Society*, p. 192.
27 A. Kassim, 'Defining and Understanding the Religious Philosophy of Jihādī-Salafism and the Ideology of Boko Haram,' *Politics, Religion & Ideology*, vol. 16, no. 2–3, 2015, pp. 173, 185.
28 P. Nesser, 'Abū Qatāda and Palestine,' *Welt des Islams*, vol. 53, no. 3–4, 2013, pp. 416–417; Q. Wiktorowicz, 'The New Global Threat: Transnational Salafīs and Jihad,' *Middle East Policy*, vol. 8, no. 4, 2001, pp. 18–38; Q. Wiktorowicz, 'Anatomy of the Salafi Movement,' *Studies in Conflict and Terrorism*, vol. 29, no. 3, 2006, p. 207; A. Moghadam, 'The Salafi-Jihad as a Religious Ideology,' *Combating Terrorism Centre at West Point*, vol. 1, no. 3, February 2008; J. Wagemakers, *A Quietist Jihadi: The Ideology and Influence of Abu Muhammad al-Maqdisi*, Cambridge: Cambridge University Press, 2012.
29 G. Kepel, *Muslim Extremism in Egypt: Prophet and Pharaoh*, London: Al Saqi Books, 1985, p. 192.
30 B. Lewis, *Islam in History: Ideas, People, and Events in the Middle East*, Chicago, IL: Open Court Publishing, 2001, p. 375.
31 This religious perception of the Pharaoh stands in contrast to the Pharaoh as a symbol of patriotism and pride for Egyptians, which emerged after the science of Egyptology made the language, literature and history of pre-Islamic Egypt known for the first time to Muslim Egyptians. Lewis, *Islam*, pp. 375–376.
32 Ibid., p. 375.
33 A. al-Salam Faraj, *al-Farida al-gha'iba*, Amman, n.d.; this pamphlet radicalized further the ideas of Sayyid Qutb.
34 Unknown author, 'The Flood of the Mubāhalah,' *Dabiq*, no. 2, 2014, p. 27.
35 See A. Maysarah ash-Shāmī, 'The Qā'idah of Adh-Dhawāhirī, Al-Harārī, and An-Nadhārī and the Absent Yemenī Wisdom,' *Dabiq*, no. 6, 'Al Qa'idah of Waziristan: A Testimony from Within,' 2014, pp. 16–25.
36 S. Maher, *Salafi-Jihadism, The History of an Idea*, London: Hurst & Company, 2016, p. 112; *al-walā'* derives from *muwālah*, meaning 'love.' It is similar to terms like *wilāyah*, meaning 'loyalty' or 'devotion' and is linked to the word *tawāli* which appears in the *Qur'ān* in the context of obedience. *Al-barā'*, on the other hand, means 'severance' or 'to be free of.'
37 Ibid., p. 113.
38 Ibid., p. 116.
39 Ibid., pp. 120–121.
40 A. Muhammad, *'Āsim Al-Maqdisī: The Religion of Ibrāhīm*, Second Edition, London: Al-Tibyān Publications, n.d.
41 Bearing witness that there is no God but Allah, and that Muhammad is the messenger of Allah.
42 Al-Maqdisī, *Millat Ibrāhīm*, p. 42.
43 Maher, *Salafi-Jihadism*, p. 120.
44 T. Izutsu, *The Concept of Belief in Islamic Theology: A Semantic Analysis of Iman and Islam*, Santa Clarita, CA: Books for Libraries, 1980, p. 11; I.A. Karawan, 'Takfir,' in J. Esposito (ed.), *The Oxford Encyclopedia of the Modern Islamic World*, vol. 5,

Oxford: Oxford University Press, 2009, p. 311. For more on the practice of *takfir* (branding one's opponents as unbelievers or *kuffar* by contemporary extremist militant groups, see M. Badar et al., 'The Radical Application of the Islamic Concept of Takfir,' *Arab Law Quarterly*, vol. 31, 2017, pp. 134–162. On *takfīr* in general, see M. Badar et al., 'The Radical Application;' see also C. Adang, H. Anṣārī, M.I. Fierro and S. Schmidtke (eds), *Accusations of Unbelief in Islam: A Diachronic Perspective on Takfir*, Leiden: Brill, 2016.

45 Izutsu, *The Concept*, p. 17.
46 Adang, *Accusations*, p. 108.
47 Izutsu, *The Concept*, p. 12.
48 A.S. Tritton, *Muslim Theology*, London: Royal Asiatic Society, 1947, p. 38. J.I. Smith, 'Faith,' in J. Dammen McAuliffe (ed.), *Encyclopaedia of the Qur'an*, vol. 2, Leiden: Brill, 2001, p. 170.
49 W. Montgomery Watt, *Islamic Political Thought*, Edinburgh: Edinburgh University Press, 1968, pp. 55–56.
50 This applies regardless of whether those resisting the ruling deny the obligation to obey it or not. Ash-Shāmī, 'The Qā'idah,' p. 19, fn. 3.
51 *Dabiq*, no. 8, 'Shari'ah alone will Rule Africa' dedicates an 18-page long article 'Irjā': The Most Dangerous Bid'ah: and its Effects on the Jihād in Shām' to denouncing the concept, 2015, pp. 39–56.
52 A group of Muslim scholars during the very first century of Islam.
53 M. Akyol, 'A Medieval Antidote to ISIS,' *New York Times*, 21 December 2015.
54 Unidentified author, 'The Soldiers of Terror,' *Dabiq*, no. 8, 2015, p. 19.
55 Ibid., p. 42.
56 Mu'awiya was the founder of the Umayyad Dynasty of the Caliphate; r. 661–680. A.C. Higgins, 'Kharijites, Khawarij,' in R.C. Martin (ed.), *Encyclopedia of Islam and the Muslim World*, London: Macmillan, 2004, p. 390; J.L. Esposito, 'Foreword,' in J.S. Hayward, *Fatwa on Terrorism and Suicide Bombings*, London: Minhaj-ul-Qur'ān International, 2010, p. 272.
57 Izutsu, *The Concept*, p. 11; P. Crone and F. Zimmermann, *The Epistle of Salim Ibn Dhakwan*, Oxford: Oxford University Press, 2001, pp. 95–97; Abū-Mansur 'Abd-al-Kahir ibn Tahir al-Baghdadi, *Moslem Schisms and Sects (al-Fark bain al-firak) Being the History of the Various Philosophic Systems Developed in Islam*, translated from the Arabic with Introduction and notes by A.S. Halkin, Tel Aviv: Palestine Publishing, 1935, p. 168.
58 A.-R. ibn Salih al-Mahmood, *Man-made Laws vs. Shari'ah*, Riyadh: International Islamic Publishing House, 2003, p. 354.
59 Ibid.
60 Ibid.
61 Ibid., p. 343.
62 Montgomery Watt, *Islamic Political Thought*, pp. 54–55; ibn Salih al-Mahmood, *Man-made Laws*, p. 347, on the opposite extreme, the *Murji'ah* did not regard the person who rejected the *Shari'āh* and replaced it with man-made laws as a *kāfir*, unless he regarded this as being permissible.
63 See J.J.G. Jansen, *The Neglected Duty: The Creed of Sadat's Assassins and Islamic Resurgence in the Middle East,* London: Macmillan Publishing, 1986.
64 Referring to the *munafiqun*, a group decried in the *Qur'ān* as outward Muslims who were inwardly concealing disbelief and actively sought to undermine the Muslim community.
65 Kassim, 'Defining,' pp. 27, 181; ibn Salih al-Mahmood, *Man-made Laws*, p. 354.
66 Kassim, 'Defining,' p. 185.
67 Y. Michot, *Muslims under Non-Muslim Rule*, Oxford: Interface Publications, 2006, p. 32, referring to writings of Muhammad 'Abd al-Salām Faraj, Shaykh 'Abs Allāh

Yūsuf 'Azzam, Muhammad b 'Abs Allāh al-Mas'ari, Shaykh 'Abd al-'Aziz b. Sālih b. Sulaymān al-Jarbū, Zuhayr Sālim, Shaykh Sa'd al-Dīn b. Muhammad al-Kibbī.

68 Ibid., p. 49.

69 Ibid., pp. 35, 53.

70 Ibid., pp. 42–43, 49, 53.

71 IS has three centralised Media units. The first was *Mu'assasat al-Furqān* (the al-Furqān Foundation for Media Production) established back in 2006 and producing DVDs, CDs, pamphlets and official statements from the organisation's leadership. In 2013 it was joined by *Mu'assasat al-I'tiṣām* (al-I'tiṣām Media Foundation) and in 2014 *Markaz al-Ḥayāt l-il-I'lām* (al-Ḥayāt Media Center) which published online magazines: *Dabiq*, in a number of different languages including English; *Konstantiniyye* in the Turkish language; *Dar al-Islam* in the French language; and *Rumiyyah*, which replaced the first three since 2016. IS also established the *Mu'assasat Ajnād*, (the Ajnād Foundation) specialising in audio recordings (see *anashīd* below). See C. Winter, 'The Virtual 'Caliphate': Understanding Islamic State's Propaganda Strategy,' *Quilliam Foundation*, July 2015.

72 L. Hinnant, 'The ISIS Radio Station Targeting European Recruits Sounds Like NPR,' *Business Insider*, 1 June 2015.

73 F. Rahim, M. Yusufzai and F.B. Bruton, 'ISIS Takes to Airwaves, Transmits Fatwas in Jalalabad, Afghanistan,' *NBC News*, 19 December 2015. 'ISIS' al-Bayan Radio Station in Mosul is Bombed into Silence by Iraqi Jets,' *NBC News*, 3 October 2016. Online. Available HTTP: <https://www.nbcnews.com/storyline/isis-terror/isis-al-bayan-radio-station-mosul-bombed-silence-iraqi-jets-n658521> (accessed 4 June 2019). D. Milto, 'The Islamic State: An Adaptive Organization Facing Increasing Challenges,' in M. al-'Ubaydi, N. Lahoud et al. (eds), *The Group That Calls Itself a State: Understanding the Evolution and Challenges of the Islamic State*, The Combatting Terrorism Centre at West Point, December 2014, pp. 47, 53–54.

74 *Dabiq* was published from 5 July 2014 (the date of the declaration of the so-called caliphate) to 31 July 2016 (the date when the town of *Dabiq* was lost), a total of 15 issues. The first issue of its successor *Rumiyah* was published in September 2016, ending with a total of 15 issues. The publisher of both magazines was Al Hayat Media Centre.

75 Winter, 'The Virtual,' p. 71.

76 Counter-Terrorism Project, 'Terrorists on Telegram,' May 2017. Online. Available HTTP: <https://www.counterextremism.com/sites/default/files/Terrorists%20on%20Telegram_052417.pdf> (accessed 4 June 2019).

77 'How ISIS Games Twitter,' *The Atlantic*, 16 June 2014.

78 E. Staub, *The Roots of Evil*, Cambridge: Cambridge University Press, 1989.

79 Ibid., p. 20.

80 Ibid, p. 22.

81 Ibid.

82 E. El-Badawy et al., 'Inside the Jihadi Mind: Understanding Ideology and Propaganda,' Centre on Religion and Geopolitics, October 2015.

83 A. Oberschall, 'Propaganda, Hate Speech and Mass Killings,' in Dojčinović (ed.), *Propaganda*, p. 172.

84 The Centre on Religion & Geopolitics has analyzed a cross section of 114 propaganda sources from IS, Jabhat al-Nusra and Al-Qaeda in the Arabian Peninsula and found that the *Qur'ān* is used five times more often in Salafī-jihādi than in mainstream material. Justifications taken from the *Qur'ān*, *hadīth* or from scholarship appeared in 87 percent of the sources analyzed. In one IS statement references to 13 different *surahs* (chapters) in the *Qur'ān* made up 26 percent of that entire statement. El-Badawy, 'Inside the Jihadi Mind,' p. 7. Online. Available HTTP: <https://institute.global/our-mission> (accessed 4 June 2019).

85 Oberschall, 'Propaganda,' pp. 172–173.
86 Founder of Al-Qaeda in Iraq, the precursor of IS and the main ideologue of IS.
87 Unidentified author, 'Dabiq Magazine,' *Dabiq*, no. 1, 'The Return of the Khilafah,' 2014, p. 4.
88 Al-Kinānī, 'It's Either the Islamic State or the Flood,' p. 9.
89 El-Badawy, 'Inside the Jihadi Mind,' p. 5.
90 Unidentified author, 'Foreword,' *Dabiq*, no. 4, 'The Failed Crusade,' 2014.
91 Ibid.
92 Ibid.
93 Ibid.
94 El-Badawy, 'Inside the Jihadi Mind,' p. 5.
95 Unidentified author, *Dabiq*, no. 4, p. 17.
96 Unidentified author, 'The Islamic State before Al-Malhamah: The Immigrants to the Land of Malāhim,' *Dabiq*, no. 3, 'A Call to Hijrah,' 2014, p. 12.
97 Unidentified author, 'The Kafir's Blood is Halal for you, so Shed it,' *Rumiyah*, no. 1, 2016, p. 36.
98 Saying (*rahimahullah*), a phrase often used after mentioning the righteous Islamic personalities who came after the companions of Prophet Muhammad.
99 Unidentified author, 'The Fight against the PKK,' *Dabiq*, no. 2, 2014, p. 13.
100 Unidentified author, 'Foreword,' *Dabiq*, no. 12, 'Just Terror,' 2015, pp. 2–3.
101 Online. Available HTTP: <https://www.ieproject.org/projects/dabiq4.pdf> (accessed 3 June 2019).
102 H.J. Ingram, 'An Analysis of *Inspire* and *Dabiq*: Lessons from AQAP and Islamic State's Propaganda War,' *Studies in Conflict and Terrorism*, vol. 40, no. 5, 2016, pp. 357–375; H.J. Ingram, 'Learning from ISIS's Virtual Propaganda War for Western Muslims: A Comparison of Inspire and Dabiq.' Online. Available HTTP: <https://icct.nl/wp-content/uploads/2017/07/INGRAM-nato-chapter-21JUL17.pdf > (accessed 4 June 2019). For more, see H.J. Ingram, 'The Strategic Logic of Islamic State Information Operations,' *Australian Journal of International Affairs*, vol. 69, no. 6, 2015, pp. 729–752.
103 P. Wignell et al., 'A Mixed Methods Empirical Examination of Changes in Emphasis and Style in the Extremist Magazines Dabiq and Rumiyah,' *Perspectives on Terrorism*, vol. 11, no. 2, 2017, pp. 4–5.
104 J. Stern and J.M. Berger, *ISIS: The State of Terror*, London: William Collins, 2015, p. 219.
105 B. Said, 'Hymns (*Nasheeds*): A Contribution to the Study of the Jihadist Culture,' *Studies in Conflict & Terrorism* vol. 35, no. 12, 2012, pp. 863, 867.
106 Ibid.
107 J. Pieslak and N. Lahoud, 'The *Anashid* of the Islamic State: Influence, History, Text, and Sound,' *Studies in Conflict and Terrorism*, 23 April 2018.
108 G. Ramsay, *Jihadi Culture on the World Wide Web*, London: Bloomsbury Publishing, 2013, p. 63.
109 Ibid., p. 64.
110 H. Gråtrud, 'Islamic State *Nasheeds* as Messaging Tools,' *Studies in Conflict and Terrorism*, vol. 39, no. 12, 2016, pp. 1050, 1052.
111 J. Chaaban, 'Youth and Development in the Arab Countries: The Need for a Different Approach,' *Middle Eastern Studies*, vol. 45, no. 1, 2009, pp. 38–47.
112 O. Roy, *Den Globaliserende Islam*, Copenhagen: Vandkunsten, 2004, p. 193.
113 Staub, *The Roots*, pp. 78, 30.
114 I. Sivan, *Radical Islam: Medieval Theology and Modern Politics*, New Haven, CT: Yale University Press, 1985, p. 65.
115 Gråtrud, 'Islamic State,' pp. 1060–1061.
116 Ibid., p. 1063.

117 A. Lemieux and R. Nill, 'The Role and Impact of Music in Promoting (and Countering) Violent Extremism,' in S. Canna (ed.), *Countering Violent Extremism: Scientific Methods and Strategies*, Air Force Research Laboratory, 2011, pp. 145–146.
118 Ibid., p. 150.
119 J. Pieslak, *Radicalism and Music: An Introduction to the Music Cultures of al-Qa'ida, Racist Skinheads, Christian-Affiliated Radicals, and Eco-Animal Rights Militants*, Middletown, CT: Wesleyan University Press, 2015.
120 Said, 'Hymns,' pp. 869–970.
121 Ibid., p. 870.
122 Pieslak and Lahoud, *The Anashid*.
123 Said, 'Hymns.'
124 N. Lahoud and J. Pieslak, 'Music of the Islamic State,' *Survival: Global Politics and Strategy*, vol. 60, no. 1, 2018, pp. 153–168, 158.
125 Ibid., pp. 158–159.
126 Al-Hayāt Media Center, 'Flames of the War,' 2014. Online. Available HTTP: <https://jihadology.net/?s=Flames+of+War+video> (accessed 4 June 2019).
127 Unidentified author, *Rumiyah*, no. 1, 2016.
128 Unidentified author, 'The World has Divided into Two Camps,' *Dabiq*, no. 1, 'The Return of the Khilafah,' 2014, p. 10.
129 Unidentified author, *Dabiq*, no. 4, citing Abu Bakr al-Baghdadi.
130 The innovators – referring to *bid'ah* or heretical innovation in religion.
131 The rebellious – referring to *Iblīs* or the devil rebelling against *Allah*.
132 The hypocrites – referring to the *munafiqūn*, a group decried in the *Qur'ān* as outward Muslims who were inwardly concealing disbelief and actively sought to undermine the Muslim community.
133 Unidentified author, *Dabiq*, no. 4.
134 T. Joscelyn, 'Islamic State Radio Tries to Quell Controversy over Takfir,' *FDD's Long War Journal*, 26 September 2017, referring to a lecture series broadcast on *Al Bayan*, 20 September 2017.
135 Unidentified author, 'Conspiracy Theory: Shirk,' *Dabiq*, no. 9, 'They Plot and Allah Plots,' 2015, p. 17; Īsā is the *Qur'ānic* name for Jesus and Maryam is the *Qur'ānic* name for Mary; Anti-Semitic discourse found in political communication across Europe from the late nineteenth century leading up to the birth of Nazi ideology included similar examples of 'religious Jewish malfeasance' (e.g., Jews are Christ killers, Oberschall, 'Propaganda,' p. 175).
136 UNHRC, 32nd Session, Human Rights Situation that Require the Council's Attention, 'They Came to Destroy: ISIS Crimes Against the Yazidis,' UN Doc. A/HRC/32/CRP.2, 15 June 2016.
137 V. Arakelova, 'Sufi Saints in the Yezidi Tradition I: Qawlē H'usēyīni H'alāj,' *Iran & the Caucasus*, vol. 5, 2001, pp. 183–192.
138 E. Basci, 'Yazidis: A Community Scattered in between Geographies and Its Current Immigration Experience,' *International Journal of Humanities and Cultural Studies*, vol. 3, no. 2, 2016, pp. 341–342; A. Mullaney, 'Wiping Out an Entire Religion: How ISIS Will Inevitably Eliminate an Ancient Culture Unless the United States Employs Military and Diplomatic Intervention,' *Suffolk Transnational Law Review*, vol. 39, no. 1, 2016, pp. 107–110.
139 A. Gökçen, *Osmanlı ve İngiliz arşiv belgelerinde Yezidiler*, Istanbul: Bilgi University, 2012, pp. 7, 11, in Basci, 'Yazidis,' p. 341.
140 E. Çelebi, *Seyahatname*, translated by T.T. Kuran and N. Akbaş, Istanbul: Üçdal Neşriyat, 1986, pp. 169–171; E. Gölbaşı, *The Yezidis and the Ottoman State: Modern power, military conscription, and conversion policies, 1830–1909* (Unpublished Master's dissertation), Istanbul: Bogazici University, 2008, both in Basci, 'Yazidis,' p. 341.

141 Basci, 'Yazidis,' p. 341.
142 Ibid.
143 Magazine Monitor, 'Who, What, Why: Who are the Yazidis?' *BBC News*, 8 August 2014.
144 Unidentified author, 'The Revival of Slavery before the Hour,' *Dabiq*, no. 4, 2014.
145 Ibid., p. 14.
146 Ibid., p. 15.
147 N. Lee, 'Convert or Die: Forced Religious Conversions and the Convention on the Prevention and Punishment of the Crime of Genocide,' *Georgetown Journal of International Law*, vol. 47, no. 606, 2015–16.
148 Unidentified author, *Dabiq*, no. 4, p. 15.
149 Ibid.
150 UNHRC, 32nd Session.
151 N. Shea, 'Falling for ISIS Propaganda about Christians,' 21 July 2016. Online. Available HTTP: <https://www.the-american-interest.com/2016/07/21/falling-for-isis-propaganda-about-christians/> (accessed 5 June 2019).
152 Unidentified author, 'Why We Hate You and Why We Fight You,' *Dabiq*, no. 15, 'Break the Cross,' 2016, p. 33.
153 Ibid., p. 31.
154 Unidentified author, 'The Ruling on the Belligerent Christians,' *Rumiyah*, no. 9, 2017, p. 5.
155 *Dabiq*, no. 15, pp. 31–32.
156 Ibid., p. 33.
157 Ibid., p. 31.
158 *Rumiyah*, no. 9.
159 Scottish Catholic Observer, 'Pope Condemns the ISIS Slaughter of 30 Christians,' 24 April 2015.
160 Ahram Online, 'Video Shows Beheading of Copts at IS Hands: Egypt Declares Week of Mourning,' 15 February 2015. Online. Available HTTP: <http://english.ahram.org.eg/News/123128.aspx> (accessed 5 June 2019). The breaking of the cross and killing of the swine is a reference to a hadith predicting the return of Jesus as a just judge in a major sign of the last days.
161 The basic idea of 'accusation in a mirror' is that propagandists 'impute to enemies exactly what they and their own party are planning to do.' A. Des Forges, *Leave None to Tell the Story: Genocide in Rwanda*, New York, NY: Human Rights Watch, 1999, p. 66. See also Akayesu TJ, para. 99. The Prosecutor v. Ferdinand Nahimana, Jean-Bosco Barayagwiza, Hassan Ngeze, Judgment and Sentence, Case No. ICTR-99-52-T, 3 December 2003, para. 111.
162 Unidentified author, *Dabiq*, no. 9, p. 51.
163 Unidentified author, 'Wilāyat Khurāsān and the Bay'āt from Qawqāz,' *Dabiq*, no. 7, 'From Hypocrisy to Apostasy: The Extinction of the Grey Zone,' 2015, p. 37.
164 Unidentified author, *Dabiq*, no. 15.
165 Unidentified author, *Rumiyah*, no. 9, p. 7.
166 European Parliament, Joint Motion, 'Resolution on the Systematic Mass Murder of Religious Minorities by the So-Called ISIS/Daesh,' 3 February 2016, 2016/2529(RSP).
167 Unidentified author, *Dabiq*, no. 4, p. 15, fn. 1.
168 Ibid.
169 Maher, *Salafi-Jihadism*, pp. 102–103.
170 Ibid.
171 Ibid.
172 S. Drennan, 'Constructing Takfir,' *Combating Terrorism Centre at West Point*, vol. 1, no. 7, July 2008.

173 Ash-Shāmī, 'The Qā'idah,' p. 19.
174 Unidentified author, 'From the Pages of History: the Safawiyyah,' *Dabiq*, no. 13, 'The Rāfidah: From Ibn Saba' to the Dajjāl,' 2016, p. 13.
175 Unidentified author, 'The "Mahdī" of the Rāfidah: The Dajjāl,' *Dabiq*, no. 11 'From the Battle of Al-Ahzāb to the War of Coalitions,' 2015, p. 16.
176 Ibid., p. 34.
177 D. Holbrook *The Al-Qaeda Doctrine: The Framing and Evolution of the Leadership's Public Discourse*, London: Bloomsbury Publishing, 2014, p. 120.
178 Unidentified author, *Dabiq*, no. 13, p. 10.
179 Ibid., pp. 10–11.
180 N. Kazimi, 'Zarqawi's anti-Shi'a Legacy: Original or Borrowed?,' *Current Trends in Islamist Ideology*, 1 November 2006, in Maher, *Salafi-Jihadism*, p. 103, fn. 78. Leading members of the Saudi *sahwa* movement, a hybrid between Qutbism and Wahhabism, echoed similar views.
181 Unidentified author, 'Foreword,' *Dabiq*, no. 11, 'From the Battle of Al-Ahzāb to the War of Coalitions,' 2015, p. 5.
182 Unidentified author, *Dabiq*, no. 13, p. 11.
183 R. Ismail, *Saudi Clerics and Shi'a Islam*, Oxford: Oxford University Press, 2016, p. 93.
184 Unidentified author, *Dabiq*, no. 13, p. 12.
185 Ibid.
186 El-Badawy, 'Inside the Jihadi Mind,'p. 4.
187 Ibid., p. 47.
188 J. Waller, *Becoming Evil. How Ordinary People Commit Genocide and Mass Killing*, Cambridge: Cambridge University Press, 2002.
189 Ash-Shāmī, 'The Qā'idah,' p. 20.
190 Unidentified author, 'The Capture of the Crusader Pilot,' *Dabiq*, no. 6, 'Al Qa'idah of Waziristan: A Testimony from Within,' 2014, p. 36.
191 Ibid., pp. 34–36.
192 *Dabiq*, no. 14, 'The Murtadd Brotherhood,' 2016, cover page.
193 Ibid., p. 43.
194 Maher, *Salafi-Jihadism*, glossary, xvii.
195 Unknown author, 'Establishing the Islamic State: Between the Prophetic Methodology and the Paths of the Deviants,' *Rumiyah*, no. 7, p. 8; unknown author, 'The Murtadd Taliban Movement: On the Footsteps of the Iraqi and Shami Sahwat,' *Rumiyah*, no. 10, p. 42.
196 The Prosecutor versus Clément Kayishema and Obed Ruzindana, Judgment, Case No. ICTR-95-1-T, 21 May 1999, para. 98. C. Stahn, *A Critical Introduction to International Criminal Law*, Cambridge: Cambridge University Press, 2019, pp. 36–37.
197 M. Degerald, 'How Daesh Talks about the World: Central Points of Daesh Discourse,' 10 March 2016. Online. Available HTTP: <https://historyxisis.wordpress.com/tag/sahwat/> (accessed 5 June 2019).
198 Ash-Shāmī, 'The Qā'idah,' p. 19.
199 Ibid.
200 Ibid.
201 Ash-Shāmī, 'The Qā'idah,' p. 19, fn. 3.
202 IS, Delegated Committee, 'That Those Who Perish Would Perish Upon Proof and Those Who Live Would Live Upon Proof,' 17 May 2017. Online. Available HTTP: <https://www.longwarjournal.org/wp-content/uploads/2018/11/17-05-17-That-Those-Who-Perish-Would-Perish-Upon-Proof-and-Those-Who-Live-Would-Live-Upon-Proof.pdf> (accessed 5 June 2019).

203 T. Joscelyn, 'Islamic State Rescinds One of Its Most Problematic Religious Rulings,' *FDD's Long War Journal*, 20 September 2017. Online. Available HTTP: <https://www.longwarjournal.org/archives/2017/09/islamic-state-rescinds-one-of-its-most-problematic-religious-rulings.php> (accessed 5 June 2019).
204 Ibid.
205 T. Joscelyn, 'Islamic State Radio.'
206 Ibid.
207 Article III(c).
208 ICTY Statute Article 4(3)(c). ICTR Statute Article 2(3)(c). ICC Statute, Article 25 3(e).
209 Prosecutor v. Radoslav Brđanin, Judgment, Case No. IT-99-36-T, 1 September 2004, paras 80, 323–332.
210 Prosecutor v. Karadžić, Judgment, Case No. ICTY-IT-95-5/18-T, 24 March 2016, para. 3514.
211 Ferdinand Nahimana, Jean-Bosco Barayagwiza, Hassan Ngeze v. The Prosecutor, Appeal Judgment, Case No. ICTR-99-52-A, 28 November 2007, para. 678 [hereinafter Nahimana et al. AJ].
212 Nahimana et al. AJ, paras 985-986; Prosecutor v. Vojislav Šešelj, MICT-16-99-A, Judgment, 11 April 2018, paras. 159, 163.
213 Nahimana et al. AJ, para. 677.
214 Akayesu TJ, para. 556.
215 Akayesu TJ, paras 557–558. See also The Prosecutor v. Tharcisse Muvunyi, Case No. ICTR-00-55A-T, Judgment, 11 February 2010, para. 502; The Prosecutor v. Eliézer Niyitegeka, Case No. ICTR-96-14-T, Judgment, 16 May 2003, para. 431; The Prosecutor v. Juvénal Kajelijeli, Case No. ICTR-98-44A-T, Judgment, 1 December 2003, para. 853; The Prosecutor v. Simon Bikindi, ICTR-01-72-T, Judgment, 2 December 2008, para. 387; Nahimana et al. AJ, para. 700.
216 Nahimana et al. AJ, para. 699; Mugesera v. Canada (Minister of Citizenship and Immigration), [2005] 2 S.C.R. 100, 2005 SCC 40, paras 87, 94.
217 Nahimana et al. AJ, para. 701.
218 As mentioned above for the Yazidi, for the Shi'a, for the Christians, and so on.
219 Unidentified author, 'The Rāfidah: From Ibn Saba' to the Dajjāl,' *Dabiq*, no. 13, 'The Rāfidah: From Ibn Saba' to the Dajjāl,' 2016, p. 45.
220 M. Badar et al., 'The Radical Application of the Islamic Concept of Takfir,' pp. 134, 136–138.
221 See Article 14(8) of the Tunisian Organic Law No. 26 of 7 August 2015 on the Fight against Terrorism and the Repression of Money-Laundering. Article 7 of Iraq's Constitution 2005.
222 Raphael Lemkin considered cultural genocide to be a component of genocide. R. Lemkin, *Acts Constituting a General (Transnational) Danger Considered as Offences against the Law of Nations*, 1933. R. Lemkin, *Axis Rule in Occupied Europe*, Concord, NH: The Rumford Press, 1944, p. 91. The drafters of the 1948 Genocide Convention, however, did not include cultural genocide in the Convention.
223 Unidentified author, *Dabiq*, no. 4, p. 17.
224 Ibid., p. 15.
225 B. Van Schaack, 'Engendering Genocide: The Akayesu Case before the ICTR,' 2008. Online. Available HTTP: <http://digitalcommons.law.scu.edu/facpubs/629> (accessed 5 June 2019).
226 Nahimana et al. AJ, fn. 1674.
227 UNHRC, 32nd Session, p. 1.
228 Nahimana et al. AJ, para. 677.
229 Nahimana et al. AJ, para. 709.

230 European Parliament, Joint Motion.
231 For example, reflecting on the sexual attacks on women Umm Sumayyah al-Muhājirah, 'Slave-Girls or Prostitutes?,' *Dabiq*, no. 9, 2015, p. 46.
232 On 'cultural genocide' or 'ethnocide' see A. Woolford, 'The Ontological Destruction of Canadian Aboriginal Peoples,' *Genocide Studies and Prevention*, vol. 4, no. 1, 2009, pp. 81–97; K. Romney, 'ISIS Destruction of Ancient Sites Hits Mostly Muslim Targets,' *National Geographic*, 2 July 2015. See also United Nations Assistance Mission for Iraq, *Report on the Protection of Civilians in the Armed Conflict in Iraq: 11 December 2014–30 April 2015*, UNAMI/OCHCR, 13 July 2015.
233 Nahimana et al. AJ, para. 719, fn. 1697.
234 Ibid., para. 719, fn. 1699.
235 Ibid. AJ, para. 726.
236 Articles 2(2) and (3) of the Statute reproduce Articles 2 and 3 of the Genocide Convention. The *travaux préparatoires* of the Genocide Convention can therefore shed light on the interpretation of Articles 2(2) and (3) of the Statute. See UN ORCA, 6th Committee, 3rd Session, 86th meeting, UN Doc. A/C.6/3/CR. 86, 28 October 1948, pp. 244–248, and UN ORGA, 6th Committee, 3rd Session, 87th meeting, UN Doc. A/C.6/3/CR. 87, 29 October 1948, pp. 248–254.
237 Nahimana et al. AJ, paras 715, 725.
238 Ibid., p. 725.
239 Ibid., para. 692.
240 Waller, *Becoming Evil*.
241 Oberschall, 'Propaganda.' See also M. Mamdani, *When Victims Become Killers: Colonialism, Nativism, and the Genocide in Rwanda*, Princeton, NJ: Princeton University Press, 2001, where the author examines the process by which a group is made to be seen as 'foreign' or 'alien' using Rwanda as a case study.
242 Oberschall, 'Propaganda' p. 174.
243 See the editorial section titled 'Extinction of the Grayzone,' *Dabiq*, no. 7, which explicitly talks about IS trying to eliminate the 'gray zone of coexistence.' See also El-Badawy, 'Inside the Jihadi Mind,' p. 16; Oberschall, 'Propaganda,' p. 179.
244 Waller, *Becoming Evil*, p. 127; C.I. Hovland, I.L. Janis and H.H. Kelly, *Communication and Persuasion: Psychological Studies of Opinion Change*, New Haven, CT: Yale University Press, 1953, p. 56. See in general A. Pratkanis and E. Aronson, *Age of Propaganda: The Everyday Use and Abuse of Persuasion*, Revised Edition, New York, NY: W.H. Freeman and Company, 2001; G.S. Jowett and V. O'Donnell, *Propaganda and Persuasion*, Fifth Edition, London: Sage, 2012.
245 Staub, *The Roots*, pp. 78, 23.
246 Oberschall, 'Propaganda,' p. 172.
247 D.F. Orentlicher, 'Criminalising Hate Speech in the Crucible of the Trial: Prosecutor v. Nahimana,' *American University International Law Review*, vol. 21, no. 4, 2006, pp. 557–596.

Chapter 2

Propaganda experts in the international criminal courtroom

Richard Ashby Wilson

Introduction

In propaganda trials at international criminal tribunals, understanding the local resonance of inciting speech acts is central to a court's judgment on the charges against the accused.

Grasping the meaning and effects of performative utterances is particularly arduous in the international context given the geographical and cognitive distance from the locale in which the crimes occurred. Adjudicating crimes where the main evidence is a speech act or acts requires a nuanced appreciation of local languages and the cultural context of their usage to establish what specific utterances mean, what the utterances encouraged the listener to do and what the consequences of the utterances were.

In order to advance their interpretation of the utterances of the accused and their overall theory of the case in a propaganda trial, both prosecutors and defense counsel have called expert witnesses on propaganda, local languages and political communication. In international criminal trials, prosecutors and defense teams often call numerous expert witnesses to testify on issues ranging from the standard protocols that forensic scientists follow when exhuming cadavers to the financial transactions of political leaders. An expert witness is defined in international law as "a person who by virtue of some specialized knowledge, skill or training can assist the trier of fact to understand or determine an issue in dispute."[1]

Official declarations by international judges explicitly indicate their preference for scientific evidence they consider 'objective.'[2] As yet, however, no one has empirically verified these proclamations. Social researchers have analyzed the impact of expert evidence in trials at the International Criminal Court (ICC),[3] the Special Court for Sierra Leone (SCSL)[4] and the International Criminal Tribunals for the former Yugoslavia (ICTY) and Rwanda (ICTR).[5]

These analyses include only a handful of cases, making generalization difficult. There has not been any comprehensive assessment, statistical or otherwise, of the aggregate significance and impact of expert witnesses in international trials.

An empirical study of propaganda experts

Before we can assess the impact of propaganda experts, we need an overall picture of the kind of experts that are called in international trials and the impact they have. To this end, I developed a database of 473 individual expert witnesses appearing at the ICTY for both the prosecution and the defense over a 20-year period (1993–2013). To enable comparison, I grouped the witnesses according to their expertise in nine areas: (1) document authentication, (2) engineering, (3) forensics, (4) finance, (5) law and human rights, (6) medicine, (7) military, police, and intelligence, (8) social research, including social science, the humanities, and Balkan studies, and (9) weapons and ballistics.[6]

On the basis of the judges' stated preferences, my working hypothesis was that material-object science (e.g., medicine, forensics and ballistics) would be favored over social research. And I expected that, as in many domestic criminal jurisdictions, international judges would prefer prosecution witnesses to defense experts.[7]

Scientific experts in medicine, forensics, ballistics and engineering were indeed called by the parties to the trial twice as often as experts outside those fields (see Table 2.1). Material-object science experts outnumbered social researchers by a factor of more than three to one. The top three categories of experts to appear in ICTY trials were medical experts, forensic scientists and social researchers. Prosecutors relied heavily on expert testimony and especially medical experts, forensic scientists and social researchers. Indeed, prosecutors commissioned experts more often in every category, with only one intriguing

Table 2.1 Total number of expert witnesses by category

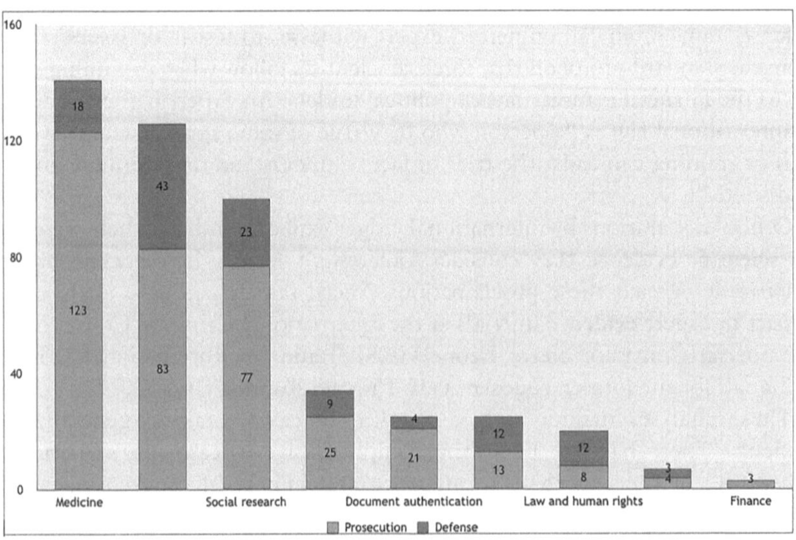

exception: legal and human rights experts. Defense counsel were more equivocal about experts and relied most on forensic scientists social researchers and medical experts.

In sociolegal scholarship, a standard measure to evaluate the significance of an expert witness is the number of times the expert is cited in the final judgment (see Table 2.2).[8] This method has its limitations; for instance, it does not account for how expert evidence provides narrative coherence. Yet the average citation rate, defined as the number of times each expert is cited in the final trial judgment, is still our best overall proxy indicator of the influence of different types of expertise. All types of experts were cited 18 times on average in each trial-chamber judgment, a startling endorsement of expert witnessing in international courts (see Table 2.3).

At the ICTY, weapons and ballistics experts have the highest citation rate, followed by legal and human rights experts and forensic scientists. In absolute terms, prosecution expert witnesses were cited in ICTY judgments nearly twice as often as defense expert witnesses. But underneath that banner headline is another, unexpected story: Defense experts had a significantly higher overall average citation rate than those for the prosecution. The prosecution, with greater resources at its disposal, could afford to call more experts, but judges preferred individual defense experts overall.

Intriguingly, social researchers (both quantitative and qualitative) have a much higher average citation *rate* than medical experts, the most frequently cited category in absolute terms. Social researchers were more frequently cited on average than military and police experts, document-verification experts, financial experts

Table 2.2 Number of citations in the final judgment per category of expert

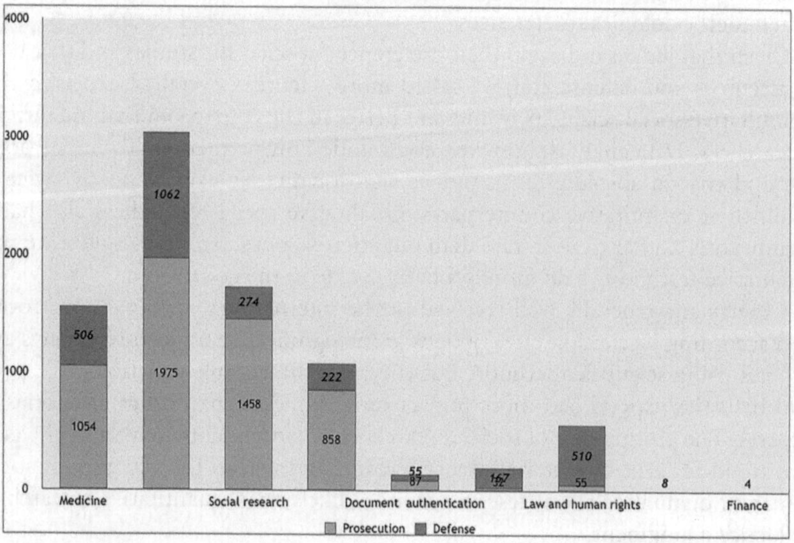

Table 2.3 Average rate of citation in final judgments per category of expert witness

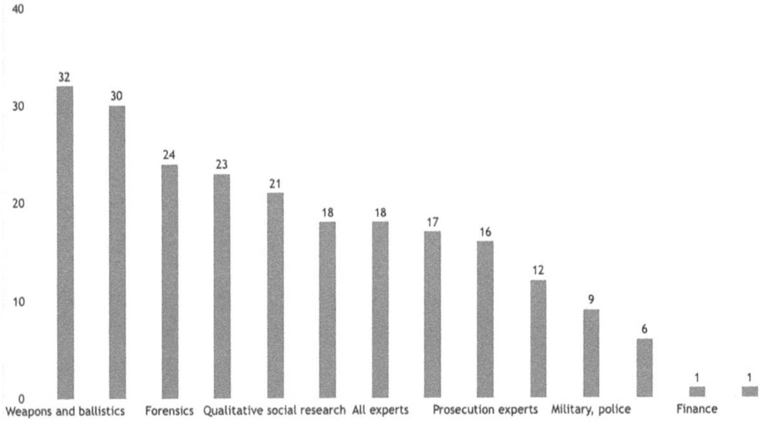

and engineers. The finding that social researchers are the third most numerous category of experts, and that their testimony is more likely to be cited than engineers' and police officers', demands further scrutiny.

To ascertain which subcategories of social research are most valued by judges, I divided the social-research category into two subcategories: those that are methodologically quantitative (economics, political science, demography and statistics) and qualitative (anthropology, cultural heritage, history, the Balkans and Eastern Europe, media, phonetics, politics and sociology). Recognizing that these categories can overlap, I distributed individual scholars based on their stated methodological preferences.

Given that judges indicated their preference for scientific studies and that both prosecutors and defense counsel called more scientists overall, I expected that quantitative social scientists would fare better in the courtroom than qualitative researchers. Data analysis, however, confounded my prediction. To my surprise, I found that in absolute terms judges cited qualitative experts nearly twice as often their quantitative counterparts. Qualitative social researchers also had a significantly higher citation rate than quantitative ones, strongly suggesting that qualitative testimony held more probative value in the courtroom.

Experts are generally well received in the international criminal courtroom, and according to citation rates, judges grant significance to defense experts and experts using scientific methods. But there are measurable variations. Weapons and ballistics experts had more impact on judgments than other categories of experts. The prominence of social researchers as experts runs counter to the general trend in favor of material-object science, and within the category of social research, qualitative social research is more likely than quantitative research to influence a judgment.

A review of the main speech-crimes trials at the ICTY and ICTR confirms the overall trend in favor of qualitative experts. In these courts, judges resisted quantitative social-science expertise yet remained open to linguists and cultural experts who commented on the meanings of the accused's utterances. Since there have not been enough propaganda trials to demonstrate this statistically, the following discussion adopts a qualitative approach and examines the role of experts in three of the most decisive speech-crimes trials at two different UN international criminal tribunals: Akayesu and Nahimana (at the ICTR) and Šešelj (at the ICTY). My argument applies primarily to these two UN tribunals and the ICC. Its relevance for 'hybrid' tribunals such as the SCSL and the Extraordinary Chambers in the Courts of Cambodia (ECCC) is for scholars of those courts to determine.

To understand why qualitative social expertise constitutes an exception to the declared pro-science policy, we must complement the quantitative data analysis with a qualitative inquiry into legal actors' strategies and motivations in international criminal trials. In doing so, we will be able to grasp the concepts and assumptions behind the raw numbers.

Enhanced translation: language expertise at the international tribunal for Rwanda

> Up to the early 1960s, the word *Inyenzi* meant "cockroach." In the early 1960s, this word acquired another meaning. […] It broadened to include the mainly Tutsi rebels who were attacking the country. […] When the *Inkotanyi* attacked the country in 1990, this second meaning was reactivated. For Hutu extremists, the word came to be generalized to Tutsis as an ethnic group.[9]

My first case study concerns a sociolinguist who testified as an expert witness for the prosecution and whose evidence was cited extensively in the final guilty verdict. The expert appeared in the trial of the first defendant convicted by the ICTR, Jean-Paul Akayesu, a town mayor accused of directly inciting villagers to commit genocide on the basis of his public speeches in 1994.

Akayesu's guilt or innocence on the charge of inciting genocide hinged on the larger question of whether the mass killing of Tutsis was motivated by an orchestrated policy to exterminate Tutsis, defined as a group protected under the UN Genocide Convention (1948) or whether the killing was secondary to the core objective of defeating the invading Rwandan Patriot Front (RPF). Akayesu openly encouraged his followers to exterminate the 'inkotanyi' (literally meaning 'warriors') and 'inyenzi,' and the judges had to parse these Kinyarwanda terms, which could constitute calls to eliminate either illegitimate civilian targets (innocent Tutsis) or lawful military ones (RPF combatants).

The judges welcomed evidence from the Rwandan linguist on the meaning of utterances in languages that they did not speak. At international criminal tribunals, a panel of three judges (rather than a jury) are the 'triers of fact,' a model that has much in common with the civil-law systems in Continental Europe, Latin America and much of Asia and Francophone and Lusophone Africa. In Akayesu's trial, the judges had to determine whether the Accused's performative utterances constituted direct and public incitement to commit genocide.

The challenge for the prosecution was that Akayesu had made few explicit appeals to exterminate Tutsis, as he mobilized his followers using euphemisms and coded statements to evade criminal liability. The panel of judges confronted a number of obstacles as they evaluated the meaning of Akayesu's speeches. For example, none of the judges spoke the local African languages or came to the tribunal with a deep knowledge of the history and culture of the African Great Lakes region, and so they were receptive to instruction by the prosecution expert on the meanings of Kinyarwanda terms in their social context.

As a practical matter, all participants faced intractable translation difficulties in the courtroom. Rwandan witnesses testified in translation from Kinyarwanda to French to English, with an occasional Swahili step added between Kinyarwanda and French, and back through the entire progression again. These circumlocutions both compounded the monotony of courtroom procedure and undermined the integrity of witness testimony. ICTR judges also found that many ordinary Rwandan witnesses were reluctant to answer direct questions such as, "What does *inyenzi* mean?" Rwandans were frequently unimpressed with the international courtroom[10] and considered the court's direct questioning 'stupid' or 'irrelevant.'[11] The paucity of witnesses considered credible by the tribunal meant that judges relied even more on expert witnesses to discern the meanings of Kinyarwanda terms than they would have otherwise.

Enter Mathias Ruzindana, a linguist at the National University of Rwanda, who was commissioned by the prosecution to submit a report and testify as an expert witness.[12] Ruzindana started with the premise that "law cannot do without linguistics,"[13] and his report set about explaining the basic meaning of Kinyarwanda terms used by the Accused. In particular, he emphasized that their meaning depended on context and how ordinary words were transformed during the 1994 genocide.[14]

Everyday Kinyarwanda terms could convey an ominous message in certain circumstances. The term *gukora*, for instance, means literally 'to work' in Kinyarwanda, but during the genocide it became a euphemism for "to kill or massacre the Tutsi."[15] According to the prosecution, the literal meaning of *inkotanyi* is 'warriors,' but in the propaganda of Hutu extremists, it came to denote the RPF army and then Tutsis in general because most RPF combatants were Tutsis. Similarly, terms like *inyenzi* (literally meaning 'cockroach'), *umwanzi* (enemy) and *icyitso* (accomplice) by extension came to stand for Tutsis as a group.

This was Ruzindana's first appearance in a criminal courtroom, and in talking to me in 2015, he reflected on the experience of testifying as an expert:

> Lawyers do not reason the way we do. They have a case to win, and they try to corner the expert. The expert is standing between two opposing sides. The opposing party asks you trick questions. When the defense got the impression that I had made a vital point, they asked a question to make me angry, to show bias. These questions are meant to test you, not to test your evidence. [...] On the other hand, the prosecution wanted me to be categorical at times and give a certain answer that I might not be sure about. As an expert, it's important to not express what you don't believe to be true. [...] At times the prosecution found this disappointing.

The tribunal convicted Akayesu of direct and public incitement to commit genocide, in large part on the evidence from Ruzindana's testimony. The judgment cited Ruzindana 14 times and acknowledged that in assessing the meaning of Kinyarwanda terms, "the Chamber has relied substantially on the testimony of Dr. Mathias Ruzindana, an expert witness on linguistics, for its understanding of these terms." On the basis of "the information provided by Dr. Ruzindana, appearing as an expert witness on linguistic issues," the trial chamber established beyond a reasonable doubt "that the population construed the Accused's call as a call to kill the Tutsi."[16]

Akayesu's defense appealed the verdict, but the Appeals Chamber affirmed the expert's evidence and the conviction. Ruzindana's interpretations of Kinyarwanda terms were consolidated in later tribunal judgments.[17] After Akayesu, it became an incontestable "fact of common knowledge" that "in the minds of Hutu hardliners, the words *Inyenzi*, *Inkotanyi*, *enemy* and *accomplice* were closely associated with the Tutsi ethnic group."[18]

Despite his effectiveness as an expert witness, Ruzindana expressed discomfort at how the prosecutors instrumentalized his report and testimony. "The prosecutors," he told me,

> were mainly interested in the use of the words as they related to proving the charges. The prosecution needed to show that words like *inkotanyi* and *inyenzi* meant Tutsis, but those words could also mean other things in other contexts. For instance, *inkotanyi* could also mean the RPF army. This causes confusion. The words are ambiguous, and we need to understand how the words were understood in their context.

For Ruzindana, ICTR judgments were not careful enough in detailing the social and cultural elements that informed their interpretations of speech acts. This indicated that, as he told me, "overgeneralization can be found in some of the judgments." Some of the trials, as Ruzindana had earlier written, "adopted a simplistic approach."[19]

Subsequently, Ruzindana's interpretations became a cornerstone of the prosecution case in the most important speech-crimes trial at the ICTR: the 'Media Trial' (hereinafter Nahimana), as it was known, against three defendants (Nahimana, Barayagwiza and Ngeze) who were the owners of Radio Télévision des Milles Collines (RTLM) and the self-described "Hutu Power" newspaper *Kangura*.[20] The Nahimana prosecution team called Ruzindana again to testify that RTLM broadcasts constituted incitement to exterminate Tutsis. Ruzindana labeled RTLM and *Kangura* "hate media"[21] that played a central role in triggering the Rwandan genocide, a view that was reinforced by historian and Human Rights Watch activist Alison Des Forges, who told the trial chamber how Rwandans were begging her to "stop RTLM."[22]

Trials in the Anglo-American adversarial tradition often become a battle of experts, and the 'Media Trial' was no exception. The defense commissioned its own expert witness, Roger Shuy, professor emeritus of linguistics at Georgetown University and a battle-hardened expert in over 50 US trials. Shuy[23] excoriated the prosecution expert's methods and conclusions, saying that Ruzindana provided no sociolinguistic evidence regarding the extended meaning of terms such as *inkotanyi* and *inyenzi*. All the Kinyarwanda terms in dispute had multiple meanings, Shuy maintained. Whereas Ruzindana interpreted a term like *inyenzi* to denote the Tutsi, it was, according to Shuy, "also very capable of meaning the army or the RPF,"[24] who were called 'cockroaches' because the insurgents were seen only at night.

Shuy, furthermore, criticized Ruzindana's qualitative methods and asserted that his claims were based not in sociolinguistics but merely on his being a native Kinyarwanda speaker who had observed the mass killing firsthand. The mantle of sociolinguistics, Shuy asserted, was simply a subterfuge for Ruzindana's personal opinions.[25] Speaking to me, Ruzindana conceded Shuy's point that he had drawn on firsthand experience:

> It's very hard to be neutral when you have experienced events before your eyes. There was a time in the courtroom testimony when I recalled to a situation where a speaker in a crowd referred to a child as an 'inkotanyi.' How could a child be an *inkotanyi*, in the sense of 'an RPF soldier'? On reflection, I shouldn't have relied on that prior personal experience.

Ruzindana prevailed in the battle of experts. The judges cited him repeatedly in the final judgment when determining the genocidal meaning of the three defendants' radio broadcasts, while they did not reference the defense expert's contributions at all. Shuy, however, might have had a point on one issue. Ruzindana's testimony on the defendants' speech was informed largely by his being a native Kinyarwanda speaker and by his contextual knowledge of Rwandan culture and the genocide itself.

What Shuy perceived as a fatal flaw might have instead granted Ruzindana an unforeseen advantage by conforming his testimony to the courtroom's conventions. For his part, Ruzindana knew he needed to present his findings in an accessible manner on the stand. "In sociolinguistics," he told me,

> meaning arises from the context of usage, and you don't always need a scientific justification. The judges were reassured when we said that a word's meaning varied according to context. That's something that everyone understands. I know the language very well as a linguistics lecturer and an educated Rwandan, and that built credibility. We looked at the context of each speech and asked the simple question, Taking into account the conditions in which the speech act occurred, what would the average Rwandan listener have understood by the words? We avoided making it too complicated and using social-science jargon. The end users were lawyers, after all.

Ruzindana's forthright testimony not only proved convincing to the judges but also, crucially, did not challenge their judicial sovereignty. Judges conventionally determine the meanings of utterances by situating them in their local context rather than by interpreting them through the prism of a technical social-science discipline such as sociolinguistics. When the meaning of allegedly threatening terms is contested, they often settle the question by asking the simple question, "What would the average listener understand by the words?"[26] Sociolinguists may ask this question as well, but they would not rely on this test alone and would ideally support their analysis with ethnographic observation and the contemporary theoretical literature.

Language experts are easily integrated into the ICC's procedural and evidentiary framework for determining facts. Sociolinguistic expertise on the pragmatic meaning of the accused's utterances represents an enhanced translation service that fits comfortably into the courtroom's prevailing legal epistemology and status hierarchy. When offered an interpretation of crucial words in a language they do not know, judges insist on remaining the ultimate arbiters of the speaker's criminal liability.

The authority of international judges is not imperiled by a local expert witness such as Ruzindana, who essentially performs the roles of both a 'fact witness' and a specialized, elite translator for the court. Translators are a perennial feature of international tribunals, and judges are accustomed to integrating their contributions into the trial in a way that comports with how law knows.[27] As we will see, judges perceive a greater threat from social-science experts who use statistical methods to understand social behavior, thus imperiling the authority of judges as finders of fact.

Judicial gatekeeping and quantitative social science

> Now, these texts were extremely straightforward. There's nothing very subtle about nationalist discourse. You know, we're not translating the poetry of Baudelaire. […] "amputate Croatia" is really what it says. I mean, it's very vivid, it's clear. There's no subtle double meaning to it.[28]

When experts use quantitative methods to analyze a political leader's discourse and the mechanisms through which his utterances prompt violence, judges are circumspect and can even be hostile. Judges are well disposed toward quantitative science in ballistics and forensics, but they do not appreciate the abstractions of sociological theories of speech and the quantitative methods employed to analyze incitement. These diverge from law's own epistemological framework, which employs ordinary commonsense reasoning to establish the facts of the case. Allowing quantitative social-science experts to determine the ultimate issue in the trial – the meaning and consequences of speech acts – palpably challenges judicial sovereignty.

An example of a social-scientist expert whose testimony was rejected comes from the trial at the ICTY of Vojislav Šešelj, a Serb nationalist politician acquitted by the Trial Chamber in 2016 of nine counts of war crimes and crimes against humanity during the conflict in the former Yugoslavia. In 2018, the Appeals Chamber reversed the trial judgment and convicted Šešelj for instigating deportation, persecution and other inhumane acts as crimes against humanity, as well as for committing persecution through hate speech as a crime against humanity, and sentenced him to ten years of imprisonment.

Because he was not charged with incitement to genocide, the issue at stake in the Šešelj trial diverged from the Rwandan cases. Šešelj's guilt or innocence hinged less on the meaning of his public speeches, which were more explicit than those of Akayesu and the RTLM broadcasters, than on the consequences of his utterances. The ultimate issue in the Šešelj trial was whether the defendant's speeches motivated his followers to murder, torture, sexually assault, and deport Croats and Bosnian Muslims and whether there was a causal nexus between his utterances and the subsequent atrocities committed by his self-avowed followers against unarmed civilians.

Enter emeritus sociology professor Anthony Oberschall of the University of North Carolina –Chapel Hill, who was called by the prosecution as an expert witness. The prosecution provided Oberschall with hundreds of the Accused's public speeches, articles and interviews that appeared in newspapers and on television and radio from 1991 to 1994[29] and used quantitative content analysis to evaluate the texts by creating a coding framework made up of recurring terms and phrases and counting their frequency. During an interview in 2013, Oberschall told me about his mandate from the prosecution team:

> We got 242 texts and conducted the content analysis. He [Vojislav Šešelj] used the same phrases again and again. [...] They [the prosecution team] not only wanted me to characterize his discourse but also decide the impact on people listening, and not only the impact of the negative stereotypes but also of the threats. He constantly talked about the threat from Croats and Albanians and how we [the Serbs] are victims in history and will be again. That was the dominant finding I had – this threat discourse in Šešelj's speech.

Oberschall's[30] expert report began with a review of the scholarly literature on nationalism, collective violence, and mass communications, and proceeded to endorse Christopher Browning's[31] 'ordinary men' thesis of collective violence, in which average, unexceptional citizens are brought by social structures and political ideologies to participate in, or at least condone, mass atrocities. As Oberschall said to me, "Ordinary people may not participate in the killings, but they vote people into power and tolerate their crimes." The report cited a survey conducted in Yugoslavia in 1990 in which 85 percent of respondents described ethnic relations in their neighborhood as 'good' or 'satisfactory.'[32] A sustained propaganda campaign by political leaders on all sides amplified threats and incited violent actions against the out-group.[33] Šešelj's threat discourse imposed a powerful cognitive schema, a "crisis frame"[34] that conjured up the history of mass atrocities in the Balkans during the first half of the twentieth century.

Oberschall's central finding was that in 99 speeches, Šešelj notified Serbs that they faced an imminent and existential threat.[35] As Oberschall quoted them, Šešelj's public speeches contained passages of classic nationalist *Sturm und Drang*:

> We will defend Serbian lands as long as we breathe [...] [against the] poisonous snake, that's the Croats. [...] This is the third time that poisonous snake has headed for us, and for the third time bit us on [*sic*] the heart. Now we need to smash its head so it never bites anyone again. [...] The Serbian revenge will come very soon, the Serbian revenge is already starting.[36]

A crisis mentality created a demand for action to remove the threat. Combined with the message that Serbs were not responsible for retaliating,[37] Šešelj claimed it also justified collective violence against non-Serbs.

Before the courtroom trial proceedings started, the defendant Šešelj, who was representing himself in the trial, objected to the report and challenged Oberschall's fitness as an expert witness. The ICTY trial chamber upheld Šešelj's objections on two grounds. First, they found that Oberschall's expertise was not specific enough to the case because he did not speak Serbian and was not an expert on Serbian mass media or nationalist propaganda. Second, the judges found fault in Oberschall's citation of 87 books and articles on nationalism, propaganda, and violence, observing, rather oddly, that these were publications that he had not written himself, which they construed as a sign that he lacked sufficient expertise in the subject. If these criteria were applied stringently, it would exclude virtually all social scientists and humanities scholars from the international criminal courtroom.

What came next, however, was highly irregular. Although the judges had ruled Oberschall unqualified as an expert, they, nevertheless, admitted his report "for practical reasons" and allowed him to testify as a prosecution witness. It is unclear on what grounds he was to testify, given that courtroom witnesses must be either an expert witness or a fact witness who was present at the crime scene, and according to the judges, Oberschall was neither.

The prosecutors plowed ahead, called Oberschall as their first witness, and referred to him as their expert. His testimony proved something of a spectacle. Šešelj furiously objected to Oberschall's very presence in the courtroom.[38] Presiding judge Jean-Claude Antonetti allowed Oberschall to proceed but pointedly reminded him that the appraisal of his evidence would depend on his performance on the stand.

Oberschall calmly noted that the quantitative social-science methods he had used were widely accepted and that scholars have analyzed the techniques of persuasion that often appear in ethnonationalist propaganda – techniques such as stereotyping, labeling, generalizing and spreading misinformation. He defended the academic practice of citing prior scholarship on a topic, explaining that sociological knowledge builds over time, as each researcher relies on the work of others. Shrewdly, he drew an analogy between academic practices and the common-law convention of relying on legal precedents.

Despite his careful comportment, Oberschall was in the hands of prosecutors who were bent on simplifying and sharpening his testimony so as to use it against the Accused. Prosecutors emphasized that speech acts directly triggered criminal acts, prompting Oberschall to make forceful claims not included in his expert report. During examination, prosecutor Christine Dahl probed for the action component of propaganda:

DAHL: How does propaganda work?

OBERSCHALL: Propaganda is a technique of persuasion that is based upon emotional appeals. [...] Through negative stereotyping, through generalizations, appeals to victimhood, creating a sense of threat, you create a demand for action, including violent action.[39]

Oberschall reiterated the link between propaganda and violent acts throughout his testimony. "The crucial part of the propaganda that sets in motion actions is actually the threat speech," he said, and the prosecution closing brief of the trial highlighted this sentence.[40] Oberschall proceeded to characterize the vivid and violent images in the Accused's speech, including his calls for the "amputation of Croatia" to recover what Serb nationalists considered Serb lands and his recurrent threats that "rivers of blood will flow." Overall, Oberschall's testimony was an unyielding condemnation of the Accused.

Šešelj opened the cross-examination by making light of his fierce speeches, pointing out that violent imagery is common in Serb nationalist narratives:

ŠEŠELJ: Mr. Oberschall, you do not know Serbian literature and Serb heroic epics that are full of passages about blood flowing, but it's about blood flowing in war. Two armies clash on the battlefield and blood flows in rivers. We have a whole cycle of these Serb popular epics that talk about that. It's one thing to talk about blood flowing in rivers, and it's another thing to say, "Go on. Kill Bosnian or Croat civilians."

OBERSCHALL: Well, that's what you say. But if you look at, actually, the military events, both in the Croatian and the Bosnian war, most of the blood that was flowing was not that of soldiers but of civilians.[41]

After a few rebarbative exchanges, the cross-examination descended into rancor as Šešelj questioned Oberschall's intelligence and credibility. When their turn to cross-examine the witness came, the three judges seemed perplexed by his quantitative methods. They expressed concern that Oberschall relied on the literature on nationalism for the keywords used in his coding and content analysis. The judges worried that content analysis neither incorporated the context of the speech acts – for example, where and when they were published or broadcast – nor assessed their persuasiveness and impact.

Oberschall replied that social inquiry does not take place in the controlled conditions of the laboratory. "It's not possible," he said, "to do this kind of experimental work in a natural historical setting."[42] Reflecting on his performance during a later interview with me, Oberschall identified an epistemological chasm between law and social science: "No matter how I explained my methods to them, I was never going to convince the judges that my social-science approach could help them. Judges are interested in a specific causal sequence that leads to a specific crime."

The judges balked at the idea that one could separate out the Accused's personal contribution to the violence from all the other voices espousing nationalist views in the media, and Oberschall acknowledged to me the validity of this line of inquiry:

> Judge [Jean-Claude] Antonetti asked a good question, saying "I can think of many prominent actors in Serbia saying similar things." But Šešelj played that card more than others, even though his speech was similar to many others at the same time. The question is, can you connect the speech of one person to the crimes? That person alone and not the others? No. It's the ensemble that does it. For propaganda to be effective, you don't need to influence 100 percent of the population. If 45–50 percent vote you into power, that's enough. In the judges' way of thinking, if it's not 100 percent, then it's not a cause.

The 'lost in translation' elements of Oberschall's court appearance result partly from the divergent understandings of causation held by lawyers and social scientists. To convict, the judges must be convinced by the prosecution's argument that there was an 'invariable sequence' of causation, in which the accused's act was the 'proximate cause' of the offence and therefore incurs criminal liability.[43] Yet in chaotic, wartime conditions, there are often multiple independent actors, and any one violation is the product of a complex set of causes and conditions.

When crimes emerge from a tangled web of causation, it is an arduous undertaking to unravel causation with the precision required to attribute individual criminal responsibility, and anthropologists and other social researchers generally disavow attributing responsibility in this manner.[44]

Judges may in theory be interested in the multiplicity of conditions relevant to understanding cause in fact, but they have an immediate task at hand: to determine specific legal causation beyond a reasonable doubt. This involves winnowing down the complex multiplicity of conditions to a single causal chain and then deciding whether the accused committed an act that constitutes the proximate cause that warrants criminal responsibility. In our interview, Oberschall criticized the law's approach to causation and liability:

> What they [the judges] didn't understand was, why does a majority of voters put people in power who then control the media and arm the military and make all those specific crimes possible? That's the relevance of the broader context and climate. If voters didn't put them in power, then the larger political events – the unwillingness to compromise, the civil war, and the violence – may not have happened. That's where I come in with propaganda studies.

In March 2016, the ICTY trial chamber acquitted Šešelj of all charges of war crimes and crimes against humanity. In so doing, the court explicitly rejected Oberschall's expert evidence, stating that even though the defendant's utterances constituted hate speech, the expert had failed to show that the speeches had caused any specific crimes. We cannot deduce from this judgment that judges are hostile to social research generally, since the aggregate data cited at the beginning of this chapter showed otherwise. It was not social research per se but the quantitative study of speech that the judges objected to.

Experts and the legal strategies of prosecutors and defense attorneys

To fully understand the role social research plays in trials, we need to delve further into the underlying assumptions, attitudes and motivating principles of prosecutors, defense counsel and judges. All experts have the same role in criminal trials – to advance the case theory of either the prosecution or the defense. While some may strive for neutrality, expert witnesses are brought into a trial only to further the goals of either party. Experienced experts do not labor under any illusions: the international criminal courtroom is quite unlike the university seminar, and the objective is not knowledge for its own sake. Experts are accessories to the prosecution or defense case, as one ICC prosecutor said to me in rather colorful terms: "Ours is an exercise in marketing, to persuade, to convince the judges that the facts assembled match the charges. I'm a prosecutor, and when I smell blood, I go for it. That's my job."

Prosecution teams call over twice as many social scientists as defense counsel. Eleven out of the 11 prosecutors interviewed for this study expressed a willingness to integrate social-science evidence into their cases. In an interview with me, Mathias Marcussen, the senior prosecutor in a succession of lead prosecutors in the eleven-year Šešelj case, remarked, "We all have our intuitions, but a propaganda expert, through empirical work that has gained wide acceptance, can show the mechanisms through which propaganda influences and mobilizes" people, thereby possibly complementing "the facts of the case."

ICTY senior trial attorney Hildegard Uertz-Retzlaff expressed confidence in both social researchers' and judges' willingness to accept their opinions. "The expert will explain what a phrase or speech will trigger in an audience," she said. "They show the effects of propaganda. They have the expertise to say whether the words will influence the listeners in the way it's intended to."

"Are the judges persuaded?" I asked. She replied,

> Yes, I think so. Look at the Nazis and Goebbels – the German population tolerated the crimes because of Nazi propaganda. Why would Serbs not protect their Croat neighbors? This is the result of propaganda. Only a small group of armed men commit the crimes, but they need all the others to keep silent and not protest.

As seen earlier, the defense commissions social scientists as expert witnesses only a third as often as prosecutors at the ICTY. The attitude of the defense attorneys I interviewed is forthrightly negative toward social researchers as experts, and none thought they were intrinsically useful. A majority indicated that they would call an expert witness only to counter the prosecution's expert, and one Belgrade-based defense attorney said, "The best way to use an expert is to neutralize the prosecution's expert."

I convened a focus group for this project of three defense attorneys with extensive experience at the ICTY, ICC and the ECCC. My initial question, "Would you call a social-science expert in a speech-crimes case?" prompted an animated exchange between focus-group participants A, B and C:

A: Me, personally? No. I have very little faith in experts. Most are myopic, and this is not an area in which I need expert testimony to be perfectly honest with you […] we're talking about things that are part of the human condition, and they're bred in the bone, and it needs to be understood that we each carry a set of prejudices, and any politician is going to figure out a way of keeping those prejudices alive in order to get elected.

B: But you would agree as a judge that the parties would have some kind of cultural expert or historian ….

C: Yeah, that I would do.

B: … to speak about the context of what these words mean, because maybe historically, culturally, the political situation ….

C: Yeah, politically ....
A: I do want to know about the political situation of the area I am dealing with, but I don't want someone necessarily to tell me what is offensive.
B: But you do want, OK, how would the objective listener, what would they derive from this particular message?
A: If I understand the history of the nation, then I'll understand that. If I am dealing with a certain part of the world and they use the word 'Turk,' then I understand it has significance in the same way that you can go through all the pejorative terms used for ethnic and racial groups.
C: I would have a historical expert for sure, and an expert on language.

Participant A asserts that hate speech is a universal attribute of the human condition, yet it needs to be understood historically and culturally. In Anglo-American law, the 'objective listener' or 'reasonable man' is a legal fiction for determining what utterances constitute incitement or what acts constitute reasonable provocation.[45] The arc of the focus group's conversation was also significant: It began with a steadfast antipathy to social-science experts on propaganda but then softened to an acceptance of enhanced language-interpretation. This maps onto the case studies in this chapter and offers a window into the rejection of Oberschall's expert testimony and the acceptance of Ruzindana's. But to more fully understand the different impact of the two experts, we need to inquire further into the thinking of international judges, the ultimate arbiters of fact and law.

Judicial gatekeeping and common sense reasoning

> The courts [...] often insist that the causal questions which they have to face must be determined on common-sense principles.[46]

An ICTY prosecutor remarked to me that the strategy of calling a social researcher as an expert to illustrate the mechanisms of propaganda might be considered "a little adventurous." But why would this be the case, given the plethora of experts appearing in international trials on a multiplicity of substantive topics, from forensics to forgeries to finance?

I interviewed four judges who had adjudicated cases at the ICC, ICTR and ICTY, and asked them if a social researcher could help the court determine the charges against defendant in a propaganda trial. Two unreservedly endorsed this kind of expertise. ICTY judge Frederik Harhoff, who served on the Šešelj case, said,

> Experts can offer a checklist of the basic elements of inciting speech and help us to analyze a speech to determine whether it is hate speech. It is not easy to determine causality, since the psychological implications in the audience are so rich and multifaceted, so putting up a checklist makes a lot of sense,

> even if it cannot offer final proof of a hate speech. That way, we can consider all the aspects that are active to determine whether incitement to violence occurred and arrive at our conclusions holistically.

Responding negatively, two other judges emphasized judges' preeminence in determining the meaning of speech acts. One drew attention to judges' role as the decision makers and gatekeepers of the courtroom: "It remains a judicial decision whether a speech had an impact beyond a reasonable doubt [...] judges shouldn't adopt the conclusions of experts and should decide cases on the basis of legal reasons. Judges have to be very careful."

Judge Wolfgang Schomburg, who served at both the ICTR and ICTY, reiterated this point:

> I am hesitant about so-called expert witnesses. Each party can buy their own expert. No, this is the genuine task of the judge to interpret the words in a situation, not the expert. It's a hard task for a judge, but it is part and parcel of our job. You can't outsource it simply by asking a so-called expert. He doesn't know any better. [...] In the end, we are the triers of fact. We have to arrive at our conclusions, and then we have to write them in a reasonable way, and then they have to be accepted by the Appeals Chamber.

The reception of expert witnesses depends on how jealously judges protect their preeminence as the triers of fact. Officially, most judges in criminal jurisdictions perform a balancing act in which they permit the "realities of scientific understanding" in the courtroom as long as they do not challenge the court's authority.[47] The quantitative analysis of political speech challenges this delicate balance, and in Oberschall's case, the judges perceived his analysis as threatening the courtroom's epistemological integrity.

Criminal law's interpretation of speech acts is neither scientific nor entirely cultural. It simply asks, what would a reasonable person understand by the speech acts? Complex contestations over meaning are decided in international courts by ordinary reasoning, not any special theory or technical language derived from scholarship, be it sociolinguistics or sociological content analysis. When asked about the relevance of experts in speech-crimes trials, one ICTY judge responded,

> It depends on the type of expert. A ballistics expert may tell me about the type of gun used in a case. The problem with speech is that its effects are difficult to measure. They are not visible. If I hit a table with a hammer, it leaves a mark. [...] Speech evidence is also different from ballistics evidence because the latter is not part of my experience, but speech is part of common human experience. [...] I'm not saying that expert evidence on speeches cannot assist, but that the distance between speech and common experience

> is less than with ballistics. A criminal law theorist told me, "Forget about psychology. You interpret what you see. Use your ordinary human experience." It's a legal, evidentiary concept. My common human experience hardly counts when it comes to ballistics.

The expressed view of some judges was this: There are times when international courts must consult expert witnesses, for instance, when the court requires specialist knowledge about the trajectories of mortar shells or the decomposition of dead bodies. But speech is not a subject that requires external expertise because judges themselves are experts on speech. This explains the differential treatment of social-science experts on inciting speech when compared to that of experts in ballistics or forensic anthropology. Underlying the rejection of Oberschall's expertise is an entrenched judicial view that speech is an element of human behavior that judges can understand without outside help. In this respect, the Šešelj trial is part of an enduring pattern in international law, since it was not the first time that the ICTY trial chamber disqualified expertise based on sociological content analysis of the public speeches of the accused. A similar incident occurred in the ICTY trial of Bosnian Serb leader Radoslav Brđanin, when Judge Carmel Agius ruled the prosecution's expert report inadmissible. The judge's indignation at the usurpation of his role was conspicuous:

> Expert evidence should be evidence on a particular matter on which the Tribunal needs expertise. But the Tribunal does not need expertise to understand or to look at a particular newspaper cutting or a particular video recording or a particular transmission or the transcript of a speech [...] an expert should never involve himself or herself in deciding a matter which the Tribunal has to decide.[48]

My interviews with judges elicited the same pattern of responses that emerged in the focus group with the defense attorney: an initial denial that social-science expertise on propaganda could be relevant, followed by the acceptance of enhanced translation from a language expert. When asked whether a language expert could help the court understand the meaning of political speech, Judge Schomburg replied,

> I would agree because we underestimated the problem of translation at the ICTR, where people testified in Kinyarwanda and then it was often translated into Swahili before going through French and finally to English. By then it's very hard to know what the witness said. A language expert can analyze the words in an appropriate way and not simply rely on the translator. Here, to be on the safe side, it would be better for the judges to call an expert, not to interpret what an alleged perpetrator said, but to understand what exactly the perpetrator said. Judges are not sensitive enough to the

> problems of translation and precise wording when it comes to hate speech and calls to genocide. If the words are hiding the true meaning – for instance, in Rwanda they called others to "Do your work" – then we may need the assistance of additional experts and an interpreter.

As with the defense attorneys in the focus group, the judge was eventually willing to accept a language expert to help the court, after having earlier rejected the idea of an expert on speech acts.

In sum, in speech-crimes trials, interpretive approaches to language and cultural meaning are preferred over statistical analyses. Judges are open to assistance from experts who discern the meaning and force of performative utterances in local languages, but they resist instruction from quantitative social scientists on the causal effects of utterances, an arena that they regard as their own special, protected domain.

Sovereignty and strategy in international criminal trials

> As a frame of thought, and a species of it, common sense is as totalizing as any other: no religion is more dogmatic, no science more ambitious, no philosophy more general.[49]

Sociolegal scholars should study international legal institutions "not merely as abstract entities, but as complex social processes," as Marie-Bénédicte Dembour and Tobias Kelly[50] have persuasively argued. The relationship between social research and international law is less a clash of abstract logics untethered to institutional processes or social interests than a complex social process in which the outcome depends on the legal actors' subjective intentions and actions.[51] Prosecutors and defense attorneys turn to qualitative expert witnesses not for exclusively epistemological reasons but for accomplishing definite legal objectives, such as proving that a speaker held genocidal intentions. An empirical, actor-oriented approach focuses our attention on the strategic and tactical terrain of the adversarial process and explains why a tribunal's handling of distinct types of expertise varies across trials.

A close empirical observation yields unexpected results that overturn the conventional expectation that quantitative social science will always outshine qualitative research in legal fact-finding. Expertise based on scientific methods is indeed dominant at international criminal tribunals, but qualitative expertise on the local linguistic and cultural context can also inform judges' deliberations. Judges often reject quantitative studies of human behavior because accepting this expertise would undermine the entire legal enterprise of an international trial that is primarily based on the (shaky) premise that a foreign cultural setting is intelligible to them and requires no further specialized scientific knowledge.

Once the defendant's utterances are translated, judges decode their meaning using the one intellectual resource they have in abundance, ordinary reason. This reflects an axiomatic principle of Anglo-American legal theory: deference to what Hart and Honoré call "the ordinary man's stock of general notions"[52] But beneath appeals to common sense, as Pierre Bourdieu[53] and Clifford Geertz[54] notably observed, there are highly normative assumptions at work that reinforce the social and cultural status quo. Common sense does double duty in criminal courts as both a cognitive frame and a bulwark against expertise that threatens judicial preeminence. The tone of common sense is "anti-expert, if not anti-intellectual," as Geertz[55] noted, and there is something unassailable about its knowledge claims. "Religion rests its case on revelation, science on method, ideology on moral passion; but common sense rests its [case] on the assertion that it is not a case at all, just life in a nutshell," Geertz maintained. "The world is its authority."[56]

Judges are tempted to adopt this kind of authority to shore up their sovereignty in the context of structurally fragile international justice institutions. Social researchers of such international institutions increasingly emphasize their geopolitical and institutional fragility.[57] This fragility relative to the continued salience and power of nation-states underlies the epistemological contestation and judicial gatekeeping prevalent in international justice institutions.

International tribunals are contested politically both in the UN Security Council and by recalcitrant nation-states such as Kenya. A number of African states, including South Africa – once the staunchest supporters of the ICC – have threatened in recent years to withdraw from the Assembly of States Parties, the body responsible for funding and managing the ICC. This would have a deleterious impact because there is no coercive state apparatus operating alongside international criminal courts, which lack the power to arrest suspects, seize evidence and imprison the convicted. International courts depend on states for these and many other basic functions. As a result, they are often buffeted by states, such as Rwanda and Croatia, that undermine their investigations and interfere with ongoing trials.

Internally, international tribunals are characterized by an uncertainty and unpredictability in fundamental law and procedure that can undermine their legitimacy. The conventional model in which a national justice system slowly accumulates legitimacy over centuries does not apply to international courts, which have had to hastily patch together an unstable amalgam of Anglo-American common law and Continental civil-law traditions.[58] The ICTY and ICTR followed the common law's adversarial process and the reasonable-doubt standard, but their rules of evidence and preference for bench trials (rather than juries) drew from civil law. Basic premises are often left undefined, and attorneys arguing before the ICC must function without clear guidance on the standard of causation needed to prove the charges against the accused.

Structural fragility has a direct impact on the knowledge-making process of international legal institutions, insofar as it generates uncertainty in evidentiary matters and compels judges to exclude evidence that threatens their precarious authority. An inordinate emphasis on the contrasting ways of knowing in law, science and social science obscures the variation in how expert witnesses are handled in international criminal trials. Even though judges regularly defer to scientists on ballistic, forensic and medical questions, when it comes to fact-finding on social behavior in a cultural context, jurists are committed less to science than to a commonsense empiricism that more readily integrates the expert testimony of anthropologists, historians, linguists and others.

We cannot assume, as many legal practitioners do, that law, science and social science are disconnected fields with their own autonomous logics, when in fact they all influence one another. The "cultures of law and science are in fact mutually constitutive," as Jasanoff[59] reminds us, and this brings us to a final, reflexive point: law and social science are mutually constitutive too, given the extent to which social researchers participate in domestic and international trials. To rephrase Jasanoff,[60] social researchers are not autonomous, self-regulating producers of information about the social world; they are, rather, embedded in global mechanisms of creating knowledge.

The next step in our inquiry is to go beyond analyzing the significance of social research for law so as to fathom how the complex interplay between law and social research is itself transformed by the experience of expert witnessing in international courts. Global justice institutions and social researchers jointly produce knowledge about armed conflict and international crimes such as genocide, and we have seen some of the consequences of this for international law.

Notes

1 Rule 94bis of the International Criminal Tribunal for the Former Yugoslavia, Rules of Procedure and Evidence. 8 July 2015, IT/32/Rev.50. The Hague: ICTY. The admissibility of expert evidence at the ICTY and ICTR is also governed by Rule 89 which states, "A Chamber may admit any relevant evidence which it deems to have probative value [89(C)]," with the only grounds for exclusion being, "if its probative value is substantially outweighed by the need to ensure a fair trial [Rule 89(D)]."

2 The Prosecutor v. Mathieu Ngudjolo Chui, Trial Chamber Judgment, Case No. ICC-01/04-02/12 52, 18 December 2012, para. 60.

3 K. Clarke, *Fictions of Justice: The International Criminal Court and the Challenge of Legal Pluralism in Sub-Saharan Africa*, Cambridge: Cambridge University Press, 2009, p. 87; R.A. Wilson, *Writing History in International Criminal Trials*, Cambridge: Cambridge University Press, 2011, pp. 192–215.

4 G. Anders, 'Testifying about "Uncivilized Events:" Problematic Representations of Africa in the Trial against Charles Taylor,' *Leiden Journal of International Law*, vol. 24, no. 4, 2011, pp. 937–959; T. Kelsall, *Culture Under Cross-Examination: International Justice and the Special Court for Sierra Leone*, Cambridge: Cambridge University Press, 2009.

5 N. Eltringham, '"Illuminating the Broader Context": Anthropological and Historical Knowledge at the International Criminal Tribunal for Rwanda,' *Journal of the Royal Anthropological Institute*, vol. 19, no. 2, 2013, pp. 338–355; Wilson, *Writing History*, pp. 170–191.

6 Most experts testified in only one area of self-reported expertise. A few experts testified in two or more areas, and all these were counted, leading to a total of 481 separate instances of expertise.
7 M.J. Saks and D.L. Faigman, 'Expert Evidence after Daubert,' *Annual Review of Law and Social Science*, vol. 1, 2005, pp. 105–130.
8 J.D. Kearney and T.W. Merrill, 'The Influence of Amicus Briefs on the Supreme Court,' *University of Pennsylvania Law Review*, vol. 148, no. 3, 2000, pp. 743–855.
9 M. Ruzindana, 'The Challenges of Understanding Kinyarwanda Key Terms Used to Instigate the 1994 Genocide in Rwanda,' in P. Dojčinović (ed.), *Propaganda, War Crimes and International Law: From Speakers' Corner to War Crimes*, Abingdon, New York, NY: Routledge, 2012, p. 155.
10 N.A. Combs, *Fact-Finding without Facts: The Uncertain Evidentiary Foundations of International Criminal Convictions*, Cambridge: Cambridge University Press, 2010, p. 79.
11 Ruzindana, 'The Challenges,' p. 147.
12 Pseudonyms are not used in this chapter for interlocutors. For those who wished to be quoted anonymously, I refer to them only by their occupations.
13 Ruzindana, 'The Challenges,' p. 146.
14 Ibid., pp. 156–162.
15 Ibid., p. 22.
16 Prosecutor v Jean Paul Akayesu, Judgment, Case No. ICTR-96-4-T, 2 September 1998, paras 361–362.
17 The Prosecutor v. Eliézer Niyitegeka, Judgment, Case No. ICTR-96-14-T, 16 May 2003, para. 273; The Prosecutor v. Clément Kayishema and Obed Ruzindana, Judgement, Case No. ICTR-95-1-T, 21 May 1999, para. 293.
18 Ruzindana, 'The Challenges,' p. 153.
19 Ibid., p. 146.
20 'Hutu Power' refers to a supremacist racial ideology advocated by Hassan Ngeze and others before and during the 1994 genocide of Tutsis that conceives of Hutus and Tutsis as separate 'races.'
21 Ruzindana, 'The Challenges,' p. 145.
22 Prosecutor v. Ferdinand Nahimana, Jean-Bosco Barayagwisa, Hassan Ngeze, Judgment and Sentence, Case No. ICTR-99-52-T, 3 December 2003, para. 458 [hereinafter Nahimana et al. TJ].
23 R. Shuy, 'Response to the March 1998 Report and Testimony of Dr. Mathias Ruzindana,' 20 January 2003. Expert report for the Defense Counsel at the International Criminal Tribunal for Rwanda, Nahimana et al. TJ. Report with Author.
24 Shuy, 'Response,' p. 26.
25 Ibid., pp. 9–11.
26 In Elonis v. United States, 13-983 U.S. (2015), the US Supreme Court considered whether a "reasonable person" would regard the rap lyrics written by Anthony Douglas Elonis as threatening.
27 E. Elias-Bursać, *Translating Evidence and Interpreting Testimony at a War Crimes Tribunal: Working in a Tug-of-War*, London: Palgrave Macmillan, 2015.
28 A. Oberschall, Šešelj trial transcripts, 11 December 2007. Online. Available HTTP: <http://www.icty.org/x/cases/seselj/trans/en/071211IT.htm> (accessed 5 June 2019), pp. 1967–1968.
29 A. Oberschall, 'Propaganda, Hate Speech and Mass Killings,' in P. Dojčinović (ed.) *Propaganda*, p. 174.
30 A. Oberschall, *Vojislav Šešelj's Nationalist Propaganda: Contents, Techniques, Aims and Impacts, 1990–1994*. Expert report for the Office of the Prosecutor at the International Criminal Tribunal for the Former Yugoslavia, 2006. The Prosecutor v. Vojislav Šešelj, Case No. IT-03-67, exhibit no. P00005.

31 C. Browning, *Ordinary Men: Reserve Police Battalion 101 and the Final Solution in Poland*, New York, NY: Harper Collins (first published 1992), 1998.
32 Oberschall, *Vojislav Šešelj's Nationalist Propaganda*, p. 14.
33 Ibid., p. 7.
34 Ibid., p. 15.
35 Ibid., p. 18.
36 Ibid., p. 21.
37 Ibid., pp. 18–21.
38 This discussion draws from the Šešelj trial transcripts, 11–13 December 2007, pp. 1950–2228.
39 Šešelj trial transcripts, 12 December 2007, p. 2054.
40 Ibid., p. 2114.
41 Ibid., p. 2126.
42 Ibid., 13 December 2007, T.2214.
43 H.L.A. Hart and T. Honoré, *Causation in the Law*, Second Edition, Oxford: Clarendon (first published 1959) 1985, p. 22.
44 Clarke, *Fictions*, p. 55. Kelsall, *Culture*, p. 255.
45 R v. Smith [2000] 4 All ER 289 at 342–343, [2001] 1 AC 146 at 11.
46 Hart and Honoré. *Causation*, p. 26.
47 J. Dressler and S.P. Garvey, *Cases and Materials on Criminal Law*, Sixth Edition, St. Paul, MN: West Academic Publishing, 2012, p. 599.
48 Prosecutor v. Radoslav Brđanin, Case No. IT-99-36-T, 23 June 2003, trial transcript, p. 17980. Online. Available HTTP: <http://www.icty.org/x/cases/brdanin/trans/en/030623ED.htm> (accessed 12 June 2019).
49 C. Geertz, 'Common Sense as a Cultural System,' in C. Geertz (ed.), *Local Knowledge: Further Essays in Interpretive Anthropology*, New York, NY: Basic Books, 1983, p. 84.
50 M.-B. Dembour and T. Kelly, *Paths to International Justice: Social and Legal Perspectives*, Cambridge: Cambridge University Press, 2007, p. 8.
51 Eltringham, 'Illuminating,' pp. 338–355. Wilson, *Writing History*.
52 Hart and Honoré. *Causation*, p. 91.
53 P. Bourdieu, *Distinction: A Social Critique of the Judgment of Taste*, translated by R. Nice, Cambridge: Harvard University Press (first published 1979), 1984.
54 Geertz, 'Common Sense,' p. 73.
55 Ibid., p. 91.
56 Ibid., p. 75.
57 R. Niezen and M. Sapignoli (eds), *Palaces of Hope: The Anthropology of the United Nations*, Cambridge: Cambridge University Press, 2017.
58 Eltringham, 'Illuminating,' p. 348.
59 S. Jasanoff, *Science at the Bar: Law, Science, and Technology in America*, Cambridge, MA: Harvard University Press, 1995, p. 8.
60 Jasanoff, *Science*, p. xv.

Chapter 3

Putting the offense of ordering in order

Toward a theory of inchoate liability

Gregory S. Gordon

Introduction

Modern atrocity speech law arguably finds its roots in the failed post-First World War international criminal law project of the Allied representatives who convened in Paris to structure a new world order after the previous four years of carnage. They set up the Commission on the Responsibility of the Authors of the War and on Enforcement of Penalties to measure liability for criminal offenses committed during the conflict.[1] The Commission's mandate included, *inter alia*, reporting on "the facts as to breaches of the laws and customs of war committed [during the war] by the forces of the German Empire and their Allies [...]"[2] The Commission found that the war's initiation was the responsibility of the Central Powers, which, in the process of prosecuting the conflict, seriously breached the laws of war and humanity.[3] It recommended bringing to justice the most senior Central Power authorities, including Kaiser Wilhelm II, who was then in exile in Holland, for *ordering* those offenses and having failed to prevent their subordinates from carrying them out (essentially a proto-version of superior responsibility).[4]

But the government in The Hague would not agree to hand over the deposed German emperor and thus the sketched-out international justice project, including its attendant 'ordering' mode of liability, would never see the light of day in a genuine international context.[5] Some 75 years later, though, after the atrocities of the Second World War, the embryonic jurisprudence of Nuremberg and the intervening Cold War period, the statutes of the ad hoc tribunals for the former Yugoslavia and Rwanda would finally criminalize 'ordering' as an offense within the modern international criminal law framework.[6] The gravamen of the crime, which would be codified as well under Article 25(b)(3) of the Rome Statute for the International Criminal Court (ICC),[7] is that "a person in a position of authority uses it to convince another to commit an offense."[8]

That ordering was ultimately criminalized was, of course, an inevitable and salutary development in the history of international criminal law – especially given its inherent link to superior–subordinate malfeasance in the military context. But concentrating more carefully on its essential nature, as described in the previous paragraph, might give one pause. In particular, that language from the modern jurisprudence suggests that liability is premised strictly on execution of the order. Why does this seem problematic? The answer is rather simple. Given the intrinsic likelihood of compliance with the order in light of the speaker's position of command, the words themselves should be deemed criminal regardless of the ordered crime's actual commission. In other words, liability for the crime of ordering should not merely be a form of parasitic complicity but rather a substantive offense in its own right. This is especially true given that incitement to genocide, which entails no definitional position of authority for the speaker, criminalizes words on their utterance.

Consequently, on the strength of both logic, policy and doctrinal coherence, this chapter contends that the crime of ordering should be modified from its present restrictive form and expanded to encompass inchoate liability. After this Introduction, Part II will explore in greater detail the doctrinal origins of the crime of ordering and its early considerations of inchoate liability. Part III will flesh out the elements of the offense through the jurisprudence of the ad hoc tribunals. And Part IV will demonstrate how, in light of the crime's history, objectives and relation to other speech modalities, ordering should criminalize commands to commit atrocities that are not carried out. It will also entertain potential objections to the expansion of liability in respect of ordering, including allegations of potential 'overcriminalization' of speech conduct and the possibility of doctrinal incoherence. In the end, given its normative moorings, sound policy considerations as well as suggested macro-fixes of the entire body of speech offenses in international criminal law, the chapter will conclude that incorporating inchoate liability within ordering's ambit will promote deterrence and enhance doctrinal harmony as part of the fight against the culture of impunity.

Ordering: background and context

Ordering in international humanitarian law

The Lieber Code

With roots in international humanitarian law, ordering is perhaps the oldest of the codified atrocity speech delicts. Going all the way back to the nineteenth century, Article 60 of the 1863 Lieber Code, history's first written systematization of the laws of war (issued during the American Civil War by President Abraham Lincoln as 'General Order 100') declared that "No body of troops has the right to declare that it will not give, and therefore will not expect, quarter [...]"[9] In essence, this provision forbade ordering that no prisoners could be taken (i.e., that captured enemy combatants be killed rather than taken prisoner).[10]

The Hague Conventions

Similarly, the Annex to the 1899 Hague Convention with Respect to the Laws and Customs of War on Land (Hague II) contains a dedicated provision prohibiting a certain kind of ordering. In particular, Article 23 of the Annex warns, "Besides the prohibitions provided by special Conventions, it is especially forbidden [...] To *declare* that no quarter will be given [...]"[11] The identical article of the Annex to the 1907 Hague Convention with Respect to the Laws and Customs of War on Land (Hague IV) is to the same effect.[12]

The Geneva Conventions

More recently, Article 49 of the First Geneva Convention (for the Amelioration of the Condition of the Wounded in Armies in the Field), Article 50 of the Second Geneva Convention (for the Amelioration of the Condition of Wounded, Sick and Shipwrecked Members of Armed Forces at Sea), Article 129 of the Third Geneva Convention (relative to the Treatment of Prisoners of War) and Article 146 of the Fourth Geneva Convention (relative to the Protection of Civilian Persons in Time of War) each have identical introductory language as regards grave breaches: "The High Contracting Parties undertake to enact any legislation necessary to provide effective penal sanctions for persons committing, *or ordering to be committed*, any of the grave breaches of the present Convention defined in the following Article" (emphasis added).[13]

Likewise, Article 40 of Additional Protocol I (AP II) to the Geneva Conventions, covering the Protection of Victims of International Armed Conflicts, declares in relevant part, "It is prohibited *to order* that there shall be no survivors [or] to threaten an adversary therewith [...]" (emphasis added).[14] A similar provision is found in Additional Protocol II (AP II), which is concerned with the Protection of Victims of Non-International Armed Conflicts. Article 4(1) of AP II provides, "It is prohibited *to order* that there shall be no survivors" (emphasis added).[15]

Ordering as treated in the courts and tribunals

The Leipzig trials

As noted above, at the end of the First World War, the victors' plans to try German war leaders before an international tribunal came to naught. But trials in 1921 of relatively lower-ranked German soldiers/officers for war crimes, based on Allied allegations, were conducted under Weimar Republic auspices at the German Supreme Court (*Reichsgericht*) in Leipzig.[16] The seventh of the twelve trials proceeded from French accusations against German Lieutenant-General Karl Stenger and his subordinate Major Benno Crusius.[17] The charges against Stenger were rooted in part, on violation of Annex Article 23 to the 1899/1907 Hague II/IV Conventions outlawing declarations of no quarter based on the killing/mistreatment of French prisoners of war.[18]

According to the French, Stenger twice issued an order to kill all French POWs under his control, which order was carried out by Crusius.[19] The alleged orders consisted of the following:

> No prisoners are to be taken from today onwards; all prisoners, wounded or not, are to be killed," and "All the prisoners are to be massacred; the wounded, armed or not, are to be massacred; even men captured in large organised units are to be massacred. No enemy must remain alive behind us.[20]

In considering the evidence, and ruling on the declaration-of-no-quarter charge, the court distinguished between an order to kill only those soldiers who were abusing POW privileges and one that enjoined executing all those who were captured or wounded. The court found that the former kind of order was in accordance with international law; but in doing so, it also had occasion to reaffirm the illegality of the latter:

> Such an order, if it were issued, would not have been contrary to international principles, for the protection afforded by the regulations for land warfare does not extend to such wounded who take up arms again and renew the fight. Such men have by so doing forfeited the claim for mercy granted to them by the laws of warfare. On the other hand, an order of the nature maintained by the accused Crusius would have had absolutely no justification.[21]

The court, while convicting Crusius, could not find beyond a reasonable doubt that Stenger had issued an order to kill wounded and unarmed POWs.[22] Thus, he was acquitted but the prohibition against ordering no quarter was, nevertheless, annealed.

Nuremberg

THE INTERNATIONAL MILITARY TRIBUNAL

Surprisingly, the Charter of the International Military Tribunal (IMT) at Nuremberg, according to which the major Nazi war criminals would be charged, makes no direct reference to ordering as a mode of liability. After setting out the substantive offenses of Crimes against Peace, War Crimes and Crimes against Humanity, Article 6 states that "Leaders, organizers, instigators, and accomplices participating in the formulation or execution of a common plan or conspiracy to commit any of the foregoing crimes are responsible for all acts performed by any persons in execution of such plan."[23] The only reference to the notion of 'orders' is found in Article 8 and framed not as a mode of liability but as a defense limitation. In particular, it declares, "The fact that the Defendant acted pursuant to order of his Government or of a superior shall not free him from responsibility, but may be considered in mitigation of punishment if the Tribunal determines that justice so requires."[24]

The IMT indictment similarly failed to charge the defendants directly pursuant to ordering as a mode of liability. Count Three, "War Crimes," did make reference to 'orders' or 'ordering' as contributing to the commission of war crimes. Thus, for example, per Count III(C), "Murder and Ill-Treatment of Prisoners of War," the indictment alluded to "Soviet prisoners of war [being] murdered en masse *on orders* from the High Command [...]" (emphasis added).[25] Under Count III(J), "Germanization of Occupied Territories," the Indictment referenced "Two *orders* from 23 to 24 August 1942 imposed by force German nationality on French citizens."[26]

The IMT's judgment took a similar approach. Ordering, qua ordering, did not serve as a specific mode of liability on which judgment was rendered. But the decision was littered with references to ordering (or, synonymously, 'directing') as part of the individual defendants' respective grounds for guilt. Thus, broadly in reference to "War Crimes and Crimes against Humanity," Hermann Göring was found to have issued a "directive" that contemplated plundering and abandonment of all industry in the food deficit regions and, from the food surplus regions, a diversion of food to German needs."[27] And, in reference to the victims of the Holocaust, by decree of 31 July 1941 he directed Himmler and Heydrich to "bring about a complete solution of the Jewish question in the German sphere of influence in Europe."[28]

And there are allusions to various infamous Nazi orders such as the Commando Order (from the High Command of the German armed forces – all captured Allied commandos must be killed immediately without trial, even if in proper uniform or attempting to surrender), the Commissar Order (another German High Command order – that any Soviet political commissar identified among captured troops be summarily executed), and the *Nacht und Nabel* Decree (or 'Night and Fog' – Hitler's order that persons in occupied territories viewed as undermining the security of German troops were to be abducted in secret and without their families/communities knowing what became of them – they were then typically tortured and killed – this was essentially an order to 'disappear' political opponents in occupied territories).[29]

THE NUREMBERG MILITARY TRIBUNALS

The so-called "Subsequent Nuremberg Trials," twelve proceedings held in the American Zone before the Nuremberg Military Tribunals (NMTs) had a much more intensive focus on the ordering modality. As noted by Kevin Jon Heller,

> Because crimes committed pursuant to the notorious Nazi orders were at the heart of a number of NMT trials – the Commando Order, the Commissar Order, the Night and Fog Decree – the tribunals devoted considerable attention to ordering as a mode of participation.[30]

Control Council Law No. 10 That more dedicated approach was immediately apparent in the NMTs' constitutive instrument, Control Council Law No. 10. After Article II(1) of that document laid out the substantive delicts of Crimes against Peace, War Crimes, Crimes against Humanity and membership in certain groups declared criminal by the IMT, subsection (2) stated as follows:

> 2. Any person without regard to nationality or the capacity in which he acted, is deemed to have committed a crime as defined in paragraph 1 of this Article, if he was (a) a principal or (b) was an accessory to the commission of any such crime *or ordered* or abetted the same [...].
>
> (emphasis added)[31]

Illegal order in a superior–subordinate context Pursuant to the rather extensive NMT jurisprudence on ordering, liability was premised on three requirements: (1) An illegal order had been issued by a superior to a subordinate; (2) the defendant was responsible in some way for that order and (3) the defendant knew or should have known that the order was illegal.[32] From these core requirements, some interesting gloss developed in the case law. In the High Command Case judgment, from the final of the twelve trials, the NMT found that the necessary superior–subordinate relationship could be either *de jure* or *de facto*, regardless of "direct command authority," provided the orders were "binding upon subordinate units to whom they were directed [...]"[33] Thus, the Tribunal rejected defendant Hermann Reinecke's claim that he could not give orders to civilian concentration camp workers because they were not directly within his chain of command as the workers felt "compelled to comply" with his directives.[34]

Issuing, drafting or transmitting orders Ordering's *actus reus* entailed the defendant's issuing, drafting or transmitting an illicit directive.[35] Issuing was fairly straightforward – Lieutenant General Walter Kuntze in the Hostage Case, for instance, was found guilty of issuing an order that set 100 Serbian civilians as a fixed reprisal number for each killed German soldier.[36] Drafting was somewhat more complex as staff officers could be liable for transcribing their superiors' directives if the officers exercised "personal initiative" during the drafting process such that an amorphous desideratum could be sufficiently transformed into a specific, executable command.[37] But being a mere stenographer would not yield ordering liability. Thus, the Hostage Case judges acquitted defendant Kurt von Geitner for typing up an order to commit illegal reprisals because he was simply carrying out his superior's instructions.[38] But defendant Walter Warlimont was convicted for his role in drafting the Commissar Order because "he contributed his part to moulding it into its final form."

Finally, a subordinate link in the chain of command transmitting a directive from a superior link also entailed ordering liability.[39] This was relatively clear-cut when the order was illegal on its face. But even a non-facially illegal directive could give rise to guilt for ordering if it was transmitted "without proper safeguards as to its application."[40] As a result, defendant Wilhelm von Leeb was convicted in respect of the Barbarossa Jurisdiction Order's issuance (an order defining how the military and security forces were to treat Soviet civilians) as "it was in [no] way clarified [...] to prevent its illegal application."[41] This liability also extended to civilians such that, in the Judges' Case, justice ministry official Franz Schlegelberger was convicted for ordering the execution of a Jew who had been sentenced for stealing eggs.[42]

Mens rea To satisfy the modality's *mens rea*, the defendant needed to know that the order was illegal or, because the order was "criminal on its face," should have known that it was.[43] In the words of the High Command Tribunal,

> [A superior] cannot be held criminally responsible for a mere error in judgment as to disputable legal questions [...] he must have passed on the order to the chain of command and the order must be one that is criminal upon its face, or one which he is shown to have known was criminal.[44]

Substantive crime? One of the most interesting issues to arise in the NMT jurisprudence concerned the handling of ordering as a substantive crime (via inchoate liability) versus a mere mode of liability. When the order was executed, the NMT treatment was uniform – it would be dealt with as a mode of participation in a crime.[45] Thus, on execution, the defendant would be responsible for the crimes committed pursuant to the order. The tribunals were divided, though, if the illegal order was never executed. Two of them – in the *Einsatzgruppen* Case and the RuSHA (SS Race and Resettlement Main Office) Case – opted for acquittal. This meant an acquittal for RuSHA defendant Heinz Brueckner, whose illicit order to force conscription of civilians was not proved to have been adopted or carried out.[46] That said, the *Einsatzgruppen* panel acknowledged Article 47 of the German Military Penal Code, which assigned liability without execution of the order if the directive "aims at the commission of a crime or offense."[47] And that is the approach adopted by the Hostage Case tribunal, which found defendant Lothar Rendulic guilty of transmitting the Commissar Order in spite of no evidence that "captured commissars were shot by troops under his command." Such a gap in the evidentiary record could serve as a "mitigating circumstance but [did] not free [Rendulic] of the crime of knowingly and intentionally passing on a criminal order."[48]

Interestingly, the tribunal in the High Command Case adopted a compromise stance. On the one hand, it took the position that a defendant could not be convicted for his part in an order that was not executed. As a result, defendant Georg-Hans Reinhardt was acquitted for distributing the Commissar Order.[49] On the other hand, quite curiously, it held that a defendant who issued an executed order was not only liable for the crimes committed pursuant to that order but also responsible for issuing the illegal order itself. Thus, under these circumstances, the tribunal assigned inchoate liability for the order, even though it was carried out. In other words, per the judges, defendant's directives as to deportations, plunder, and forced labor "were criminal orders and they were fully implemented by him. He is criminally responsible for issuing the orders *and* for the acts done in implementation of them" (emphasis added).[50]

The ad hoc tribunals

Ordering is a mode of liability in the statutes for the *ad hoc* Tribunals for the former Yugoslavia and Rwanda (the jurisprudence interpreting these statute provisions will be considered in the following section). International Criminal Tribunal for the former Yugoslavia (ICTY) Statute, Article 2 (Grave Breaches of the Geneva Conventions of 1949), states that the "International Tribunal shall have the power to prosecute persons committing or *ordering to be committed* grave breaches [...]" (emphasis added).[51] Moreover, Article 7 (Individual Criminal Responsibility), which is explicitly linked to Article 2 (Grave Breaches) and Article 3 (Violations of the Laws or Customs of War), provides that "a person who planned, *instigated*, *ordered*, committed, or otherwise aided and abetted in the planning, preparation or execution of a crime referred to in articles 2 to 5 of the present Statute, shall be individually responsible for the crime" (emphasis added).[52]

International Criminal Tribunal for Rwanda (ICTR) Statute Article 4 (Violations of Article 3 Common to the Geneva Conventions and of AP II) contains an analogous provision governing non-international armed conflict. It declares that the "International Tribunal for Rwanda shall have the power to prosecute persons committing or *ordering to be committed* serious violations" of Common Article 3 and AP II.[53] Also parallel to the ICTY "Individual Criminal Responsibility" provision, Article 6 of the ICTR Statute provides that a "person who planned, *instigated, ordered*, committed or otherwise aided and abetted in the planning, preparation or execution of a crime referred to in articles 2 to 4 of the present Statute, shall be individually responsible for the crime" (emphasis added).[54]

The hybrid tribunals

As regards the hybrid tribunals, the Statute of the Special Court for Sierra Leone (SCSL) had the same provisions as the ICTR Statute regarding violations of Common Article 3 and AP II (SCSL Statute, Article 3) and Individual Responsibility (SCSL Statute, Article 6) (emphasis added).[55] Article 6 of the Law on the Establishment of the Extraordinary Chambers in the Courts of Cambodia (ECCC) declares that "[t]he Extraordinary Chambers shall have the power to bring to trial all Suspects who committed or *ordered the commission of* grave breaches of the Geneva Conventions" (emphasis added).[56] The statute for the ECCC also deals with speech in connection with individual criminal responsibility. Thus, Article 29 declares that "Any Suspect who planned, *instigated, ordered*, aided and abetted, or committed the crimes referred to in article 3 new, 4, 5, 6, 7 and 8 of this law shall be individually responsible for the crime" (emphasis added).[57]

The International Criminal Court

As the founding statute of the sole *permanent* court among the current assortment of ICL institutions, the Rome Statute must be considered in respect of ordering.[58] Consistent with the other constituent instruments reviewed, there is a paucity of relevant text. Within Article 8 ("War Crimes"), there is one provision related to speech. Article 8(2)(b)(xii) describes as a serious violation of "the laws and customs applicable in international armed conflict, within the established framework of international law" any act of "*Declaring* that no quarter will be given [...]" (emphasis added).[59]

Otherwise, the Rome Statute configures its ordering (and instigating) provisions differently from the other ICL foundation documents. Instead of grafting language directly onto specific war crimes articles and then laying out a separate, and redundant, individual responsibility article, the Rome Statute fuses all substantive war crimes provisions into a unified Article 8 and then deals with individual criminal responsibility uniquely in Article 25.[60] Subsection (3)(b) of that Article declares that

> a person shall be criminally responsible and liable for punishment for a crime within the jurisdiction of the Court if that person [...] orders, solicits or induces the commission of such a crime which in fact occurs or is attempted [...][61]

The elements of ordering in the modern cases

Overview

Although, as we saw in the previous section, the Nuremberg Charter did not contain an explicit 'ordering' mode of liability, the responsibility of certain Nuremberg defendants was clearly predicated on the functional equivalent of 'ordering.' For instance, Göring's guilt for war crimes and crimes against humanity was predicated, in part, on the fact that he "signed a directive concerning the treatment of Polish workers in Germany" and "directed Himmler and Heydrich to 'bring about a complete solution of the Jewish question in the German sphere of influence in Europe.'"[62] Further, as we have seen, the ordering mode of liability was integral to findings of guilt in several judgments of the Nuremberg NMTs (and it played an important role in the post-First World War Leipzig trials).

'Ordering,' as discussed in the previous section, was embedded into the individual responsibility provisions of the *ad hoc* Tribunal statutes as well as the Rome Statute.[63] And modern jurisprudence setting forth the elements of ordering is found in judgments issued by the ICTY and ICTR. The essence of the offense, as reflected in these judgments, is that a "person in a position of authority uses it to convince another to commit an offence."[64] This then subdivides into three separate components: a circumstance element (i.e., a superior–subordinate relationship), an *actus reus* element (the transmission of an order) and a *mens rea* element (awareness of a substantial likelihood that an international crime or crimes will be committed in execution of the order). Each of these shall now be considered in turn.

Superior–subordinate relationship

Regarding the first element, the prosecution need not establish a formal superior–subordinate relationship.[65] Rather, proof of the defendant's authority such that he could compel another to commit a crime in following his order is enough.[66] In fact, the requirement boils down to "the *implied* existence of a superior–subordinate relationship" (emphasis added)[67] and, distinguishing it from command responsibility, establishing effective control is not required.[68] This allows for establishing ordering liability in the context of a civilian superior–subordinate relationship.[69]

Actus reus

Transmission

Ordering's *actus reus* amounts to transmitting an unlawful command to one or more subordinates.[70] An order is deemed unlawful if it is in breach of general international criminal law or international humanitarian law, "even if it is in conformity with the domestic law of the State of the person who issued it."[71] It may be in written or oral form and meant for either a particular individual or individuals or to unknown recipients.[72] Not needing to be illicit on its face for liability to attach,[73] the order may also be channeled to its intended recipients through a chain of intermediaries.[74] Consistent with this, there is no requirement that an individual be the original author of the order – passing it to the next link in the chain of command may be sufficient to generate culpability.[75]

Proof of transmission

The *actus reus* can be established via circumstantial evidence.[76] For example, an order's transmission can be proved through a substantial number of similar actions over disparate locations within a compressed time frame.[77] Moreover, to sustain a conviction, the order need not be written or tape-recorded – testimony or other secondary evidence can suffice.[78]

The target crime: omission, commission and causal link

According to the Appeals Chamber decision in Prosecutor v. Galić, a superior's omission to act cannot give rise to ordering liability for the superior.[79] Such grounds for guilt are covered under ICTY Statute Article 7(3) (as well as ICTR Statute Article 6(3) and Rome Statute Article 28) under the rubric of superior responsibility.[80] *Ad hoc* tribunal jurisprudence has specified that responsibility for ordering will lie only when the ordered crime is actually perpetrated.[81] And there is a requirement that the order substantially contribute to the commission of the offense (but need not be a *sine qua non*) – in other words, a causal link must be demonstrated.[82] The Rome Statute's Article 25(3)(b) is to the same effect – ordering is considered a form of secondary liability triggered exclusively when the target offense "occurs or is attempted."[83]

Mens rea

The Appeals Chamber judgment in Prosecutor v. Blaškić represents the ICTY/ICTR consensus regarding the ordering offense's *mens rea*: "the awareness of the substantial likelihood that a crime will be committed in the execution of that order [...]"[84] That judgment concluded, "Ordering with such awareness has to be regarded as accepting that crime."[85] That said, as discussed *supra*, an order need not be explicitly criminal to establish guilt.[86] Cryer observes that this is "consonant with the point that a mistake of law that does not affect *mens rea* is not exculpatory, and a mistake about whether certain conduct is criminal does not *per se* affect *mens rea*."[87] Finally, liability is measured per the *mens rea* of the person who issued (or passed on) the order, not that of the person who executed it.[88]

Ordering and inchoate liability

As we just considered, the ordering offense mandates a causal link between the directive and perpetration of the target offense. This has two doctrinal implications that are arguably problematic. First, even if the subordinate committed the target offense, *ad hoc* tribunal case law specifies that the order must have "a direct and substantial effect on the commission of the illegal act."[89] Thus, a superior could be absolved of all responsibility if the link between the order and the commission of the substantive crime is perceived as attenuated.

Second, *a fortiori*, failure to execute the ordered crime would similarly result in the superior's acquittal.[90] Why is this problematic? In light of the requisite element of the superior–subordinate relationship, where refusal to comply with a command is normatively verboten, "the likelihood of the occurrence of the ordered offence [is] high."[91] As a result, ordering "*per se* creates a significant risk of commission of an offense, probably more so than simple instigation or encouragement."[92]

As noted above, this creates a knotty doctrinal issue since incitement carries inchoate liability notwithstanding the lack of a formal relationship between speaker and listener while ordering, necessarily within the superior–subordinate context, does not. The solution to this problem is simple: Convert ordering into a substantive (i.e., inchoate) offense. As explained by Robert Cryer,

> It is the hierarchical relationship that provides us with an insight into the special harm of ordering, and thus why there is a strong case for a separate inchoate crime of ordering. The Rome Statute […] contains a lacuna in this regard […] There is also a further cumulative form of harm that argues in favour of an inchoate crime of ordering. This is that, unlike incitement […] ordering offenses against international law also involve an abuse of authority.[93]

And, as previously considered, in addition to the policy rationales, there is some precedent in the post-Second World War jurisprudence for treating the ordering modality as an inchoate crime. This was how the NMT handled ordering in the Hostage Case, where defendant Rendulic was convicted of transmitting the Commissar Order even though it was not proved to have been executed by soldiers within his chain of command. A post-Second World War British Military Court took a similar stance. It convicted General Nickolaus von Falkenhorst, commander-in-chief of the German Armed Forces in Norway, on the grounds that he ordered his subordinates to transfer Jewish prisoners of war to the Security Police for purposes of having them murdered.[94] The order was not executed. Still, a British Military Court convicted von Falkenhorst of war crimes for issuing the order.[95] Thus, per Antonio Cassese and Paula Gaeta,

> Although the ICTY and ICTR have treated ordering […] exclusively as [a mode] of liability for participating in a completed crime, there is considerable historical authority supporting ordering […] as [an inchoate crime]. When ordering is conceived of as an inchoate offence, an authority figure issuing an illegal order may be found guilty even if the order is not carried out by the subordinates […] Ordering makes most sense as an inchoate crime […][96]

Looking beyond the strict confines of the ordering offense itself, broadening its scope to include inchoate liability makes sense within the larger framework of international criminal law. As I have suggested elsewhere in my scholarship, speech offenses should be considered as a distinct and interrelated body of law within that larger framework.[97] From that perspective, we can see that there are many liability gaps within that body. More specifically, it is useful to point out that pre-crime speech in international law can be broadly classified into two large conceptual categories: (1) persuading speech and (2) directing speech.

Persuading speech would entail communication meant to encourage the recipient to commit an offense. This, in turn, would bifurcate into speech that leads to the commission of the offense and speech that does not. The former can be defined as 'instigation' – the prompting of another to commit an offense where there is a causal connection between the prompting and the perpetration of the offense.[98] The latter can be defined as incitement – "urging another to commit a [crime] when the crime is not subsequently perpetrated."[99] In this sense, persuading speech is symmetrical in terms of its coverage – it can be charged with or without the commission of the target crime.

Directing speech has a monolithic penal designation – ordering. But it lacks the same kind of symmetry. In particular, while liability will attach to directing speech that results in a crime's commission, the same is not true for directing speech that does not. My 'Unified Liability Theory' for atrocity speech is an effort to create symmetry and fill in gaps with respect to this body of law. Pursuant to that theory, if non-catalytic *persuasion* creates liability, then so should non-catalytic *direction*. This is in line with other recommended atrocity speech symmetry-creation/gap-filling nostra. For example, it is consistent with extending speech-related inchoate liability (i.e., incitement) to the core international offenses of crimes against humanity and war crimes when that modality is currently limited to the crime of genocide.

Some have suggested that this approach would "overcriminalize behavior and make distinctions in relation to hate speech even more difficult."[100] But this position is untenable on two independent grounds. First, assuming it even applied, "overcriminalization" inheres in the *current* doctrinal structure, where we assign inchoate liability to mere *persuading* non-catalytic speech. Given the inherent likelihood of compliance with an order, punishment for *directing* a subordinate to commit a crime, regardless of compliance, certainly does not represent normative overreaching.

Moreover, in light of the law's current incitement/instigation configuration, the change recommended herein promotes overall consistency as it puts executed/non-executed directing speech on the same footing as executed/non-executed persuading speech. For that reason, the charge that any such change would "make distinctions in relation to hate speech even more difficult" is similarly unfounded. To the contrary, in enhancing uniformity across the relevant speech delicts, this chapter's proposal would reinforce the "principle of fair warning," which is necessary to achieve two of the criminal law's chief aims – deterring future criminal conduct and punishing those who choose to pursue wrongful ends in disregard of the law.[101] In effect, the law would be more efficacious for being less murky – permitting the global community to make distinctions based on principle, not pursuant to the random historic development of the law. As noted in my book *Atrocity Speech Law: Foundation, Fragmentation, Fruition*,

> [It] would seem the current legal landscape is the result of a complete lack of global vision or intentionality in formulating the various modalities that

> comprise atrocity speech law. The reactive and doctrinally haphazard manner in which atrocity speech law has been framed was apparent from its earliest origins. [It] grew [...] in a piecemeal, disconnected fashion with no teleological guideposts [and with] a series of golden opportunities [to harmonize it] squandered. Penal treatment of weaponized words in the context of atrocity, a body of law misshapen and riddled with gaping holes thanks to diplomacy trumping legislative reason, [has] simply calcified.[102]

Creating executed crime/non-executed crime symmetry with regard to persuading and directing speech is an important step in updating atrocity speech law to help it achieve its prime objectives of notice and deterrence. This is not about degrading normative efficacy through overcriminalization and penal-contour blurring; rather, it is about promoting normative efficacy through harmonization and penal-contour coherence.

Conclusion

Likely compliance with an order in the context of a superior–subordinate relationship is the foundational premise for this chapter. From that simple cornerstone, it builds an argument that the current law's shielding from liability the issuance of non-executed orders to commit international crimes is problematic on different levels. Not only does it implicitly overlook the probability of compliance as a compelling rationale for criminalization, but it fails to consider that a sister set of provisions, treating what I have termed 'persuading speech,' takes a quite different approach. How can we reconcile not punishing a person with *authority* over someone, who ineffectually *directs* that person to commit a crime when we punish a person with no authority over someone and who merely ineffectually *persuades* that person to commit a crime? The consequences for lack of success when directing, as opposed to persuading, should certainly be direr.

As has been demonstrated, the proper adjustment is tantamount to assigning inchoate liability for ordering. And, as we have seen, such an approach is not without precedent. It was adopted by American and British military tribunals in prosecutions against German war criminals after the Second World War. Moreover, it is no stranger to municipal law, and it has been supported by eminent publicists. Some critics might contend that conversion to a substantive offense amounts to inadvisable overcriminalization. If anything, however, it is the current law that seems excessive in freighting unfulfilled persuading speech with criminal liability. Thus, to the contrary, extending such liability to *directing* speech is quite logical and sound from a policy perspective. As explained in this chapter, ordering's elements have otherwise been sensibly formulated. Incorporating inchoate liability will, at long last, put the ordering offense in order. And it will bring us one step closer to the vision of a Unified Liability Theory for atrocity speech law. Given the increasing brutality of ordered atrocities in the years since Nuremberg, it is high time we take that important step.

Notes

1 Y. Khushalani, *The Dignity and Honour of Women As Basic and Fundamental Human Rights*, The Hague: Martinus Nijhoff Publishers, 1982, pp. 11–12.
2 Violations of the Laws and Customs of War: Report of Majority and Dissenting Reports of American and Japanese Members of the Commission on Responsibilities, Conference of Paris, 1919, reprinted in *American Journal of International Law*, vol. 14, no. 1–2, 1920, p. 95.
3 Ibid., pp. 107, 114–115.
4 Ibid., pp. 129.
5 W.A. Schabas, *The Trial of the Kaiser*, Oxford: Oxford University Press, 2018, pp. 290–291. As we will see *infra*, however, there were some trials of lower-ranking German military personnel for WWI war crimes in the German Supreme Court in Leipzig. Although Allied lawyers identified the defendants and the charges, the proceedings were within the German domestic jurisdiction. In light of German animosity toward the proceedings, the limited scope of defendants and charges, the many acquittals, the slap-on-the wrist punishments and anemic post-conviction enforcement, most experts agree that the trials did not represent a legitimate justice enterprise. See Y. Dinstein, *The Defence of 'Obedience to Superior Orders' in International Law*, Oxford: Oxford University Press, 2012, p. 11.
6 G.S. Gordon, *Atrocity Speech Law: Foundation, Fragmentation, Fruition*, New York, NY: Oxford University Press, 2017. Updated Statute of the International Criminal Tribunal for the Former Yugoslavia (ICTY), Article 7(1), [hereinafter ICTY Statute]. Statute of the International Criminal Tribunal for Rwanda (ICTY), Article 6(1), [hereinafter ICTR Statute].
7 Rome Statute of the International Criminal Court (ICC), Article 25(b)(3), [hereinafter Rome Statute].
8 The Prosecutor v. Jean-Paul Akayesu, Judgment, Case No. ICTR-96-4-T, 2 September 1998, para. 483 [hereinafter Akayesu TJ].
9 Article 60, F. Lieber, *Instructions for the Government of Armies in the United States in the Field*, Washington, DC: Government Printing Office, 1898. D. Scheffer, *All the Missing Souls: A Personal History of the War Crimes Tribunals*, Princeton, NJ: Princeton University Press, 2012, p. 422.
10 P.K. Sharma, A. Ratnam and T. Madhusudhan, 'Misconduct Behaviours in Armed Forces,' in N. Maheshwari and V.V. Kumar (eds), *Military Psychology: Concepts, Trends and Interventions*, New Delhi: Sage Publication India, 2016, p. 125.
11 Convention (II) with Respect to the Laws and Customs of War on Land and its annex: Regulations concerning the Laws and Customs of War on Land, The Hague, 29 July 1899, 32 Stat. 1803, 187 Consol. T.S. 410 [hereinafter 1899 Hague Convention]. Regulations Respecting the Laws and Customs of War on Land were attached as Annexes to both the 1899 Convention and the later 1907 Convention.
12 Convention (IV) respecting the Laws and Customs of War on Land and its annex: Regulations concerning the Laws and Customs of War on Land, The Hague, 18 October 1907, 36 Stat. 2277, 205 Consol. T.S. 277 [hereinafter 1907 Hague Convention].
13 Article 49, Geneva Convention for the Amelioration of the Condition of the Wounded and Sick in Armed Forces in the Field, 12 August 1949, 6 U.S.T. 3114, 75 U.N.T.S. 31 [hereinafter First Geneva Convention]. Article 50, Convention (II) for the Amelioration of the Condition of Wounded, Sick and Shipwrecked Members of Armed Forces at Sea. Geneva, 12 August 1949, 6 U.S.T. 3217, 75 U.N.T.S. 85 [hereinafter Second Geneva Convention]. Art 129, Convention (III) relative to the Treatment of Prisoners of War. Geneva, 12 August 1949, 6 U.S.T. 3316, 75 U.N.T.S.

135 [hereinafter Third Geneva Convention] (emphasis added). Article 146, Convention (IV) relative to the Protection of Civilian Persons in Time of War. Geneva, 12 August 1949, 6 U.S.T. 3516, 75 U.N.T.S. 287 [hereinafter Fourth Geneva Convention] (emphasis added).

14 Article 40, Protocol Additional to the Geneva Conventions of 12 August 1949, and Relating to the Protection of Victims of International Armed Conflicts, 8 June 1977, 1125 U.N.T.S. 3 [hereinafter Protocol I].

15 Protocol Additional to the Geneva Conventions of 12 August 1949, and relating to the Protection of Victims of Non-International Armed Conflicts (Protocol II), 8 June 1977, 1125 U.N.T.S. 609 [hereinafter Protocol II].

16 J. Matthäus, 'The Lessons of Leipzig: Punishing German War Criminals after the First World War,' in P. Heberer and J. Matthäus (eds), *Atrocities on Trial: Historical Perspectives on the Politics of Prosecuting War Crimes*, Lincoln, NE, London: University of Nebraska Press, 2008, p. 9.

17 G.D. Solis, *The Law of Armed Conflict: International Humanitarian Law in War*, Cambridge: Cambridge University Press, 2016, p. 118. Solis refers to this as the last of the Leipzig trials but the historical record does not bear this out. See C. Mullins, *The Leipzig Trials: An Account of the War Criminals' Trials and a Study of German Mentality*, Forgotten Books, 1921, p. 151. See also M. Neuner, 'When Justice is Left to the Losers: The Leipzig War Crimes Trials,' in M. Bergsmo, C.W. Ling and Y. Ping (eds), *Historical Origins of International Criminal Law: Volume* 1, Oslo: Torkel Opsahl Academic ePublisher, 2014, pp. 334–335.

18 Mullins, *The Leipzig*, p. 151.

19 J. Rikhof, 'The Istanbul and Leipzig Trials: Myth or Reality?' in Bergsmo, *Historical Origins*, p. 272.

20 Mullins, *The Leipzig*, p. 153.

21 Ibid., p. 152.

22 Rikhof, 'The Istanbul,' in Bergsmo, *Historical Origins*, p. 272.

23 Article 6, London Charter of the International Military Tribunal, 8 August 1945, 59 Stat. 1544, 1547, 82 U.N.T.S. 279 [hereinafter London Charter].

24 Ibid., p. 288.

25 Indictment of the International Military Tribunal (Count III) in 1 Trial of the Major War Criminals Before the International Military Tribunal, 1947, p. 54 [hereinafter Nuremberg Indictment].

26 Ibid., p. 64.

27 Judgment of the International Military Tribunal (Göring) in 22 Trial of the Major War Criminals Before the International Military Tribunal, 1947 [hereinafter Nuremberg Judgment], pp. 279–282.

28 Ibid., p. 282.

29 Nuremberg Judgment, pp. 288–291 (noting that defendant Wilhelm Keitel reaffirmed the [Commando Order], and later extended it to Allied missions fighting with partisans), pp. 232–233 (observing that Keitel signed and executed the *Nacht und Nebel* Decree). See also p. 352:

> From Fritzsche's testimony in Court it is obvious that already in May 1942, while in the Propaganda Section of the 6th Army, he was aware of Hitler's decree ordering execution for all Soviet political workers and Soviet intellectuals, the so-called 'Commissar Decree.'
>
> [dissent of Soviet Judge Nikitchenko]

30 K.J. Heller, *The Nuremberg Military Tribunals and the Origins of International Criminal Law*, Oxford: Oxford University Press, 2011, p. 254.

31 Control Council Law No. 10, Article II(2)(a) and (b), reprinted in T. Taylor, *Final Report to the Secretary of the Army on the Nuremberg War Crimes Trials under*

Control Council Law No. 10, Washington, DC: U.S. Government Printing Office, 1949, pp. 251–252.

32 Heller, *The Nuremberg*, p. 254.

33 *High Command Case* Judgment, XI Trials of War Criminals Before the Nuremberg Military Tribunals under Control Council Law No. 10, 651, 1949 [hereinafter TWC].

34 Ibid.

35 Heller, *The Nuremberg*, p. 255.

36 *Hostage Case* Judgment, XI TWC, pp. 1277–1278.

37 *High Command* Judgment, XI TWC, p. 683.

38 *Hostage Case* Judgment, XI TWC, p. 1288.

39 Heller, *The Nuremberg*, p. 257.

40 *High Command* Judgment, XI TWC, p. 525.

41 Ibid., pp. 560–561.

42 *Judges' Case* Judgment, III TWC, p. 1085.

43 *High Command* Judgment, XI TWC, p. 511.

44 Ibid.

45 Heller, *The Nuremberg*, p. 258.

46 *RuSHA Case* Judgment, V TWC, p. 147.

47 *Einsatzgruppen Case* Judgment, IV TWC, p. 487.

48 *Hostage Case* Judgment, XI TWC, p. 1294.

49 *High Command* Judgment, XI TWC, pp. 615–616.

50 Ibid., p. 614.

51 ICTY Statute.

52 Ibid., Article 7(1).

53 ICTR Statute.

54 Ibid., Article 6.

55 SCSL Statute [hereinafter SCSL Statute].

56 Law on the Establishment of the Extraordinary Chambers in the Courts of Cambodia for the Prosecution of Crimes Committed during the Period of Democratic Kampuchea, Royal Decree No. NS/RKM/1004/006, Article 6 (27 October 2004) [hereinafter ECCC Law].

57 Ibid., Article 29.

58 See generally Rome Statute.

59 Ibid., Article 8(2)(b)(xii).

60 Ibid., Articles 8, 25.

61 Ibid., Article 25(3)(b). It should be noted that, relative to the other ICL individual responsibility provisions previously considered, Article 25(3)(b) enlarges the ambit of culpable acts by adding 'soliciting' and 'inducing' to simple 'ordering.'

62 Nuremberg Indictment, p. 282.

63 ICTY Statute, ICTR Statute, Rome Statute.

64 Akayesu TJ, para. 483.

65 Prosecutor v. Dario Kordić and Mario Čerkez, Judgment, Case No. IT-95-14/2-A, 17 December 2004, para. 28.

66 Ibid.

67 The Prosecutor v. Laurence Semanza, Judgment and Sentence, Case No. ICTR-97-20-T, 15 May 2003, para. 342.

68 Jean De Dieu Kamuhanda (Appellant) v. The Prosecutor (Respondent), Appeals Chamber Judgment, Case No. ICTR-99-54A-A, 19 September 2005, para. 75 [hereinafter Kamuhanda AJ].

69 I. Bantekas and S. Nash, *International Criminal Law*, London: Routledge-Cavendish, 2007, p. 24. ("An order is a command for action or omission that is

issued by a superior to a subordinate, irrespective of whether the relationship is military or civilian.")

70 Prosecutor v. Radoslav Brđanin, Judgment, Case No. IT-99-36-T, 1 September 2004, para. 270.

71 Bantekas and Nash, p. 24.

72 Ibid.

73 Prosecutor v. Tihomir Blaškić, Trial Judgment, Case No. IT-95-14-T, 3 March 2000, para. 281 [hereinafter Blaškić TJ].

74 Ibid., para. 282.

75 Prosecutor v. Zoran Kupreškić, Mirjan Kupreškić, Vlatko Kupreškić, Drago Josipović, Dragan Papić, Vladimir Šantić aka "Vlado," Judgment, Case No. IT-95-16-T, 14 January 2000, paras 827, 862 [hereinafter Kupreškić *et al.* TJ].

76 Blaškić TJ, para. 281.

77 R. Cryer, H. Friman, D. Robinson and E. Wilmshurst (eds), *An Introduction to International Criminal Law and Procedure*, Third Edition, Cambridge: Cambridge University Press, 2014, p. 375.

78 Ibid.

79 Prosecutor v. Stanislav Galić, Appeal Judgment, Case No. IT-98-29-A, 30 November 2006, paras 90, 103–104.

80 ICTY Statute, Article 7(3); ICTR Statute, Article 6(3). Blaškić TJ, para. 282.

81 Blaškić TJ.

82 Prosecutor v. Milan Milutinović, Nikola Šainović, Dragoljub Ojdanić, Nebojša Pavković, Vladimir Lazarević, Sreten Lukić, Judgment, Case No. IT-05-87-T, vol. III, 26 February 2009, para. 1213.

83 Rome Statute, Article 6(3).

84 Prosecutor v. Tihomir Blaškić, Appeal Judgment, Case No. IT-95-14-A, 29 July 2004, para. 42.

85 Ibid.

86 Ibid.

87 Cryer, *An Introduction*, p. 376.

88 Blaškić TJ, para. 282.

89 Kamuhanda AJ, para. 75. A somewhat softer standard of the order having a 'substantial factor' in the commission of the crime had been applied previously. See, for example, Kupreškić et al. TJ, para. 862.

90 M.G. Karnavas, 'Forms of Perpetration,' in P. Behrens and R. Henham (eds), *Elements of Genocide*, London, New York, NY: Routledge, 2013, p. 104. ("A causal link must be shown between the order and the actual commission of the crime.")

91 R. Cryer, 'General Principles of International Criminal Law,' in D. McGoldrick, P. Rowe and E. Donnelly (eds), *The Permanent International Criminal Court: Legal and Policy Issues*, London: Hart Publishing, 2004, p. 246.

92 Ibid.

93 Ibid.

94 Trial of Generaloberst Nickolaus von Falkenhorst, British Military Court, Brunswick 29th July–2nd August 1946.

95 Ibid.

96 A. Cassese and P. Gaeta, *International Criminal Law*, Third Edition, Oxford: Oxford University Press, 2013, p. 204. Cassese and Gaeta cite the case of General Jacob A. Smith, a US commander, in connection with inciting his troops during counter-insurrectionary operations in the Philippines. Apart from his incitement, Cassese and Gaeta point out that in 1902 "a US Court Martial held that General Smith was guilty of ordering that no quarter should be given to the enemy in the Philippines, even though in fact his troops did not comply with the order." It should

be noted that Cassese and Gaeta suggest that, for inchoate liability to attach, the *mens rea* of the crime should be that "the superior intended the order to be executed and knew that the order was illegal, or else the order was manifestly illegal." Such liability, they note, should also be limited to situations of "formal authority, such as the military context." The position of this chapter, impliedly accepted by Cryer, is that inchoate liability should attach consistent with the current *mens rea* standard and formulation of the superior–subordinate relationship requirement. Cryer, *An Introduction*, p. 246. Elies van Sliedregt is in accord, noting that the *dolus eventualis* standard is sufficient. Van Sliedregt explicitly points out that it is appropriate to impose liability if the result was foreseen and accepted even in "situations where there is divergence between the order and the executed offence." E. van Sliedregt, *International Criminal Law*, Oxford: Oxford University Press, 2012, p. 106.

97 Gordon, *Atrocity*, p. 367.

98 Blaškić TJ, para. 280. The Prosecutor v. Ignace Bagilishema, Judgment, Case No. ICTR-95-1A-T, 7 June 2001, para. 30.

99 Gordon, *Atrocity*, p. 380.

100 C. Stahn, *A Critical Introduction to International Criminal Law*, Cambridge: Cambridge University Press, 2019, p. 50.

101 J. Child and D. Ormerod, *Smith, Hogan and Ormerod's Essentials of Criminal Law*, Oxford: Oxford University Press, 2017, pp. 24–25.

102 Gordon, *Atrocity*, pp. 368, 373, 375.

Chapter 4

International speech crimes following the *Šešelj* appeal judgment

Wibke K. Timmermann

Introduction

On 11 April 2018, the Appeals Chamber (AC) of the Mechanism for International Criminal Tribunals (MICT) rendered its judgment in the Šešelj case. Because of the Trial Chamber (TC) judgment's many serious flaws,[1] the AC's judgment had been eagerly awaited. This chapter assesses the AC's judgment in light of the status of international speech crimes before Šešelj, and of the TC judgment in that case. It considers whether the appeal judgment achieved a clarification of the status of speech crimes in international law.

Vojislav Šešelj, president of the Serbian Radical Party from 23 February 1991 and member of the Assembly of the Republic of Serbia from June 1991, had been charged with persecution, deportation and other inhumane acts (forcible transfer) as crimes against humanity, as well as various war crimes. He was alleged to have planned, ordered, instigated, committed or otherwise aided and abetted these crimes, as well as participated in a joint criminal enterprise.[2]

Šešelj was alleged to have committed, or participated in, the above crimes mainly through his speeches, in addition to recruiting and organizing volunteers who were integrated into the Serb forces. The indictment made specific references to four speeches by the Accused, through which he allegedly persecuted non-Serbs and instigated the commission of various crimes against them. In the first two speeches, made in Vukovar, Šešelj publicly stated on or about 8 November 1991 that "[t]his entire area will soon be cleared of Ustaša," and, approximately five days later, that "Not one Ustaša must leave Vukovar alive."[3] In the third speech, in March 1992 in Mali Zvornik, Šešelj spoke at a rally, stating, *inter alia*, "Dear Chetnik brothers, especially you across the Drina river, you are the bravest ones. We are going to clean Bosnia of pagans and show them a road which will take them to the east, where they belong."[4]

In the fourth speech, delivered on 6 May 1992 in Hrtkovci, Šešelj declared that there was "no room for Croats in Hrtkovci."[5] He announced that "we will drive them to the border of Serbian territory and they can walk on from there, if they do not leave before of their own accord."[6] Directly addressing Croatians who might consider returning to Hrtkovci, he emphasized that they had "nowhere to return to" and stated his conviction that the Serbs from Hrtkovci and surrounding villages would "promptly get rid of the remaining Croats in your village and the surrounding villages."[7] All of the four speeches allegedly resulted in various violent crimes against non-Serb civilians.

On 31 March 2016, a majority of the TC acquitted Šešelj of all charges. However, the difficulties inherent in this decision were already discernible in the fact that not only did Judge Lattanzi dissent on virtually all issues, but Judge Niang also appended an 'Individual Statement' primarily outlining the difficulties he encountered in being appointed to the TC after all the evidence had been heard, and Judge Antonetti composed a 500-page-long concurring opinion. The judgment was widely criticized; many of its findings were controversial. Thus, the Chamber had found that it had not been proven that there had been a widespread or systematic attack against the non-Serbian civilian population in either Croatia or Bosnia and Herzegovina or Vojvodina. Consequently, it held that the *chapeau* elements of crimes against humanity had not been met.[8]

The AC rendered its judgment on 11 April 2018. It reversed Šešelj's acquittals for instigating persecution (forcible displacement), deportation and other inhumane acts (forcible transfer) as crimes against humanity and for committing persecution (violation of the right to security) as a crime against humanity, found him guilty for those offences and sentenced him to ten years of imprisonment. The AC declared that in view of the time Šešelj had spent in custody pending trial, his sentence had been served.

This chapter focuses on the impact of the AC's findings on instigation and the use of language to stir up hatred or violence (also called 'hate speech,' 'incitement to hatred' or 'incitement to violence').

When direct and public incitement meets instigation

The instigation of international crimes is criminalized in Article 7(1) of the Statute of the International Criminal Tribunal for the former Yugoslavia (ICTY), as well as Article 6(1) of the Statute of the International Criminal Tribunal for Rwanda (ICTR). Article 25(3)(b) of the Rome Statute declares that an individual is criminally responsible if he or she "solicits or induces" the commission of an international crime.

Instigation, as opposed to direct and public incitement to commit genocide, is a mode of liability – a form of participation in another individual's crime. This means that the substantive crime, the commission of which is sought to be achieved through the act of instigation, must actually be committed (or, in the case of the Rome Statute, at least be attempted). A causal connection to the substantive crime must therefore be proven.

The International Criminal Tribunals have repeatedly defined instigation as "prompting another person to commit an offence."[9] The instigator's words must have made a "substantial contribution" to the conduct of the principal perpetrator. However, there is no need to prove that the crime would not have been committed but for the instigation.[10] The act of instigation must involve more than merely facilitating the commission of the offence; the principal perpetrator must be influenced in some way to commit the offence. At the same time, the original plan need not have originated with the instigator, and even where the principal perpetrator was already contemplating the commission of the offence, instigation can be present where the final determination to go ahead with it was brought about by "persuasion or strong encouragement of the instigator."[11] In terms of the required *mens rea*, the instigator must either directly intend for the principal offence to be committed or be aware of the substantial likelihood that a crime will be committed in the execution of the acts or omissions instigated.[12]

According to ICTY and ICTR jurisprudence, instigation can be done in private or in public. This can lead to an overlap in the case of direct and public incitement to commit genocide. The latter, of course, is an inchoate crime – no causal link needs to be proven between the inciting speech and any crime which it seeks to bring about. In fact, direct and public incitement to commit genocide is punishable as soon as the speech is uttered. By contrast, as noted above, instigation is a mode of liability which derives its criminality from the substantive offence it seeks to bring about. Where public speech acts are charged as instigation, certain significant problems can arise, as the Šešelj case demonstrated. Where a speaker publicly addresses a large crowd of people, stirs up their emotions and calls for the commission of violence or various crimes, the group of addressees is typically undefined. Consequently, where crimes are committed following the inciting speech, a causal link between a particular crime and the speech in question is much more difficult to establish than in a case of more private instigation, where an individual persuades a specific individual or limited number of individuals to commit a particular offence.[13] This difficulty is especially marked where the temporal or spatial distance between the speech and the crimes in question is rather large. In the Nahimana case, the AC found that

> the longer the lapse of time between a broadcast and the killing of a person, the greater the possibility that other events might be the real cause of such killing and that the broadcast might not have substantially contributed to it.[14]

In the Šešelj case, the TC was confronted with this issue with respect to speeches which the Accused made in Mali Zvornik as well as before the Serbian Parliament. In mid-March 1992, Šešelj delivered a speech in Mali Zvornik, in which "he called 'on the Serbs to 'clear up' Bosnia of the 'pogani' and the 'balijas,' the former meaning 'waste' or 'faeces.'"[15] Nearly three weeks later, on 8 April 1992, Serbian forces commenced its takeover of Zvornik, which allegedly involved the killing of civilians. Further, on 1 and 7 April 1992, Šešelj had delivered two speeches in the Serbian Parliament, which the TC had found "clearly constituted calls for the expulsion and forcible transfer of Croats."[16]

The TC had found that the Mali Zvornik speech and the speeches before the Serbian Parliament did not amount to instigation because their impact was too insignificant and/or the possibility could not be excluded that their aim was to contribute to the war effort or Šešelj's political campaign.[17] The AC rejected this conclusion; it referred to the "widespread and systematic mistreatment of civilians" which accompanied the Serbian forces' violent takeover of Bosnian municipalities and pointed out that Šešelj had "called on *Chetniks* to 'show the *balijas*, the Turks and the Muslims [...] the direction to the east' as '[t]hat's where their place is.'"[18] Given this and other evidence, the AC held that "no reasonable trial chamber could have found that Šešelj's speech in March 1992 in Mali Zvornik did not call for ethnic cleansing but was instead 'contributing to the war effort by galvanizing the Serbian forces.'"[19]

However, the AC concluded with respect to Mali Zvornik that

> The crux of the Prosecution's argument on appeal is the temporal link between Šešelj's statements and the contemporaneous or subsequent commission of crimes in various locations. The Appeals Chamber considers that a reasonable trier of fact could find such a link to be tenuous in circumstances where there was a significant lapse of time between the statement and the offences, allowing for the reasonable possibility that Šešelj's statement did not substantially contribute to the commission of the specific crimes and that other factors may have influenced the conduct of the perpetrators.[20]

With respect to the speeches in the Serbian Parliament, the AC noted that "the Prosecution did not demonstrate at trial the breadth of their dissemination and the specific impact that they had on the commission of crimes in Zvornik and other areas."[21]

The Šešelj case demonstrates the problems associated with charging instigation in relation to acts of public incitement. In such cases, the speeches are often held in front of large crowds rather than specific individuals; frequently, the speech calls for violence in general without specifying the acts with precision; and there is no individual relationship between the speaker and a specific person who is tasked with committing a specific offence. Consequently, where there is a large time lapse between the inflammatory speech and the criminal acts, it becomes difficult to prove that there is a connection between the two.

Similar problems have arisen before the International Criminal Court (ICC), for instance in the case of Ruto and Sang. In the *Decision on Defence Applications for Judgments of Acquittal*,[22] Judge Fremr could find no evidence that would be able to support a conviction on the basis of soliciting or inducing (essentially equivalent to instigating). While there was evidence that Ruto "used language at public events which denigrated Kikuyu and other perceived PNU (Party of National Unity) supporters and expressed the political goal of having them expelled from the Rift Valley," this was "not sufficient to support a possible finding that Mr Ruto *actively called upon any of those present to engage in criminal conduct to bring about this goal*" (emphasis added).[23] Moreover, a sufficiently causal link between the language and the violent conduct had not been proven; the mere fact that "crimes were actually committed against Kikuyu and other perceived PNU supporters in the Rift Valley" did not permit "a strong enough inference" against the Accused: "The geographic and temporal distance between Mr Ruto's alleged speeches and the commission of the crimes" was too large.[24]

Interestingly, in the Brđanin case, the TC held that where the instigating acts are in the shape of public statements or written decisions, they must be "specific enough to constitute instructions [...] to the physical perpetrators to commit" the substantive offences.[25] In determining whether or not the statements are sufficiently specific, the context in which they are made is important.[26] In the Brđanin case, the TC considered whether decisions by the ARK (Autonomous Region of Krajina) Crisis Staff dated 28 and 29 May 1992 instigated the municipal authorities and police to commit the crimes of deportation and forcible transfer, which were carried out subsequent to those decisions. While the decisions were "framed in terms of voluntary compliance," the Chamber, nonetheless, found that "to the municipal authorities and the police they could have only meant a direct incitement to deport and forcibly transfer non-Serbs from the territory of the ARK."[27] This was 'the only reasonable conclusion' when the context was taken into account. This context included "the Accused's unambiguous public statements, made repeatedly from early April 1992 onward, calling on the non-Serb population to leave the Bosnian Krajina and stating that only a small percentage of non-Serbs would be allowed to stay."[28] These findings were upheld by the AC.[29]

The only speech in respect of which the AC in the Šešelj case found that it constituted instigation was Šešelj's speech in Hrtkovci. On 6 May 1992, at an electoral campaign rally, the Accused had called for the expulsion of the Croatian population. Addressing his "Serbian brothers and sisters," he declared that "there was no room for Croats in Hrtkovci," and that "we will drive them to the border of Serbian territory and they can walk on from there, if they do not leave before of their own accord."[30] He told Croatians directly that they had "nowhere to return to" and ended his speech by proclaiming,

> I firmly believe that you, Serbs from Hrtkovci and other villages around here, will also know how to preserve your harmony and unity, that you will promptly get rid of the remaining Croats in your village and the surrounding villages.[31]

Following Šešelj's speech, which was attended by approximately 700 Serbian Radical Party sympathizers and citizens of neighboring villages,[32] the crowd chanted "Croats, go to Croatia" and "[t]his is Serbia."[33] Croatians and other non-Serbians experienced increased harassment and violence and regular threats to leave Hrtkovci.[34] Many non-Serbian civilians left Hrtkovci as a result of housing exchanges with Serbian refugees in a "context of coercion, harassment, and intimidation."[35] Local authorities remained largely inactive.[36]

The AC held that these facts did not leave open the conclusion that the non-Serbian civilians "genuinely consented" to departing from Hrtkovci.[37] It was, moreover, clear that the perpetrators intended the civilians' deportation from an area in which they were lawfully present.[38] It was also evident that the acts of forcible displacement fulfilled the requirements of the crime of persecution, as they "amounted to discrimination in fact, were carried out with discriminatory intent on ethnic grounds, and constituted part of a widespread or systematic attack against the non-Serbian civilian population."[39] In view of the content of Šešelj's speech and the events which were taking place at the time in Bosnia and Herzegovina, the perpetrators were unquestionably aware that their acts formed part of the attack.[40]

It can first be noted that Šešelj's words in this case could be described as "specific enough to constitute instructions" to the principal perpetrators to commit certain offences, as per the requirement suggested in the Brđanin case. In the instant case, Šešelj specifically explained that the "Croats in Hrtkovci" should be driven to the border of Serbian territory, from where they could walk. Again, he stated that his listeners should "promptly get rid of the remaining Croats in [their] village[s]."[41]

In relation to the issue of causation – whether Šešelj's words substantially contributed to the crimes which followed – the TC had not been satisfied that Šešelj's speech "was the reason" for the Croatians' departure from Hrtkovci or the persecutory acts which were alleged to have followed the speech.[42] The AC disagreed. It noted that the speech represented "a clear appeal for the expulsion of the Croatian population in Hrtkovci"[43] and concluded,

> [S]oon after Šešelj's speech, many Croatians and other non-Serbians left for Croatia either out of fear, or by way of fraudulent housing exchanges with Serbian refugees in a context of coercion, harassment, and intimidation, which was met with inaction by the local authorities. Additionally, Serbians, including the Mayor Sibinčić who attended the rally, regularly threatened non-Serbians who still remained in the village. The Appeals Chamber considers that, in light of Šešeljs influence over the crowd and the striking parallels between his inflammatory words and the acts subsequently perpetrated by, *inter alia*, members of the audience, no reasonable trier of fact could have found that, through his speech, he did not substantially contribute to the conduct of the perpetrators.[44]

In the case of the Hrtkovci speech, then, several factors allowed the AC to conclude that instigation was made out: the specificity of Šešelj's words; the short time lapse between the speech and the substantive crimes; regular threats to non-Serbians remaining in the village by Serbians, including individuals who had attended the rally; Šešelj's visible influence over the crowd and the fact that the criminal acts corresponded closely to the content of the speech.

The Šešelj case therefore demonstrates the problems with the way in which instigation and incitement are currently treated in international criminal law. Because public incitement is limited to the crime of genocide – that is, direct and public incitement to commit a crime is only punishable if that crime is genocide – public incitement to commit any other international crime is addressed through the mode of liability of instigation (or solicitation and inducement in the case of the Rome Statute). This has been interpreted in a broad enough manner to encompass both public incitement before large crowds and more private acts of instigation of specific individuals. Because no specific link could be demonstrated between many of Šešelj's inciting speeches and crimes committed subsequently, these speeches went unpunished. The result is a lack of accountability as well as doctrinal confusion and imprecision.

As suggested previously by this author, the doctrinally tidiest way of rectifying the current legal situation would be to have regard to the way in which German (and in a similar way, Swiss)[45] doctrine has addressed this issue. German law differentiates between '*Anstiftung*' (instigation or solicitation) and '*öffentlicher Aufforderung zu Straftaten*' (public call for the commission of crimes). The former is punished in s. 26 of the German Criminal Code which states, "Anyone who intentionally determines another person to intentionally commit an unlawful act, shall be punished in the same way as a principal."[46] The latter is encoded in s. 111(1) which reads, "A person who calls publicly, in a meeting, or through the distribution of written materials, for the commission of unlawful acts, is punished in the same way as an instigator (s. 26)."[47] German doctrine has drawn clear distinctions between these two offences.

Instigation is characterized by the fact that the instigator 'determines' another specified individual or determinable group of persons to commit an unlawful act. The instigator not only causes the commission of the offence but corrupts the principal perpetrator. He or she puts pressure on him in order to influence the existing value system of the addressee. The instigator's words or conduct in some way threaten a certain sanction or promise a kind of reward, which causes an inner conflict for the instigatee who is now in a position where he or she is forced to choose between two desired values (the interest in avoiding the commission of a criminal offence on the one hand, and the avoidance of the threatened consequence or the achievement of the desired reward outlined by the instigator).[48] In order to establish the required pressure to motivate the principal perpetrator to act in the desired way, it is necessary that the threatened sanction can reach the perpetrator, that is, that he or she is unable to evade it. This necessitates an intensive personal relationship between the instigator and the recipient. The recipient must be personally addressed; he or she must be 'individualizable.'[49]

By contrast, the dynamic which prevails in a case of public incitement before a large group of anonymous individuals is completely different. Here the speaker does not possess the possibility of personally influencing the recipient. He or she is unable to increase the pressure to act or adapt it to a specific individual.[50]

The public inciter metaphorically throws a match, unsure whether it will light the fire. By contrast, because of his or her close, personal relationship with the principal perpetrator, the instigator is in a position to 'throw more wood on the fire' to really ensure that the fire is lit.[51] As Michael Redmann explains, for instigation under s. 26 to apply rather than the public call for crimes under s. 111, the crucial element is the development of a personal relationship in the context of the act which constitutes the exertion of influence over the principal perpetrator.[52] If there is such a relationship, then the principal perpetrator can be said to be determinable.[53] As soon as the large number of recipients makes it impossible for the speaker to exert a personal influence on every individual, it would turn into a case of public incitement under s. 111,[54] and instigation under s. 26 would not apply.[55] Where the appeal is to a large, anonymous group of people, individual addressees experience the pressure to act as less strong and can withdraw from such pressure more easily.[56]

Furthermore, public incitement sets in motion certain psychological processes inherent in group dynamics, which render the causal sequence of events unpredictable and uncontrollable.[57] Here, the inciter cannot take back what he or she said – because of the intrinsic characteristics of a group, he or she lacks any further influence over the crowd once it disperses. He or she does not know who among the listeners, who are largely anonymous to him, will go on to commit offences. Due to the lack of a personal relationship with the listeners, he or she lacks any ability to influence them.[58] The inciter does not know how many people may act on his or her words; nor is it clear whether the listeners will restrict themselves to committing those acts which he or she specifically called for, or commit further offences. The intensity of the actions is also out of the inciter's hands.[59] Public incitement, particularly if it avails itself of modern mass media, including the Internet, has the potential to reach an unforeseeably large number of people.[60] As a result, incitement is punishable even if no one acts on it; if it is successful, this is merely relevant for sentencing purposes – that is, it is regarded as an aggravating circumstance because the success lies outside the speaker's influence.[61]

Public incitement also involves other serious dangers, which justify punishing such conduct. These are grounded in the characteristics of crowds, which have famously been described by Gustave Le Bon and Sigmund Freud, among others. One such characteristic is the disappearance of the individuals' conscious personality and the diversion of every group member's thoughts and feelings into the same, specific direction.[62] Any idea which becomes part of the unconscious of the group members assumes an irresistible power.[63] Because in crowds, the affectivity of each individual is increased, while his or her intellectual output is simultaneously decreased.[64] These characteristics render crowds particularly dangerous. In crowds, a process of depersonalization takes place, which results in the loss of a sense of self in favor of the group identity. In this context, "socially acquired inhibitions to attack others" are weakened.[65]

Some authors, including this one,[66] have therefore proposed conceiving of soliciting/inducing under Article 25(3)(b) of the Rome Statute, as well as instigating, in a similar way to the concept of *Anstiftung* in German law, and extending the offence of direct and public incitement to encompass not only genocide, but also other international crimes such as crimes against humanity, war crimes and aggression. Thus, referring also to the American Model Penal Code,[67] Kai Ambos has suggested that 'solicits' is conceptually closer to s. 26 of the German Criminal Code than to s. 111 of the same because it is directed at a specific or specifiable circle of perpetrators.[68]

As noted above, the Brđanin trial judgment's requirement that where acts of instigation are in the form of public statements or written decisions, they must be sufficiently specific so as to amount to 'instructions,' goes some way toward such a definition. Interestingly also, in its judgment in the Šešelj case, the ICTY TC erroneously added a further requirement. It stated that "it should also be demonstrated that the instigator used different forms of persuasion such as threats, enticement or promises to the physical perpetrators of the crimes."[69] The AC in its judgment noted that it could "not exclude that proof of threats, enticement, or promises to physical perpetrators may have some relevance in assessing whether a particular conduct amounts to instigation."[70] Yet it confirmed, in conformity with consistent international jurisprudence, that this was "not a legal requirement, and the TC erred in stating so."[71] Practically, however, this erroneous statement by the TC made no difference; as the AC held, the TC did "not appear to have applied this requirement in its assessment of Šešelj's speeches."[72]

Yet while the TC's additional requirement is mistaken in terms of the current status of international law, it is interesting in that the listed examples of instigation all represent ways of specifically determining or corrupting the principal perpetrator. They imply a close personal relationship between the instigator and the principal perpetrator, as a result of which the latter is unable to evade the pressure exerted on him or her by the former. Threats, enticements and promises perfectly fit within the definition of instigation here advocated.[73]

Incitement to hatred and/or to violence as persecution

The Prosecution had charged Šešelj with persecution by means of "[d]irect and public denigration through 'hate speech' of the Croat, Muslim and other non-Serb populations in Vukovar, Zvornik and Hrtkovci on the basis of their ethnicities."[74] As with any other crime against humanity, it needed to be proven that the acts of persecution had been committed as part of a widespread or systematic attack against a civilian population, with knowledge of the attack. Persecution has been defined as a discriminatory act or omission which involves a gross or blatant denial of a fundamental right laid down in international customary or treaty law.[75] It must, moreover, reach the same level of gravity as other crimes against humanity, whether considered in isolation or in combination with other acts.[76] The underlying act of persecution does not need to be specified in the ICTY Statute[77] and, in fact, need not even be a crime in international law.[78] The Prosecution must also prove that the persecutory act or omission was carried out with the intention to discriminate on a prohibited ground.[79]

Prior to Šešelj, the ICTY had seen a guilty plea by Milan Babić, who admitted to contributing to a campaign of persecutions against non-Serb civilians through his propaganda. Before the ICTR, the journalist Ruggiu pleaded guilty to direct and public incitement to commit genocide and persecution in relation to broadcasts. Most significantly, in its judgment in the Nahimana case, the ICTR AC held that hate speech directed against a group on discriminatory grounds violated the right to respect for the group members' human dignity and, in fact, amounted to discrimination.[80] Moreover, where the speech incited to violence against a group of people on discriminatory grounds, it also violated the group's right to security.[81] In the Nahimana case, there was a combination of incitement to hatred and incitement to violence and even genocide, which occurred in "the context of a massive campaign of persecution directed at the Tutsi population of Rwanda, this campaign being also characterized by acts of violence (killings, torture and ill-treatment, rapes [...]) and of destruction of property."[82] The AC found that considered as a whole and in this context, the speeches were of equivalent gravity to other crimes against humanity. Consequently, the speeches made after the widespread and systematic attack began against the Tutsi (which the Chamber determined was after 6 April 1994), "themselves constituted underlying acts of persecution."[83]

However, the AC failed to resolve the question as to whether incitement to hatred and violence *outside of such a context* could be of equal gravity to other crimes against humanity, nor did it consider whether hate speech which did not incite violent acts at all could in itself be of such gravity.

The majority opinion in the Šešelj trial judgment found that there was no widespread or systematic attack against a civilian population.[84] As a result, it did not consider in any detail whether Šešelj's acts could have amounted to persecution. The Chamber also criticized the Prosecution for "often conflat[ing] the calls by the Accused aimed at rallying the Serbian forces and fighters in the face of the enemy [...] and the calls that were directed against the non-Serb civilians."[85] While it acknowledged that the Hrtkovci speech amounted to a clear call for the expulsion of the Croatian population in that location,[86] it alleged that the Prosecution had failed to point to any contextual elements which would permit the Chamber to assess the impact of the Hrtkovci and Vukovar speeches. Finally, the Chamber noted that it considered relevant the distinction between "speeches and actions that stem from a conflict between the communities and actions that stem from deliberate and discriminatory criminal violence."[87] These comments by the TC are not entirely clear. Of course, any act of persecution must involve discriminatory consequences, and there must be an intent to discriminate. However, violence is not an element of the offence of persecution.

In relation to the Vukovar speech, the TC, moreover, found that the evidence before it failed to establish beyond a reasonable doubt the content of Šešelj's speeches. This finding was upheld by the AC, which held that the TC's conclusions had not been demonstrated to be unreasonable.[88] As a result, the AC only considered whether the TC erred in holding that Šešelj did not "physically commit persecution (violation of the right to security) as a crime against humanity" in relation to the speech in Hrtkovci.[89]

The AC set out by citing the Nahimana appeal judgment as authority for when speech may constitute an underlying act of persecution: "Speech inciting to violence against a population on the basis of ethnicity, or any other discriminatory ground, violates the right to security of the members of the targeted group and therefore constitutes 'actual discrimination.'"[90]

Referring to Šešelj's statement that "there is no room for Croats in Hrtkovci"; his appeal to the Serbian population to give every Serbian refugee family the address of a Croatian family, leading to a population exchange which would be facilitated by driving the Croatian families to the border of Serbian territory from where they would be able to walk[91]; his message to Croatians that they had "nowhere to turn to"; his statement that he believed the Serbian population of Hrtkovci and surrounding villages would "promptly get rid of the remaining Croats" and the crowd's chants at the end of the speech "Croats, go to Croatia,"[92] the AC concluded that "no reasonable trier of fact could have found that Šešelj's speech did not incite violence that denigrated and violated the right to security of members of the Croatian population."[93]

The AC held that "by instigating the forcible expulsion of Croatians from Hrtkovci, Šešelj incited violence against them, in violation of their right to security."[94] Furthermore, his speech "denigrated the Croatians of Hrtkovci on the basis of their ethnicity" and thereby also violated their "right to respect for dignity as human beings."[95] The level of gravity of the speech "amount[ed] to the *actus reus* of persecution as a crime against humanity."[96]

Interestingly, the AC referred to the TC's finding that at the time of the speech, there was a "lack of a specific war context in Vojvodina," which indicated that "Hrtkovci had known relative peace from the ongoing attacks in Croatia and Bosnia and Herzegovina."[97] It was Šešelj's speech which put an end to this "sense of safety" and "infect[ed] the village with hatred and violence," causing "the departure of Croatian civilians in the ensuing months, [and] thereby expanding the wider attack against the non-Serbian population in Croatia and Bosnia and Herzegovina."[98]

These comments by the AC are remarkable, as they indicate that in its finding that Šešelj's speech amounted to persecution, the AC went a step further than the Nahimana AC. In the instant case, there were no *explicit* calls for violence (although the advocated acts of expulsion could certainly be expected to involve or lead to violence). In the Nahimana case, the AC's findings related to incitement to hatred, violence and genocide, in a *context of violent crimes*. The Šešelj AC effectively held that incitement to forcible expulsion in a *context of "relative peace,"* governed by a "sense of security," violated the rights to security and respect for dignity and was of a level of gravity equivalent to other crimes against humanity. The AC made clear that there was no need for an immediate context of violence and crimes; *the speech itself*, calling as it did for forcible expulsion, was sufficiently serious and of equal gravity to other crimes against humanity.[99] This constitutes a significant step forward and is an important clarification of the status of hate speech as persecution.

The AC's finding that Šešelj's speech also "denigrated the Croatians of Hrtkovci on the basis of their ethnicity, in violation of their right to respect for dignity as human beings" is less clear. The AC does not explain which specific words by the Accused it relies on to come to this conclusion. The words quoted by the AC do not seem to denigrate Croatians in an obvious way; no denigrating or dehumanizing language is used, nor are Croatians depicted as, in any way, inferior, threatening, and morally corrupt or as possessing any other negative characteristics. Šešelj does make clear that Croatians are not welcome in Hrtkovci ("there is no room for Croats in Hrtkovci;" "you have nowhere to return to"), and should be expelled ("I firmly believe that you, Serbs from Hrtkovci and other villages around here, [...] will promptly get rid of the remaining Croats in your village and the surrounding villages").[100] He also refers to them as "Croats," a reference to their ethnicity (but not a derogatory term).[101]

It would have been desirable for the AC to be more specific on this point, particularly given that the Nahimana appeal judgment similarly failed to elaborate on the specific content of the right to respect for human dignity and on when exactly hate speech or incitement to hatred amounts to a violation of this right. It appears obvious that there is a connection between incitement to hatred and a violation of respect for human dignity; thus, the Committee on the Elimination of All Forms of Racial Discrimination (CERD) has held that "the fundamental principle of respect for human dignity requires all States to combat dissemination of racial hatred and incitement to racial hatred."[102]

By contrast, the Nahimana trial judgment had provided some clarification regarding the connection between hate speech and violation of human dignity. The Chamber had found that

> Hate speech is a discriminatory form of aggression that destroys the dignity of those in the group under attack. It creates a lesser status not only in the eyes of the group members themselves but also in the eyes of others who perceive and treat them as less than human. The denigration of persons on the basis of their ethnic identity or other group membership in and of itself, as well as in its other consequences, can be an irreversible harm.[103]

As an example of hate speech amounting persecution, the TC referred to the so-called "Ten Commandments," which had formed part of an article published in the virulently anti-Tutsi magazine *Kangura* in December 1990.[104] This document accused Tutsi, among other things, of being "dishonest in their business dealings" and of "only seeking ethnic supremacy."[105] It advised Hutu to "cease having any pity for the Tutsi," and called for solidarity among Hutu.[106] The TC found that "[t]he Tutsi were portrayed as the enemy, as evil, dishonest and ambitious" and that "contempt and hatred for the Tutsi ethnic group" were advocated.[107] Clearly, these descriptions would have been likely to create a "lesser status" both in the eyes of members of the Tutsi group, as well as "others who perceive[d] and treat[ed] them as less than human."

Turning to the Šešelj case, the Accused's words in his speech in Hrtkovci do not on the face of it create a perception of Croatians as less than human. Šešelj did not make any comments or claims about any alleged inherent characteristics of theirs, which would supposedly have defined them as Croatians. By contrast, his language in Vukovar and Mali Zvornik was much more obviously degrading of other ethnic groups, as is demonstrated by his use of denigrating terms such as 'Ustaša,' 'pagans,' 'pogani' (which, according to Šešelj himself in his testimony in the Milošević case, was to be translated as "waste" or "faeces"),[108] and 'balijas.'

At this point, it is useful to briefly explore the concept of dignity; what is its content and how does incitement to hatred violate the right to protection of one's dignity? Respect for human dignity has often been viewed as connected to treating individuals always as end in themselves; the right to respect for human dignity is violated when an individual is treated as merely a means to an end. For instance, in the Israeli case Ploni v. Minister of Defence,[109] the court found that the prolonged detention of Lebanese nationals in Israeli prisons as bargaining chips to negotiate the return of Israeli soldiers from Lebanon amounted to "a severe violation of human dignity, since the detainee is perceived as a means for achieving an end and not as the end itself."[110]

Human dignity has also been perceived to be rooted in human freedom.[111] What truly distinguishes us as human beings is our freedom of will, our capacity to choose the kind of life we wish to lead, and to change our life from any moment on. As the philosopher Avishai Margalit has written, human dignity, and the need to respect human beings, is grounded in each individual's ability "to reevaluat[e] one's life at any given moment, as well as the ability to change one's life from this moment on."[112] Incitement to hatred presents individuals belonging to the group under attack as defined by certain negative characteristics, which are alleged to be inherently unchangeable. Such incitement thereby treats those individuals in a way that denies their quintessential human capacity to be free and therefore rejects them as human beings.[113]

Respect for human dignity also means that individuals must not be deprived of their ability to control their own lives. For instance, as Corinna Mieth explains, severe poverty is humiliating and violates human dignity because it involves such a loss of control. The poor become dependent on others; both the feeling of self-worth based on a life plan worthy of being followed and trust in their own capacities suffer.[114] Similarly, if someone is tortured, their dignity is violated because the infliction of pain deprives them of their capacity for self-control.[115]

Turning from this brief sketch of the concept of dignity to the Šešelj case, it is difficult, first, to interpret his language as obviously degrading or dehumanizing. In the speech in question, Šešelj did not use language which ascribed negative (or any other) characteristics to Croatians. If at all, his speech could be said to have *implicitly* created a lesser status of Croatians, by virtue of the fact that his words implied that they could, and should, be treated in a certain way. They had no rights – or at least not the right to stay in their homes; they could be expelled at will. These actions, which Šešelj undeniably promoted, as a matter of fact denied their freedom to choose. His words thus promoted a situation where Croatians would be unable to control their own lives. Arguably, they were also treated as means to an end, and not as ends in themselves.

Finally, the AC in Šešelj went on to find that "following Šešelj's speech, members of the Croatian population of Hrtkovci were increasingly harassed and subjected to repeated mistreatment, threats, and violence, resulting in a large percentage of them leaving Hrtkovci."[116] According to the AC, this evidence demonstrated that Šešelj's speech, in fact, constituted discrimination and that he spoke with discriminatory intent.[117] This is correct and corresponds to the ICTY's finding in previous case law that the act or omission in question "must have discriminatory consequences."[118]

Conclusion

The Šešelj appeal judgment rectified the most blatant mistakes of the trial judgment and clarified the situation of international speech crime law in some important respects. Thus, it went farther than the AC in Nahimana had done, effectively holding that incitement to forcible expulsion in itself, without *explicit* calls for violence (although violence could be expected to follow), in an immediate context of "relative peace" and security, could constitute persecution. Such incitement was of a level of gravity equal to other crimes against humanity and violated the rights to security and respect for dignity.

However, it also left a number of matters unsettled. First, it is still unclear whether incitement to hatred in and of itself, without a call for certain crimes to be committed, and without a context of violence, can amount to persecution. Given that the Hrtkovci speech, with its unequivocal calls for expulsion, was the only one which the AC considered in this context, this result is not surprising. Second, the AC finding that the Hrtkovci speech denigrated the Croatians of that locality on the basis of their ethnicity and thereby violated their right to respect for their human dignity is unclear. How was the speech degrading? How exactly did it violate the victims' right to respect for their dignity, and how exactly is human dignity to be defined? This author has highlighted two important aspects of human dignity, the right never to be treated purely as a means to an end, but always as an end in oneself, and the idea of freedom – such as freedom to change one's life from any point on. In the excerpt of the Hrtkovci speech relied on by the AC,[119] Šešelj did not use any obviously degrading language, but arguably the actions he advocated limited the Croatians' freedom, refused to give them any choice over what was to happen to them and treated them as mere means to an end defined by the Accused.

Lastly, the Šešelj case again demonstrated a fundamental problem with the way in which instigation is defined in international criminal law. Because direct and public incitement as an inchoate crime only applies to genocide, the mode of liability of instigation has been interpreted to encompass both public and private acts of instigation. It therefore includes both inciting speeches before large crowds and situations in which the instigator has a personal relationship with the principal perpetrator and seeks to persuade him or her by exerting a certain influence over him or her. This is problematic, as it is often exceedingly difficult to prove causation in cases of public incitement. Here, the addressees – members of large crowds of listeners – are frequently unknown to the speaker, and particularly where there is a large temporal or spatial distance between the speech and the criminal acts in question, proving a causal link is virtually impossible. Consequently, the AC in Šešelj was able to find that the Accused instigated offences in only one instance, his speech in Hrtkovci.

The same problem has also plagued other international criminal tribunals, and this author therefore advocates drawing a clear distinction between instigation and direct and public incitement. Instigation would be defined as a mode of liability which is marked by a speaker addressing a specific or specifiable individual or small group of individuals who are known to him or her personally and over whom he or she is able to exert sufficient influence to persuade them to commit an offence. By contrast, direct and public incitement is defined as a speech act in public, before a large crowd or through mass media, where the addressees are not known to the speaker and he or she is therefore unable to control the subsequent sequence of events. Direct and public incitement would then, of course, need to be extended to all other international crimes, such as crimes against humanity, war crimes and aggression. This, it is submitted, would result in a more logical framework and greater accountability.

Notes

1 For critical assessments outlining some of these flaws, see, for example, G.S. Gordon, *Atrocity Speech Law: Foundation, Fragmentation, Fruition*, New York, NY: Oxford University Press, 2017, pp. 239–242, 245, 247, 248–250; M. Milanović, 'The Sorry Acquittal of Vojislav Šešelj,' *EJIL: Talk! Blog of the European Journal of International Law*, 4 April 2016. W.K. Timmermann, 'Inciting Speech in the Former Yugoslavia: The Šešelj Trial Chamber Judgment,' *Journal of International Criminal Justice*, vol. 15, no. 1, 2017, pp. 133–155.

2 Prosecutor v. Vojislav Šešelj, Appeal Judgment, Case No. MICT-16-99-A, 11 April 2018, paras 2–3 [hereinafter Šešelj AJ]; The Prosecutor of the Tribunal against Vojislav Šešelj, Third Amended Indictment, Case No. IT-03-67, 7 December 2007 [hereinafter Šešelj TAI].

3 Šešelj TAI, para. 20.

4 Ibid.

5 The Prosecutor v. Vojislav Šešelj, Trial Judgment, Case No. IT-03-67-T, 31 March 2016, para. 331 [hereinafter Šešelj TJ]; Šešelj AJ, paras 146, 161.
6 Šešelj TJ, para. 331; Šešelj AJ, paras 146, 161.
7 Šešelj AJ, paras 146, 162.
8 Šešelj TJ, paras 192–198.
9 Šešelj AJ, para. 124; Ferdinand Nahimana, Jean-Bosco Barayagwiza, Hassan Ngeze v. The Prosecutor, Appeal Judgment, Case No. ICTR-99-52-A, 28 November 2007, para. 480 [hereinafter Nahimana et al. AJ]; Prosecutor v. Dario Kordić and Mario Čerkez, Appeal Judgment, Case No. IT-95-14/2-A, 17 December 2004, para. 27 [hereinafter Kordić AJ].
10 Kordić AJ, para. 27.
11 Prosecutor v. Naser Orić, Judgment, Case No. IT-03-68-T, 30 June 2006, para. 271.
12 Kordić AJ, paras 29, 32.
13 See also Timmermann, 'Inciting Speech,' pp. 153–154.
14 Nahimana et al. AJ, para. 513.
15 Šešelj AJ, para. 127.
16 Šešelj TJ, para. 335.
17 Ibid., paras 303, 318, 328, 338–343; Šešelj AJ, para. 127.
18 Šešelj AJ, para. 130.
19 Ibid., para. 130.
20 Ibid., para. 132.
21 Ibid., para. 132.
22 Situation in the Republic of Kenya in the Case of The Prosecutor v. William Samoei Ruto and Joshua Arap Sang, Public redacted version of Decision on Defence Applications for Judgments of Acquittal, Case No. ICC-01/09-01/11, 5 April 2016.
23 Situation in the Republic of Kenya in the Case of The Prosecutor v. William Samoei Ruto and Joshua Arap Sang, Public redacted version of Decision on Defence Applications for Judgments of Acquittal, Case No. ICC-01/09-01/11, 5 April 2016, para. 134.
24 Ibid., para. 135.
25 Prosecutor v. Radoslav Brđanin, Trial Judgment, Case No. IT-99-36-T, 1 September 2004, paras 468, 527, 662 [hereinafter Brđanin TJ].
26 Ibid., para. 574.
27 Ibid.
28 Ibid.
29 Prosecutor v. Radoslav Brđanin, Appeal Judgment, Case No. IT-99-36-A, 3 April 2007, paras 315–316.
30 Šešelj AJ, para. 146; see also Šešelj TJ, paras 330–331.
31 Šešelj AJ, para. 146.
32 Ibid., para. 147.
33 Ibid.
34 Ibid., paras 148–150.
35 Ibid., para. 150.
36 Ibid. However, there were exceptions to this – far from remaining inactive, Ostoja Sibinčić, the president of a local commune in the municipality of Hrtkovci, who is erroneously referred to in the judgments as "former mayor of Hrtkovci," threatened the life of non-Serbs in Hrtkovci and forced them to leave the locality or exchange properties. Šešelj AJ, paras 147, 154, and fn. 533. In this case, the authorities of the Federal Republic of Yugoslavia (FRY), more specifically, the Ruma Municipal Court in Serbia, tried and sentenced Sibinčić for, *inter alia*, his participation in the persecution of non-Serbs.

37 Ibid.
38 Ibid.
39 Ibid.
40 Ibid.
41 Ibid., para. 146.
42 Ibid., para. 153. Šešelj TJ, para. 333.
43 Šešelj AJ, para. 154.
44 Ibid.
45 See, for example, G. Stratenwerth and W. Wohlers, *Schweizerisches Strafgesetzbuch: Handkommentar*, Bern: Stämpfli, 2007, p. 119.
46 My translation; the original reads: *"Als Anstifter wird gleich einem Täter bestraft, wer vorsätzlich einen anderen zu dessen vorsätzlich begangener rechtswidriger Tat bestimmt hat."* Note that Prof. Dr. M. Bohlander translates this section as follows: "Any person who intentionally induces another to intentionally commit an unlawful act (abettor) shall be liable to be sentenced as if he were a principal." Online. Available HTTP: <https://www.gesetze-im-internet.de/englisch_stgb/englisch_stgb.html#p0151> (accessed 1 November 2018).
47 My translation; the original reads: "*Wer öffentlich, in einer Versammlung oder durch Verbreiten von Schriften, zu einer rechtswidrigen Tat auffordert, wird wie ein Anstifter (§ 26) bestraft.*" Note that Prof. Dr. M. Bohlander translates this section as follows: "Whosoever publicly, in a meeting or through the dissemination of written materials (section 11(3)) incites the commission of an unlawful act, shall be held liable as an abettor (section 26)." Online. Available HTTP: <https://www.gesetze-im-internet.de/englisch_stgb/englisch_stgb.html#p1144> (accessed 1 November 2018).
48 See M. Redmann, *Anstiftung und anstiftungsähnliche Handlungen im StGB unter Berücksichtigung linguistischer Aspekte*, Berlin: Duncker and Humblot, 2014, pp. 106–107.
49 Ibid., p. 167.
50 Ibid., p. 170.
51 Ibid., p. 171.
52 Ibid., p. 172: "Wichtig ist allein das Entstehen einer persönlichen Beziehung im Rahmen der Einwirkungshandlung."
53 Ibid., p. 173.
54 Ibid., p. 210.
55 Ibid., p. 212.
56 Ibid.
57 K. Ambos, *Der Allgemeine Teil des Völkerstrafrechts: Ansätze einer Dogmatisierung*, Second Edition, Berlin: Duncker and Humblot, 2004, pp. 652–653.
58 Redmann, *Anstiftung*, pp. 171–172.
59 Ibid., p. 199.
60 Ibid., p. 202.
61 Ibid., p. 200.
62 G. Le Bon, *Psychologie des Foules*, Paris: Quadrige/Presses Universitaires de France, 1963, p. 9. See also W.K. Timmermann, *Incitement in International Law*, London, New York, NY: Routledge 2015, p. 23.
63 Ibid., p. 33.
64 S. Freud, *Massenpsychologie und Ich-Analyse*, Seventh Edition, Frankfurt am Main: Fischer Verlag, 2005, p. 51.
65 S. Savage and J. Liht, 'Radical Religious Speech: The Ingredients of a Binary World View,' in I. Hare and J. Weinstein (eds), *Extreme Speech and Democracy*, Oxford: Oxford University Press, 2010, pp. 488, 504.

66 Timmermann, *Incitement*, pp. 227–241.
67 Section 5.02 states that a person is guilty of soliciting a crime if he or she "with the purpose of promoting or facilitating its commission [...] commands, encourages or requests another person to engage in specific conduct that would constitute such crime or an attempt," as cited in K. Ambos, *Der Allgemeine Teil des Völkerstrafrechts*, p. 646.
68 Ibid., 647.
69 Šešelj TJ, para. 295.
70 Šešelj AJ, para. 124.
71 Ibid.
72 Ibid.
73 This author would however take issue with the TC's requirement that the instigator must employ 'different forms of persuasion,' which is incorrect, unclear and unnecessary.
74 Šešelj TAI, para. 17(k).
75 Prosecutor v. Miroslav Kvočka, Mlađo Radić, Zoran Žigić, Dragoljub Prcać, Appeal Judgment, Case No. IT-98-30/1-A, 28 February 2005, para. 320; Kordić AJ, para. 101; Šešelj AJ, para. 159; see also R. Cryer, H. Friman, D. Robinson and E. Wilmshurst (eds), *An Introduction to International Criminal Law and Procedure*, Third Edition, Cambridge: Cambridge University Press, 2014, p. 256.
76 Prosecutor v. Mladen Naletilić a.k.a. "Tuta" and Vinko Martinović a.k.a. "Štela," Appeal Judgment, Case No. IT-98-34-A, 3 May 2006, para. 574.
77 Prosecutor v. Dario Kordić and Mario Čerkez, Trial Judgment, Case No. IT-95-14/2-T, 26 February 2001, para. 194; Brđanin TJ, para. 994.
78 Prosecutor v. Momčilo Krajišnik, Trial Judgment, Case No. IT-00-39-T, 27 September 2006, para. 735; Brđanin TJ, para. 995.
79 Prosecutor v. Milomir Stakić, Appeal Judgment, Case No. IT-97-24-A, 22 March 2006, para. 328; Kordić AJ, para. 101.
80 Nahimana et al. AJ, para. 986.
81 Ibid.
82 Ibid., para. 988.
83 Ibid.
84 Šešelj TJ, para. 192.
85 Ibid., para. 283.
86 Ibid., paras 197, 333. See also Šešelj AJ, para. 156.
87 Ibid.
88 Ibid., para. 137.
89 Ibid., para. 141.
90 Nahimana et al. AJ, para. 986; Šešelj AJ, para. 159.
91 Šešelj AJ, para. 161.
92 Ibid., para. 162.
93 Ibid., para. 163.
94 Ibid.
95 Ibid. However, in its summary in para 165, the AC fails to reiterate its finding that the speech violated the Croatians' right to respect for dignity, merely stating that "Based on the foregoing, the Appeals Chamber finds Šešelj responsible [...] for committing persecution, based on a violation of the right to security, as a crime against humanity."
96 Ibid.
97 Ibid.
98 Ibid.
99 Of course, there was a wider context of war and attacks in Croatia and Bosnia and Herzegovina.

100 Šešelj AJ, paras 146, 161–162.

101 Note, however, that in its judgment, the AC was only able to rely on those parts of the Hrtkovci speech which the TC addressed in its assessment of the evidence. In other parts of his speech, Šešelj does refer to Croats in obviously derogatory terms. Thus, he equates local Croats with 'Ustasha,' which constitutes a more unequivocal denigration of Croats on the basis of their ethnicity:

> Just two years ago, none of us could have dreamt that we would also, and so quickly, hold the largest parts of Serbian Dalmatia, Lika, Banija, Kordun, Slavonija and Baranja in Serbian hands, and that they would be definitively freed from *Ustasha* control. [...] In this village, too, in Hrtkovci, in this place in Serbian Srem, there is no room for Croats [...].
>
> (emphasis added)

See Šešelj TJ, para. 331, exhibit no. P00547, and Šešelj AJ, para. 147, exhibit no. P00547.

102 *Report of the Committee on the Elimination of Racial Discrimination: Sixty-Fourth Session (23 February–12 March 2004), Sixty-Fifth Session (2–20 August 2004), General Assembly, Official Records, Fifty-Ninth Session, Supplement No. 18 (A/59/18)*, New York, NY: United Nations Publications, 2004, p. 48.

103 The Prosecutor v. Ferdinand Nahimana, Jean-Bosco Barayagwiza, Hassan Ngeze, Trial Judgment and Sentence, Case No. ICTR-99-52-T, 3 December 2003, para. 1072 [Nahimana et al. TJ].

104 Nahimana et al. TJ, para. 138.

105 Ibid., para. 139.

106 Ibid.

107 Nahimana et al. TJ, 3 December 2003, para. 152.

108 Šešelj TJ, para. 325.

109 Ploni v. Minister of Defence, Dinim-Elyon, 1994, vol. LVI, no. 921.

110 Ibid., cited in D. Kretzmer, 'Human Dignity in Israeli Jurisprudence,' in D. Kretzmer and E. Klein (eds), *The Concept of Human Dignity in Human Rights Discourse*, Alphen aan den Rijn: Kluwer Law International, 2002, pp. 161, 171.

111 For more, see Timmermann, *Incitement*, pp. 44–46.

112 A. Margalit, *The Decent Society*, translated by N. Goldblum, Cambridge, MA: Harvard University Press, 1996, p. 70.

113 Ibid., p. 117.

114 C. Mieth, 'Menschenwürde und soziale Gerechtigkeit,' in C. Thies (ed.), *Der Wert der Menschenwürde*, Paderborn: Ferdinand Schöningh Verlag, 2009, pp. 133, 139–140.

115 Ibid., p. 138.

116 Šešelj AJ, para. 164.

117 Ibid.

118 Prosecutor v. Vidoje Blagojević and Dragan Jokić, Trial Judgment, Case No. IT-02-60-T, 17 January 2005, para. 583 Brđanin TJ, para. 993.

119 As noted above (see endnote 101), in other parts of his speech, Šešelj does use more obviously derogatory language.

Chapter 5

Prosecuting speech acts

An examination of the trial of the Prosecutor v. William Samoei Ruto and Joshua Arap Sang*

Clare Lawson and Rogier Bartels

Introduction

Joshua Arap Sang (Sang) was a broadcaster on Kenyan radio station KASS FM, where he hosted a popular call-in show called 'Lene Emet.'[1] In 2011, after the Pretrial Chamber of International Criminal Court (ICC) authorized the ICC Office of the Prosecutor (Prosecution) to open an investigation,[2] Sang was charged with the crimes against humanity of murder, deportation or forcible transfer and persecution.[3] The charges arose out of postelection violence occurring in Kenya's Rift Valley after the 2007 general election, where over 700 people died and more than 400,000 were forcibly displaced.[4] In January 2012, Pretrial Chamber II, by majority, confirmed the charges against Sang, as well as William Samoei Ruto (Ruto), and declined to confirm the charges against the third suspect, Henry Kiprono Kosgey.

The Prosecution alleged that the accused "planned and organized the violence in an attempt to seize political power should they not succeed in the elections."[5] According to the Prosecution, Ruto headed a network for this purpose, of which Sang was part.

Ultimately, the Prosecution was unsuccessful. On 5 April 2017, following a motion by the defense teams contending that there was no case for them to answer (NCTA, 'no-case-to-answer'), Trial Chamber V(A), by majority, vacated the charges against the accused and discharged them.[6]

This chapter addresses the speech act aspects of the case against Ruto and Sang. Following a brief background, it analyzes the charged modes of liability, before turning to the evidence relied on by the Prosecution and how that evidence materialized (or failed to materialize) at trial. Thereafter, the particular speech acts alleged are discussed, focusing on the use of metaphors and coded language. The chapter addresses, in particular, the charges against Sang but

* The authors are the Legal Officer Team Leader at the Kosovo Specialist Prosecutor's Office and Legal Officer in Chambers (Trial Division) of the International Criminal Court, respectively. All views expressed are solely those of the authors and do not necessarily represent the views of the aforementioned institutions or any other organization.

also discusses specific words or phrases allegedly used by Ruto to illustrate the challenges and limitations of prosecuting alleged speech acts in the manner attempted by the Prosecution.

The case against Sang

Background

When the incumbent Party of National Unity (PNU) candidate Mwai Kibaki was announced as the winner of the Kenyan presidential election on 30 December 2007, a wave of violence erupted. The ICC Prosecution alleged that the violence was aimed at permanently expelling PNU supporters (predominantly members of the Kikuyu, Kamba and Kisii ethnic groups) from the Rift Valley in order to establish a pro-Kalenjin voting bloc.[7] The violence was allegedly planned and orchestrated by a network of key individuals and entities, within the Kalenjin ethnic community, who were supportive of the PNU's main political rivals, the Orange Democratic Movement (ODM).[8] The network, led by Ruto, was alleged to include pro-ODM political figures, media representatives (including Sang), financiers; tribal elders, local leaders, and former members of the Kenyan police and army.[9]

In immediate response to the violence, mediation between the PNU and ODM occurred under the auspices of a panel chaired by former United Nations Secretary General Kofi Annan. On 28 February 2008, a power-sharing agreement, for a coalition government comprising the PNU and ODM, was reached. By the time the trial against Ruto and Sang commenced at the ICC, in September 2013, Ruto had been elected vice president of Kenya.[10]

The charges

Of particular relevance in analyzing the speech components of the case against Ruto and Sang are two factual aspects underlying the charges: (i) the media component of the alleged network, which was stated to include Sang and to have contributed to the crimes by way of public broadcasts and (ii) the anti-PNU rhetoric allegedly used by Ruto at public meetings and rallies leading up to the election, in order to incite anti-PNU sentiment among direct perpetrators of the crimes.

Ruto, as an alleged key member of the network,[11] was charged with co-perpetration of the crimes against humanity of murder, deportation or forcible transfer and persecution, all pursuant to Article 25(3)(a) of the ICC Statute.[12] The speech aspects of his conduct – including the alleged use of derogatory language against PNU supporters (discussed further in the final section) – were charged merely as one factor in a wider range of conduct which cumulatively amounted to the 'essential contribution' required for co-perpetration.[13]

By contrast, Sang was charged under Article 25(3)(d) of the ICC Statute. Article 25(3)(d) has been described as a 'residual form of accessory liability,' which acts as a catchall for criminal contributions which would not fulfill the requirements of other accessory forms of liability, such as ordering, soliciting, inducing and aiding or abetting.[14] It requires proof of the following elements, three objective (*actus reus*) and two subjective (*mens rea*)[15]:

i A crime within the jurisdiction of the ICC was committed (or attempted).
ii A group of persons acting with a common purpose committed (or attempted to commit) that crime.
iii The individual in question made a significant contribution to the crime, in any way other than those set out in Article 25(3)(a) to (c).
iv The individual's contribution was intentional.
v Was made either (a) with the aim of furthering the criminal activity or criminal purpose of the group or (b) in the knowledge of the intention of the group to commit the crime.

While the ICC Statute includes a separate mode of liability for incitement in Article 25(3)(e), it only applies to the crime of genocide.[16] Although proposals were made to extend the draft of what would become Article 25(3)(e) to cover incitement to commit war crimes and crimes against humanity, "[a] clear majority of delegations to the Rome Conference in 1998 rejected [these] proposals."[17] However, even if paragraph (3)(e) had included crimes against humanity, the Prosecution may still have opted to bring charges under (3)(d). Consistent with its role as a residual form of liability, Article 25(3)(d) presents a number of potential advantages relative to other modes of liability, especially in the context of speech acts. First, although in this case the Prosecution made factual assertions that Sang was a member of the alleged network,[18] proof of such membership is not required for prosecution under Article 25(3)(d). It is necessary to prove that a group of persons acting with a common purpose (in this case the alleged network) existed, but a person charged under Article 25(3)(d) need not necessarily be a member of that group.[19]

Second is the issue of causation, which is typically considered in the context of the degree of contribution that an accused's act made to the commission of the crime(s). In contrast to a charge of co-perpetration under Article 25(3)(a), where the accused must make an 'essential contribution,'[20] or of aiding and abetting or instigation under Article 25(3)(b) or (c),[21] where a 'substantial' contribution is required,[22] under Article 25(3)(d) only the lesser standard of a 'significant' contribution must be proven.[23]

As can be seen from the Mbarushimana case at the ICC, even the significant contribution standard under Article 25(3)(d) can be difficult to achieve in the context of certain speech acts. Callixte Mbarushimana was charged with contributing to the commission of crimes by the FDLR (Forces Démocratiques pour la Liberation du Rwanda) "by encouraging the troops on the ground through his press releases and speeches."[24] The Pretrial Chamber, by majority, did not find there to be substantial grounds to believe that Mbarushimana had done so, and "therefore, he could have not provided through his radio communications and press releases a significant contribution to the commission of crimes by the FDLR within the meaning of article 25(3)(d) of the Statute."[25] However, the potential relevance of the distinction between the different standards of contribution has become apparent in a number of cases, including that against Charles Blé Goudé at the ICC and against Vojislav Šešelj at the International Criminal Tribunal for the former Yugoslavia (ICTY). Blé Goudé held official positions in various so-called "Pro-Gbagbo groups" in Côte d'Ivoire and was appointed by then President Laurent Gbagbo as the Minister for Youth, Vocational Training and Employment. Blé Goudé had been charged in the alternative under the modes of liability provided for in Articles 25(3)(a), (b), (c) and (d) of the ICC Statute. A key component of Blé Goudé's alleged conduct was that in speeches broadcast by pro-Gbagbo media, he had used his "charisma and oratorical skills" to mobilize youth for violent acts. Further, through the use of xenophobic and other rhetoric, Blé Goudé had incited hatred against perceived opposition supporters, identifying them as the enemy and as legitimate targets for attack. In considering the charges, the ICC Pretrial Chamber found that certain of Blé Goudé's alleged contributions did not meet the essential contribution standard required for Article 25(3)(a).[26] Similarly, Vojislav Šešelj was convicted by the IRMCT/ICTY (International Residual Mechanism for Criminal Tribunals) Appeals Chamber of instigating the crimes of persecution, deportation and other inhumane acts, through speech acts which made a 'substantial' contribution to those crimes.[27] However, the Appeals Chamber simultaneously acquitted him of a charge of having physically perpetrated those crimes, having not been persuaded that Šešelj's speech was an "integral part" of what caused the Croatian population of Hrtkovci to leave.[28]

It has, consequently, been noted that,[29] given the difficulty in proving that crimes would not have been committed without speech act contributions,[30] Article 25(3)(d) presents a potential alternative means of nonetheless prosecuting such acts as contributions to a crime. And, as mentioned above, it was the mode of liability initially charged in respect of Sang's conduct.

In confirming the charges against Sang, the Pretrial Chamber had, by majority, found substantial grounds to believe that, by virtue of his position as a key broadcaster within KASS FM, Sang intentionally contributed to the commission of the crimes against humanity by doing the following:

i Placing his show Lene Emet at the disposal of the network.
ii Advertising the meetings of the network.
iii Fanning the violence through the spread of hate messages explicitly revealing desire to expel the Kikuyus.
iv Broadcasting false news regarding alleged murders of Kalenjin people in order to inflame the atmosphere in the days preceding the elections.
v Broadcasting instructions during the attacks in order to direct the physical perpetrators to the areas designated as targets.[31]

However, on 8 September 2015, just two days before the Prosecution formally closed its presentation of evidence, it filed a request asking the Trial Chamber to issue a notice of possible variation of the charges against Sang to include the possibility of, alternatively, finding Sang criminally responsible under Articles 25(3)(b) (ordering, soliciting or inducing) or (c) (aiding, abetting or otherwise assisting).[32] As discussed above, Articles 25(3)(b) and (c) require proof of a higher level of contribution than Article 25(3)(d) does. Nonetheless, amending the charged mode of liability in the manner requested could, in particular, have enabled Sang to be found guilty regardless of whether or not the existence of a group of persons acting with a common purpose was proven. The Trial Chamber did not rule on the request for notice of possible recharacterization prior to consideration of the defense 'no case to answer' motions, instead advising the parties to address those additional modes of liability in their submissions.

The evidence

The nature of the evidence presented at trial

In respect of the evidence presented to support the charges against Sang, in so far as they related to speech acts, the following portion of Judge Fremr's reasons for vacation of the charges is particularly instructive (footnotes omitted):

> Care, in particular, must be taken to ensure that proof of a criminal broadcast or publication does not depend mostly or entirely on the oral evidence of witnesses whose own biases and sense of offence about the subject matter of discussion may have clouded their perception. The primary evidence of the actual broadcast or writing itself – rather than second-hand accounts of them – would be the safest basis for the proper evaluation of the material element of the criminality of the broadcast or publication charged as a crime. In this case, the Prosecution has not produced any recording of a broadcast by Mr Sang in which he made the type of statements he is accused of. Instead, the Prosecution asks the Chamber to rely on the testimony of a number of witnesses who claim to have heard Mr Sang's radio show at relevant times. In my view, this evidence is not sufficiently reliable in this context. When it comes to allegations of solicitation or inducement through the media, it is of great import to know the exact words used by the accused [...][33]

From the outset, the Prosecution case had been built primarily on the basis of witness evidence, including a number who claimed to have heard Sang's broadcasts. In confirming the charges against Sang, the Pretrial Chamber relied specifically on the evidence of five witnesses, four of whom were 'insider' witnesses who had admitted participation in the postelection violence.[34] However, even at the pretrial stage, the accounts of those witnesses were being challenged by the production by the defense teams of (unauthenticated) documentary evidence, including what was purported to be schedules of programs and transcripts of peace messages broadcast on KASS FM during the time period when the crimes were committed.[35] At trial, the case against Sang continued to rest on the testimony of a relatively small number of witnesses.[36] This left the case vulnerable to a range of challenges, including – as will be discussed below – the risk of recantation.

The broadcasting ban

Evidence disclosed and presented by the Prosecution indicated that a ban on live broadcasting had been imposed by the Kenyan government on 30 December 2007, in the immediate aftermath of the announcement of the election results. The defense teams naturally argued that the existence of this ban severely undermined the evidence of Prosecution witnesses who claimed, among other things, that (i) as the election result was being broadcast live on 30 December 2007, Sang called on his Kalenjin listeners to be ready "to demand their rights," (ii) on 31 December 2007, Sang called on people to "fight for their rights" and for those who has stolen the vote "to be punished," (iii) he congratulated people for a "good job" in Kisumu, which had already been attacked and (iv) called on Kalenjin to "show resentment" and "demonstrate against the stolen vote," which the listeners understood to refer to "violent demonstration."[37]

Indeed, certain of the Prosecution witnesses appeared to acknowledge the existence of the ban. For example, one witness apparently stated that KASS FM was only playing music while violence was occurring in Nairobi.[38] Similarly, Witness P-0268 – albeit recanting from his prior statement to the Prosecution – stated before the Trial Chamber that "for a while immediately after results were announced, I didn't listen to KASS FM. I heard somebody say that KASS FM is no longer there for a while."[39] The Defense also introduced the statement of a witness relating to events at KASS FM in the aftermath of the election, which included assertions that at KASS FM the broadcasting ban lasted at least eight days, during which people could not come to the studio and normal programming could not continue.[40]

The Prosecution countered that there was no evidence that the ban was "anything more than a government directive" or that it, in fact, prevented media from broadcasting.[41] The Permanent Secretary of the Ministry of Information had stated that the ban was "resisted" by media at the time. A government spokesperson had explained that the ban was designed to require vernacular radio stations, in particular, to listen to their own content before broadcasting it, as people calling-in live were inciting others to take up arms and burn houses. Moreover, the District Commissioner covering the Central Rift Valley area had stated that he could not monitor vernacular stations such as KASS FM, as he did not speak Kalenjin. The Prosecution therefore submitted that the ban was merely intended to impose self-censorship by the broadcasters, and there was nothing to suggest it had, in fact, prevented broadcasting on KASS FM. While the Prosecution pointed to evidence that at least one radio station had defied the ban and continued to operate, only the testimony of witnesses who claimed to have heard the broadcasts was relied on in respect of KASS FM specifically.[42]

Recordings/transcripts of broadcasts

The Prosecution did not have any recordings or transcripts of the actual broadcasts allegedly made by Sang on KASS FM and was reliant on witness accounts of those broadcasts. By contrast, the defense teams used their cross-examination of Prosecution witnesses to introduce documentary and audio evidence. These included audios and transcripts of various peace messages allegedly broadcast on KASS FM during the relevant time period, such as:[43]

1 January 2008: recordings of appeals for peace by notable members of the Kalenjin community, as well as members of the KASS FM staff, including Sang, who was recorded saying:

- "[…] This is Joshua Arap Sang, telling you we are fine, and to implore that we keep peace everywhere – peace in Kenya. May peace be promoted today and forever. Let us keep on maintaining peace;" and
- "We should keep the peace. To all people, or anyone in Kenya who may be engaged in wrongdoing and is not keeping peace, or is breaching the peace, we would like to pray for peace; that please, all of us, let us keep peace as Kenyan people. Let us keep peace wherever we are. Peace is what we need. […] So we are pleading for peace, peace, peace. Please, please, at Kass FM we are appealing for peace […]"

3 January 2008: two recordings of Ruto saying, amongst other things:

- "ODM believes that the loss of live, the destruction of property that is ongoing in our country is unnecessary, unwarranted and should stop immediately;" and
- "[…] I would like to appeal to the Kalenjin people wherever they are, and the people of Kenya to persevere and renounce violence. Let us desist from any action that may ruin peace in our country Kenya, so that we may find a peaceful solution to these issues and that every voter in the just concluded elections may find justice. […] We appeal that, please, let us exercise restraint: let there be peace in this land. We do not want to use unlawful methods. We want to use peaceful means, until we find justice. So I would like to appeal to the Kalenjin people, wherever they are, and all the people of Kenya that we refrain from violence and pursue peace so that our country may prosper […]"

4 January 2008: a recording of an appeal by Sang for people to "open the roads" so that people could travel, including for food and medical assistance.

The Sang defense also introduced audio recordings purportedly demonstrating that from August-November 2007, in the lead up to the election, a number of PNU and other non-ODM politicians were featured on Sang's radio shows.[44] These recordings were presented in response to the allegation of certain Prosecution witnesses that Sang would not allow PNU supporters to call-in or appear in his show to express their views, and "when that occurred unexpectedly he would immediately change tone, cut them off, ridicule, openly attack or verbally insult them."[45]

Several Prosecution witnesses had referred to reports on KASS FM of fake ballot papers being transported on 25 and 26 December 2007. For example, a witness known as P-0658 claimed that Sang called on people to 'be on alert' for vehicles carrying fake ballots, and that Sang had read out the number plates of the vehicles suspected of being involved. The Sang defense, in addition to arguing that Sang was merely covering what was, in fact, a news story at the time,[46] produced an audio recording in respect of the incident. The audio confirmed that Sang had invited one of his callers to read out the vehicle registration plates but also included Sang stating that people should remain peaceful.[47]

Admission of material into evidence is without prejudice to the weight that will ultimately be attached to it, especially where there may be limited authentication information available to the Trial Chamber, as appears to have been the case with certain of these recordings. Further, it is clear that the mere existence of such public peace messages may carry little weight where it is established that the speakers in question were otherwise actively engaged in directly contrary conduct. In such circumstances, depending on the facts, it may be possible to prove that the public statements were merely a 'show' for political or other purposes. The Prosecution, in fact, argued that in the historical context of long-standing ethnic tension between the Kalenjin and Kikuyu in the Rift Valley, where there was a real possibility for violence, and when considered against Sang's prior inciting statements, any calls for peace he may have made were mere 'window dressing.'[48]

A full weighing of evidence, which would consider such factors, normally occurs only on conclusion of the presentation of evidence by both parties, and at the time of issuance of the final judgment. The case against Ruto and Sang concluded at the end of the Prosecution case by way of a successful 'no case to answer' motion by the defense teams.[49] It is therefore not known what weight the Trial Chamber would ultimately have given to the recordings and transcripts presented by the Sang defense, or any other similar material which may have been presented during the course of a defense case. Nonetheless, it is apparent from the remarks of Judge Fremr, as quoted above, that, where specific statements of the accused were at issue, he considered reliance on witness recollection alone insufficiently reliable in the particular circumstances. An additional factor in this case, as noted in the following section, is that in a context of intimidation and active witness interference many of the witnesses recanted their prior statements to the Prosecution when called to testify at trial.

Witness evidence

An atmosphere of witness intimidation and interference was a key feature of the trial from the outset. The witness interference efforts were summarized by Judge Eboe-Osuji in his reasons for vacation of the charges, which included sections entitled 'Direct Interference with Witnesses' and 'Indirect Pressure on Witnesses.'[50] For example, during the testimony of the very first witness, who had been granted protective measures, there were concerted efforts made on social media to establish and publish the witness's identity. Subsequently, in the context of a request to introduce into evidence the prior statements of certain recanting Prosecution witnesses, the Trial Chamber made findings that improper direct interference occurred in respect of at least four witnesses, some of whom themselves acted as intermediaries to interfere with other witnesses.[51] During the course of the trial, three individuals were charged by the Prosecution with obstruction of justice offences.

The case also suffered from what Judge Eboe-Osuji termed "political meddling." He referred in that context to aggressive anti-ICC sentiment and "hostile rhetoric" promoted by Kenyan politicians, which he considered many witnesses were likely to have found intimidating.[52]

Ultimately, approximately half of the relatively small number of witnesses relevant to the case against Sang recanted their prior statements to the Prosecution when called to testify. The Prosecution has stated that, in fact, 17 witnesses who had agreed to testify against the two accused withdrew their cooperation entirely.[53] Notably, the context of interference was such that Judge Eboe-Osuji indicated it had been impossible to determine whether or not the Prosecution case had collapsed simply as a result of its own inherent weakness.[54]

The risk of witness interference and recantation is a vulnerability that will attach to any case that is solely or predominantly reliant on evidence in the form of witness testimony. However, as highlighted by Judge Fremr, sole reliance on witness testimony may create additional evidentiary challenges in the context of charges relating to speech acts. Recordings or transcripts of the actual words used are likely to be the most reliable form of evidence for the purpose of ascertaining what was actually said. Alternatively, other contemporaneous records, such as press or official reports, addressing the speech acts may be available, especially where the speeches were publicly broadcast. Witness testimony will form a crucial evidentiary component in confirming that the speech acts were heard by their intended audience, in explaining how the words were understood by that audience and in demonstrating that the words, in fact, had a connection to the crimes by influencing the direct perpetrators. But for the purpose of proving the nature of the speech itself, witness testimony is vulnerable to difficulties in recollection and particular (conscious or unconscious) biases of the witnesses in question. Certain of these may be overcome, for example, where especially distinctive or memorable phrasing is alleged, or where there is a high degree of consistency among the accounts of multiple witnesses. However, the allegations in the case against Ruto and Sang were that coded and metaphorical speech was used. As considered in the following section, that in itself gives rise to further evidential challenges.

The nature of the alleged speech acts

Metaphors or coded language

The Prosecution alleged, and the Pretrial Chamber found there to be substantial grounds to believe, that Sang and Ruto had incited those listening to KASS FM, or attending rallies, to commit crimes against the Kikuyu and associated ethnic groups,[55] *inter alia*, by using messages that did not call for any direct criminal conduct but instead used metaphors. In addition, Sang was alleged to have "broadcast instructions during the attacks through the use of coded language in order to direct the physical perpetrators to the areas designated as PNU targets."[56] The relevant speech acts thus consist of two different parts: (i) inciting language and (ii) veiled or coded instructions.

As noted above, demonstrating the connection between speech acts and subsequent crimes is challenging. This is even more so in the case of speech acts that do not directly call for the commission of crimes. Indirect incitement, for example, may also be done by stating that committing a particular crime is morally justified or to be applauded, or by communicating messages using metaphors.[57] The present section will not address the legal classification of the use of speech metaphors or the standard for when such metaphors may qualify as incitement. Instead it will consider the evidentiary challenges and consequences of alleging inciting language based, in part, on metaphors or – what was referred to by the Prosecution as – "coded" or "veiled" language.

Generally, coded language forms part of an unrelated body of information, which acts as the carrier of the code, meant to obscure the use of the code for anyone else than the intended recipient(s). It is therefore suitable and, indeed, often used, to transmit information about (planned) criminal conduct, including international crimes. Indeed, a well-known scholar has observed that "history shows that those who attempt to incite genocide speak in euphemisms."[58] Those who know the 'key' can encode the language and have the real meaning revealed to them. Some form of prior relation or contact between the person deciphering the code and the encoder is therefore required. Such was, indeed, alleged in Ruto and Sang case. According to the Prosecution, Sang had "broadcast coded language signalling that PNU supporters were to be attacked [...] Listeners who had attended the previous meetings or events understood the coded language and proceeded to the previously identified locations to execute their plans for attack."[59] Incitement or hate speech cases generally address situations where inciting of hateful language is used to persuade persons outside any preexisting organization[60] to commit crimes,[61] the Rwandan genocide being a case in point. However, the way the Prosecution charged Sang's conduct meant that his (alleged) coded speech acts were not what persuaded or, indeed, incited the direct perpetrators but rather the mere indication for persons (who – apparently – had already been persuaded to commit crimes) to commence their criminal conduct.

Metaphors can be used in a context that leaves no doubt as to their meaning. Indeed, Julius Streicher, who was convicted for incitement to persecution of Jews by the International Military Tribunal at Nuremberg, was found to have written in *Der Sturmer*, *inter alia*, that "[t]he Jews in Russia must be killed. They must be exterminated root and branch."[62] However, when the allegedly inciting language is less straightforward and the meaning to be given to metaphors or (allegedly) coded language depends on the cultural context, it may be appropriate for the prosecution, or for the chamber, to call expert witnesses to explain the cultural meaning of the words used.[63] In the case against Akayesu, at the International Criminal Tribunal for Rwanda (ICTR), for example, the Trial Chamber relied on the testimony of an expert witness on Kinyarwanda linguistics, called by the prosecution.[64] The term 'Inkotanyi,' which was used by Akayesu in his public speaking, translates as 'warriors.' However, according to the expert witness, "it should be assumed that the basic meaning of the term Inkotanyi is the RPF army," but at the time it had more extended meanings, namely, "RPF sympathizer or supporter" or it would even refer to the "Tutsi as an ethnic group."[65] Relying on the expert's explanations, the Akayesu Trial Chamber found that the Accused urging a crowd to fight the 'Inkotanyi' was construed by the addressees "as a call to kill the Tutsi in general."[66]

Alleged use of metaphors and coded language

Sang was charged with encouraging and coordinating the attacks against PNU supporters through his broadcasts on KASS FM.[67]

Inciting messages allegedly used on his radio show included asserting shortly before election day that "the Kikuyu would rig the election,"[68] stating that "if Kibaki[69] wins, we will carry out our work," adding that "we will give the instructions."[70] With regard to the latter, the Pretrial Chamber observed that the relevant witness indicated that during the three months preceding the election, the word "work" was used "instead of explicitly using to the word 'kill.'"[71] "[T]o carry out the work" was alleged to have meant "mak[ing] sure that Kikuyus 'have been evicted [...] [and] have been killed.'" Following the announcement of the election results, declaring Kibaki as the winner, Sang supposedly said that "the elections had been stolen and our rights denied," calling listeners to "get their weapons from where they were kept and, if necessary, to use any arm at their disposal to evict the Kikuyus."[72]

The latter statement leaves little room for misinterpretation and could – if he had, indeed, made such a statement – constitute incitement to use violence against the Kikuyu, had it been charged in that manner. However, Sang's alleged instructions also included far more ambiguous statements, such as, when the violence was already ongoing, "come out, go to Turbo, you know their whereabouts in Turbo."[73]

Ruto was similarly alleged to have used metaphors or coded language to incite crowds of supporters and convey instructions. In its pretrial brief, the Prosecution alleged that Ruto, in a rather direct way, incited a crowd by "holding a toy hammer, telling them that they needed to walk with a hammer and a matchbox so they can demolish the houses of the Kikuyu and then set them alight."[74] During the same speech, he was alleged to have used the word *madoadoa*, which translates as "stains," indicating that he did not want any *madoadoa*.[75]

Prior to the commencement of the trial stage, the Prosecution had alleged that during ODM rallies, Ruto "addressed the crowds passionately and incited them, declaring either directly or through parables that non-ODM supporters should be evicted from the Rift Valley." It submitted that he

> used parables, stating that the Kikuyu were birds whose nests needed to be destroyed, weeds growing near Kalenjin houses which needed to be removed, or witches who should be burned. He said further that if the ODM won the elections they would 'uproot the tree stumps that are among the people' and they would 'get rid of and send back to where they came from' all the people who had taken over local farms and businesses.[76]

Only a part of the evidence the Prosecution had relied on at the pretrial stage remained following presentation of its case at trial. For example, according to a witness who testified at trial, Ruto had used phrases at a rally such as not wanting the "trees which were brought by the white people" and "do not allow the grass [or 'weeds'][77] to creep right into your houses."[78] Sang was claimed to have said similar things on his radio show, but that evidence was removed from the case record following an Appeals Chamber ruling that prior recorded testimony could not be admitted.[79] Ruto allegedly further asked the crowd "to do the work that I asked you to do."[80]

During the same rally, he allegedly referred to *madoadoa* and had stated that "[w]e do not want two different types of clothing."[81] The latter is interesting in light of the fact that the Prosecution had charged both Sang and Ruto with referring to the Kikuyu as *madoadoa*, alleging that this was a derogatory term.[82] *Madoadoa* was supposedly used in combination with another metaphor: 'a three-piece suit.' However, the Ruto Defense submitted that the phrase "three piece suit" referred to "three piece voting," which was supposed to symbolise the ODM desire to win the elections for both the parliament and the presidency.[83]

Following presentation of its case at trial, and the withdrawal or recantation of a number of key witnesses, the Prosecution appeared to acknowledge that no evidence about Sang using code was, in fact, before the trial chamber.[84] Nonetheless, Judge Fremr considered that some witnesses had "testified that the alleged language used by the accused was not a straightforward call for crimes to be committed, but rather a sort of coded language, which the witnesses understood to mean as instructions to act against the Kikuyu."[85] He mentioned as examples the testimony of a witness that Sang spoke about people in Kisumu being 'authorized to' call for their rights, 'good work' being done in Kisumu, and that 'people should not remain quiet' but instead 'call out and insist upon their rights.'[86]

The allegations of the Prosecution, and findings of the Pretrial Chamber, had relied on the meaning that fact witnesses had given to particular words/phrases. No expert witness was called either during the pretrial or trial stage to explain the use of certain words at the relevant time. With regard to the concept of 'work,' for example, it is interesting to note that the *Akayesu* Trial Chamber of the ICTR, guided by the testimony of the expert witness on Rwandan linguistics, interpreted Akayesu's use of the phrase 'go to work' as meaning "go kill the Tutsis and Hutu political opponents of the interim government."[87] The interpretation of euphemisms by that trial chamber may have been referred to as "capacious,"[88] but at least it was grounded on evidence by an expert witness who interpreted the meaning of the relevant words in the applicable context. Conversely, in Ruto and Sang case, Judge Fremr noted that in case of indirect or coded language, there is a "risk that the witnesses provide their own, incorrect, interpretation of the obscure wording."[89]

As discussed above, the use of witness testimony alone meant that the Chamber could not itself assess the manner in which the metaphors were used. Judge Fremr observed that it is "especially important for a chamber to have access to the actual words used by the accused, in order to assess whether such 'coded language' would amount to inflammatory or instigating speech."[90] In Ruto and Sang case, the witnesses concerned therefore had to recount both the actual words, as well as their interpretation of these words in the relevant context. Witnesses may be able to testify about the reaction of other persons to the speeches and/or broadcasts, on the basis of which it could have been possible to somewhat objectify the understanding given by the witness to the words used. However, Judge Fremr's observation raises the question of whether the use of metaphors or words that do not in and of themselves have a clear and objective derogatory meaning, or inciting appearance, can ever be adequately proven on the basis of the testimony of one or a few witnesses alone.

A further challenge may arise if not all speech is inflammatory or inciting. In the case of Sang, his radio show purportedly broadcast peace messages during the relevant days, and – due to the time of the year – his shows included many (ostensibly peaceful) Christmas carols.[91] The Pretrial Chamber considered that evidence indicating the broadcasting of "peaceful appeals" by Sang does "not rule out the possibility that, beside these peaceful messages, the instructions and speeches reported by Witnesses 1, 2, 4, 6 and 8 could have also been broadcasted."[92] It is certainly true that a broadcast would not need to be inciting in its entirety, and broadcasting nonviolent information may be purposely done to obscure the inciting messages for the general public. Yet where the majority of the speech concerned, in fact, says the opposite of what is allegedly being incited (namely, peace rather than violence), a question arises as to whether the language can actually work in an inciting manner. Can potentially inciting language that is fully enclosed in nonviolent words be considered as having an inciting effect? Moreover, if the alleged inciting language is not straightforward, but instead uses metaphors and must be interpreted in a certain manner in order to consider it inciting, it may be argued that in analyzing whether the metaphor actually called for unlawful behavior, one must take the context in which the words were used, namely, an otherwise nonviolent message, into account.

Conclusion

The case against Ruto and Sang presents a case study of the multiple challenges that can arise in prosecuting speech acts. Recent guidelines, drawn up by a group of scholars and practitioners,[93] in part in reaction to the failure to successfully prosecute alleged hate speech before the court in the case against Mbarushimana and in the case against Ruto and Sang,[94] recommended including hate speech in the *actus reus* of the crime against humanity of persecution,[95] and amending and extending the mode of liability of incitement included in Article 25(3)(e) of the ICC Statute.[96] These are useful proposals, which – if adopted by the Assembly of State Parties – may assist the prosecution of speech acts in the future, but even if already in place at the time would not have made a difference in the Ruto and Sang case, where evidentiary deficiencies let to the acquittal following the presentation of the prosecution case. Some of the challenges in that case, such as the risk of politicization, are hazards of any high-profile case. Witness intimidation and recantation are similarly not risks that are unique to the prosecution of speech acts. However, the Prosecution's almost exclusive reliance on witness evidence in this case made it particularly vulnerable to such factors, and the contrast between the evidence presented at the confirmation stage and that which materialized at trial underline the associated risks. Moreover, the limitations of exclusive reliance on the testimony of witnesses to prove speech act components are evident. This is especially so where the alleged speech is ambiguous, metaphorical or coded. The use of social media and mobile phones (with cameras) may reduce the need to rely on witness testimony in future speech act cases. The Ruto and Sang case is, nonetheless, a pertinent reminder of the need for careful attention to the particular characteristics of speech, including in making charging decisions, evidencing the allegations and contextualizing the speech acts in question. While the absence of a final trial judgment may limit the jurisprudential value of the case, significant evidentiary and practical lessons can and should still be drawn from it.

Notes

1 There are a range of alternative spellings including Le Nee Emet, Lee Ne Emet, Leneemet and Lee Nee Emet. It was variously translated as 'How is the country?' or 'What is the opinion of the country?'

2 Kenya Situation, Decision Pursuant to Article 15 of the Rome Statute on the Authorization of an Investigation into the Situation in the Republic of Kenya, Situation No. ICC-01/09, 31 March 2010.
3 The Prosecutor v. William Samoei Ruto and Joshua Arap Sang, Updated Document Containing the Charges Pursuant to the Decision on the Confirmation of Charges (UDCC), Case No. ICC-01/09-01/11, 21 August 2012. References to filings and transcripts in these endnotes refer to those in the *Ruto and Sang* case, unless indicated otherwise.
4 UDCC, para. 17.
5 Public redacted version of Prosecution's Updated Pretrial Brief, Case No. ICC-01/09-01/11, 9 September 2013 (Pretrial Brief), para. 3.
6 Decision on Defence Applications for Judgments of Acquittal, Case No. ICC-01/09-01/11, 5 April 2016 (Decision on NCTA), p. 1.
7 UDCC, para. 20.
8 UDCC, para. 21. The ODM had also run a presidential candidate, Raila Odinga, in the 2007 elections.
9 UDCC, para. 21. A second case arising from the Kenyan postelection violence was also brought before the ICC. However, the charges against Mohammed Hussein Ali, Commissioner of the Kenyan police, were not confirmed, and the charges against Francis Kirimi Muthaura, chairman of the National Security and Advisory Committee, and Uhuru Muigai Kenyatta, a leading politician during the relevant time and current president of Kenya, were both withdrawn by the Prosecution prior to the trial.
10 Ruto ran for election in a "Jubilee Alliance" with Uhuru Muigai Kenyatta, who, as noted above, was also, at that time, facing prosecution before the ICC.
11 See, for example, Decision on the Confirmation of Charges Pursuant to Article 61(7)(a) and (b) of the Rome Statute, Case No. ICC-01/09-01/11, 23 January 2012 (Confirmation Decision), paras 352–353 (referring to the 'major role played by Mr. Ruto in creating the group, leading the group and organizing its criminal activities').
12 Confirmation Decision, para. 349; UDCC, Section VIII. However, shortly after the start of trial the Trial Chamber gave notice of the possibility of recharacterization of the charges against Ruto, in particular, to include the modes of liability provided for under Article 25(3)(b), (c) and (d), see Decision on Applications for Notice of Possibility of Variation of Legal Characterisation, Case No. ICC-01/09-01/11, 12 December 2013.
13 The charges against Ruto were based on conduct including having allegedly created the network, supervised overall planning for the common plan to carry out the crimes, provided/assisted in obtaining funding, weapons and other logistics. See, for example Confirmation Decision, paras 309–311.
14 See, for example, Confirmation Decision, para. 354; The Prosecutor v. Thomas Lubanga Dyilo, Decision on the Confirmation of charges, Case No. ICC-01/04-01/06, 29 January 2007, para. 337; *The Prosecutor v. Callixte Mbarushimana*, Decision on the confirmation of charges, Case No. ICC-01/04-01/10, 16 December 2011 [hereinafter *Mbarushimana DCC*], paras 278–279; The Prosecutor v. Germain Katanga, Judgment, Case No. ICC-01/04-01/07, 7 March 2014, para. 618 [hereinafter Katanga TJ].
15 ICC Statute, Article 25(3)(d). See, for example, Confirmation Decision, para. 351; Katanga TJ, paras 1616–1620; *The Prosecutor v. Bosco Ntaganda*, Decision on the Confirmation of charges, Case No. ICC-01/04-02/06, 14 June 2014, para. 158
16 ICC Statute, Article 25(3)(d) reads, in relevant part, "[A] person shall be criminally responsible and liable for punishment for a crime within the jurisdiction of the Court if that person [...] [i]n respect of the crime of genocide, directly and publicly incites others to commit genocide."

17 I. Peterson, 'International Criminal Liability for Incitement and Hate Speech,' in M. Böse, M. Bohlander, A. Klip and O. Lagodny (eds), *Justice without Borders: Essays in Honour of Wolfgang Schomburg*, Leiden: Brill Publishers, 2018, p. 340, referring, *inter alia*, to W. Schabas, *Genocide in International Law*, Second Edition, Cambridge: Cambridge University Press, 2009.
18 See, for example, UDCC, paras 21, 40, 44.
19 See, for example, Katanga TJ, para.1631; *Mbarushimana DCC*, paras 272–275.
20 *The Prosecutor v. Thomas Lubanga Dyilo*, Appeal Judgment, Case No. ICC-01/04-01/06, 1 December 2014, paras 469, 473 [hereinafter Lubanga AJ]. The Appeals Chamber held that an essential contribution to a crime entailed the 'power to frustrate its commission' (para. 473). However, the essential contribution need not be made during the execution of the crime. It could, for example, also be made during the planning or preparation stage (paras 469, 473).
21 The term 'instigation' is not directly used in the ICC Statute, however, an ICC Trial Chamber has held that soliciting and inducing, as used in Article 25(3)(b), fall under the concept of 'instigating,' see Prosecutor v. Bemba et al., Judgment, Case No. ICC-01/05-01/13, 19 October 2016, para.73.
22 Confirmation Decision, para. 354.
23 See, for example, Katanga TJ, paras 1620, 1632–1633; *Mbarushimana DCC*, para. 284.
24 *Mbarushimana DCC*, para. 312 and further.
25 *Mbarushimana DCC*, para. 339.
26 *The Prosecutor v. Charles Blé Goudé*, Decision on the confirmation of charges, Case No. ICC-02/11-02/11, 11 December 2014, paras 145–148.
27 Prosecutor v. Vojislav Šešelj, Appeal Judgment, Case No. MICT-16-99-A, 11 April 2018, para. 154 [hereinafter Šešelj AJ].
28 Šešelj AJ, para.151. Šešelj was, however, separately found guilty of having committed the act of persecution by violating the right to security of the Croatian population of Hrtkovci through his speech acts. See Šešelj AJ, paras 163–165.
29 Group of authors, *The Hartford Guidelines on Speech Crimes in International Criminal Law*, The Hague: Peace and Justice Initiative, 2018, paras 222, 243.
30 As noted above, the ICC Appeals Chamber defined an essential contribution as one that gives a person the power to frustrate the commission of the crime. See Lubanga AJ, paras 469, 473.
31 Confirmation Decision, para. 355.
32 Prosecution's Request for notice under regulation 55(2) of possibility of variation with respect to individual criminal responsibility of Mr Joshua Arap Sang, Case No. ICC-01/09-01/11, 8 September 2015.
33 Decision on NCTA, Reasons of Judge Fremr, para. 142.
34 Referred to at the pretrial stage as witnesses 1, 2, 4, 6 and 8.
35 Confirmation Decision, para. 362.
36 In identifying the scope of the Prosecution case which it needed to address in making arguments for a judgment of acquittal, the Sang Defense highlighted ten (10) prosecution witnesses. See Public Redacted Version of Sang Defence 'No Case to Answer' Motion, Case No. ICC-01/09-01/11, 23 October 2015 (Sang Defence NCTA Motion), paras 130–131.
37 Second Public Redacted version of 'Prosecution's consolidated response to the "Corrigendum of Ruto Defence Request for Judgment of Acquittal" and "Sang Defence 'No Case to Answer' Motion,"' (ICC-01/09-01/11-2000-Conf), Case No. ICC-01/09-01/11, 20 November 2015 (public redacted version filed on 22 December 2015) (Consolidated Response), paras 341–345.
38 Sang Defence NCTA Motion, para. 194.
39 Transcript of hearing of 30 October 2013, ICC-01/09-01/11-T-62-Red2-ENG, p. 50.

40 The identity of this witness is not public. See reference to this evidence in Sang Defence NCTA Motion, para. 195.
41 Consolidated Response, para. 348.
42 Consolidated Response, paras 348–352.
43 Sang Defence NCTA Motion, paras 200–202.
44 Sang Defence NCTA Motion, para. 143.
45 Consolidated Response, para. 313.
46 A newspaper article from 24 December 2007 was presented to demonstrate that ODM politicians were making allegations of vote rigging, which were being reported on in national newspapers, before the matter was mentioned on KASS FM.
47 Consolidated Response, para. 322; Sang Defence NCTA Motion, para. 153.
48 Consolidated Response, para. 322.
49 A consideration of the "no case to answer" standard, and its application by the Trial Chamber in the case against Ruto and Sang, is beyond the scope of this chapter.
50 Decision on NCTA, Reasons of Judge Eboe-Osuji. See also Statement of the Prosecutor following vacation of the charges, in which she highlighted that the case had been "severely undermined by witness interference and politicisation of the judicial process," and referred to "a relentless campaign to identify individuals who could serve as Prosecution witnesses in this case and ensure that they would not testify." (*Statement of the Prosecutor of the International Criminal Court, Fatou Bensouda, regarding Trial Chamber's decision to vacate charges against Messrs William Samoei Ruto and Joshua Arap Sang without prejudice to their prosecution in the future*, 6 April 2016.)
51 Decision on the Prosecution Request for Admission of Prior Recorded Testimony, Case No. ICC-01/09-01/11, 19 August 2015.
52 Decision on NCTA, Reasons of Judge Eboe-Osuji, paras 161–164.
53 Online. Available HTTP: <https://www.icc-cpi.int/Pages/item.aspx?name=otp-stat-160406> (accessed 8 June 2019).
54 Decision on NCTA, Reasons of Judge Eboe-Osuji, para. 155.
55 UDCC, paras 61, 99, 101, 116, 130.
56 UDCC, p. 42, para. 128.
57 See J. Jaconelli, 'Incitement: A Study in Language Crime,' *Criminal Law and Philosophy*, vol. 12, no. 2, 2018, p. 248. Gordon refers to speaking in coded language as a 'separate incitement technique': G.S. Gordon, *Atrocity Speech Law: Foundation, Fragmentation, Fruition*, New York, NY: Oxford University Press, 2017, p. 289, referring to S. Benesch, 'Vile Crime in Inalienable Right: Defining Incitement to Genocide,' *Virginia Journal of International Law*, vol. 48, no. 3, 2007, p. 506.
58 W.A. Schabas, 'Hate Speech in Rwanda: The Road to Genocide,' *McGill Law Journal*, vol. 46, no. 141, 2000, p. 160.
59 UDCC, para. 46.
60 Organisation as used to assign criminal liability.
61 Jaconelli observes that "[t]he most salient characteristic of incitement … is the existence of a communication that is made with a view to persuading the addressee(s) to commit an offence." Jaconelli, 'Incitement,' p. 245.
62 *International Military Tribunal, Nuremberg, Trial of the Major War Criminals before the International Military Tribunal*, 14 November 1945–1 October 1946, Vol. 1, Published at Nuremberg, Germany 1947, pp. 302–303.
63 For such a call to rely on expert witnesses, albeit with regard to domestic hate speech cases, see T. Carney, 'Being (im)polite: A Forensic Linguistic Approach to Interpreting a Hate Speech Case,' *Language Politics in Africa*, vol. 45, no. 3, 2014, pp. 325–341.
64 Prosecutor v Jean Paul Akayesu, Case No. ICTR-96-4-T, Trial Chamber Judgment, 2 September 1998, para. 146 [hereinafter Akayesu TJ].

65 Akayesu TJ, para. 147.
66 Akayesu TJ, para. 673.
67 UDCC, para. 25.
68 Confirmation Decision, para. 357.
69 Kibaki was running for the party mostly supported by Kikuyu.
70 Confirmation Decision, para. 358.
71 Ibid.
72 Ibid.
73 Confirmation Decision, para. 359. Turbo was known as a Kikuyu town.
74 Pretrial Brief, para. 68.
75 Ibid.
76 Pretrial Brief, para. 59. See also UDCC, para. 87.
77 Ambiguity arose about the translation of the relevant Kalenjin word used by Ruto. See Prosecutor v William Samoei Ruto and Joshua Arap Sang, Transcript of hearing of 24 February 2014, ICC-01/09-01/11-T-93-Red-ENG.
78 Ruto and Sang case, transcript of hearing of 24 February 2014, pp. 7, 16, 21, 24, 25. Decision on NCTA, Reasons of Judge Fremr, footnote 208.
79 As noted by the Prosecution in the Consolidated Response, a witness heard Sang calling the Kikuyu 'labotwet' (i.e., alleged to mean 'weeds') and calling for them to be rooted out: "Remove that plant. It is not supposed to enter your compound. You are not a man if you let this plant in." The Prosecution submits that a reasonable Trial Chamber could conclude that, in the context, this was a veiled call for the expulsion of the Kikuyu from the Rift Valley, which was considered to be the ancestral home of the Kalenjin people. Consolidated Response, para. 309.
80 Ruto and Sang case, transcript of hearing of 24 February 2014, p. 20. See also Reasons of Judge Fremr, footnote 208.
81 Ruto and Sang case, transcript of hearing of 24 February 2014, p. 27.
82 UDCC, para. 22.
83 Public redacted version of "Corrigendum of Ruto Defence Request for Judgment of Acquittal," Case No. ICC-01/09-01/11, 26 October 2015, para. 102.
84 Consolidated response, para. 359, in which the Prosecution states,

> Although there is no specific evidence on record that Mr Sang's statement described above was broadcast using specific codes, the evidence establishes that in general Mr Sang spoke guardedly, using veiled language that would only be understood by ethnic Kalenjin. In any event, even if the use of coded language is not established [...].
>
> (footnote omitted)

85 Decision on NCTA, Reasons of Judge Fremr, para. 141.
86 Ibid., Decision on NCTA, Reasons of Judge Fremr, footnote 208. Judge Fremr further noted that "the main evidence against Mr Sang in this regard, the prior recorded testimony of Witness 789, is no longer part of the record and the witness has disavowed this entire statement under oath."
87 Akayesu TJ, para. 349.
88 R.A. Wilson, *Incitement on Trial: Prosecuting International Speech Crimes*, Cambridge: Cambridge University Press, 2017, p. 36.
89 Decision on NCTA, Reasons of Judge Fremr, para. 141.
90 Ibid.
91 See the messages listed above under "(ii) Recordings/Transcripts of Broadcasts." See also the transcript of the testimony of Witness 326 for a discussion of recordings of portions of Sang's Lene Emet radio show, which contained peace messages and

Christmas songs. Transcript of hearing of 11 October 2013. ICC-01/09-01/11-T-47-Red2-ENG. See further Sang Defence NCTA Motion, para. 94.

92 Confirmation Decision, para. 363.

93 Group of authors, *The Hartford Guidelines.*

94 See the blog post by R.A. Wilson, 'The Hartford Guidelines on Speech Crimes in International Criminal Law,' *EJILTalk!*, 31 August 2018.

95 Rome Statute of the International Criminal Court, Article 7(2)(h).

96 Group of authors, *The Hartford Guidelines*, para. 101. The recommendation is to amend Article 25(3)(e) to read as follows:

> Intentionally, directly, and publicly incites others to commit any of the crimes in the Statute, thereby significantly increasing the likelihood of their occurrence. For the purpose of this provision it is not necessary that the incited crime(s) be committed or attempted.

Chapter 6

Beyond takedown

Expanding the tool kit for responding to online hate*

Molly K. Land and Rebecca J. Hamilton

Introduction

The current preoccupation with 'fake news' has spurred a renewed emphasis in popular discourse on the potential harms of speech. In the world of international law, however, 'fake news' is far from new. Propaganda of various sorts is a well-worn tactic of governments, and in its most insidious form, it has played an instrumental role in inciting and enabling some of the worst atrocities of our time. The essays in this book, which consider the role of propaganda in mass atrocity crimes and international criminal law, are, in fact, a testament to the power – and danger – of speech. Yet as familiar as propaganda might be in theory, it is raising new issues as it has migrated to the digital realm.

Technological developments have largely outpaced existing legal and political tools for responding to the use of mass communications devices to instigate or perpetuate human rights violations. With hate spreading at a virulent pace online, social media platforms like Facebook and Twitter have mostly operated in reactionary mode – seeking to take down content or ban users after concerns have been aired in high-profile public forums. This, we contend, is insufficient. In this chapter, we look to a future where the policies and practices of major social media platforms are reimagined to proactively support a healthy speech environment.

We are not addressing all propaganda, which is a capacious term that encompasses a number of different kinds of state and non-state communicative activities.[1] Nor are we addressing speech that constitutes incitement to genocide or other international crimes. The legal frameworks established by Facebook and others by and large provide an adequate basis for responding to such speech, even if their enforcement policies fall short. Rather, the real Achilles' heel for social media companies, we contend, is the massive amount of speech that falls somewhere between the two – pervasive and coordinated online speech, often state-sponsored or state-aligned, denigrating a particular group that is used to justify or foster impunity for violence against that group.

* The authors wish to thank Jessica Blasnick for excellent research assistance in the preparation of this chapter.

This category of speech is a problem for social media companies because they cannot possibly remove it all (nor would we want them to), and attempting to do so on an individualized basis harms free expression far more than it helps protect vulnerable groups. In other words, policies designed to stamp out hate speech are inevitably both overbroad and underinclusive. They are overbroad because they establish a very broad definition of hate speech that goes far beyond what international human rights law requires or even permits to be removed. They are underinclusive because the individualized and user-focused enforcement models that Facebook and other companies have adopted end up concentrating their energies in all the wrong places. More often than not, they end up mediating disputes between private individuals about racial slurs in the context of discussions that are clearly in the public interest, while missing pervasive denigrating speech with corrosive environmental effects.

This is not to say that social media companies should ignore racial and other slurs on their platforms in established democracies characterized by the rule of law. It is to say, however, that such an approach may be a poor fit for the many other scenarios in which social media platforms have served as conduits for hate. By way of illustration, we look in this chapter to the role of Facebook in the recent genocide against the minority Muslim Rohingya population in Myanmar. Suffice to say, one cannot possibly respond to anti-Rohingya sentiment in a country where an authoritarian military government is engaged in genocidal acts against that population, using the same framework that one adopts to tackle the use of racial slurs in conversations between individuals in an established democracy. These are not the same things.

Facebook's experience in responding to how its platform was being abused in Myanmar provides a helpful illustration of the gaps in hate speech policies that attempt to address the legal gray zone of pervasive denigrating speech. Using the example of the Myanmar case, we argue that the policies and practices of social media companies responding to hate speech need to be more broadly conceptualized, and to factor in guidance from both international human rights law and international law on remedies, which emphasize that responses to harmful speech must be proportional. This kind of reorientation would require two specific changes to social media policies and practices on hate speech. First, the companies would need to proactively police their networks for coordinated speech campaigns against vulnerable groups, in conditions that might indicate such speech could contribute to impunity for violence. Second, their toolkit would need to be expanded beyond outright bans and content removal. To this end, this chapter documents a range of innovative techniques that would give social media platforms the flexibly to intervene earlier, but with a much lighter touch.

The chapter first considers Facebook's role in the Rohingya genocide as an example of coordinated speech campaigns and the limitations of current social media policies. The chapter then provides an overview of international human rights law and the law on remedies that require proportionality in responses to harmful speech. Finally, the chapter discusses new and innovative responses to hate speech that go beyond content takedowns or user bans. These alternative remedies offer a way of responding to harmful speech that are less burdensome on speech and thus can be applied more liberally to reduce the chance that platforms will be used to incite atrocity crimes.

New directions in propaganda

This section discusses the case of Myanmar and what it illustrates about the gaps in social media polices on hate speech. What we term 'conditioning speech' – coordinated speech campaigns that create the conditions in which human rights violations are easier to justify – falls short of direct threats but are too pervasive to be handled on an individualized basis. The answer, however, is not more enforcement, since full enforcement of Facebook's hate speech prohibitions would cut deeply into expressive rights. Rather, this section argues that the case of Myanmar illustrates the need for a new policy that would address conditioning speech as something separate from individualized hate speech and also deploy a broader range of responses that could be tailored more proportionally to the nature of the threat.

Facebook dominates the social media environment in Myanmar, with over 20 million users in a country of just over 55 million.[2] A UN-sponsored Independent International Fact-Finding Mission on Myanmar (hereinafter Fact-Finding Mission) noted that for many in Myanmar, "Facebook is the Internet."[3] Low levels of technological and social media literacy combined with Facebook's offering of basic services outside data plans means that many have come to rely on Facebook as their primary source of news and information. In addition, "the Government's use of Facebook for official announcements and sharing of information further contributes to users' perception of Facebook as a reliable source of information."[4]

As early as 2015, the Allard K. Lowenstein International Human Rights Clinic found "strong evidence that genocide [was] being committed against Rohingya,"[5] a Muslim-minority population located primarily in Rakhine State within the Buddhist-majority Myanmar. Speech on Facebook is believed to have contributed both to specific acts of violence against the Rohingya as well as a general climate in Myanmar that made the genocide possible. The Fact-Finding Mission documented over 150 online public social media accounts, pages, and groups on Facebook that "regularly spread messages amounting to hate speech against Muslims in general or Rohingya in particular."[6] The Fact-Finding Mission noted that there were a number of these accounts that were "particularly influential" in light of "the number of followers (all over 10,000, but some over 1 million), the high levels of engagement of the followers with the posts (commenting and sharing), and the frequency of new posts (often daily, if not hourly)."[7]

Over several years, the government deployed anti-Rohingya propaganda on social media and through other channels to fuel fear in the general populace that would justify military action in Rakhine State against the Rohingya.[8] These online narratives drew on several different themes about the supposed threat posed by the Rohingya Muslims, describing "an existential threat to the country," "a threat to Burmese racial purity" and "a threat to Buddhist religious sanctity."[9] According to the Fact-Finding Mission, "[s]uch narratives latch onto long-standing anti-Muslim prejudices and stereotypes; they are designed to stoke fear."[10]

Although the Fact-Finding Mission was unable to reach a definitive answer to the question of direct causality between online hate speech and violence, it nonetheless concluded that "the linkage between offline and online hate speech and real world acts of discrimination and violence is more than circumstantial."[11] The Fact-Finding Mission also emphasized, however, that apart from specific incitement, anti-Rohingya speech on social media "contributed to and exacerbated a climate in which hate speech thrives and in which individuals and groups may be more receptive to calls of incitement to violence."[12]

By its own admission, Facebook was "too slow" to respond to the concerns of UN officials and human rights advocates. An open letter from Myanmar human rights advocates to Mark Zuckerberg of Facebook in April 2018 cited numerous deficiencies in Facebook's response, ranging from a lack of sufficient Burmese-speaking staff to the absence of procedures for identifying and escalating harmful speech. The letter described efforts to engage with Facebook dating back to September of 2017.[13] The Mission itself described Facebook's "slow and ineffective response" to its requests to remove posts targeting a human rights defender, posts which were first deemed not to violate Community Standards and eventually only removed via unofficial channels.[14] Facebook did not begin implementing a more robust and coordinated response until August 2018.

It is unclear why Facebook was so slow to respond. Although the speech documented by the Fact-Finding Mission may not necessarily rise to the level of a credible threat of violence,[15] it is easily a violation of the platform's prohibition on hate speech, which Facebook defines as "a direct attack on people based on what we call protected characteristics" which include not only race and ethnicity but also religion[16] – all of which would have been triggered by anti-Rohingya posts. One aspect of the problem beyond our ability to address here is that much of this speech was coded and thus difficult to identify as triggering Facebook's policies.[17] As the Mission Report notes, "[s]ubtleties in the Myanmar language and the use of fables and allegories make some potentially dangerous posts difficult to detect."[18] But once these coded threats were brought to Facebook's attention and it began working with individuals with appropriate language and cultural expertise,[19] why was this not an easy case?

One possibility is that Facebook initially relied on the same model of content moderation that it developed for responding to hate speech in democratic societies. Such an approach looks an individual instances of hate speech in isolation. A user (or increasingly an algorithm) identifies and flags a particular instance of speech as a violation of the company's Community Standards. This post is then escalated through a series of review processes, yielding a determination as to whether the speech should be removed or may remain on the platform. This approach, though, simply could not work in Myanmar. There were no users ready or willing to flag this speech – users were, in fact, largely willing consumers of the government's propaganda. Nor is it clear, in light of the pervasiveness of the speech, whether individual users could have physically or technologically identified all instances of this speech rapidly enough for it to be removed before spreading. Even when the speech was identified by activists, it may have been difficult for Facebook to determine how best to apply rules designed for racial slurs to a government-sponsored campaign of genocide.

Ultimately, in August 2018, and in the face of widespread public condemnation, Facebook began identifying accounts and pages that were the source of the anti-Rohingya campaign and removing them from the platform as hate figures or hate organizations or, later, for coordinated inauthentic behavior.[20] Facebook summarizes the steps it took as follows:

- In August 2018, it removed accounts and pages followed by almost twelve million people, banned 20 individuals and removed an additional 46 pages and twelve accounts for covertly pushing the messages of the military.[21]
- On 15 October 2018, Facebook announced the removal of "13 Pages and 10 accounts for engaging in coordinated inauthentic behavior on Facebook in Myanmar," noting that about 1.35 million unique people followed at least one of these 13 pages.[22]
- On 18 December 2018, Facebook announced that it had removed an additional "425 Facebook Pages, 17 Facebook Groups, 135 Facebook accounts and 15 Instagram accounts in Myanmar for engaging in coordinated inauthentic behavior on Facebook."[23] According to Facebook, "Approximately 2.5 million people followed at least one of these Facebook Pages, Approximately 6,400 people belonged to at least one of these Facebook Groups, Approximately 1,300 people followed at least one these Instagram accounts."[24]

Faced with such pervasive harmful speech, individualized moderation based on Community Standards was in all likelihood simply impossible. In Myanmar at least, the most effective solution appears to have been to simply identify the pages and accounts most responsible for circulating the speech in question and banning them from the platform – not for hate speech but for coordinated inauthentic behavior.

What lessons might we draw from this experience? The answer is not greater enforcement of hate speech policies more generally. Leaky enforcement of the kind already employed is likely sufficient for most environments, and in fact, the leakiness of social media flagging may be what prevents hate speech policies from affecting expressive freedoms more than they already do. Instead, the Myanmar case reveals the need for social media companies to develop a new policy for pervasive hate speech in environments where the rule of law is weak. This kind of speech may both contribute to a culture that accepts impunity for political violence, and also a signal that such violence is about to occur – and in such contexts, regular enforcement mechanisms are insufficient.

Second, the Myanmar case also indicates the need for more tailored remedies in situations of pervasive hate speech against vulnerable groups. Removal of accounts and organizations is a radical step that is hard to justify until hate speech against a vulnerable group has already caused harm.[25] Having an array of more tailored responses that could be deployed in ways proportional to the risks presented by each particular situation would give social media companies the ability to intervene earlier and more frequently to counter widespread and pervasive speech campaigns against vulnerable minorities – before they do real harm.

Proportionality in responding to online hate

Proportional responses are required both by international human rights law as well as the law of remedies in international law more generally. Content removal should still be an available and commonplace remedy in appropriate situations. But particularly in the early stages of pervasive hate speech campaigns in low rule of law contexts, when the impact and source of the speech may be unclear, a broader set of remedies might be introduced to allow this speech to be countered much earlier.

We take as a starting point the recommendation of David Kaye, the UN Special Rapporteur on Freedom of Expression and Opinion, that the content moderation policies and procedures of social media companies should be based on international human rights law.[26] International human rights law takes as its starting point that while expression may be limited to achieve important public policy goals, any such limits must comply with the principles of legality, necessity and proportionality, and legitimacy.[27] The requirement of necessity and proportionality provides that the restriction in question must be one that "imposes the least burden on the exercise of the right and actually protects, or is likely to protect, the legitimate state interest at issue."[28]

Proportionality is also required by the law of remedies. Companies that provide a platform for speech that is used to support or incite human rights violations have a responsibility under the UN Guiding Principles on Business and Human Rights to avoid, mitigate and remediate such harms.[29] The right to a remedy includes both the right to fair procedures and the right to a substantive remedy.[30] Although remedies for human rights harms are directed to a variety of objectives, a central principle of the law on remedy is proportionality. Any remedy chosen must be proportional to the gravity and harm of the violation.[31]

The response of a company to hate speech on its platform may be thought of not only as mitigation of harm but also as part of the remedy owed to victims of violations linked to that speech. As a remedy, the response should be directed not only toward cessation of the violation but also to guarantees of non-repetition. Remedies can be both "intended to benefit the individual victim" as well as "remedies of a systemic nature intended to prevent future violations of the rights of others."[32] Thus, a remedy includes the duty to take appropriate measures to prevent future violations, including through the creation of "processes and institutions designed to prevent reoccurrence of the violation" such as "human rights education, the institution of codes of conduct, and mechanisms for monitoring violations."[33] Victims are also entitled to information about the violation.[34]

Alternatives to takedown

Social media companies require a broader range of tools to intervene earlier in pervasive hate speech directed to vulnerable populations. The purpose of this section is to survey possibilities for alternatives to either the takedown of content on the one hand or the banning of users on the other. Removing offending speech and speakers remains an important tool, but those seeking to ensure platforms are not abused require a significantly expanded toolkit, one that considers the various actors, methods and time frames of hate speech.

Expanding our lens to consider the actors, methods and time frames of hate speech suggests a range of new remedies that might be deployed beyond simply takedown. Online speech regulation arises from a process of tripartite contestation between platforms, states and users – including individuals, nonprofits and businesses.[35] The remedy of takedown alone gives a privileged place to platforms, at the expense of states and users. With respect to methods of influence, a focus on takedowns directs attention to online responses to hate speech, but remedies might suggest exploration of offline methods as well. Finally, in terms of time frames, concentrating on takedowns addresses one salient-but-fleeting moment in the life span of hate speech. Methods that aim to prevent hate speech before it occurs, and counter it after it occurs, could vastly expand the toolkit of responses available to social media companies.

The following surveys a range of initiatives that involve a broader range of actors and which draw on a mix of online and offline methods to both prevent hate speech before it occurs and to minimize its impact after it occurs. Although we begin with prevention-focused approaches, there is inevitable overlap – countering existing hate speech and preventing future hate speech go hand-in-hand.

Prevention by design

Two distinct but related factors contribute to the striking pervasiveness of hate speech in an online environment – and designing platforms to minimize these features could be an essential element of curbing such speech.

First, from the perspective of the speaker, the barriers to uttering hate speech are often lower in the online world thanks to a phenomenon that researchers have called 'online toxic disinhibition.'[36] Aspects of the online environment, including lack of eye-contact and the ability to be anonymous facilitate such toxic disinhibition, leading people to communicate in harmful ways online that they may not do offline.[37] And the instantaneous nature of social media exacerbates these tendencies, enabling the so-called 'spontaneous hate speech' that people, if forced to reflect on what they were doing, might not have posted.[38] Further, algorithms that determine what content to prioritize are also often tailored to promote the most extreme and controversial content, since that is the content that is likely to garner the platform more views.[39]

The second feature that distinguishes the spread of online hate from its offline equivalent is the ease and speed of dissemination.[40] The online environment enables hate speech to go viral, almost instantly, at no cost to those who spread it. The widespread availability of tools for sharing information without the need for journalistic intermediaries means that speech spreads rapidly without any filters in place to manage it.

These characteristics, however, are not inevitable. Anonymity, for example, is not inherent in online communications, and some have suggested supporting real-name requirements – a policy that Facebook has always insisted on.[41] Platforms could be designed in ways that work to minimize the online disinhibition effect, such as through the use of cues reminding users of their shared humanity.[42] Already, platforms can create interfaces that nudge users toward responsible speech choices.[43] Algorithms could be tweaked to deprioritize particularly extreme or virulent content, either as a general matter or in places where such content may be linked to offline violence. Indeed, Facebook already does this for spam, "deprioritize[ing] links that are aggressively shared by suspected spammers, on the theory that these links 'tend to include low quality content such as clickbait, sensationalism, and misinformation.'"[44]

Platforms also have the technical capability to add 'friction' into their user interface. Warnings or other kinds of prompts that question the user as to whether they really want to post certain content may be enough to deter at least some of those who would otherwise post hate speech.[45] Initial findings from an experiment in a reddit sub-community found that simply notifying users of a rule about prohibited comments in the same space as the posts themselves (as opposed to a separate location on the site) significantly increased compliance with the rule.[46] And Facebook juxtaposes items from a user's Newsfeed with other selected 'Related Articles' to "give people more perspectives and additional information" that may deter them from spreading false content.[47]

Similar methods could also be used to help dissuade users from reposting hateful content. Indeed, YouTube already takes this approach by removing its sharing tools from videos that – although not meeting its threshold for takedown – nonetheless contain inflammatory or supremacist content.[48] Facebook has also begun introducing friction into its WhatsApp messenger service. In response to claims that its platform was being used to circulate misinformation contributing to communal violence in India, WhatsApp began limiting the number of users who could be forwarded any particular news report, as well as labeling more clearly information that has been forwarded as opposed to authored by the sender.[49]

Some of these design changes could have serious costs, of course. Digital activists make strong arguments that real-name requirements harm those seeking to build social movements or find affiliations among the most marginalized in different societies.[50] Further, users are often able to circumvent real-name policies, and such requirements do nothing to curb speakers who either do not view their speech as hateful or embrace the controversy associated with their speech being labeled as such.[51] Both concerns may make real-name requirements an ineffective and harmful design choice. But at the very least we must begin a conversation about what those design choices might be – and how companies could design platforms less hospitable to speech.

User education

To the degree that online and offline hate speech have a unified core, it seems unlikely that there is a technical 'quick fix' that will comprehensively address the problem of hate speech online. As with offline hate speech, the key to its ultimate reduction lies in long-term educative work. As one of us notes in a recent essay, speech rights come with speech responsibilities – and such responsibilities do not lay exclusively at the feet of individual users.[52]

To take just one example, MediaSmarts, a non-profit Canadian organization, has built a digital literacy curriculum for children from kindergarten through high school, including a guide for responding to hate online,[53] and interactive games designed to increase students' ability to "recognize bias, prejudice and hate propaganda on the Internet."[54] Such material lays preventive ground, training young people how to identify hate speech and how to respond if they encounter hate speech online.[55] And while this particular curriculum comes out of the non-governmental sector, there is equally a role for States to play in integrating such curricula into the public education system.

User education – conceived of as a remedy for hate speech and an essential element of guarantees of non-repetition – must be tailored to the specific context in which it is deployed. For example, in an effort to reduce the risk of violence in the buildup to the 2013 elections in Kenya, advocates teamed up with the cast and crew of *Vioja Mahakamani*, a long-running comedy series that is one of the most popular shows on Kenyan television. A post-intervention assessment found that by watching four 'edutainment' episodes, viewers gained a greater understanding of the way leaders can use inciting language to manipulate their followers as well as the legal consequences that flow from such speech.[56]

User education must be distinguished from mere fact-checking. Some platforms, such as WhatsApp, have introduced verification efforts in an attempt to combat misinformation online. Research indicates, however, that fact-checking – rather than helping to dissuade people from factually incorrect beliefs – can, in fact, makes them more likely to hold to their original ideas.[57] Moreover, fact-checking does not necessarily inhibit content sharing. As Marwick notes,

> in many cases, what matters is the affective or emotional appeal of a particular story or claim, rather than its factual accuracy. In many cases, the sharer may be aware that the story is false, but still choose to share it for its identity-signaling properties.[58]

Counter-speech

Concerns about electoral violence in Kenya provided fertile ground for another innovative project to both prevent and counter hate speech, *Sisi ni Amani* ('We are peace' in Swahili).[59] The project used the same mobile phone technology that helped to spread hateful and inciting messages during the 2007–08 Kenyan elections to instead spread messages of peace and community in the buildup to future elections. Drawing heavily on local leaders, the project receives real-time information about rumors and hate speech in rural communities and then distributes peace messaging to counter the spread of hate. Importantly, such rapid-response work is paired with ongoing efforts to reduce conflicts over land, which lie at the heart of some of the worst violence in recent Kenyan history.[60] In a follow-up study of the campaign, more than half the respondents said they felt that the rapid-responses "actively aided in preventing violence."[61]

The conditions needed to make counter-speech effective may not exist in all contexts. The idea of counter-speech is a touchstone of U.S. First Amendment law, which justifies the limits it puts on the state's ability to regulate speech by reference to the marketplace of ideas. As Justice Brandeis argued in Whitney v. California, "If there be time to expose through discussion the falsehood and fallacies, to avert the evil by the processes of education, the remedy to be applied is more speech, not enforced silence."[62] Yet there are good reasons to fear that counter-speech may fail precisely in situations when hate speech is most inimical. Faced with massive power disparities that characterize pervasive vilification of a minority group, the marketplace of ideas simply does not work.[63] As Susan Benesch explains,

> by the time incitement to genocide is possible, there is such a disproportion in access to the means of disseminating information that protests by the targeted group, or even by sympathizers among the audience, would be extremely unlikely to stop incitement from taking effect.[64]

Participatory enforcement

Turning to the direct countering of hate speech, interesting work is being spearheaded by non-profit groups to address the problem with the support of artificial intelligence (AI). The scale of online activity makes it impossible to identify even a fraction of online hate speech through the use of human moderation alone. Just as platforms enforce their takedown policies by relying on AI to help identify content for review, so too have nonprofit organizations begun to develop AI tools to identify hate speech.

The process is not a simple one; hate speech is an inherently contextual matter, and words that may be hateful in one context are benign in another.[65] To develop a "lexicon of online hate speech" in the South Sudan context, for example, PeaceTech Lab triangulated words commonly found in online hate speech with data visualization of networks through which such language spreads as well as a 'ground truth' process of interviews with users throughout South Sudan.[66]

Once validated, such lexicons can train an algorithm to at least make a first pass at identifying hateful content.

This approach, of combining technical tools with the knowledge of actual users, is also being taken in a major initiative spearheaded by the Anti-Defamation League in partnership with the University of California at Berkeley's D-Lab, to develop an index of online hate speech. Although it is still in development, the researchers have concluded that "the most powerful tool we have to understand the scope and spread of hate speech online is the experience of those who have been targeted by it"[67]

Although platforms have used such approaches to help them identify content for takedown, civil society organizations are developing more creative responses. #WeCounterHate is a project that draws on AI-identified content to triage material posted to Twitter for human review.[68] If the human moderator determines the content is, indeed, hate speech, they generate a response that combines both the benefits of adding 'friction' to the user experience and engaging in user education. Specifically, they reply with the following message: "This hate tweet is now being countered. Think twice before retweeting. For every retweet, a donation will be committed to a non-profit fighting for equality, inclusion, and diversity."[69] The tweet also provides a link to the recipient nonprofit, Life After Hate, where users can access information on the impact of hate speech.

In its pilot initiative, #WeCounterHate claims to have reduced the retweet rate of hate tweets by 66 percent.[70] Further, one in five hateful tweets that were countered by the project were subsequently deleted by their original authors.[71] Although these results are preliminary and anecdotal, the initiative suggests that these tools – friction, user education and user participation in enforcement – might even be combined to develop new and innovative responses to online hate speech.

Conclusion

Responding to online hate speech is an extraordinarily difficult challenge. And putting greater responsibility on social media companies to fix this problem risks exacerbating an already problematic delegation of vast regulatory authority. Greater incorporation of principles of proportionality and remedy, however, would not only broaden the responses companies have available to them when their platforms are misused but would also provide guidance for ensuring greater transparency and accountability of these efforts.

Broader tools are essential for creating online spaces that better serve their intended goals. Takedown is a remedy that, by definition, can only come into force after hate speech has already been posted online. And once shared, speech can be stubbornly persistent. Even after the original speech is removed, it is difficult if not impossible to track down every reposting. Thus, from the perspective of the victim, takedown is often cold comfort, since the harm of the speech lives on – and indeed, this persistence is what makes pervasive hate campaigns, such as that seen in Myanmar, so difficult to stop. We need tools to respond at the threshold of speech rather than after the fact.

Although efficacy assessments in this area are in their infancy, the array of approaches currently being tested to prevent online hate speech seem promising. Of course, it is unrealistic to prevent all online hate speech. But this is why methods of countering hate speech and, crucially, limiting the degree to which others spread the speech, are also vital. Indeed, from the perspective of individual victims, such approaches may provide a more meaningful remedy to the harm they suffered than a takedown can provide. Moreover, empowering local communities who have been affected by hate speech to engage in solutions to the problem is not only likely to be more effective[72] but has the added advantage of amplifying the very voices that hate speech seeks to marginalize.

Once we widen our lens beyond the current focus on takedown, it is easier to see that the creation of a safe online environment is not simply in the hands of platforms but rather is a shared responsibility between platforms, states and users. Developing more robust and effective responses to online hate speech requires responses that account for and take advantage of this shared responsibility.

Notes

1 A. Addis, 'International Propaganda and Developing Countries,' *Vanderbilt Journal of Transnational Law*, vol. 21, 1988, p. 492.
2 'Report of the Detailed Findings of the Independent International Fact-Finding Mission on Myanmar,' U.N. Doc. A/HRC/39/CRP.2, 17 September 2018, para. 1344 [hereinafter Myanmar Report]; *The World Factbook.*
3 Myanmar Report, para. 1345.
4 Ibid.
5 A.K. Lowenstein International Human Rights Clinic, *Persecution of the Rohingya Muslims: Is Genocide Occurring in Rakhine State? A Legal Analysis*, New Haven, CT: Yale Law School for Fortify Rights, 2015, p. 1.
6 Myanmar Report, para. 1310.
7 Ibid.
8 P. Mozur, 'A Genocide Incited on Facebook, With Posts from Myanmar's Military,' *New York Times*, 15 October 2018.
9 Myanmar Report, paras 1315–1317.
10 Ibid., para. 1314.
11 Ibid., para. 1326.
12 Ibid., para. 1327.
13 'Open Letter from Myanmar Civil Society Organizations to Mark Zuckerberg,' 5 April 2018. Online. Available HTTP: <https://perma.cc/3ZJB-XL3Z> (accessed 9 June 2019).
14 Myanmar Report, para. 1351.
15 Facebook, 'Credible Violence,' *Community Standards.* Online. Available HTTP: <https://perma.cc/F5NA-ADWD> (accessed 9 June 2019).
16 Facebook, 'Hate Speech,' *Community Standards.* Online. Available HTTP: <https://perma.cc/W8YN-62VW> (accessed 9 June 2019).
17 'International Law and Human Rights Clinic,' *Invisible Threats: Mitigating the Risk of Violence from Coded Hate Speech against Human Rights Defenders in Guatemala*, 2019, pp. 19–23.
18 Myanmar Report, para. 1311.
19 Ibid., para. 1352.

20 Ibid., para. 1353.
21 'Removing Myanmar Military Officials from Facebook,' *Facebook Newsroom*, 28 August 2018.
22 Ibid.
23 Ibid.
24 Ibid.
25 S.B. Starr, 'Rethinking "Effective Remedies": Remedial Deterrence in International Courts,' *New York University Law Review*, vol. 83, 2008, p. 695.
26 D. Kaye, *Report of the Special Rapporteur on the Promotion and Protection of the Right to Freedom of Opinion and Expression*, U.N. Doc. A/HRC/38/35, 6 April 2018, para. 41.
27 Ibid., para. 7.
28 Ibid.
29 *UN Guiding Principles on Business and Human Rights*, 2011, pp. 13–16, 31–32. Online. Available HTTP: <https://perma.cc/6D9C-VQ5X> (accessed 9 June 2019).
30 D. Shelton, *Remedies in International Human Rights Law*, Oxford: Oxford University Press, First Edition, 1999, pp. 14–15. T.M. Antkowiak, 'Remedial Approaches to Human Rights Violations: The Inter-American Court of Human Rights and Beyond,' *Columbia Journal of Transnational Law*, vol. 46, no. 2, 2008, p. 402.
31 *Basic Principles and Guidelines on the Right to a Remedy and Reparation for Victims of Gross Violations of International Human Rights Law and Serious Violations of International Humanitarian Law*, U.N. Doc. A/RES/60/147, 21 March 2006, para. 15. *Report of the Working Group on Enforced or Involuntary Disappearances*, U.N. Doc. E/CN.4/1998/43, 12 January 1998, p. 16. C. Sandoval and M. Duttwiler, 'Redressing Non-Pecuniary Damages of Torture Survivors: The Practice of the Inter-American Court of Human Rights,' in G. Gilbert, F. Hampson and C. Sandoval (eds), *The Delivery of Human Rights: Essays in Honour of Professor Sir Nigel Rodley*, New York, NY: Routledge, 2012, p. 124.
32 G.L. Neuman, 'Bi-Level Remedies for Human Rights Violations,' *Harvard International Law Journal*, vol. 55, no. 3, 2014, p. 330.
33 Basic Principles, Principles 3a and 23.
34 Shelton, *Remedies*, p. 17; D. Valeska, 'The Expansive Right to an Effective Remedy: Common Developments at the Human Rights Committee and the Inter-American Court,' *British Journal of American Legal Studies*, vol. 3, no. 1, 2014, p. 261.
35 R. Hamilton, 'Governing the Public Square,' forthcoming, on file with authors.
36 J. Suler, 'The Online Disinhibition Effect,' *CyberPyschology & Behavior*, vol. 7, no. 3, 2004, p. 321.
37 N. Lapidot-Lefler and A. Barak, 'Effects of Anonymity, Invisibility, and Lack of Eye-Contact on Toxic Online Disinhibition,' *Computers in Human Behavior*, vol. 28, no. 2, 2011, pp. 436–437.
38 A. Brown, 'What Is So Special About Online (as Compared to Offline) Hate Speech?' *Ethnicities*, vol. 18, no. 3, 2018, p. 304.
39 A. Taub and M. Fisher, 'Facebook Fueled Anti-Refugee Attacks in Germany, New Research Suggests,' *New York Times*, 21 August 2018.
40 N. Syed, 'Real Talk about Fake News: Towards a Better Theory for Platform Governance,' *Yale Law Journal Forum*, vol. 127, 9 October 2017, p. 354.
41 E. Armijo, *Meet the New Governors, Same as the Old Governors*, New York, NY: Knight First Amendment Institute, Columbia University, 2019.
42 M.K. Land, 'Speech Duties,' *The American Journal of International Law Unbound*, vol. 112, 2018, p. 329.
43 R. Thaler and C. Sunstein, *Nudge: Improving Decisions about Health, Wealth, and Happiness*, New York, NY: Yale University Press, 2008.
44 Syed, 'Real Talk,' p. 354.

45 *Harmful Content: The Role of Internet Platform Companies in Fighting Terrorist Incitement and Politically Motivated Disinformation*, New York, NY: NYU Stern Center for Business and Human Rights, 2017, p. 26.
46 J.N. Matias, 'Posting Rules in Online Discussions Prevents Problems & Increases Participation,' *Civil Servant*, 8 October 2016.
47 S. Su, 'New Test with Related Articles,' *Facebook Newsroom*, 25 April 2017.
48 K. Walker, 'Four Ways Google Will Help to Tackle Extremism,' *Financial Times*, 18 June 2017.
49 V. Ananth, 'WhatsApp Races against Time to Fix Fake News Mess Ahead of 2019 General Elections,' *The Economic Times*, 24 July 2018.
50 J.C. York and D. Kayyali, 'Facebook's Real Name Policy Can Cause Real-World Harm for the LGBTQ Community,' *Electronic Frontier Foundation*, 16 September 2014.
51 K. Roose, 'Facebook Banned Infowars. Now What?' *New York Times*, 10 August 2018.
52 Land, 'Speech Duties,' p. 332.
53 'Responding to Online Hate,' *Media Awareness Network*, 2012, pp. 1–19. Online. Available HTTP: <https://mediasmarts.ca/sites/mediasmarts/files/guides/responding_online_hate_guide.pdf> (accessed 9 June 2019).
54 Allies and Aliens: A Mission in Critical Thinking, *Media Smarts*, 2005.
55 'Responding to Online Hate.'
56 L. Kogen, *Testing a Media Intervention in Kenya: Vioja Mahakamani, Dangerous Speech and the Benesch Guidelines*, Center for Global Communication Studies, 2013, p. 3.
57 A.E. Marwick, 'Why Do People Share Fake News? A Sociotechnical Model of Media Effects,' *Georgetown Law Technology Review*, vol. 2, 2018, p. 508.
58 Ibid., p. 509.
59 'About,' *Sisi ni Amani Blog*, 13 July 2011. Online. Available HTTP: <https://perma.cc/ZK8B-5USL> (accessed 9 June 2019).
60 SNA-K is Featured on the iHub's blog!, *Sisi ni Amani Blog*, n.d. Online. Available HTTP: <https://perma.cc/L98Y-U3AW> (accessed 9 June 2019).
61 S. Shah and R. Brown, 'Programming for Peace: Sisi Ni Amani Kenya and the 2013 Election,' *ICTs, Statebuilding and Peacebuilding in Africa*, 2014.
62 Whitney v. California, 274 U.S. 357, 377 (1927) (J. Brandeis, concurring).
63 Syed, 'Real Talk,' p. 340. D. E. Bambauer, 'Shopping Badly: Cognitive Biases, Communications, and the Fallacy of the Marketplace of Ideas,' *University of Colorado Law Review*, vol. 77, 2006.
64 S. Benesch, 'Vile Crime or Inalienable Right: Defining Incitement to Genocide,' *Virginia Journal of International Law*, vol. 48, no. 3, 2008, pp. 496–499.
65 T. Davidson et al., 'Automated Hate Speech Detection and the Problem of Offensive Language,' *Proceedings of the Eleventh International AAAI Conference on Web and Social Media*, 2017.
66 'Social Media and Conflict in South Sudan: A Lexicon of Hate Speech Terms,' *Peace Tech Lab*, vol. 2–18, 2016, p. 2.
67 Online Hate Index, *Center for Technology & Society*, vol. 4–19, 2018, p. 17.
68 POSSIBLE Agency, 'WeCounterHate: How to Identify Hate Speech,' 2018. Online. Available HTTP: <https://perma.cc/24YN-VA5Y> (accessed 9 June 2019).
69 C. Jarrett, 'AI Could Make Trolls Think Twice Before Retweeting Offensive Content,' *VentureBeat*, 4 February 2018.
70 POSSIBLE Agency.
71 Ibid.
72 Online Hate Index, p. 17.

Part II

Science to law

Chapter 7

From creativity to conflict

Semantic innovation in the Bosnian Serb national movement of the 1990s

Robert J. Donia

Introduction

> [Mafia] is a term with multiple meanings [...] referring to different events depending on the context, circumstances, and intentions and interests of those who use it.[1]
>
> Salvatore Lupo

> [...] dog, for the Arabs, is an unclean animal, just like pigs [...] A pigsty by the door of the house and dog-kennel or wicker basket for one's lap-dog are Christian inventions, it is not by accident that the Moslems refer to the warriors of the cross as dogs [...][2]
>
> José Saramago

The Socialist Federal Republic of Yugoslavia (SFRY) broke apart in the early 1990s into several independent successor republics governed principally by elected national populists. In the tri-ethnic Republic of Bosnia and Herzegovina (hereinafter Bosnia), leaders of nationalist parties representing the republic's three largest ethnonational groups employed semantic innovation – the purposeful manipulation of words and their meanings – to expand their national movements and compete with one another politically and militarily. This chapter examines how one organization, the Serb Democratic Party (SDS) used semantic innovations to prevail in the elections of 1990 and thereafter to strengthen their movement and eventually seize much of the republic by force of arms.

The purpose and notional foundations of the study

My purpose here is to show that tracking a movement's semantic innovations can yield valuable insights into its leaders' guiding principles, intentions and plans that might not be apparent from their utterances and writings. The Bosnian Serb nationalists were hardly alone: Leaders of many social movements employ semantic innovations that reveal their goals and strategies. (Conservative American intellectuals, for instance, relabeled the 'Estate Tax' a 'Death Tax' in the 1990s, when the tax applied to all estates over 600,000 dollars, and successfully swung public against the tax such that in 2019 it applies only to estates of 11 million dollars or more.)

The dynamics of many national movements can be better understood by examining the semantic innovations of its proponents. Jurists at the International Criminal Tribunal for the former Yugoslavia (ICTY) would likely have better and more readily understood the motivations and deeds of the accused who stood before them had they heard from expert linguistic witnesses in the trials. Translators and interpreters provided invaluable assistance to the court on several key linguistic issues, but they were prevented by rules and conventions from making more helpful contributions, as Ellen Bursać relates in her account of the work of interpreters and translators at the ICTY.[3] In contrast, Mathias Ruzindana, a Rwanda-born sociolinguist and expert witness at the International Criminal Tribunal for Rwanda (ICTR), provided invaluable insights in a trial whose judges wrote that they "relied substantially on the testimony of Dr. Mathias Ruzindana."[4] Unfortunately, judges at the ICTY heard very little such evidence.

I chose to examine the Bosnian Serb national movement in the 1990s principally because its leaders generated a rich trove of documentary evidence that became public on being accepted as evidence in war crimes trials at the ICTY. Those documents detail the activities of the SDS from its founding in July 1990 until the end of the war in Bosnia in 1996. The early documents reveal a great deal about the SDS campaign prior to the democratic multiparty elections of November 1990. In those elections, the SDS and the leading party of Croat nationalists, the Croatian Democratic Community (HDZ), and the Bosnian Muslims' Party of Democratic Action (SDA) combined to defeat soundly their non-nationalist rival parties.[5] Once in power, the three victorious parties formed a shaky alliance (which they called a 'partnership'), but their squabbling soon doomed their power-sharing arrangements. All parties transitioned from cooperation to intense rivalry in 1991 and eventually entered into armed conflicts that lasted from spring 1992 until early 1996. Central to this study, and to a general understanding of the conflicts in the former Yugoslavia, is the foundational concept of the *narod*, a word usually translated into English as *a people* or (less accurately) *a nation*.[6] There is a widespread understanding in the Balkans that every *narod* is a neatly bounded, homogeneous human group with ancient origins, a common biological lineage, and cultural practices that are stable over time. In contrast, some Western scholars have recently argued that a *narod* is a social construct, an imagined community that is dynamic, malleable and constantly being redefined and modified as circumstances change.[7] In a recent study, Edin Hajdarpašić amplifies this interpretation, noting that South Slav national movements are unpredictable, turbulent generators of cultural production in forms such as ethnographic knowledge, visual representations, poetry and prose, myths, symbols and linguistic practices.[8] Semantic innovations, the subject of this inquiry, are yet another form of the prolific cultural production Hajdarpašić describes.

This study also builds on recent research across several disciplines that has reconceptualized everyday interpersonal communication and the derivation of meaning from words. Scholars have feasted for the past few decades on the fraught, complex relationship between signifiers – uttered or written – and their intended referents, the meanings that can be imputed to such signifiers. Scholars across several disciplines are critical of *literalism*, the idea that the meaning of any given lexical element is fixed, stable and readily knowable.[9] They argue that a speaker's or writer's *intended* referent is typically elusive, and they urge careful examination of each signifier's abundant connotations and context in which a communication takes place. Their studies have shown that communicators may use a variety of linguistic devices, such as shifters, floating signifiers, codes, gestures, metaphoric speech and irony to convey meanings quite at variance from those suggested by the literalism inherent in unambiguous definitions.[10]

In a recent study, Mark Grdešić shows how Serbs in the Republic of Serbia adroitly exploited the ambiguity of multiple meanings to mobilize Serbs in the movement that brought the late Serbian President Slobodan Milošević to power in the late 1980s. Grdešić identifies three "discursive affinities" – concepts or lexical elements common to both communist and nationalist discourse – as instrumental in smoothing Serbia's transition from Yugoslav communism to the Serb nationalism that superseded it in the 1980s.[11]

Erving Goffman has brought a modicum of order to alternatives to literalism by proposing the *frame* as a conceptual tool to identify and select those contextual elements relevant to a given signifier's meaning.[12] (So, for example, in the second epigram above, the signifier 'dog' in a Christian frame appears as a welcome companion and household member, whereas 'dog' in an Islamic frame refers to a filthy, unwelcome invader of the home.) The *frame* will be invoked in this article to clarify how Serb national activists – poets, artists, composers, sloganeers, intellectuals, political leaders, ideological promoters and linguistic innovators – developed semantic innovations to shape and strengthen the Bosnian Serb national movement.

The Serb *narod*

Bosnian Serb national activists enhanced the everyday meaning of *Serb narod* by attributing to it semantically the qualities of elasticity, anthropocentricity, suffering and congenital impossibility of committing genocide, as outlined below. Whereas most *narods* in Europe are distinguished by the mother tongue of its members, Serb, Croat and Bosniak *narods* are distinguished mainly by self-identified loyalty to a secular name, adherence to a religion or religious tradition (particularly as evidenced by first names taken from saints and other revered figures) and cultural practices. In the eighteenth through twentieth centuries, secular national movements of the Croats, Bosnian Muslims and Serbs arose, respectively, among members of the Catholic, Muslim and Serbian Orthodox communities. Those of each *narod* insist that they speak a distinct language

(Croatian, Bosnian or Serbian), but all three languages are mutually intelligible and so close that they went by the hyphenated name 'Serbo-Croatian' before 1990 and have been known as BCS (Bosnian/Croatian/Serbian) since then.[13] One recent study described BCS as "the common core underlying Bosnian, Croatian, and Serbian" and concluded that "the language is simultaneously one and more than one."[14]

Activists of all *narods* in the former Yugoslav lands held an essentially biological conception of their group. Serb activists held *narods* in general, and their *narod* in particular, to be the highest and morally superior form of human organization. Aleksa Buha, foreign minister of the Republika Srpska during the war, summed up the premise that only the *narod*, "the fundamental unit of individual and collective life," could fulfill basic human needs:

> Neither theory nor historical experience can demonstrate that the civil aspect of the individual or the collective is as strong and as detached from the national aspect that it could offer a solid base for the overall development of the individual and collective life.[15]

As their movement advanced, Serb activists elaborated and glorified the referent of the signifier 'Serb *narod*' through periodic amplification and clarification. Specifically, they imputed to the Bosnian Serb *narod* the qualities of elasticity, anthropocentricity, suffering and victims of genocide, to be discussed in that order.

Elasticity

SDS leaders expanded the meaning of Serb *narod* to prosecute their claim that Serbs made up the largest portion of Bosnia's population and therefore deserved to control the most territory. Leaders of the Bosnian Serbs naturally wanted to awaken the national consciousness and Serb loyalty of those vacillating or indifferent to their national identity. Between the election in November 1990 and the decennial census of 1 April 1991, national activists urged as many people as possible to declare themselves *Serbs*. They particularly targeted those who had previously declared themselves Yugoslavs in hopes they would awaken instead to an identity as Serbs. In the census, the category 'Yugoslav' consisted of an eclectic mixture of Yugoslav army officers, civil servants, the offspring of mixed marriages, those with no preferred identity and opponents of national identity as a category of political participation. Their census declarations loomed particularly significant in competitive municipalities where Serbs and Bosnian Muslims lived in approximately equal numbers. In the demographically contested municipality of Prijedor, SDS local leader Šavanović identified the campaign's objective: "The problem is making the Serbs realize that they are of Serbian nationality, and not Yugoslavs."[16]

Whether because of the SDS campaign or for other reasons, Bosnians identifying themselves as Yugoslavs constituted a lower percentage and number in 1991 (5.5 percent or 242,682) than in 1981 (7.9 percent or 326,316). But the decline in self-declared Yugoslavs did not translate into a proportionate increase in Serbs. 1,369,258 declared themselves Serbs in 1991, only 3.7 percent more than the 1,320,738 self-declared Serbs in 1981, while the number of Bosnian Muslims increased 16.9 percent, from 1,630,738 to 1,905,829, between the two censuses. Many Serbs believed a higher birth rate among Bosnian Muslims was responsible for their faster growth rate, but demographic expert witnesses at the ICTY demonstrated that there was no significant difference in the birth rates among those of the two *narods.* The increase in Bosnian Muslim numbers is better explained by substantial immigration of Bosnian Muslims into Bosnia from a Muslim-inhabited region that straddled the border of Serbia and Montenegro to the east. Serb national activists admitted as much by demonizing Muslim immigrants from that area as fanatical, hate-filled Muslims, thereby arousing fear and hatred of them among Serbs.

Once the census was complete, national activists turned to other semantic innovations to increase the number of Serbs in some Bosnian municipalities. In areas where self-declared Serbs fell just short of constituting a majority, SDS leaders simply rejected the census declarations and arrogated unto themselves the authority to determine others' national identity. They simply proclaimed that self-declared Yugoslavs were in reality Serbs. By counting both Yugoslavs and Serbs as part of their *narod*, Serb leaders claimed a demographic majority in several contested municipalities.[17] In this they were not alone. Some SDA leaders asserted that self-declared Yugoslavs were in fact Bosnian Muslims.[18] None of these self-appointed census revisers was particularly successful, as journalists and diplomats generally accepted the census results rather than speculative assertions of *narod* leaders.

In a bid to solidify Serb claims, Radovan Karadžić, president of the SDS and of the self-declared Bosnian Serb entity Republika Srpska, urged his fellow SDS members to conflate 'absolute' (over 50 percent) and 'relative' (less than 50 percent but still largest number) majorities when speaking in public. He told the assembly that he had reached an agreement with Croat leaders that "where they constitute a relative majority, we shall define the areas as theirs, and where we constitute this relative majority, ours."[19] Most laypersons, in Bosnia or anywhere else, assume that the word 'majority,' unmodified by an adjective, refers to an absolute majority. If followed and believed, Karadžić's instruction would have diminished the Bosniaks' demographic strength as portrayed on maps but substantially expanded the numbers of Croats and Serbs. Serbs generally observed Karadžić's proposed elision, particularly when under his watchful eye, but most foreign diplomats and journalists lent little credence to this transparently deceptive Serb claim.

Anthropocentricity

Bosnian Serb activists, following the practice of other national leaders and of Serbs themselves in earlier times, portrayed the Serb *narod* as possessing the characteristics of a living human being. SDS President Radovan Karadžić thrived on eloquently articulating the *narod*'s anthropomorphic character. At various times, he characterized the Serb *narod* as willful, generous, gracious, patient, sensitive, angry, righteously indignant, vengeful, disputatious and willing to sacrifice. With the regular exercise of his fertile imagination, poetic command of language and considerable rhetorical skills, Karadžić brought the Serb *narod* into a frame of life-changing vitality for his listeners and readers.

Having placed the Serb *narod* in an anthropomorphized frame, Karadžić claimed the oracular power to know the *narod*'s will, and he freely spoke with authority on its behalf. He became the Serb *narod*'s chosen ventriloquist, lending his voice to proclaim its will and bringing life to an otherwise abstract concept of the Serb *narod* to make it more intuitively appealing. Karadžić explained his relationship with the Serb *narod* in a conversation with a regional SDS leader in November 1991. "I'm not creating the policy and the political will of the Serb narod, I interpret it for you," he said.[20] His interlocutor, Božidar Vučurević, replied in agreement, "You are conveying the aspirations of a people." Miroslav Toholj, editor of the SDS's official weekly newspaper *Javnost* (Public) and a long-time friend of Karadžic, noted the mutually empowering reciprocity between Karadžić and the Serb *narod*, saying that he "quickly mastered the skill of communicating with the people" and had "stumbled on a sort of catharsis which the Serb people of Bosnia shared."[21]

Karadžić's own speech patterns reveal that at times he conceived of himself and the Serb *narod* as one and the same. He veered between speaking of the Serb *narod* in the third person singular and referring to himself and the Serb *narod* collectively as 'we,' as if he and the Serb *narod* were identical:

> *The Serb narod* around Sarajevo, as you know, will not be defeated. [...] *We* never allowed forces from Central Bosnia to connect with the forces in Sarajevo [...][22]
>
> (emphasis added)

By shifting seamlessly from 'the Serb narod' to 'we,' Karadžić subtly suggested a oneness among himself, his listeners, and the Serb *narod*, a oneness that would prove useful when he called for war or praised Serbs for committing war crimes. The animated Serb *narod*, as interpreted and represented by Karadžić, implored each individual to carry out his or her organic role as an integral part of a robust, energetic entity. With the sacrifice and dedication of each individual, the Serb *narod* would realize its destiny and create a single, unified Serb-governed state free of the influence of non-Serbs.

The suffering narod

As part of their prolific cultural production, national activists typically develop historical narratives that transform selected historical episodes into powerful metaphors for the *narod's* virtues. For Serbs in Bosnia, their *narod's* poignant experiences in the Second World War encoded into a powerful metaphor for suffering. The Ustasha, a group of fascists who ruled Bosnia and Croatia on behalf of the German and Italian occupiers, became metaphorically the generic oppressor of Serbs, South Slavs who betrayed them in exchange for the benefits of serving for stronger powers to the west. The organized Ustasha killing of hundreds of thousands of Serbs became a metaphor for the *narod's* agony throughout history; its suffering took so many lives and reached such depths that its agony amounted to "genocide."

On 28 March 1992, three days before Serb paramilitaries launched armed assaults on Eastern Bosnian towns, national activists from Serbia and Bosnia convened as the "Congress of Serb Intellectuals" at the Holiday Inn in Sarajevo.[23] At this congress, professors and researchers from Serbia and Bosnia attested in detail to past Serb suffering, particularly in the Second World War, and took their listeners to the precipice of preemptive war by linking past suffering with the imminent threats to the *narod's* further existence. Milorad Ekmečić, a highly respected Serb professor of history at the University of Sarajevo, told those present that Serbs had suffered more than almost any other *narod*. "The historical right of Serbs is great [...] because in the history of the world only the Jews have paid a higher price for their freedom than Serbs," he declared. "Serbs bear the invisible brand of the struggle for biological existence."[24] To politically conscious Bosnian Serbs, such inflammatory descriptions of past genocides became incentives to launch a preemptive war to preserve the Serb *narod* as a biological community.

A genocidal narod?

In addition to valorizing their nation's positive qualities, Bosnian Serb leaders actively discouraged the use of 'genocide' to characterize Serb actions against those of other *narods*. Serb activists hoped the Croat *narod* would be perceived as genocidal, but they campaigned against the idea that Serbs could commit genocide. They argued that Serbs, by their very biological makeup, were incapable of committing genocide. The Croat *narod*, on the other hand, whom they conceived as 'genocidal,' were congenitally predisposed to committing genocide whenever circumstances permitted.

Bosnian Serbs sought to ban in their assembly any mention of Serb *genocide* against others. By controlling the assembly's agenda and applying peer pressure whenever a delegate crossed the lexical line, assembly leaders quashed mention of possible genocide by Serbs. In examining the transcripts of 44 searchable assembly sessions from October 1991 to December 1995, I found that delegates used the word 'genocide' well over 100 times in reference to genocide committed by others against Serbs, but in only two instances did a delegate voice the word 'genocide' in reference to acts committed by Serbs against Croats or Muslims.

To deflect allegations of international negotiators that Serbs were committing genocide, Karadžić and other SDS leaders transferred the allegation to claim that Serbs were the real victims of genocide carried out by Croats and Muslims. In a few judgments at The Hague Tribunal, judges mentioned the Second World War events without characterizing them as justification for Serb deeds in the 1990s. The Serb nationalists' efforts to silence any mention of Serb-committed genocide was a creative and unusual variant of semantic innovation, but it did not succeed. Neither did Serb efforts to justify their own crimes by alleging that those of other *narods* had committed atrocities against them.

Serb land

Land in socialist Bosnia (1945–91) was either 'socially owned' or 'privately owned.' Accounting for 53.26 percent of Bosnia's land as of 1991, socially owned land consisted of natural features such as mountains, rivers, parks and public grazing land, as well as large-scale extraction and production facilities such as factories, transportation infrastructure, and mines. The state, acting on behalf of all Bosnian citizens, held legal title to such lands but delegated to municipalities or enterprises the right to manage them. Individuals of any race, religion, social status or *narod* could own land privately, but a category of *narod*-owned land – territory belonging collectively to a single *narod* – did not exist. Nationalist-minded Serbs, unhappy that they could not claim land for their *narod* using definitions of Yugoslav socialism, formulated several different referents for 'Serb land' in an effort to satisfy their party's growing demand for more territory.

Some Serb national ideologues held expansive notions of 'Serb land' identified with the Great Serbia project, the program to have all Serb lands united in a single state covering much of the territory of socialist Yugoslavia. Vojislav Šešelj, a Bosnian-born Serb, championed a single Serb state that would sprawl from eastern Serbia over all of Bosnia and most of Croatia to the "Karlovac-Ogulin-Karlobag-Virovitica line"[25] far to the west. SDS leaders never officially endorsed such a far-flung notion of Serb land, though many longed in their hearts to join large parts of Bosnia with the Republics of Serbia and Croatia to form Great Serbia.

Expansion by projection

As early as 1971, a few nationally minded Serbs devised an expanded referent for 'Serb land.' Working outward from core properties owned by individual Serbs, they projected Serb collective ownership onto surrounding uninhabited areas classified as 'socially owned.' In August 1993, Vladimir Lukić, the then prime minister of Republika Srpska, explained to the Bosnian Serb Assembly that after the 1971 census, the Military-Geographical Museum invited a few Serb demographers to determine just how much land was owned by Serbs. The demographers, as Lukić explained, employed a generous definition of 'Serb land' as consisting of individual "Serb properties *and* socially owned property in their surroundings."[26] Using this definition, Lukić explained, "we came to the area of 62.5 percent, 63 percent, later on 64 percent, so, we rounded figures and said it was somewhere between 63 and 64 percent [of the territory] that belongs to the Serbs."[27] The claim of 63–64 percent Serb land was conceptually impossible, since 53.26 percent of Bosnia was socially owned and therefore belonged to all.

These semantic acrobatics proved remarkably successful in changing perceptions of Serb land, particularly among outside observers and international diplomats. Serb leaders and activists recited the 64 percent figure repeatedly in internal communications and in public, and most foreigners either adopted a figure of 64 percent or employed an even higher one, essentially conceding that Serbs owned a majority of Bosnian territory despite making up only 33 percent of the population.

Serb demographers in the 1990s turned to semantic innovations to expand further the referent of *Serb land*. In municipalities where the majority of inhabitants declared themselves Serbs in the 1991 census, activists declared the entire municipality to be Serb land, no matter how small the percentage of land owned privately by individual Serbs. By depicting entire municipalities in one color, depending on the *narod* with the most inhabitants, cartographers produced appealing and understandable but oversimplified representations of Bosnia's territory. Since Serbs constituted a demographic majority in many large but sparsely populated municipalities, Serb demographers could claim large blocks of land as belonging to Serbs based on a relatively few widely scattered peasant villages. The resulting maps misleadingly tended to validate the claims of earlier demographers that Serbs owned about two thirds of Bosnia even though they accounted for less than a third of the population. Like those of other *narods*, Serb activists weaponized cartography by choosing the jurisdictional units that magnified their claims to land. Krajisnik captured the value of such an approach in a very few words: "Every Serb has a pistol and a map."[28]

Expansion by regionalization

Serb negotiators found colored maps of the Republic of Bosnia useful in prosecuting their territorial claims. But since the political and military battles for Bosnia in the 1990s were fought one municipality at a time, activists turned to various forms of gerrymandering at the local and regional level. Karadžić stated that their primary objective was to link Serb-inhabited areas by following "the principle of ethnic distribution of peoples, which would be the only proper way."[29] This was transparently a step in the direction of separating the three *narods* that might have been accomplished peacefully had SDA and HDZ leaders concurred, but they did not. Bosniak and some Croat leaders staunchly opposed every Serb effort to divide Bosnia, be it by political agreement or force of arms.

In January 1991, local Serb activists initiated a campaign to bring Serb-inhabited municipalities in northwest Bosnia under a single regional body, the "Community of Municipalities of Bosnian Krajina."[30] As precedent, SDS leaders pointed to the socialist-era 'Community of Municipalities of Banja Luka,' an association of municipalities that facilitated regional economic development. But the SDS-initiated communities of municipalities of the 1990s were intended to extend Serb political authority and obstruct the Bosnian central government's exercise of jurisdiction. Among others, Vojo Kuprešanin, the community's president, unabashedly proclaimed its primary purpose: "The task of the Region of Krajina was to destroy Alija's [Izetbegović] state."[31]

Expansion for strategic security

On 12 May 1992, the Bosnian Serb Assembly codified a new referent for *Serb land* by accepting Karadžić's proposed Six Strategic Goals of the Serb *narod*.[32] The goals departed from previous concepts of Serb land that expanded outward from Serb settlements. They identified a large part of the Republic they believed was required to meet their *narod's* strategic need for a compact, contiguous, resource-rich territory. The goals were sufficiently far-reaching but vague enough to encompass potential future conquests and to accommodate possible Serb losses in territorial exchanges. Karadžić and the assembly solemnly proclaimed the six goals in May 1992 and treated them as mandatory guidelines for all Serbs for the remainder of the war.

The first goal expressed the Serb desire for "separation from the other two *narods*." It affirmed, if somewhat cryptically, that the core purpose of the Bosnian Serb project was to secure a separate, ethnically homogeneous territory ruled by and for Serbs. The goals also made clear that Serb nationalists did not aspire to take over all of Bosnia. They accepted the need to grant to each of the other *narods* a territory of its own, however small it may be.

By May 1992, the map of Serb holdings in Bosnia resembled two bulging saddlebags in Western and Eastern Bosnia, linked by an east-west strip of land along the Sava River called the Posavina (which literally means "along the Sava River"), which the Bosnian Serbs insistently called the "corridor" *(koridor)*. Karadžić described its strategic significance:

> The first strategic goal was separation, not occupation of 60 percent of it. The second strategic goal was to get the land in one piece, inter-connected and we got the corridor, so that was the strategic goal.[33]

The subtle lexical switch from *Posavina* to *corridor* served to underline the narrow strip's indispensability to the Bosnian Serbs. It appears to have made an impression on international peace negotiators and had its desired effect. The war-ending Dayton Agreement awarded the corridor to the Bosnian Serbs, giving them a link between their eastern and western lands and securing unimpeded passage between the Republic of Serbian Krajina (the self-declared Serb stronghold in Croatia) to the west and Republic of Serbia to the east. *Serb land*, as described in the six goals, also included most of Eastern Bosnia (expressed as the elimination of the Drina River as a border with Serbia) (goal three), a substantial portion of the city of Sarajevo (goal five) and an outlet to the sea (goal six).[34]

By elaborating the concept of Serb land as a legal and discursive category in a Serb nationalist frame, activists strengthened the basis for their claim to conquer and govern most of Bosnia.

Slurs: vilifying adversaries

Vilifying one's enemies is a time-honored if dishonorable practice among those seeking to instill hatred and rally their followers to a cause. Following common practice among scholars, I will refer to such pejorative labels as *slurs*. In using slurs, a speaker creates moral distance between one's wicked adversaries and one's virtuous own. Serb leaders had their choice of slurs to employ and encourage among their followers: Many were already in common use among Serbs long before the SDS came to power.

Each slur had unique properties and a history of its own. Many slurs originated as a term of collective self-description for one's own *narod* with a prideful and positive meaning. Sometimes those of rival groups, finding that label to be alien, 'othered' their adversaries by calling them by the same term but with the pejorative implications of a slur. For example, Albanians have for centuries used the signifier *Shiptars* pridefully to refer to themselves and longed for others to call them by that same name with positive connotations. In a 1965 appeal, an Albanian author pleaded that his group be universally recognized '*Shiptars* or Albanians.'[35] But by that time, Serbs had likely recognized *Shiptar* as an alien word and loaded onto it all the loathsome negative stereotypes of a group they considered an adversary.

In 1974, the government of Yugoslavia, to encourage replacing a slur with a neutral descriptive term, ordered official government media to use the Serbo-Croatian term *Albanac* in place of *Shiptar*. For a dozen years thereafter, *Albanac* was used in government documents and official media in Yugoslavia. But after Slobodan Milošević came to power in the Republic of Serbia in 1987, his government reversed the decision and again allowed Albanians to be called *Shiptars*, thereby giving license to Serbs to use the slur publicly and officially. The decision coincided with a full-scale propaganda campaign to vilify the Albanians of Kosovo for allegedly repressing the Serbs who lived there.

In the late 1990s, several Albanian witnesses at the ICTY testified that Serb nationalists had insulted them during the war by calling them 'Shiptars.' In the same spirit, translators and interpreters at the ICTY followed the word *Shiptar* with "pejorative for Albanian" in parentheses. But soon Serb witnesses appeared to claim that, because Albanians themselves used the term *Shiptar* only as a neutral or positive descriptor, the term could not possibly be a slur. The judges temporarily appeared baffled by the apparent contradictions in sworn testimony. Eventually a translator, called as a witness, explained (without using the word) that *Shiptar* was understood differently in two distinct frames. The term was a prideful self-ascription if uttered by an Albanian, but was a slur if spoken by a Serb. Court transcripts show that the issue was definitively clarified by Geoffrey Nice, the prosecutor, with an example: "It is as offensive to use the word *šiptars* by a Serb as it would be for non-Poles to use the word Polaks to and about Polish people, although that is itself a Polish term."[36] There is no indication either in the court transcript or the judgment of whether or not the judges accepted Nice's interpretation.

Thus, the same word can be a term of pride in one national frame but a vicious slur in another. The case of the Albanian–*Shiptar* dichotomy also shows that national activists ineluctably generate new slurs and different meanings for existing ones, just as they create other cultural content. Furthermore, semantic innovations appear to proliferate when an accepted term proves inadequate or inappropriate for its intended purpose. We now turn to examining the history and usage of other slurs in the former Yugoslav space.

Turk

The history of the term *Turk* in Europe goes back to the Middle Ages. Europeans used *Turkish* interchangeably with *Ottoman* as adjectives to identify the empire that invaded and conquered Southeast Europe in the fourteenth century. Both words were appropriately descriptive, since the empire was ruled by the House of Osman (rendered adjectivally as *Osmanli* in BCS and *Ottoman* in English), whose members spoke Turkish as their native language. But from 1453, when the Ottomans conquered Constantinople (now Istanbul) and posed a grave threat to all of Europe, most Europeans framed *Turks* as ferocious, bloodthirsty, decadent and sensually depraved adversaries.[37] The Turk's religion, Islam, came in for particular derision and was disparaged for encouraging Turks to pursue their wars of conquest.

After 230 years of intermittent Ottoman advances into Southeast Europe, a coalition of Christian forces began to reverse the trend by driving Ottoman armies back from the gates of Vienna in 1683. The Ottomans lost territory periodically thereafter, and the *Turk* lost ferocity in the public mind as the Islamic threat receded. Europeans reframed him as an exotic but unthreatening curiosity, much like a colorful museum display of an alien land. The Turk became even kinder and gentler in the mid-1800s as the Ottoman reform movement gave rise in Western Europe to a Turk recognizably European in attire and behavior. Turks appeared in many European operas in supporting roles as colorful and intriguing but harmless entertainers.[38]

While the image of the Turk was becoming benign in Western European, developments in the Balkans were creating two different frames in which he was perceived there. Throughout the nineteenth century, several Balkan *narods* rose in rebellion against the Ottoman Empire to create new independent states of their own. As Muslims they had little sympathy for the emerging Christian Balkan states, but as South Slavs they had come to see themselves as different from other Ottoman subjects. They began to self-identify as 'Turks,' meaning that they practiced the Islamic faith,[39] but in doing so they also distinguished themselves "from 'foreign' Ottoman citizens, whom they viewed pejoratively."[40] In a Muslim Balkan frame, the Bosnian Muslims proudly called themselves *Turks*.

Their Christian neighbors in the Balkans also took to calling the Muslims *Turks*, but they intended it as a slur. As the Serb national movement took root, Serb activists disparaged Slavic-speaking Muslims, believing their forefathers had left Serbdom by converting to Islam and were therefore apostates. But Serb activists also hoped that the 'Turks' would return to the Serb fold by renouncing the Islamic faith and reconverting to Orthodoxy. They used the term 'poturk,' meaning a biological Serb who had converted to Islam, to capture the paradox of a Muslim mortal enemy who could be redeemed through reconversion. Edin Hajdarpašić has proposed the term *(Br)other* to capture the *poturk's* dual qualities (or two frames) as a despised apostate who converted to an alien faith and as a potentially beloved brother and ally.[41]

While most Serbs probably understood the term *poturk*, it was rarely used in everyday discourse, much to the chagrin of devoted Serb activists who valued the term for its distinctiveness and clarity. In 1993, Vojislav Maksimović, Bosnian Serb information minister, complained that many Serbs mistakenly used 'Turk' when they should say 'poturk':

> President Krajišnik is very skilled in conducting these talks with Turks [Turci] and poturks [poturci]. To tell the truth we praise them too much and give them too much importance by calling them Turks by habit although they are actually poturks.[42]

He need not have worried. By semantic conflation in popular use, *Turk* and *Poturk* both referred to a Bosnian Muslim whose ancestors had converted to Islam but could rejoin the Serb *narod* if they converted to Orthodoxy. Maksimović's preference for *poturk* did not win popular acceptance, probably because most speakers saw little to be gained by its use in everyday discourse, but it revealed that some SDA leaders yearned to instill in their followers the notion that the Islamic faith was a superficial conceit for Muslims that they might be persuaded to abandon.

The duality of the Turk's identity in the Balkan frame gave some Christians the idea that they would be justified in using violence against Muslims to force them to reconvert to Orthodoxy. Such violence was described in detail in the epic poem *The Mountain Wreath* penned by the Montenegrin ruler and writer Petar Petrović Njegoš in 1847. In Njegoš's story, Serbs in Montenegro rounded up local Muslim chieftains, threatened them with torture and death if they did not convert, and slaughtered them *en masse* after they refused. Some have interpreted Njegoš's tale as approval for Serbs either to force Muslims to renounce their faith or to slaughter them if they declined.

Delegates in the Bosnian Serb Assembly of the 1990s followed Njegoš in expressing their contempt for "Turks," as summarized by assembly president Momčilo Krajišnik:

> The Assembly has taken the position that the Muslims are a communist creation and a religious group of Turkish orientation. [...] They are unbelievers, a *narod* that is not a *narod*, that, a *narod* that would like to be a *narod* but has no arguments for being a *narod*.[43]

Some particularly heinous acts committed during the Bosnian war appear to have been inspired by the wish of Serbs to forcibly reconvert Bosnian Muslims to Orthodoxy. Subjected daily to their leaders' shrill contempt for Muslims, their faith and their identity, some Serbs in the 1990s engaged in ritual reconversions of Muslim prisoners of war by forcing them to sing Serbian songs. In some cases, guards committed symbolic reconversions against the dead as well as the living, by carving crosses in their skin and mutilating the bodies of Muslims they had killed. These acts ceremonially desecrated their Muslim faith, leaving them (in Serb eyes) stripped of their superficial Muslim identity and nakedly Serb.

Many Bosnian Muslims conceived these desecrations as further proof that genocide was being perpetrated against them, and they longed for an international court ruling to validate their claim of being victims of the 'crime of crimes.' Whatever the specific motivations behind them, the atrocities and symbolic reconversions speak to the leaders' need to instill contempt among Serbs for the Bosnian Muslims and for the Islamic faith.

Begotten of the Turk: clones and cognates

By 1990, *Turk*, in its Balkan frame, referred to a multitude of negative referents that Serb activists wished to ascribe to the Bosnian Muslim *narod*. But as a Muslim witness in the case of the Prosecutor v. Zdravko Tolimir[44] suggested, the gnawing historical ambiguity of the term rendered it less than ideal as a slur. "When they say a Turk, what I could say is that they probably believe that we have some Turk ancestry,"[45] he testified. But *Turk* was not the only slur available to malign the Bosnian Muslims. Cognates such as 'balija,' 'Islamic fundamentalists' and 'Mujahedeen' proliferated in public usage among Serbs. The term *Turk*, together with its several synonyms, entered the 1990s as so threatening as to justify violence against a Muslim.

Balija, a word of Arabic origin, first appeared in Bosnia as the given name of a male Muslim.[46] Perhaps because it was pronounced similarly to the South Slavic word *balav* (slimy, wet-nosed), it had become a slur by the nineteenth century. It referred to the most primitive and destitute Muslim peasants, with a connotation similar to *lout*. Elite Muslims as well as Orthodox and Catholics used the term pejoratively for Muslim peasants, suggesting that the term demeaned Muslim peasants because of their occupation and class as well as their religion. *Balija* was more insulting than *Turk*, according to the Bosnian Muslim witness at the ICTY cited above: "If someone calls you 'balija,' it means that you are the lowest of the low and that that person does not see you as a human being, or anything positive, for that matter."[47]

According to the ICTY's website index of testimony and documents, *balija* was used 763 times in court proceedings, while *Turk* appeared 806 times.[48] (Those numbers should be regarded as rough approximations owing to variations in spelling in court documents.) Anecdotally, it appears from snippets in the ICTY index that *balija* was most frequently used by Serb soldiers while torturing Bosnian Muslim prisoners, often accompanied with "f… your *balija* mothers" or similar expressions. That suggests that the slur *balija* was a genderized term with implications of sexual sadism as well as class and religious hatred. In contrast, Serbs of all classes and occupations used *Turk* in a wide variety of situations. *Balija* was the most demeaning slur of all, often spoken or shouted at defenseless Muslims as they faced imminent death or great bodily harm.

At the beginning of the 1940s, Ustasha was the signifier for a small group of Croatian fascists invited by German and Italian occupiers to govern all of Bosnia and most of Croatia. But the term became slippery after the Ustasha came to power. A small number of Bosnian Muslims joined the movement or went to work for the Ustasha-run Independent State of Croatia, so the Ustasha referent broadened to include Croats and Bosnian Muslims. During the war, German officers organized an all-Muslim brigade, the Handžar (sword) Division, that committed atrocities against Serbs. Serbs thereafter identified both Croats and Bosnian Muslims as Ustasha.

In the 1990s, Serbs used *Ustasha* as a slur against Croats, but after the war in Croatia temporarily ended in 1991, Serbs saw the Bosnian Muslims as their primary adversaries and used the term *Ustasha* to refer to both Croats and Bosnian Muslims. The term *Ustasha* became even less appropriate in late 1992 when Croats cautiously began cooperating with Serb forces in an informal alliance. In everyday usage, Serbs preferred to use slurs that referred only to Muslims, often highlighting their Islamic faith and associating them with Islamic fundamentalism in Middle East.

The words *Islamic fundamentalists* rolled effortlessly off the tongues of both Serb and Croat national activists, among whom Karadžić was the most effective proponent. As noted below in the discussion of 'Green Transversal,' Serb activists worked relentlessly to persuade international players that the Bosnian Muslims were under the influence of fanatical fundamentalists from Middle East. They adopted the *fundamentalist* signifier in part because international diplomats and journalists would instantly think of militant fundamentalists in Middle East. By adopting this universally understood signifier, Serbs and Croats managed to bring some disrepute on the Bosnian Muslims. Several widely read English-language books, published mainly after the war, painted Bosnian Muslims as threats to civilization in the same category as Al-Qaeda, Daesh and the Taliban.

Mujahedeen, a signifier for Islamic volunteers who had joined other Islamic fighters in Algeria, was rightly and logically assigned to the several thousand volunteers who began entering Bosnia in 1993 to join the Army of the Republic of Bosnia and Herzegovina (ARBiH) in fighting Serb and Croat forces in rural areas. Not surprisingly, Serb and Croat activists generalized its referent to include all Muslim combatants in Bosnia, including the many native Muslims who themselves objected to the presence of the foreign Muslim warriors. Although most foreigners knew better, Serb and Croat activists persuaded some journalists and publicists to adopt the term as a synonym for the ARBiH or even for all Bosnian Muslims, whether in uniform or not. By generalizing the referent of this and other terms, the Bosnian Serb activists helped stoke Islamophobia throughout the region.

The Green Transversal

The signifier 'Green Transversal' (*Zelena transverzala*, also translated into English as Green Transverse, Green Corridor or Green Belt) came into widespread use in Sarajevo in the 1980s. While planning infrastructure changes in advance of the 1984 Winter Olympics, the city's political leaders proposed to establish a north-south ecologically protected greenbelt on the city's near west side. They envisioned the greenbelt stretching from the Skenderija Sports Center (completed in 1969) at its southern end,[49] to another sports complex to be built several hundred meters to the north. The new sports stadium was called 'Zetra,' a portmanteau containing the first two letters of the Serbo-Croatian word for 'green' (ZElena) and the first three letters of 'transversal' (TRAnsverzala). Zetra was completed in time for the Olympics, but the Green Transversal remained no more than a proposal on the drawing board.

Nothing came of the Green Transversal after the Olympics ended. Sarajevans' hopes for a green corridor were dashed by a crippling economic crisis that beset Yugoslavia in the 1980s, and the unrealized project gradually faded from their aspirations. But to their dismay, within a few years Serb national activists co-opted the name and transformed it into a trope that sullied Bosnia and the Bosnian Muslims by suggesting that Muslims had controlled the process of planning a Green Transversal and selected the color green. One Serb nationalist ideologue later claimed that the Olympic Committee had been "dominated by Bosnian Muslim members of the Communist Party,"[50] who had deliberately chosen 'Green' for the corridor because it was the globally acknowledged color of Islam. That claim was false: Only one Muslim served on the multiethnic five-member Olympic Organizing Committee.[51]

In the Serb amplification of its referent, the Green Transversal became a corridor through which Islamic countries in Middle East conveyed arms, people and toxic Islamic fundamentalism to the Bosnian Muslims. The alleged corridor followed an imagined route from Western Bosnia through the Eastern Balkans to an undesignated terminus in Middle East that even Serb activists could not agree on. General Ratko Mladić claimed that the transversal went "all the way to the Great Wall of China."[52] Srđa Trifković defined it in 2009 as extending from northwestern Bosnia only to eastern Turkey, well to the west of locations favored by other writers. Such differing viewpoints reveal the many different meanings that can emerge as national movements prolifically generate new cultural forms.

In the fertile imaginations of Serb nationalists, the Green Transversal evoked many exaggerations, myths and fantasies. Mladić falsely believed that the military operations of Bosnian government forces were intended to secure that part of the corridor within Bosnia. Others claimed that the corridor was obstructing the unification of Serb states. Karadžić emphasized the strategic dangers posed by the Green Transversal. "The Drina is of great strategic importance, [...] if the Green Transversal is cut off at the Drina, Muslim Bosnia will lose in importance," he stated.[53]

Despite their euphoric proclamations of the myth, a few Serb activists recognized that the Green Transversal was marred by internal inconsistencies and sheer impracticality. Muslim settlements that supposedly made up the corridor were not geographically contiguous. To link them, Serb cartographers drew maps of the transversal using sweeping elliptical arrows to suggest that goods and ideology leapt from one cluster of Muslim inhabitants to the next. The concept was so unrealistic that in the early twenty-first century its proponents conceded that the corridor was only aspirational, the "long-term goal of Islamic ideologues [...] to create a geographically continuous chain of majority Muslim or Muslim-dominated polities [...]."[54]

Despite the logical inconsistencies in the Green Transversal myth, Serb activists deployed it with considerable success to induce fears of Islamic fundamentalism among non-Muslims. The myth outlived the wars that had given rise to it. Initially embraced principally by Serb and Croat nationalists, the transversal myth has been made into a metonym for Islamic fundamentalism's most despicable qualities. It has been elaborated in books, articles and blogs by Orientalist and Islamophobic ideologues in many countries, many of them admirers of Samuel Huntington's book, *The Clash of Civilizations*.[55] The benevolent ecological ideal of leafy urban parks traversed by nature-loving Sarajevans was hijacked and transplanted to the Serb nationalist imaginary as an intercontinental threat to Serbdom and a *casus belli* for war against Islam.

Conclusion

Semantic innovations were an important element in the Bosnian Serb political and cultural efflorescence in the 1990s. The originality and range of semantic innovations reveal activists' unrelenting commitment to forge a new nationalist discourse to replace the class-oriented lexicon of communism. Semantic innovations reveal that Bosnian Serbs frequently expanded their ambitions while still observing certain externally imposed constraints, such as the need to allocate some of Bosnia to non-Serbs. These innovations are vivid evidence of the Serb *narod's* ever-expanding ambitions and of its leaders' ingenuity in vilifying their adversaries.

National activists employed many different variants of semantic innovation. They purposefully mutated, conflated and elided signifiers. They revived long-forgotten signifiers as slurs to vilify adversaries and adopted new referents as adversaries changed. And they used semantic co-optation to link their adversaries with movements considered odious elsewhere on the globe. But acceptance of any given innovation depended not on its originality and cleverness but on whether it appealed intuitively to its intended audience and was consistent with other traits the audience already believed to typify the 'other.'

With some important exceptions, jurists at the ICTY learned little about semantic innovations and thus were denied the insights they might yield. In accordance with the fact that many jurists are inclined to follow the doctrine of 'plain meaning' and lean toward the judicial variant of literalism, jurists at the ICTY were not predisposed to raise questions about mutations in signifiers and referents. But judges at the Rwanda Tribunal proved receptive to explanations of an effective expert witness and found they had considerable probative value. Prosecutors of future complex war crimes cases should consider calling linguistic expert witnesses in addition to relying on the work of court translators and interpreters. Omission of linguistic evidence robbed the triers of fact at the ICTY of relevant evidence that might have affected their judgments on the guilt or innocence of the accused.

Notes

1 S. Lupo, *History of the Mafia*, translated by A. Shugaar, New York, NY: Columbia University Press, 2009, p. 1.

2 J. Saramago, *The History of the Siege of Lisbon*, translated by G. Pontiero, New York, NY: Harcourt Brace, 1996, p. 17.

3 E. Elias-Bursać, *Translating Evidence and Interpreting Testimony at a War Crimes Tribunal: Working in a Tug-of-War*, New York, NY: Palgrave McMillan, 2015, pp. 130–161.

4 The Prosecutor vs. Jean-Paul Akayesu, Judgment, Case No. ICTR-96-4-T, 2 September 1998, para. 146. See also M. Ruzindana, 'The Challenges of Understanding Kinyarwanda Key Terms Used to Instigate the 1994 Genocide in Rwanda,' in P. Dojčinović (ed.), *Propaganda, War Crimes Trials, and International Law: From Speakers' Corner to War Crimes*, Abingdon, New York, NY: Routledge, 2012, pp. 145–169.

5 S. Arnautović, *Izbori u Bosni i Hercegovini; Analiza izbornog procesa*, Sarajevo: Promocult, 1996, pp. 90–92, 103–127; and N. Anđelić, *Bosnia-Herzegovina: The End of a Legacy*, London: Frank Cass, 2003, pp. 159–171.

6 Neither English term adequately captures the immanence and cultural prolificity inherent in the word *narod* in the South Slavic original, so I will continue to use *narod* for the singular form while using *narods* for the plural and *national* or *nationalistic* for the word's adjectival form.

7 B. Anderson, *Imagined Communities: Reflections on the Origin and Spread of Nationalism*, Revised Edition, London: Verso, 1998, pp. 5–7. E.J. Hobsbawm and T. Ranger (eds), *The Invention of Tradition*, Cambridge: Cambridge University Press, 1983. R. Brubaker, *Ethnicity without Groups*, Cambridge, MA: Harvard University Press, 2006, p. 11. R. Brubaker, *Nationalism Reframed: Nationhood and the National Question in the New Europe*, Cambridge: Cambridge University Press, 1996, pp. 13–14, especially fn. 4. E. Gellner, *Nations and Nationalism*, Ithaca, NY: Cornell University Press, 1983, pp. 124–125.

8 E. Hajdarpašić, *Whose Bosnia? Nationalism and Political Imagination in the Balkans, 1840–1914*, Ithaca, NY: Cornell University Press, 2015, pp. 2–3.

9 V. Crapanzano, *Serving the Word: Literalism in America from the Pulpit to the Bench*, New York, NY: New Press, 2000.
10 M. Silverstein, 'Shifters, Linguistic Categories, and Cultural Description,' in K.H. Basso and H.A. Selby (eds), *Meaning in Anthropology*, Albuquerque, NM: University of New Mexico Press, 1976. B. Urciuoli, 'Strategic Deployable Shifters in College Marketing, or Just What Do They Mean by "Skills" and "Leadership" and "Multiculturalism"?' Online. Available HTTP: <http://language-culture.binghamton.edu/symposia/6/index.html> (accessed 18 December 2018).
11 M. Grdešić, 'Serbia's Anti-Bureaucratic Revolution as Manipulation? A Cultural Alternative to the Elite-Centric Approach,' *Comparative Studies in Society and History*, vol. 58, no. 3, 2016, pp. 774–803.
12 E. Goffman, *Frame Analysis: An Essay on the Organization of Experience*, Cambridge, MA: Harvard University Press, 1974. T. Scheff, 'The Structure of Context: Deciphering *Frame Analysis*.' Online. Available HTTP: <http://www.soc.ucsb.edu/faculty/scheff/main.php?id=43.html> (accessed 7 April 2013).
13 The ICTY's translation services section adopted 'BCS' as a pragmatic solution to trial-related ethnonational disputes about its appropriate name. Elias-Bursać, *Translating Evidence*, pp. 67–68.
14 R. Alexander, *Bosnian, Croatian, Serbian: A Grammar with Sociolinguistic Commentary*, Madison, WI: University of Wisconsin Press, 2006, p. 379.
15 Prosecutor v. Radovan Karadžić, Trial Judgment, Volume I of IV, Case No. IT-95-5/18-T, 24 March 2016, para. 50, fn. 113, exhibit no. D00086 [hereinafter Karadžić TJ]. Bosnian Serb Assembly [hereinafter BSA], 4th Session, 21 December 1991, Aleksa Buha.
16 Prosecutor v. Milomir Stakić, Judgment, Case No. IT-97-24-T, exhibit no. 12 A.
17 Karadžić TJ, exhibit no. D00088, para. 78, fn. 200, para. 86, fn. 219, 220. Karadžić, exhibit no. P01370, p. 83.
18 Karadžić TJ, exhibit no. P01385, para. 2747, fn. 9110, paras 2766–2767, fn. 9167–9170, para. 2768, fn. 9173–9174, para. 2768, fn. 9175. Karadžić, "The Muslims Tend to Consider Yugoslavs as Muslims, Even the Croats Consider the Yugoslavs as Croats," p. 117.
19 Karadžić TJ, exhibit no. P01350, para. 78, fn. 200.
20 The Prosecutor of the Tribunal Against Slobodan Milošević, Case No. IT-02-54-T, exhibit no. P613.
21 M. Toholj, 'O osnivanju SDS i…,' in Lj. Bulatović, *Radovan*, Belgrade: Evro, 2002, p. 116.
22 Karadžić TJ, exhibit no. D00092, paras 2786–2791, fn. 9218–9230.
23 *Oslobođenje*, 29 March 1992, p. 2. See also R.J. Donia, *Radovan Karadžić: Architect of the Bosnian Genocide*, New York, NY: Cambridge University Press, 2015, p. 184.
24 Ibid.
25 P. Dojčinović, 'The Shifting Status of Grand Narratives in War Crimes Trials and International Law: History and Politics in the Courtroom,' in D. Zarkov and M. Glasius (eds), *Narratives of Justice In and Out of the Courtroom: Former Yugoslavia and Beyond*, Heidelberg: Springer, 2014, pp. 70, 73–75.
26 Karadžić TJ, exhibit no. P01379, para. 83, fn. 213.
27 Ibid.
28 Karadžić TJ, exhibit no. D00089, para. 53, fn. 120.
29 R.J. Donia (ed.), *From the Republika Srpska Assembly, 1991–1996: Excerpts from Delegates' Speeches as Body of Evidence for the International Criminal Tribunal at The Hague*, Sarajevo, Tuzla: University Press, 2012, excerpt 48, pp. 136–137.
30 Donia, *Radovan Karadžić*, pp. 76–84.
31 Donia, *From the Republika Srpska Assembly*, excerpt 183, pp. 134–137.
32 Ibid., excerpt 48, pp. 52–55.

33 Karadžić TJ, exhibit no. P01385, para. 2747, fn. 9110, paras 2766–2767, fn. 9167–9170, para. 2768, fn. 9173–9174, para. 2768, fn. 9175.
34 Karadžić TJ, exhibit no. P00956, P00955, para. 57, fn. 127–128, 'Decision on Strategic Objectives of the Serbian People in Bosnia and Herzegovina.'
35 H. Hodža, 'National Renaissance of Shiptars (Albanians) in the Socialist Federal Republic of Yugoslavia. Statement Made to the United Nations Human Rights Seminar on Multi-National Society,' manuscript in author's possession.
36 Elias-Bursać, *Translating Evidence*, p. 157.
37 A.N. St. Clair, *The Image of the Turk in Europe*, New York, NY: Metropolitan Museum of Art, 1973.
38 L. Wolff, *The Singing Turk: Ottoman Power and Operatic Emotions on the European Stage from the Siege of Vienna to the Age of Napoleon*, Palo Alto, CA: Stanford University Press, 2016.
39 M. Imamović, *Pravni položaj i unutrašnjo-politički razvitak Bosne i Hercegovine od 1878. do 1914*, Second Edition, Sarajevo: Bosanski kulturni centar, 1997, p. 127. Arhiv Bosne i Hercegovine, Präsidial Index, Austria-Hungary Joint Ministry of Finance, 390/PrBH 1896. 'Abschrift eines Berichtes des Bezirksamtes Livno vom 8. April 1896 nro. 144.' A Livno Muslim told a local Austro-Hungarian official, "I am a Turk because I accepted my former name Mujo and pray in the mosque but no more in the church."
40 H. Grandits, *Multikonfesionalna Hercegovina: vlast i lojalnost u kasnoosmanskom društvu*, Sarajevo: Institut za istoriju, 2014, p. 79. First published as *Herrschaft und Loyalität in der spätosmanischen Gesselschaft: Das Beispeil der multikonfessionallen Herzegovina*, Wien: Bohlau, 2008.
41 Hajdarpašić, *Whose Bosnia?*, p. 80.
42 Karadžić TJ, exhibit no. P01388, paras 166–167, fn. 448, 451.
43 Donia, *From the Republika Srpska Assembly*, excerpt 26, pp. 40–41.
44 Prosecutor v. Zdravko Tolimir, Case No. IT-05-88/2.
45 Prosecutor v. Zdravko Tolimir, Trial Judgment, Case No. IT-05-88/2-T, 12 December 2012, para. 179, fn. 641, para. 186, fn. 668, para. 240, fn. 929–930, 932, 934, para. 315, fn. 1372, para. 315, fn. 1374, witness Osman Salkić, 22 November 2010 [hereinafter Tolimir TJ].
46 A. Škaljić, *Turcizmi u srpsko-hrvatskom jeziku* (Turcisms in Serbo-Croatian Language), Sarajevo: Svjetlost, 1973, p. 118.
47 Tolimir TJ, testimony of Osman Salkić, 22 November 2010, para. 863, fn. 3443.
48 Online. Available HTTP: <http://www.icty.org/en/search-results?as_q=balija> (accessed 11 September 2018).
49 R.J. Donia, *Sarajevo: A Biography*, London: Hurst and Co., and Ann Arbor, MI: University of Michigan Press, 2006, p. 234.
50 S. Trifković, 'U.S. Policy and the Geopolitics of Jihad: The Green Corridor in the Balkans.' Online. Available HTTP: <http://gatesofvienna.blogspot.com/2009/05/green-corridor-in-balkans.html#readfurther> (accessed 10 June 2019).
51 'The XIVth Olympic Winter Games, Sarajevo 1984, The Members of the Organizing Committee.' Online. Available HTTP: <http://library.la84.org/OlympicInformationCenter/OlympicReview/1981/ore170/ORE170p.pdf> (accessed 30 August 2018).
52 J. Jančić, *Srpski General Ratko Mladić*, Novi Sad: Matica Srpska, 1996, p. 99.
53 Karadžić TJ, exhibit no. D00092, para. 2787, fn. 9225.
54 Trifković, 'U.S. Policy and the Geopolitics of Jihad.'
55 S.P. Huntington, *The Clash of Civilizations and the Remaking of World Order*, New York, NY: Simon and Schuster, 1996.

Chapter 8

In the mind of the crime

Proving the *mens rea* of genocidal intent in the words of Ratko Mladić and other members of the joint criminal enterprise*

Predrag Dojčinović

The words of genocide: an ontological preliminary

This chapter may as well start with a sweeping statement. Unlike some other crimes, the ontology of all mass atrocity crimes is ultimately decided in and by words. That is why the key to understanding the evidentiary complexities of genocide and its central cognitive initiator intent should begin at its conceptual, linguistic foundations. Genocidal intent, *dolus specialis* or 'specific intent,' resides in the internal world of the individual mind. As the requisite element of 'the crime of crimes,' genocidal intent can be classified as internal emergent property of the mind. Evidence of genocidal intent should, consequently, always be sought in the external world of its manifestations, the "acoustic blasts,"[1] or speech acts, the "minimal units of linguistic communication."[2] A single speech act can be evidence of genocidal intent.

The Genocidal Intent Project: purpose and objectives

In 2012, a special team of researchers and analysts of the Office of the Prosecutor (OTP) at the International Criminal Tribunal for the former Yugoslavia (ICTY), under the supervision of this author, undertook a special project defined primarily within the scope of the two genocide charges brought against the Bosnian Serb General Ratko Mladić.[3] The principal objective of the project was to identify,

* I would like to express my extraordinary gratitude to Nadan Hadžić, a linguist and a former researcher on the OTP-ICTY special projects team, for his work and comments without which parts of this chapter could not have been written. Also, from 2017 to 2019, I had a unique opportunity to give a series of lectures and seminars dealing with some of the themes included in this chapter. I have benefited greatly from the insights offered to me on these occasions by the scholars and students of the Princeton Institute for International and Regional Studies at Princeton University, the School of Law at the University of Greenwich, the Faculty of Humanities at the University of Oslo, the Department of Justice Studies at Montclair State University and the School of Law at the University of Connecticut.

analyze, categorize and contextualize the evidence on the prosecution exhibit list[4] relating to the elements of genocidal intent emerging from the speech acts[5] of Ratko Mladić and other members of the joint criminal enterprise (JCE).[6]

The project initially relied on the context and evidence-based knowledge of an OTP team of researchers and analysts acquired in the course of the investigations conducted in other JCE-related cases, as well as on the preliminary pre-trial investigative, research and analytical, projects in the Mladić case, which indicated that the speech acts of the Accused carried content expressing both *direct* and *indirect* forms of genocidal intent. The prosecution believed that the value of such evidence would be of critical importance for the final determination of Mladić's *mens rea* and the degree of his culpability, relevant to the counts of genocide and persecution charged in Articles 1, 2 and 8 of the Indictment.[7] Moreover, the linkage between Mladić's *mens rea* captured in his speech acts and the evidence emerging from the crime-base witnesses, both *viva voce* and written witness submissions,[8] as well as from all other categories and sources of evidence, would become more explicit. Most importantly, as envisaged by the project outline, such a concentrated body of evidence would not allow, neither qualitatively nor quantitatively, for the inferences of Mladić's genocidal intent to be drawn exclusively from the physical circumstances of the crimes. In other words, the mind of the Accused, as the central location where the physical crimes were initially conceived and intended, was placed at the epicenter of the *mens rea* required for the proof of genocidal intent.

Due to the inherent nature of the mental element of *mens rea*, including its derivative of genocidal or special intent,[9] the temporal and spatial criteria of the project were not limited to the time-period (from at least October 1991 until 30 November 1995) and locations covered by the Indictment. As a result, given the contextual, temporal factors present in the historical records relating to the speech crime components in international criminal trials,[10] this element of the project additionally relied on the jurisprudence addressing the temporal aspects of *mens rea*, such as the related reasoning found in the most recently developed International Criminal Tribunal for Rwanda (ICTR)[11] and ICTY case law.[12] The Mladić Genocidal Intent Project [hereinafter MGIP] analysis thus sought to identify all speech acts relevant within the scope of the prosecutorial interest, as captured by its comprehensive list of exhibits. The secondary objective of the project, as part of its JCE component, was the identification of the speech acts of the key JCE members (e.g., Radovan Karadžić, Momčilo Krajišnik, Radoslav Brđanin and others), including the JCE 'tools,'[13] expressing the same or similar cognitive forms and degrees of genocidal intent.

The methodology and procedure: from linguistics to law

The research and analysis team created the search criteria in the form of key words and phrases, or speech acts,[14] which carried the content of both *direct* and *indirect* semantic indications of and references to 'the deliberate and systematic destruction, in whole or in part' of the specific groups identified in the Genocide Convention,[15] as well as specific references to the various forms of discrimination on political, racial, national, ethnic, cultural, religious, gender and other grounds, including hate speech[16] and calls for violence,[17] directed against the non-Serb population in Bosnia and Herzegovina (BiH). The purpose of the search criteria was to identify all forms of genocidal intent residing in the most comprehensive selection of the specific speech acts or utterances.

The initial cluster of words and phrases, selected and searched for, is shown in the following example: *Turci* (Turks, a derogatory term referring to Bosnian Muslims); *poturice* (a convert to Islam, connoting also a renegade and a traitor); *Ustaše* (also spelled in English as Ustashas or Ustashe, a Croatian Second World War extreme nationalist military organization which committed mass atrocities against Serbs, Jews, Roma, political adversaries and other groups); *balija* (a derogatory term for a simple and ignorant Muslim peasant; a Muslim in general)[18]; *tući, tucite* (to beat; to pound at); *Dahije* (Dahis, Turkish word referring to janissary officers who seized power in Serbia in 1801; a violent person)[19]; *džamahirija* (Jamahiriya, 'state of the masses,' a uniquely Islamic system of governing introduced in Libya by Muammar al-Gaddafi); *čišćenje* (cleaning; cleansing; mopping up; sweeping); *handžar* (a short sword carried by Ottoman law enforcement agents during the Ottoman reign in the region; also reference to the 'Handžar Division,' a Second World War pro-Nazi military formation composed of predominantly local Muslim combatants); *osveta* (revenge, retribution, reprisal, retaliation); *džihad* (Jihad, the spiritual struggle for and within Islam; the physical struggle and/or war against the enemies of Islam); *kama* (a Turkish curved knife associated by the Serbs with Ustashas) and dozens of other words and phrases.

Direct and *indirect* semantic references: the meaning and definition

As earlier indicated, the list of key words and phrases were divided into a list with *direct* and *indirect* semantic references at the outset. The word 'references' denoted references to the semantic content of the key words and phrases, that is, utterances or speech acts, indicative of the mental element of special intent.

The central analytical premise of the MGIP was based on the idea that the cognitive, linguistic and, most importantly, related legal concept of *intent* is placed on the *intentional use* and *actionability* of the specific words and phrases by the speaker.[20] In other words, the choice and the use of speech acts by the speaker acting under the psychological conditions generally recognized as reasonable are virtually always by and within itself *intentional* and *volitional.*

The meaning of direct semantic references[21]

The content of the category of *direct semantic references* can essentially be determined and interpreted in a twofold manner. One is the directness of the semantic content of the message communicated to the intended recipient. The second indicates that direct semantic references are closely related to or derived from the crime of 'direct and public incitement to commit genocide.'[22] While the first meaning suggests a semantic universality and translatability of the speech acts, that is, the common conceptual grounds for all parties involved, the second meaning clearly indicates that some of the speech acts may have been communicated on public occasions, such as political and military conventions, or rallies, media appearances or similar events, which would have regularly resulted in threatening or otherwise direct messages indicating genocidal intent.[23] Other related evidence may have been recorded as part of intercepted telephone conversations, audio and video recordings, minutes from closed meetings, personal diaries, as well as other types of documents or artifacts. As an illustration, some of the direct semantic references used by Mladić were conveyed through speech acts such as *destroy*, *vanish*, *extinguish* and *disappear*,[24] all of them contextually unambiguous references to the intended fate of the non-Serb population, and most frequently the Muslims of BiH.

It should be noted, however, that the element of 'directness' in Mladić's and JCE members' speech acts was more often than not concealed behind a wide range of culture-specific and "standardized coded language,"[25] or figures of speech, such as metaphors, metonymies or euphemisms. In other words, the 'directness' of such speech acts can be found in their implicit content and meanings as *directly* understood by the intended audiences.[26] As a fact firmly established in the ICTR's jurisprudence and case law,[27] the MGIP followed a corresponding line of reasoning and deliberation as found in the relevant ICTR judgments. The consequence of such jurisprudential records relating primarily to 'direct and public incitement to commit genocide' is that a number of specific speech acts, such as *Turks*, *balijas* and *Ustashas*, both key elements of the emerging speech patterns identified by the research team, can be, and indeed were, under the specific conditions, understood as *direct* by the native speakers. This key aspect of their semantic content, or their 'directness' as perceived and possibly acted on by the native speakers, that is, their actionability, required additional corroboration in the *viva voce* and documentary evidence, introduced through both expert and fact witnesses equally. This approach was adopted and proven successful in various international criminal trials, such as the ones tried before the International Military Tribunal (IMT)[28] and ICTR.[29]

The meaning of indirect semantic references[30]

The category of *indirect semantic references*, on the other hand, can initially be interpreted within the scope of derogatory hate speech, or inflammatory and discriminatory speech acts. This broad definition places emphasis on the genocidal intent of specific speech acts with a manifestly emotional, intentional and propagandistic content. The 'indirectness' of indirect semantic references can first and foremost be found in the implicit content of 'coded' and semantically culture-determined messages circulated through the JCE network of associates or co-conspirators, as part of their standard mode of communication. The 'indirectness' of these types of speech acts most frequently stems from metaphorical, metonymical, idiomatic or euphemistic expressions. The first judgment issued by the ICTR in 1996 in the Akayesu case stated that "the direct element of incitement should be viewed in the light of its cultural and linguistic content. A particular speech may be perceived as 'direct' in one country, and not so in another, depending on the audience."[31]

In the evidence found by the prosecution, Mladić repeatedly used the following, both historically and culturally determined, 'indirect' references to the Muslim and Croat civilians and combatants: *Turks*, *Ustashas* (often uttered as conceptual blends,[32] such as *Ustasha dragon*, *Islamic hordes* and *Muslim Ustashas*), *poturice*, and many other terms. Other JCE members used the same or similar speech acts, particularly in combination with terms such as *Turks* and *Ustashas*. Along these lines, it has been established that genocide is indeed a crime based on the "depersonalization of the victim,"[33] indicating that individuals are, or can be, first 'identified' by particular names, or labels, and then, as a matter of generalization, pigeonholed as members of the group recognized by that same name. As part of the process of labeling, a cognitive process of intentional conversion of an individual or a group from a subject to an object occurs. Consequently, the true identity of the targeted individuals and/or groups, otherwise identifiable only through official personal records, becomes irrelevant. The analysis of the prosecution's research team offered strong indications that this was indeed the manner in which Mladić and other JCE members used the derogatory terms *Turks* or *Ustashas*.[34] For Mladić and other JCE members, the Muslim civilian population and BiH forces were 'Turks,' whereas the Croat civilian population and the Croat forces, including occasionally Muslims, were 'Ustashas.' In other words, the critical difference between the enemy forces as potentially legitimate targets on the one hand and the civilians on the other hand ceased to exist. The semantic labels eventually became the shooting targets.

Hybrid of direct/indirect *semantic references*

As part of the analytical process, a third category of speech references has emerged, that is, 'direct/indirect' references as a symbiotic extension of the two previously defined basic semantic types of references. Ambiguous speech acts that could not be clearly defined into one of the other two categories were placed into this category. Examples of 'direct/indirect' references include, among others, the following speech acts: *liberating*, *cleansing* and *genocide*. Mladić and other JCE members regularly used the concept of *liberation* as a euphemism for the conquest of territories that could neither administratively nor ethnically belong to the Bosnian Serbs. With its multiple meanings, the fluid polysemic concept of *čišćenje*, suggesting the process of cleaning, cleansing, mopping up or sweeping,[35] was more often than not a matter of debate between the parties in various trials, including Mladić's. The concept of *genocide* was frequently used by Mladić and other JCE members as a historical reference to the genocidal acts committed against the Serbs by the Croats and Muslims during the Second World War. This usage was propagandistic and its basic intention was to warn and consequently mobilize Serbs to fight against another allegedly imminent "genocide." In the ICTR jurisprudence, such usage became known as the 'accusation in a mirror.'[36] At the same time, Mladić demonstrated a full *knowledge* and *awareness* of the potentially genocidal acts, as planned and ultimately executed within the Bosnian Serb political and military structures against the non-Serbs of Bosnia and Herzegovina.[37]

The central place in the constellation of concepts constituting an offense of special intent was reserved for the specific speech acts uttered by Mladić. The corroboration of a guilty mind was sought in the relationship, or along the lines of a causal (e.g., orders, directives and similar speech acts) and non-causal nexus (e.g., speech acts demonstrating collective intentionality, such as shared intent or shared objectives, common plan or common purpose), between the speech acts and *other* physical acts[38] of the Accused[39] and other members of the JCE. Individual speech acts, as much as speech act patterns, played a crucial role within the totality of evidence determining the relevance and probative value of each (special) intent-related exhibit identified by the prosecution.

The speech act patterns in the MGIP emerged as a particularly strong and persuasive type of cumulative evidence. The recurring use of words such as *Turks* and *Ustashas* by Mladić and other JCE members belong to this type of evidence. Apart from forming patterns, through their consistent use in military and political documents, such evidence manifested itself as a strong contributing factor in creating the context for the subsequent interplay between those speech acts and other physical acts, that is, the commission of the physical crimes, within an increasingly extended context.[40] In other words, by sharing specific speech acts and related patterns, as the evidence indicated, some of the JCE members undeniably shared at least part of the same *common plan* and *purpose* and, ultimately, the same genocidal intent.[41] In brief, the specifics of their speech acts exposed the specifics of their special intent.

Construal, contextualization and status of culture-determined speech acts indicating genocidal intent

As part of the earlier outlined methodology and procedure, the prosecution research and analysis team construed and contextualized each selected speech act identified as a meaning, or set of meanings, linguistically, historically, culturally and politically specific to the region. Mladić's and JCE members' references to the Bosnian Muslims and their identity stand out in this context. Some of the following examples played a key role in determining the forms and faces of specific intent in the Mladić case and other related JCE cases.

Poturica

The use of the term *poturica* (a convert to Islam, connoting also a renegade and a traitor) by the Serbs belongs to the category of derogatory or pejorative references to the Muslims of BiH. Its historical meaning is derived from the period under the Ottoman Empire, when a number of Slavs, mainly Christians (Serbs and Croats), converted to Islam. The best known use of the word *poturica* (singular of *poturice*) in Montenegrin and Serbian culture is recorded in the epic poem *The Mountain Wreath* by Petar II Petrović Njegoš from 1847. This poem is considered to be the most influential work of literature in Montenegrin and Serbian literary tradition. The poem's main theme is a struggle against the Ottoman rule and, more specifically, the *poturice* themselves. The poem also relates to a historically uncorroborated event known as *istraga poturica*, which can be translated in its archaic form as 'annihilation' (or extermination, or eradication) of the converts to Islam, that is, *poturice*. ICTY trial records contain numerous references to this particular epic poem. Mladić used the term *poturice* in a 1993 interview at a time when his subordinates were actively involved in committing mass atrocity crimes against Bosnian Muslims:

> We all know who the Turks are. As a matter of fact, these Muslims are not even Turks, they are converts [*poturice* in the original]. They have betrayed the Serb people and repressed them for 500 years. They are the worst scum – the Serb people who changed their religion. To change a religion means to betray one's own people, to betray oneself.[42]

The Mladić Trial Chamber (TC) correctly but inadequately considered this term to imply merely a discriminatory intent.[43] Such simplistic classification could, for example, be decisive in shifting and relegating the characterization of an act with specific intent from the crime of genocide to persecution as a crime against humanity. On one occasion, in the trial of Radovan Karadžić, both the Accused, the former Bosnian Serb president, and a defense witness made multiple explicit references to *The Mountain Wreath*. The prosecution seized the moment during the cross-examination and, having read a transcript of large parts of the poem to the court, asked whether the witness was reminded of "the fact that this poem celebrates the killing of Muslims, the destruction of their homes, and destruction of their mosques?"[44] On this occasion, the prosecution clearly sought to establish the elements of genocidal intent of the Accused.

It should be emphasized again that Radovan Karadžić and Ratko Mladić were both members of the same JCE. The fact that they used the same, or similar, language can be regarded as relevant in establishing the type and degree of *mens rea* and, more specifically, genocidal intent required within the framework of their two virtually identical indictments.

Balija

Another term frequently used by the Bosnian Serb political and military leadership is *balija*, a strong derogatory reference to a simple and ignorant Muslim peasant, a Muslim in general.[45] The prosecution research and analysis team has, however, extended the explanation of the bare meaning of the term to a meaning with broader context-dependent semantic resonances in the minds of the native speakers.[46] The new description indicated that the term *balija* is one of the most derogatory terms for Muslims used by non-Muslims. Originally, the Turkish word *balija* was used in the Muslim community to denote a simple, rude, indecent, uneducated and wretched person. Commonly, when used within the Muslim community, the word was used by urban, city-dwelling Muslims to denote those from rural areas. In ethnology, the name is also used for an ethnic group of Muslims from a certain region of Herzegovina. In modern, colloquial use the term invariably has a pejorative meaning, particularly strong when used by non-Muslims.

"In fact, *balija* is such an offensive word that non-Muslim defendants have generally avoided using it in the courtroom," or, as shown in the testimony of the Bosnian Serb General Radislav Krstić,[47] "have even denied ever using it," writes Ellen Elias-Bursać, a scholar and former ICTY translator.[48] Indicted for genocide, crimes against humanity and violations of the laws and customs of war, Krstić was considered to be the prosecution's seminal case on genocidal intent. During the trial, the prosecution presented evidence that "General Krstić and his superiors also manifested genocidal intent by using inflammatory rhetoric and racist statements that presented the VRS (Army of Republika Srpska) as defending the Serbian people from a threat of genocide posed by 'Ustasha-Muslim hordes.'"[49] Shifting the attention from the complex historical, political and military conceptual blend between the 'Ustashas' and the 'Muslims,' the defense strategically argued that only *direct* references or "calling for killings" could qualify as an expression of genocidal intent.[50] Although the TC was satisfied as to the existence of the requisite genocidal intent, the Appeals Chamber (AC) took a different view. It accepted the TC's conclusion that "charged language is commonplace amongst military personnel during war," but inferred therefrom that "no weight can be placed upon Radislav Krstić's use of derogatory language in establishing his genocidal intent."[51] While confirming that genocide had occurred, the AC found that Krstić did not have the requisite genocidal intent for commission and convicted him only of aiding and abetting.

The first reason for the prosecution's failure to prove the existence of genocidal intent in Krstić's use of primarily *indirect* derogatory semantic references to their intended victims, the Bosnian Muslims in and around Srebrenica, was that it did not employ a cognitive linguistic expert witness to explain the meaning, gravity and impact of these types of speech acts on the perpetrators.[52] Second, it did not specifically and persuasively argue the culture-specific genocidal *mens rea* component of the case. The prosecution simply overlooked the fact that the crime of genocide can only be conceived and intended in the mind of the perpetrator evidenced through the use of his language. The Krstić case illustrates an intellectual and legal failure by both the prosecution and the appeal judges to appreciate the key ontological principle of the crime of genocide embodied in its inchoate nature. The crime of genocide could not and would not have occurred in Srebrenica and other Bosnian municipalities without its cognitive, linguistic blueprint.

Dahija

The historical concept of *Dahias*, another pejorative term used by Mladić and other Bosnian Serbs as a reference to the present-day Bosnian Muslims, denotes leaders of the Ottoman Empire units led by the Janissaries (forcibly recruited young men mainly from the non-Turkish population; they were recruited to serve in the military; some of them were initially outlaws, but later all Christians could be recruited as Janissaries). As the first step toward independence from the Ottoman Empire, present-day Serbs, including the general population, still glorify a historical event called the Uprising against the Dahias from 1804.

One of the most telling examples of this veneration is the television footage showing General Ratko Mladić after the takeover of the Bosnian town of Srebrenica in July 1995. While making his way into the town, Mladić is recorded as saying,

> Here we are on 11 July 1995 in Serbian Srebrenica. On the eve of one more great Serbian holiday [Saint Peter and Paul, one of Serbian Orthodox Patron Saints Days, celebrated on July 12 every year], we present this town to the Serbian people. After the rebellion against the *Dahis*, the moment has finally come for us to take *revenge* on the *Turks* here.[53]
>
> (emphasis added)

It should be emphasized that the reference to the Serbian 'uprising against the Dahis' (Serbo-Croatian: *buna protiv Dahija*) has traditionally been, and still remains, part of the Serbian elementary school curriculum. It is also a commonly accepted phrase used by local speakers to express revolt against anything perceived as pronouncedly hostile and oppressive. Evocation of this historical event therefore has particularly strong historical and emotional resonance among the thus cognitively conditioned Serbs. In other words, this phenomenon can, by and of itself, be used and construed as a *direct* and unambiguous call for action. On this occasion, Mladić intentionally conveyed a set of historically, politically and culturally coded, but meaningful, messages to his audience.

Turk

The noun *Turk*, as used by the non-Muslim population of BiH, and particularly Serbs, is one of the oldest and most commonly employed strong derogatory references to the Bosnian Muslims. This term can be regarded as a single token containing the resonances of all other strong pejorative anti-Muslim concepts, such as *balija* or *poturica*. The word *Turk* has been the common denominator of all genocidal and persecutory speech acts emerging from the ICTY's Bosnian Serb trials. In the Mladić trial, the prosecution explained the meaning of this term through the *viva voce* testimony of the historian Robert Donia, a fluent speaker of the local language. Here is how the expert witness contextualized this word for the TC:

> [...] in the course of the 20th century, and possibly even a little bit before, it ["Turk"] began to be used by those peoples who had lived under the Ottoman Empire pejoratively to describe the empire that they regarded as having oppressed them in the 19th century and before. So that by the time the – let's say the elections of 1990 came along, the term "Turk" had acquired severe pejorative connotations and Bosnian Serbs and Bosnian Croats began to use it to refer to the Muslims of Bosnia-Herzegovina, and that then brought with it the negative connotations of the Ottoman Empire's behaviour toward other peoples and also associated the term with, broadly speaking, Turkish ambitions which they believed existed in the region.[54]

Having thus provided an abridged historical account of the semantic evolution of the term in the region, Donia concluded that during the relevant period it was "a pejorative term that implied enemy, an enemy that posed a direct and immediate threat to the very existence of the Serb people."[55] The key to this explanation is indeed offered in the suggested link between the repeated, and therefore *intentional*, use of the term *Turk* by Mladić, and his military and political associates, and the connotations suggested by the expert witness.

Ustaša

Last but not least, one of the strongest historically determined expressions of contempt, fear and hatred, directed particularly at the Croats, can be found in the multiple utilization of the term *Ustaša* (Ustasha). For operational reasons, the prosecution's research and analysis team in the Mladić trial adopted the definition of this term as defined by Mark Thompson, the prosecution expert on propaganda in the ICTY's trial of Momčilo Krajišnik. Having historically contextualized the semantic range and impact of the term in the region, in his book *Forging War*, Thompson concluded the following: "Since 1990 or earlier, the term and its cognates (ustašoid, ustašism) have been widely used in Serbia to describe all Croat nationalists."[56]

As correctly noted by Thompson, this term was used to 'describe all Croat nationalists,' but also all Croat forces and, more often than not, all Croat civilians throughout the region. The research and analysis team showed that Mladić and other JCE members used the term as a reference to both the enemy forces and civilians of Croat ethnic origin, occasionally incorporating the Muslims of Bosnia into the particular wording. From the records stored by the research and analysis team, the prosecution ultimately utilized a selected number of speech acts referring to the 'Ustashas,' such as Mladić's references to "[…] Ustasha and Islamic hordes which have, for decades, in secret and from within the bosom of our people, been preparing its extermination,"[57] and characterized the VRS as protecting Serbs "from the Nazi-Ustasha and fundamentalist genocide and enslavement."[58] These two exhibits offer the examples of a complex historical, political and military conceptual blend between the *Ustashas* and *Muslims*, as implied by Mladić in his references to the 'Islamic hordes' and the 'fundamentalist genocide and enslavement.' Coming from someone in a position of authority, that is, the Commander of the Bosnian Serbs forces himself, this type of *mens rea* evidence can be assessed as a strong contribution to the creation of a context and atmosphere required for the commission of crimes 'with intent to destroy, in whole or in part, a national, ethnical, racial or religious group.'

Introducing speech acts as evidence of genocidal and persecutory intent

On 7 May 2013, based on the research and analytical work recorded in the MGIP database, the prosecution initially tendered a selected number of 30 exhibits through a bar table motion (BTA).[59] The general purpose of the motion was to demonstrate (i) patterns of speech reflective of Mladić's *mens rea* and (ii) relevant connections between Mladić's utterances reflective of his *mens rea* and the crimes committed by Serb forces under his command.

The motion introduced evidence of Mladić's and JCE members' speech acts containing *direct*, *indirect* and hybrid of *direct/indirect* semantic references to genocidal and persecutory intent.[60] On many occasions, as argued by the prosecution,[61] Mladić *directly* expressed his intent by explicitly calling for the destruction of non-Serbs through speech acts such as 'destroy,' 'vanish,' 'extinguish,' 'disappear,' but also through extended utterances such as those related to the early siege of Sarajevo, "[W]henever I come by Sarajevo, I kill someone in passing. That's why the traffic for Sarajevo was disrupted […] snipers. I go, kick the hell out of the Turks, who gives a fuck for them!"[62]

The prosecution further argued that the connection between the use of derogatory and violent terms and both genocidal and persecutory intent has been broadly recognized in the ICTY and ICTR jurisprudence. In the case of Zdravko Tolimir, who was Mladić's Assistant Commander for Intelligence and Security, as part of the discussion relating to the requisite element of genocidal intent, the judgment referred to a "pattern of verbal abuse on account of affiliation with the Islamic faith inflicted by Bosnian Serb Forces on the Bosnian Muslims," such as the Bosnian Serbs' use of the term *balija*, when they commanded or threatened Bosnian Muslims.[63] In the case of Milomir Stakić, president of the Serb-controlled Prijedor Municipality Crisis Staff and head of the Municipal Council for National Defence in Prijedor in 1992, the trial judgment considered the humiliation and degradation of non-Serbs by members of Serb forces in finding persecutory intent, including Stakić's use of derogatory terms such as *Ustaša* and *balija*.[64] In the ICTR case of Sylvestre Gacumbitsi, the TC held that "the use of derogatory language toward members of the targeted group"[65] can give rise to an inference of genocidal intent.

The exhibits tendered by the prosecution included both derogatory language and utterances which were *directly* linked to the campaigns of persecution, ethnic cleansing and genocide in Srebrenica, the campaign of terror against Sarajevo and other municipalities listed in the indictment. The *mens rea* and the *actus reus* were approached and defined as separate and yet clearly linked elements of genocide and crimes against humanity charged in the Mladić indictment.

Apart from documentary evidence (e.g., media interviews, public and private speeches, video and audio recordings, intercepted radio and telephone conversations, Mladić's notebooks, political and military documents), the prosecution team designed a generic set of questions for both prosecution and defense witnesses. The responses from both categories of witnesses created the required linkage evidence between the genocidal *mens rea* and the *actus reus* of the two genocide charges brought against Mladić. This set the pace of a steadily growing cumulative pattern of evidence demonstrating the existence of Mladić's genocidal intent. In his *viva voce* testimony, for example, the first prosecution witness repeatedly referred to the language used by the perpetrators, all members of the Overarching JCE[66]:

> [...] they were screaming and yelling, Oh, we got the *balijas*. [...] she grabbed me and pulled me on the ground and had a knife. She put it on my neck. She said, Let me kill one *balija* [...][67]
>
> (emphasis added)

The same testimonial pattern, including the corroborative documentary evidence, repeated itself in numerous other cases throughout the Mladić trial. In virtually all instances, the perpetrators used specific slurs and derogatory speech acts as the victim group signifiers and identifiers before, during and after committing the physical act of the crime. In other words, the essential elements of *mens rea* and *actus reus* received an adequate evidentiary description and indication of the causal feedback loop from the mental to the physical component of the crime. The victims in this and numerous other cases were clearly targeted *because* they were 'balijas.' Given the number of recorded situations, this body of evidence created sufficiently strong grounds for the prosecution to argue its case in relation to both genocide charges and for the TC to draw the clear inferences of the existence of both *direct* and *indirect* semantic forms of genocidal intent originating from Mladić and other JCE members.

Ultimately, following the trail of evidence recorded in its MGIP database, the prosecution persuasively argued during the 98 bis submission[68] that the linguistically analyzed evidence demonstrated the existence of genocidal intent in the speech acts of Mladić and other JCE members:

> Both *direct* and *indirect* evidence provide a sufficient basis for a reasonable chamber to conclude that the accused and other JCE members intended to physically destroy the groups. […] Mladić stated his intent with respect to Bosnian Muslims in 1994 at the 37th Assembly session. […] He said: "My concern is not that they will create a state. My concern is to have them *vanish* completely." […] Mladić brought and endorsed a lexicon of derogatory terms and eliminationist rhetoric when referring to the targeted peoples in Bosnia. […] His use of the terms "Ustasha" and "Turks" was directed at enemy forces but also civilians.[69]
>
> (emphasis added)

The prosecution's closing brief, the trial judgment and genocidal intent: a summary review and conclusions[70]

In its Closing Brief, following the totality of the *mens rea* and linguistically generated categories of evidence, the prosecution argued that Mladić "depicted Muslims and Croats *generally* as the VRS' enemies"[71] (emphasis added). This clearly indicated that Mladić's utterances referring to the targeted groups of non-Serbs often did not distinguish between the enemy combatants and the civilians. The prosecution further offered a long litany of evidence with discriminatory, both direct and indirect, semantic references to the Muslims and Croats in BiH as well as throughout the region.[72] In the section of the Closing Brief titled 'The Crimes Within the Common Purpose Included Genocidal Acts Committed with Genocidal Intent,' the prosecution argued that the hitherto enumerated circumstances

> […] reflect the convergence of thousands upon thousands of genocidal acts with the requisite genocidal intent. This intent is revealed both by a concerted attack on the very foundation and fabric of the group through acts prohibited under the Genocide Convention and other culpable acts, as well as by *direct evidence of intent found in the statements* of Mladić, Karadžić and other members of the JCE.[73] […] it most clearly illuminates the application of the Genocide Convention and Article 4 to the acts of Mladić's forces and, *coupled with the statements* of Mladić and other JCE members, the accompanying *intent.*[74]
>
> (emphasis added)

In the section titled '*Mens Rea* of Genocide: The Intent to Destroy,' the prosecution correctly stated that "The intent to destroy does not have to be realized to any particular degree or level. It is the intent to destroy which is the 'key factor' – not the result."[75] This argument clearly indicated the relevance of the crime as conceived and intended in the mind of the perpetrator and not necessarily the physical execution of the crime. The concept of intent was pertinently placed at the epicenter of a cognitive process logically untying and not automatically linking the *mens rea* and the *actus reus* as two legally detachable elements of a crime.

In the section 'Direct Expressions of Genocidal Intent'[76] the prosecution somewhat weakened its strong linguistically generated *mens rea* evidence and once again shifted its full attention to the physical facts on the ground. This line of reasoning is best exemplified through the following statement: "Although even one killing coupled with genocidal intent would suffice to establish genocide, in Prijedor, the number of killings was massive."[77] As a matter of law, however, the inchoate nature of the crime of genocide, as defined by the Genocide Convention,[78] does not require a single physical crime for the prosecution of genocide. In theory, the only and most basic requirement is, or can be, a single speech act as the sole physical evidence of genocidal intent.[79]

In the Conclusion of the Trial Judgment, the judges summarized the linguistic component of the genocidal *mens rea* evidence and its relationship with the physical crimes as follows:

> While the statements and speeches [...] were inflammatory, caused fear, and incited ethnic hatred against their war-time enemy, the TC must consider whether they demonstrated intent to destroy either of the protected groups. Considering the disparate dates, meetings, and purposes of the speeches and statements, the TC is careful not to combine them to give a semblance of a *collective intent* to destroy where no such collective intent existed or to read individual *statements and speeches in isolation and without context.* [...] The TC considers that the speeches and statements could have been directed to the *military enemy* and have been used as *propaganda*, rather than to demonstrate an expression of a genocidal intent. [...] In that regard frequent references to 'ethnic cleansing' and other similar expressions by Karadžić, Krajišnik, and others do not necessarily indicate intent to physically destroy the protected group. In this respect, the TC notes for example that during the 16th Session of the Bosnian-Serb Assembly, Mladić used the word 'eliminate,' but added 'either temporarily or permanently.' The *rhetorical speeches and statements* assisted in the task of ethnic separation and division rather than the physical destruction of the protected groups.[80] [...] *having assessed the entire trial record*, including the statements, speeches, and conduct of Mladić and the Bosnian-Serb leadership as well as the prohibited and other culpable acts committed by the physical perpetrators, the TC is

> not satisfied that the only reasonable inference that can be drawn from the evidence is that the crime of genocide formed part of the objective of the Overarching JCE.[81]
>
> (emphasis added)

In its summary conclusion, the TC makes a series of unduly erroneous and inaccurate statements. First, by addressing the concept of 'collective intent' to destroy, the TC ignored the fact that, as demonstrated by the voluminous evidence submitted by the prosecution, the language shared by Mladić and other JCE members overwhelmingly evidenced *common goals* and *shared objectives* with 'intent to destroy, in whole or in part, a national, ethnical, racial or religious group, as such.' When a group of speakers share the same language, if in general agreement, they usually share the same intentional stance.[82] Individuals and groups "in pursuance of a policy,"[83] who share the same common plan and purpose, the same goal or objective, generally share the same criminal plan. The evidence in the Mladić trial showed that the JCE members recurrently and consistently used the same or synonymous words and phrases, or speech acts, to design and define their shared common plan to destroy the non-Serb population in BiH. Second, Mladić's and JCE members' 'statements and speeches' were not offered 'in isolation or without context,' as stated in the TC's reasoning. All of the statements, both *direct* and *indirect*, semantically referred either to the specific crime base, including political and military plans, or the 'national, ethnical, racial or religious groups,' or both within the same speech act, as earlier specified in this chapter. Third, the evidence directly and conclusively proves that Mladić's and other JCE members' language targeted both the enemy combatants and the civilian population of non-Serb ethnic origin. Fourth, even if some of Mladić's statements are to be construed as propagandistic, the use of propaganda, as enshrined in international treaties[84] and addressed in recent jurisprudence,[85] can be regarded as a substantial contributing factor to both mental and physical acts of genocidal nature. Fifth, Mladić's speech act records were not merely 'rhetorical speeches and statements,' but unambiguous expressions of a desire and intent to destroy and exterminate the specific non-Serb groups in the crime-based areas charged by the indictment. This was not a set of decontextualized, incoherent ramblings or inner conflicts of the Accused, but a series of consistent, rationalized and self-justified intentional speech acts targeting the specific groups of the non-Serbs in BiH. Virtually all of these speech acts, both statements of discriminatory nature and specific directives and orders, overwhelmingly correspond to the crimes committed in the municipalities charged in the indictment.

The conclusions of the TC addressing the substantiation of genocidal intent through Mladić's and JCE members' statements can therefore be described as grossly incomplete, inaccurate and erroneous in terms of factual and related legal findings. They indicate the intellectual and legal failure of the judges to comprehend and assess the gravity of the meanings and implications of the overwhelming amount of linguistically relevant genocidal *mens rea* evidence. It is a firm conviction of this author that future research and analysis of the existing trial record will show a considerable level of factual, legal and intellectual misinterpretation introduced by the Mladić TC into the branch of case law and jurisprudence addressing genocidal intent in international criminal trials.

Notes

1 J.R. Searle, *Speech Acts: An Essay in the Philosophy of Language*, Cambridge: Cambridge University Press, 1969, p. 3.
2 Ibid., p. 16.
3 Online. Available HTTP: <http://www.icty.org/case/Mladić/4> (accessed 25 January 2019).
4 The initial prosecution exhibit list contained approximately 35,000 exhibits of all categories amounting to several hundred thousand pages of original evidence.
5 The concept of 'speech acts' is used as originally explained in Searle, *Speech Acts.*
6 Prosecutor v. Duško Tadić, Appeal Judgment, Case No. IT-94-1, 15 July 1999, para. 226. For more on JCE, see Prosecutor v. Radoslav Brđanin, Appeal Judgment, Case No. IT-99-36-A, 3 April 2007, paras 363–364.
7 Online. Available HTTP: <http://www.icty.org/x/cases/Mladić/ind/en/111216.pdf> (accessed 25 January 2019).
8 ICTY Rules 92 *bis*, 92 *ter* and 92 *quarter*, Rules of Procedure and Evidence, 8 July 2015.
9 W.A. Schabas, *Genocide in International Law*, Second Edition, Cambridge: Cambridge University Press, 2009, pp. 260–287. R. Cryer, H. Friman, D. Robinson and E. Wilmshurst (eds), *International Criminal Law and Procedure*, Third Edition, Cambridge: Cambridge University Press, 2014, pp. 220–228. M.E. Badar, *The Concept of Mens Rea in International Criminal Law: The Case for a Unified Approach*, Oxford, Portland, OR: Hart Publishing, 2013, pp. 299–302.
10 The IMT records indicate that numerous admitted exhibits are dated years and sometimes decades prior to the crimes charged in the Indictment. Similar examples can be found in the ICTR and ICTY records (e.g., Akayesu, Case No. ICTR-96-4, Nahimana et al., Case No. ICTR-99-52, and Šešelj, Case No. IT-03-67).
11 Ferdinand Nahimana, Jean-Bosco Barayagwiza, Hassan Ngeze v. The Prosecutor, Judgment, Case No. ICTR-99-52-A, 28 November 2007, Partly Dissenting Opinion of Judge Shahabuddeen, para. 25: "Influence is a function of the processes of time" [hereinafter Nahimana et al. AJ].
12 "The Trial Chamber notes that while the incident in June 1993 is *outside the temporal scope* in which prohibited act were alleged to have occurred, [...] prohibited acts were *relevant considerations for their specific intent*" (emphasis added). The Prosecutor v. Ratko Mladić, Judgment, Volume 3, Case No. IT-09-92-T, 22 November 2017, para. 3461, fn. 13365 [hereinafter Mladić TJ].
13 'Tools' are individuals who may have carried out the *actus reus* itself.
14 J.L. Austin, *How to Do Things with Words*, Cambridge, MA: Harvard University Press, 1962. Searle, *Speech Acts*, and J.R. Searle, *Mind, Language and Society: Philosophy in the Real World*, London: Phoenix, 1999.
15 Online. Available HTTP: <https://www.ohchr.org/en/professionalinterest/pages/crimeofgenocide.aspx> (accessed 26 January 2019).
16 Nahimana et al. AJ, paras 692–693, 697, 986–987, and Prosecutor v. Vojislav Šešelj, Appeal Judgment, Case No. MICT-16-99-A, 11 April 2018, paras 159, 163.

17 Cryer et al., *International Criminal Law*, p. 258.
18 *Rečnik srpskohrvatskoga književnog jezika*, Novi Sad, Zagreb: Matica Srpska, Matica Hrvatska, 1967, p. 133.
19 *Rečnik*, p. 621.
20 J.R. Searle, 'The Intentionality of Intention and Action,' *Cognitive Science*, vol. 4, no. 1, 1980, pp. 47–70.
21 This definition originates from P. Dojčinović, 'The Chameleon of *Mens Rea* and the Shifting Guises of Culture-Specific Genocidal Intent in International Criminal Proceedings,' *Journal of Human Rights*, vol. 15, no. 4, 2016, pp. 454–476.
22 Article III (c), Convention on the Prevention and Punishment of the Crime of Genocide.
23 W. Timmermann and W.A. Schabas, 'Incitement to Genocide,' in P. Behrens and R. Henham (eds), *Elements of Genocide*, London, New York, NY: Routledge, 2013, pp. 155–156.
24 See Prosecutor v. Ratko Mladić, Case No. IT-09-92-T [hereinafter Mladić Case], Prosecution Motion to Admit Evidence from The Bar Table: Mladić's Statements Indicating Genocidal and Persecutory Intent, 7 May 2013, and Mladić Case, Decision on Prosecution Motion for Admission of Documents from the Bar Table, 19 July 2013. See also Mladić Case, Decision on Prosecution Motion for Admission of Documents from The Bar Table, 19 July 2013.
25 International Court of Justice, Reports of Judgments, Advisory Opinions and Orders, Case Concerning Application of the Convention on the Prevention and Punishment of the Crime of Genocide (Bosnia and Herzegovina v. Serbia and Montenegro) Judgment of 26 February 2007, p. 124.
26 "[…] even implicit messages or utterances may amount to incitement, as long as the addressees immediately grasp the implications of the message in light of its cultural and linguistic content." A. Cassese, *International Criminal Law*, Second Edition, Oxford: Oxford University Press, 2008, p. 229. See also The Prosecutor Versus Jean-Paul Akayesu, Judgement, Case No. ICTR-96-4-T, 2 September 1998, para. 558 [hereinafter Akayesu TJ]. The Prosecutor v. Juvénal Kajelijeli, Judgment, Case No. ICTR-98-44A-T, 1 December 2003, para. 853 [hereinafter Kajelijeli TJ], and Prosecutor v. Ferdinand Nahimana, Jean-Bosco Barayagwiza, Hassan Ngeze, Case No. ICTR-99-52-T, Trial Chamber Judgment, 3 December 2003, paras 1004–1006 [hereinafter Nahimana et al. TJ].
27 Nahimana et al. AJ, para. 527. Sylvestre Gacumbitsi v. The Prosecutor, Judgment, Case No. ICTR-2001-64-A, 7 July 2006, para. 43 [hereinafter Gacumbitsi AJ]. Kajelijeli TJ, para. 531.
28 See, for example, the case of Julius Streicher. Online. Available HTTP: <http://avalon.law.yale.edu/imt/judstrei.asp> (accessed 29 January 2019).
29 See, for example, Akayesu TJ, and Nahimana et al. TJ.
30 Dojčinović, 'The Chameleon of *Mens Rea*,' pp. 454–476.
31 As quoted in Schabas, *Genocide*, p. 331. See also Akayesu TJ, para. 556. As noted by Schabas, see also The Prosecutor v. Simon Bikindi, ICTR-01-72-T, Judgment, 2 December 2008 [hereinafter Bikindi TJ], Decision on Defence Motion for Judgment of Acquittal, Rule 98 bis of the Rules of Procedure and Evidence, 26 June 2007, para. 29.
32 P. Dojčinović, 'A Mouthful of Crimes: Facing the Challenges of Culture-Specific Propaganda as Evidence in International War Crimes Trials,' Princeton University, May 12, 2017. Online. Available HTTP: <https://ssrn.com/abstract=2991038> (accessed 29 January 2019).
33 A. Cassese, 'The Subjective Elements,' *International Criminal Law*, Second Edition, Oxford: Oxford University Press, 2008, p. 137.
34 Referring to The Prosecutor v. Clement Kayishema and Obed Ruzindana, Judgment, Case No. ICTR-95-1-A, 1 June 2001 [hereinafter Kayishema AJ], in 'Genocide,'

International Criminal Law, p. 143, Cassese writes: "The utterances of the two defendants were also taken into account (for instance, Tutsis had been called 'cockroaches,' had been referred to as 'dirt' or 'filth') [...]," para. 538.

35 See, for example, the trial discussion regarding the meanings of the polysemic word *čišćenje*, referred to as "cleaning, cleansing, mopping [...]" by the Presiding Judge, in the Prosecutor v Momčilo Krajišnik, ICTY Case No. IT-00-39-T, pp. 9906–9908. Online. Available HTTP: <http://www.icty.org/x/cases/krajisnik/trans/en/050304IT.htm> (accessed 29 January 2019).

36 "[...] a person accuses others of what he or she does or wants to do." Akayesu TJ, para. 99. Nahimana et al. TJ, para. 111.

37 See how the prosecution addressed Mladić's use of the word 'genocide' in May 1992 as cognitive elements of awareness and knowledge. Online. Available HTTP: <http://www.icty.org/x/cases/Mladić/trans/en/130822ED.htm> (accessed 29 January 2019), pp. 15514–15516.

38 This author understands 'speech acts' as physical acts of uttering sounds and meanings, as in Austin, *How to Do Things with Words*, and Searle, *Speech Acts*.

39 The Prosecutor v. Ignace Bagilishema, Judgment, Case No. ICTR-95-1A-T, 7 June 2001, para. 63. Also, The Prosecutor v. Jean de Dieu Kamuhanda, Case No. ICTR-95-54A-T, Judgment, 22 January 2004, para. 626. As quoted in Schabas, *Genocide*, p. 266, fn. 110: "The Chamber is of the opinion that the Accused's intent should be determined, above all, from his words and deeds [...]."

40 For the meaning of 'context' and 'manifest,' see, for example, Article 6(a)(b), Genocide, *Elements of Crimes*. Online. Available HTTP: <https://www.icc-cpi.int/nr/rdonlyres/336923d8-a6ad-40ec-ad7b-45bf9de73d56/0/elementsofcrimeseng.pdf> (accessed 29 January 2019).

41 "[...] the accomplice who knows of the principal offender's intent and who assists or encourages must necessarily share the genocidal intent," Schabas, *Genocide*, p. 302. W.A. Schabas, 'The Jelisić Case and the *Mens Rea* of the Crime of Genocide,' *Leiden Journal of International Law*, vol. 14, no. 1, 2001, pp. 125–139.

42 Prosecutor v. Ratko Mladić, Case No. IT-09-92-PT, 16 December 2001, exhibit no. P07719.

43 Mladić TJ, para. 3275.

44 Prosecutor v. Radovan Karadžić, Case No. IT-95-5/18, exhibit no. P06666.

45 *Rečnik*, p. 133.

46 The author owes the specific explanation of the term 'balija' to Nenad Fišer.

47 Open Session (2000). Online. Available HTTP: <http://www.icty.org/x/cases/krstic/trans/en/001027it.htm> (accessed 25 April 2015).

48 E. Elias-Bursać, *Translating Evidence and Interpreting Testimony at a War Crimes Tribunal: Working in a Tug-of-War*, New York, NY: Palgrave McMillan, 2015, p. 145.

49 Prosecutor v. Radislav Krstić, Judgment, Case No. IT-98-33-T, 2 August 2001, para. 592.

50 Ibid., para. 593.

51 Prosecutor v. Krstić, Appeal Judgment, Case No: IT-98-33-A, 19 April 2004, para. 130 [hereinafter Krstić AJ].

52 Ibid. See also Schabas, *Genocide*, p. 266, fn. 110.

53 Prosecution Opening Statement (2000). Online. Available HTTP: <http://www.ictytranscripts.org/trials/krstic/000313it.htm> (accessed 23 January 2015).

54 Open Session (2013). Online. Available HTTP: <http://www.ictytranscripts.org/trials/Mladić/130822ED.htm> (accessed 23 January 2015).

55 Ibid.

56 M. Thompson, *Forging War*, London: Article 19, 1994, p. 271.

57 Mladić Case, exhibit no. P00359, p. 150.
58 Ibid., exhibit no. P05080.
59 First introduced in The Prosecutor v. Tihomir Blaškić, Judgment, Case No IT-95-14-T, 3 March 2000, para. 35, BTA is a form of written motion which allows parties to seek admission of a large number of exhibits without calling *viva voce* witnesses to comment on the relevant documents.
60 Prosecutor v. Zoran Kupreškić, Mirjan Kupreškić, Vlatko Kupreškić, Drago Josipović, Dragan Papić, Vladimir Šantić aka "Vlado," Judgment, Case No. IT-95-16-T, 14 January 2000, para. 636.
61 This section includes a revised version of the arguments presented in the BTA 'Prosecution Motion to Admit Evidence from The Bar Table: Mladić's Statements Indicating Genocidal and Persecutory Intent,' 7 May 2013.
62 Mladić Case, Notice of Filing of Corrigendum to Updated Public Redacted Version of Prosecution Final Trial Brief, 13 October 2017, paras 154, 229, 635.
63 Prosecutor v. Zdravko Tolimir, Judgment, Case No. IT-05-88/2-T, 12 December 2012, paras 313, 378, 522, 773 [hereinafter Tolimir TJ].
64 Prosecutor v. Milomir Stakić, Judgment, Case No. IT-97-24-T, paras 105, 199, 807–808, 826 [hereinafter Stakić TJ].
65 Gacumbitsi AJ, para. 253. See also Kayishema AJ, para. 93.
66 The Overarching JCE, which existed between 1991 and November 1995, had the objective of permanently removing Bosnian Muslims and Bosnian Croats from Bosnian Serb-claimed territory through the commission of crimes in municipalities throughout BiH.
67 Online. Available HTTP: <http://www.icty.org/x/cases/Mladić/trans/en/120709IT.htm> (accessed 29 January 2019), p. 581.
68 Rule 98 *bis*, ICTY, Rules of Procedure and Evidence, 24 July 2009.
69 Available Online: <http://www.icty.org/x/cases/Mladić/trans/en/140318ED.htm> (accessed 30 January 2019), pp. 20866–20867.
70 At the time of the writing of this chapter, the Appeal Judgment in the trial of Ratko Mladić was still pending.
71 Mladić, Prosecution Closing Brief, paras 226–228.
72 Ibid.
73 Ibid., para. 351.
74 Ibid., para. 352.
75 Ibid., para. 366, pp. 152–153. See also Stakić TJ, para. 522; Krstić AJ, paras 25,32; Tolimir TJ, para. 746; Prosecutor v. Vujadin Popović, Ljubiša Beara, Drago Nikolić, Radivoje Miletić, Vinko Pandurević, Appeal Judgment, Case No.: IT-05-88-A, 30 January 2015, para. 822 [hereinafter Popović et al. AJ]; Prosecutor v. Radoslav Brđanin, Judgment, Case No. IT-99-36-T, 1 September 2004, para. 694. See also Prosecutor v. Slobodan Milošević, 98 *bis* Decision, Case No. IT-02-54-T, para. 124.
76 Mladić, Prosecution Closing Brief, paras 378–382.
77 Mladić, Prosecution Closing Brief, para. 354.
78 The three inchoate offenses listed in the Genocide Convention are conspiracy, direct and public incitement, and attempt to commit genocide. See also E. van Sliedregt, *Individual Criminal Responsibility in International Law*, Oxford: Oxford University Press, 2009, pp. 179–181.
79 "[…] the crime of direct and public incitement to commit genocide is an inchoate offense, punishable even if no act of genocide has resulted therefrom." Nahimana et al. AJ, para. 678.
80 Online. Available HTTP: <http://www.icty.org/x/cases/Mladić/tjug/en/171122-4of5_1.pdf> (accessed 29 January 2019), para. 4235.

81 Ibid., para. 4237.
82 P. Dojčinović, 'The Shifting Status of Grand Narratives in War Crimes Trials and International Law: History and Politics in the Courtroom,' in D. Zarkov and M. Glasius (eds), *Narratives of Justice In and Out of the Courtroom: Former Yugoslavia and Beyond*, Heidelberg: Springer 2014, pp. 72–73.
83 Cassese, *International Criminal Law*, p. 189.
84 Article 20(1)(2) of the International Covenant on Civil and Political Rights (ICCPR). For more, see M.G. Kearney, *The Prohibition of Propaganda for War in International Law*, New York, NY: Oxford University Press, 2007, p. 217. For relevance of the ICCPR in genocide cases, see for example Nahimana et al. TJ, paras 984–991, and Bikindi TJ, paras 380, 384. See also Article 4 of the International Convention on the Elimination of All Forms of Racial Discrimination (CERD), as per reference in Nahimana et al. TJ, para. 985.
85 See Section 'War Propaganda, Misleading Information and Threats,' in Popović et al. AJ, paras 1812–1836. See for example D. Saxon, 'Propaganda as a Crime under International Humanitarian Law: Theories and Strategies for Prosecutors,' pp. 118–141, and M.G. Kearney, 'Propaganda in the Jurisprudence of the International Criminal Tribunal for the Former Yugoslavia,' pp. 231–253, in P. Dojčinović (ed.), *Propaganda, War Crimes Trials and International Law: From Speakers' Corner to War Crimes*, Abingdon, New York, NY: Routledge, 2012.

Chapter 9

The neuroscience of dehumanization and its implications for political violence

Celia Guillard and Lasana T. Harris

Why is it that situations arise in which some people fail to recognize the humanity inherent in their fellow human beings? What factors must collide to permit a person to commit some of the most heinous atrocities in human history? Dehumanization is the failure to recognize another person or group of people as being fully human – to spontaneously neglect to consider the mind of another person.[1] There are both cognitive mechanisms and social conditions that enable dehumanization. Psychological studies and historical examples have repeatedly reaffirmed that that many people are susceptible to this process. In this chapter, we discuss the psychological phenomenon of dehumanized perception and consider the implications for human rights law specifically and legal systems more broadly.

Dehumanization is not always harmful; in certain circumstances, it is a necessary process that can lead to benefits to both the social target and the social perceiver. Dehumanizing targets, to some degree, protects countless individuals including medical professionals, social workers, teachers, therapists and the like from empathy exhaustion (also known as compassion collapse or fatigue, or secondary traumatic stress). Humans naturally suffer from emotional exhaustion when assisting others, and dehumanization is one mechanism of protecting oneself. Even the act of simply anticipating emotional costs can result in individuals being dehumanized.[2]

While dehumanization can occasionally serve a beneficial purpose, at other times it can be extremely harmful. This can occur on a small scale or in larger, systematic acts of violence. Dehumanization is arguably most detrimental when it occurs during conflict in the form of systematic violence perpetrated against a group or groups of people. Violence of this nature is often politically motivated, with the aim of accomplishing a political goal. The most serious mass atrocity crimes, that is, war crimes, crimes against humanity and genocide are frequently the products of political violence. Recent advances in social neuroscience may assist in explaining cognitive mechanisms that facilitate dehumanization and other processes that permit violent behavior.

This chapter examines dehumanization research from a number of perspectives, all while discussing applications of this research for international criminal trials. The chapter first delves into current cognitive neuroscience research to examine brain regions that permit individuals to spontaneously dehumanize out-group members. Second, we evaluate how language shapes perception. Next, we investigate two dueling hypotheses within the dehumanization literature in psychology, before discussing how these two theories conflict, and how they might be combined to provide possible explanations for mass human rights abuses. Then, we review how human rights violations can result in severe psychological trauma for perpetrators, as well as victims. Lastly, we provide a brief summary of current data on political partisanship and how bias arising from this can shape and warp basic cognitive functioning and views of reality.

Brain correlates

Social cognition – inferring the mental state or 'getting into the mind' of another – occurs spontaneously in daily life, and is crucial to comprehend if one wishes to understand how dehumanization occurs. Social cognition is not limited to only human targets; humans can spontaneously infer the mental states of animals and even inanimate objects.[3,4] This mechanism allows us to imagine what other people are thinking and feeling. Several neuroscience studies have identified key brain regions that work in unison to effortlessly facilitate this process. It is possible that these regions disengage during dehumanization to obfuscate the contents of a social target's mind. Although studying war crimes in a laboratory setting would pose significant ethical challenges, there are ways of studying dehumanization and group cognition in an ethical manner, which could reflect actual cognitive patterns present during conflict.

Neuroimaging studies have used functional magnetic resonance imaging (fMRI) to demonstrate activity (or lack thereof) in these brain regions when presented with stereotypical images of various groups of people, including people belonging to routinely dehumanized populations, such as people who use drugs or people who are homeless. When participants were confronted with such images, regions of their brain that would typically become active during social cognition were not engaged, specifically the medial prefrontal cortex (mPFC) – a portion of the prefrontal cortex which, as a whole, is crucial to personality and executive functioning.[5] Similarly, participants exhibited increased activation in other regions, namely, the insula, that are consistent with feelings of disgust. They also demonstrated increased activation in the amygdala – a region that has long been implicated in fear responses.[6] Other experiments demonstrated that participants used far fewer mental-state verbs when imagining a day in a dehumanized person's life, when compared with the other people pictured – indicating less engagement of social cognition. They also rated these individuals lower than other people pictured in terms of competence, similarity, articulateness and intelligence, and, perhaps most troubling, as being less than typically human. These findings suggest that, without even being aware of it, humans are apt to dehumanize certain people and think less about their thoughts, feelings, needs and daily concerns.

Neural correlates of dehumanization are not as simple as the mere reduction in brain activity in social cognition regions. In some instances, dehumanization *increases* activation in certain regions. For instance, another fMRI study examined brain activity when participants evaluated ten categories of high- and low-status social groups, animals and inanimate objects. These researchers found that the inferior frontal cortex (IFC) appears to be involved in making assessments about social status and seems to play a distinct role in blatant dehumanization of animals or low-status groups of humans (Roma, homeless, etc.).[7] It is worth noting that dehumanization is a somewhat flexible mechanism that can be regulated to some degree without the conscious awareness of an individual. For example, players of violent first-person shooter games dehumanize their opponent just prior to killing their avatars, suggesting that it may be possible to humanize and dehumanize the same social target at different times.[8]

Such research demonstrates that dehumanization can affect people to such an extent that their brains do not spontaneously recognize certain individuals as fully human. To the best of the authors' knowledge, studies of this exact nature have not been conducted on populations who have experienced intense conflict, such as genocide, either as perpetrators or victims. It is understandable that such studies could potentially pose ethical or logistical difficulties. It is possible that the same cognitive processes that fail to activate or show heightened activation when confronted with systematically dehumanized populations might exhibit the same pattern during systematized atrocities directed toward a population who has been routinely marginalized within a society over a lengthy period of time. There is hope, however; fortunately, there is evidence of re-humanization. When specifically requested to infer mental states of habitually dehumanized social targets, participants experienced increased activation in two key social cognition regions.[9] Similarly, there is data to suggest that individuals are more likely to *humanize* out-groups after first learning that the out-group views them in humanizing ways.[10] Perhaps methods that employ re-humanization strategies will prove integral to reducing prejudice and preventing future atrocities.

Although not exactly dehumanization, there is neuroimaging evidence to demonstrate that in-groups and out-groups are represented differently in the brain. One study found that when people were arbitrarily divided into teams, with no prior history of social interaction or any association with stereotypes of those team differentiations, their brain activation demonstrated an encoding of group membership that spontaneously reflected differences in activation when considering in-group and out-group members.[11] In contrast, when the researchers tested members of rival political orientations (Republican and Democrat), political affiliation provoked activation in a different series of regions that was distinct from the former arbitrary group divisions. In either case, this research suggests that to some extent humans are wired to perceive the world in terms of 'us' and 'them' when social distinctions arise.

Cognitive bias can influence other players as well; preferred outcomes can inadvertently sway judgment.[12] When confronted with ambiguous stimuli, people are more likely to report observing something "that assigned them to a preferable outcome."[13] In fact, some researchers have gone as far as to state, "people literally are prone to see what they want to see."[14] This becomes especially problematic when compounded with existing implicit bias (stereotypes and assumptions that one holds without conscious awareness of these beliefs). For example, implicit racial bias associating individuals of predominantly African descent with threat can be measured using the weapons identification task (WIT), a task where participants identify pictures of tools or guns after first being primed with faces of individuals of predominantly African or European descent.[15] More biased individuals experience a greater likelihood of misidentifying benign objects as weapons. Additionally troubling, if one already possesses implicit bias, physiological cues from within the body may continue reinforcing this during times of perceived threat. Specifically, this occurs when the primary channel of communication between the heart and brain processes frightening stimuli. When this happens, the brain receives heightened threat signals during a cardiac systole (at the exact moment when the heart beats) and less so during a cardiac diastole (the time between beats). Because of this, researchers found that individuals with racial bias are more likely to experience the sensation of threat during a systole and thereby more likely to misidentify objects as weapons.[16]

This body of research is important because it demonstrates that dehumanization is a spontaneous and involuntary psychological reaction. While not an excuse for atrocities, it is important to be aware that there are underlying biological mechanisms that shape human reactions to the world that are not always fully within voluntary control.

Language matters

Exposure to messages in our environment shapes how we view the world. Frighteningly, the vast majority of this influence occurs without conscious awareness. Messages, such as those in media, can impact beliefs and actions by instilling implicit prejudice. In 1975, psychologist Albert Bandura demonstrated how labeling informs implicit prejudice, both positive and negative. Using key phrases, he primed students either to humanize or dehumanize or view targeted individuals neutrally. Then, students were instructed to punish these targets with electric shocks. Despite never having interacted with the targets prior to the experimental session, and thus having had no opportunity to make their own personal evaluations about these targets, the students exhibited strikingly consistent patterns in how intensely targets were punished. These labels and the implicit prejudice they created dictated the extent to which targets were punished, with the dehumanized targets being shocked with escalating intensity over time.[17]

This pattern was observed in both directions, with humanized targets receiving less punishment than neutral or dehumanized targets. A key finding of Bandura's research is that dehumanizing language enables maltreatment of out-groups because it denies cognition to the target. The assumption is that they are not cognizant enough to perceive mistreatment.[18] Subsequently, Bandura found that humans are more apt to morally justify punishment of individuals who have been dehumanized because they have been assigned lower levels of worth than non-dehumanized individuals.[19]

This is significant because dehumanizing language has far-reaching implications for policies, legal decision-making and shaping public opinion. It can also influence actions and, possibly, provoke atrocities. Substantial psychological research has examined the extent to which dehumanizing phrases can alter perception. This research demonstrates that dehumanizing language may go so far as to alter basic cognitive processes and have real-life consequences. Dehumanizing words and phrases can elicit both cognitive and emotional reactions from its target audience.[20] The mere exposure to words that individuals have strong, pre-existing negative reactions to, can impact evaluations of politics and politicians, regardless of context.[21] In this way, word choice by politicians and the media can influence political judgments.[22] Even more troubling is that this process can be extremely subtle and require very little exposure in order to be harmful, as even short texts can negatively influence political attitudes.[23]

In one telling study, psychologists demonstrated that subtle exposure to racist, dehumanizing language of Americans of predominantly African descent has real-life consequences and impacts acceptance of violence toward such Americans.[24] These researchers systematically analyzed data from two decades' worth of newspaper articles, examining reports of over 150 cases where the defendant was eligible to receive the death penalty. They searched for the presence of words that suggested animal-like qualities such as 'savage,' 'stalk,' 'monster' and even 'animal,' and analyzed the outcomes of these cases. American defendants of predominantly African descent who were dehumanized in media presentations were statistically more likely to be executed than those who were not. This pattern was also seen among defendants of prominently European descent who were sentenced to death versus those who escaped this fate, although American defendants of predominantly African descent were significantly more likely than defendants of prominently European descent to be described using dehumanizing language.[25] These findings suggest that basic cognitive processes such as decision-making over choices as serious as life and death situations can be altered by dehumanizing language.

Dehumanizing language has a clear impact on creating negative emotional responses and negative attitudes toward dehumanized groups. Another study of American citizens found that dehumanizing language has the capacity to heighten anger and disgust toward immigrants, thus generating anti-immigrant public opinion.[26] This research showed that dehumanizing of immigrants through the use of disease and virus metaphors exhibits a tangible influence on political attitudes. Specifically, dehumanization increased levels of disgust, and disgust then mediated the effect of dehumanization on attitudes. These attitudes then manifested in increased tendency to support anti-immigrant policies. After reading brief texts with subtle dehumanizing cues, participants reported that they were more likely to support strengthening border security and less likely to support amnesty programs to assist immigrants in gaining legal status, than participants who had read a neutral text.[27] As with language employed in Nazi Germany and during the conflicts in Rwanda and the former Yugoslavia, this research demonstrates that dehumanizing language increases xenophobia and support for strong national security.

Dehumanizing language is not the only type of dialogue to elicit emotionally charged reactions. In, perhaps, the only study of psychophysiological reactions to specific incendiary phrases used during the conflict in the former Yugoslavia, a team of researchers devised a study that highlights how even minimal exposure to racist political rhetoric and propaganda can influence subconscious reactions that people feel toward an out-group. The researchers created composite speeches from 242 real addresses given by the Serbian nationalist and propagandist Vojislav Šešelj.[28] These composite texts were organized by themes Šešelj frequently employed, including revenge and dehumanization. To ensure unbiased responses, all references to region and nationality were replaced with innocuous fictionalized countries. Participants read these texts, or a control text, and then responded to a series of questionnaires. Surprisingly, the researchers found that overall negative attitudes toward the out-group were only moderated by revenge speech – not nationalism, dehumanization or any other of a collection of probable incendiary topics. The researchers then measured spontaneous, involuntary movement of facial muscles associated with disgust and aggression. They found that participants responded with disgust to the out-group after reading the revenge composite speech. In contrast, the dehumanization text did not provoke a disgust reaction any stronger than that seen in the control condition.[29] Only revenge speech had the capacity to increase measurable feelings of disgust toward out-group members, questioning whether dehumanization plays a causal role in mass atrocity crimes.

Again, language can alter cognitive processes and shape perception without any conscious awareness of this process. Unlike residents of regions affected by conflict, these participants had the advantage of not being exposed to vitriolic condemnations of this particular out-group throughout their lives by friends, family and the media. Yet they still exhibited signs of having developed an implicit bias after very limited exposure to political messages. It is not difficult to imagine how years or decades of this type of language could severely impact one group's perception of another group.

This body of psychological research is significant for its application in international war crimes trials. Significantly, this research suggests that humans may have much less autonomy over their thoughts than commonly believed. Humans are highly susceptible to stimuli in their environment that can subtly sway opinions and actions in discernible ways. Individuals perpetrating atrocities may be influenced by factors outside of their control (via exposure to societally based implicit bias) or within their control (such as by selecting the types of media they consume).

Dueling hypotheses

That said, not all dehumanization literature agrees. Two somewhat diverging theories of dehumanization exist – with different implications with regard to intent. The first is the traditional view of dehumanization which contends that when harm occurs, most often, the perpetrator has engaged in some degree of cognitive acrobatics in order to view the victim as subhuman. This theory posits that dehumanization enables moral exclusion, which then permits abuse. The second contends that dehumanization is not so essential a component to inflicting intentional harm, as moral outrage. This theory suggests that atrocities are fueled by the belief that the target of harm is morally corrupt, deserving of punishment and fully human. A final theory is that these two views are not in conflict but to some extent are working in combination.

Theory one: dehumanization is essential for harm

The dominant theory of dehumanization is predicated on the assumption that in order to be successful in abusing another human being, perpetrators must first dehumanize their victims. The theory contends that without this, abuse is unlikely to occur, especially on a large scale such as genocide. One key component of this view is that dehumanization is often a crucial precursor to moral exclusion. It is supported by decades of psychological and legal theory.

The consistent element of dehumanization involves viewing 'others' as subhuman, not possessing key characteristics that distinguish humans from less evolved species. For example, *animalistic dehumanization* is a specific type of dehumanization that involves denying uniquely human traits to out-group members, such as the ability to feel emotions and have capacity for critical thinking.[30] One's 'humanness' is determined by having typically human traits and if one believes that members of another group or groups somehow fail to possess these attributes, it becomes increasingly easier to deprive them of their humanity. Likewise, *implicit dehumanization* is a process that can be measured through implicit association tests (IATs) and captures unconscious ways in which individuals attribute less humanness to out-group members than in-group members. For instance, one study demonstrated that Christian participants implicitly dehumanize Muslims and found that intensity of implicit dehumanization is associated with participants' willingness to support torture of Muslim prisoners of war.[31] One example of *implicit dehumanization* is *infrahumanization* theory that contends that complex secondary emotions such as sympathy, hope, embarrassment or jealousy are systematically denied to out-group members because acknowledging

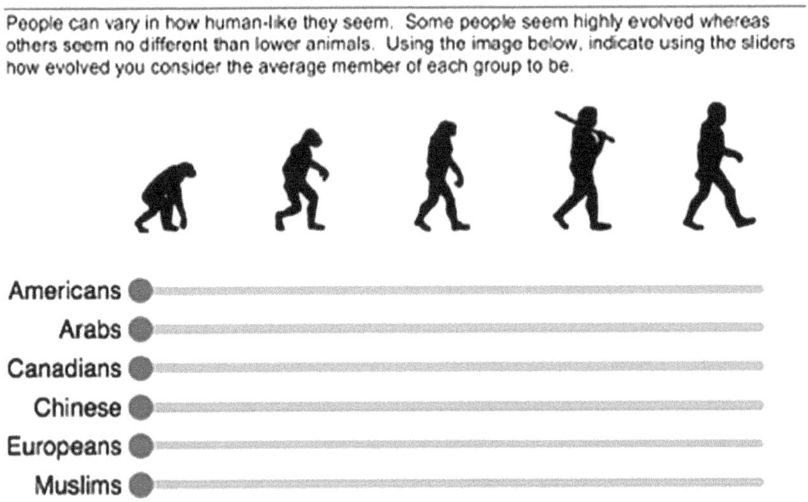

Figure 9.1 The Ascent of Man measure of blatant dehumanization, used by Kteily et al. (2015). Courtesy of Dr. Emile Gabriel Bruneau.

that someone possesses secondary emotions is crucial for increased altruism and empathy for that individual.[32] Research on infrahumanization has found that individuals tend to associate more positive and negative secondary emotions with members of their own group, than members of out-groups. Finally, *blatant dehumanization*, as the name would suggest is the most direct and aggressive form of dehumanization. Researchers have studied blatant dehumanization using a novel method through the 'Ascent of Man' graphic to depict various stages of human evolution. This test adeptly measures overt beliefs about the inferiority of out-groups relative to one's in-group. These researchers found that instances of blatant dehumanization increase immediately following intergroup violence and "strongly predicts support for aggressive actions like torture and retaliatory violence."[33] Another study using the 'Ascent of Man' scale of blatant dehumanization found that 74 percent of people surveyed reported holding the belief that their political opponents are less evolved than members of their own party.[34]

Theory two: violence is morally motivated, without the need for dehumanization

The second theory of dehumanization is less dominant due to its relative novelty. It is founded on the principle that violence often falls into one of two categories: *instrumental violence* and *moral violence.* In the former, violence may not be desirable but is viewed as justifiable for instrumental reasons because it somehow facilitates a greater systemic good. In the latter, violence is justified by the sentiment that its victims *are* fully human and are morally deserving of abuse.

In this theory, dehumanization is an essential component of instrumental violence. Dehumanization permits an attenuation of moral inhibitions and immunizes perpetrators to victims' suffering, so that they might proceed with the violence in order to achieve a secondary objective.[35] In contrast, moral violence is *not* facilitated by dehumanization. It is the belief that perpetrators are fueled by morality that is rational within their social context, and believe that their actions are morally justified. According to this theory, perpetrators have no need to dehumanize their victims because although they recognize their victims as human, the perpetrators believe that the target is *deserving* of abuse. Researchers suggest that when someone is dehumanized, they are viewed as an object; this objectification predicts indifferences toward their well-being.[36] In contrast, large-scale systematic abuse, such as genocide, is often characterized by an intense desire and even delight in causing suffering.[37] Furthermore, mass atrocity crimes are often characterized by "a moral outcry to decontaminate the in-group polluted by the out-group."[38] Indeed, the portrayal of out-groups as filthy contaminants, viruses or other types of pollutants is a reoccurring theme in political propaganda.[39] Julius Streicher infamously incited fear through racist propaganda of a 'racial contamination' that Jews would pollute German blood.[40] Immigrants too are often portrayed in language that evokes images of contaminants, engendering anger and disgust.[41,42] This suggests that dehumanizing language contributes to dehumanizing attitudes and thus giving rise to disgust, anger and other negative emotions that fuel political outrage.[43]

However, it is possible that although dehumanizing language was employed, dehumanization itself may not have occurred. It is possible that these terms provoked moral outrage, which in turn produces anger and disgust, and may even serve to *justify* the violence once it is ongoing, not *cause* the violence. This theory is consistent with the research discussed in a previous section, which found that following exposure to short composite texts of Vojislav Šešelj's speeches, *only* revenge speech produced negative attitudes toward the out-group. Dehumanization, among others, had no effect. Other research that supports the post-hoc justification role of dehumanization comes from a study of Americans of predominantly European descent and their perceptions of Native Americans. When these participants were told that the Native Americans were felled at the hands of European settler violence (genocide versus disease), participants were more likely to dehumanize Native Americans, perhaps to ease their moral guilt.[44] Therefore, brief exposure to speeches dealing with themes of revenge noticeably "intensified the participant's propensity to morally justify violence" and ignited feelings of disgust toward the out-group.[45] It is possible that revenge provokes to moral outrage in way that dehumanizing language does not.

Contrary to other dehumanization research, researchers of this theory do not believe that dehumanizing language is used with the intent of removing the target's humanity. Rather, they argue that when dehumanizing language is employed to characterize victims as animals, it is effective because perpetrators recognize that their target *is* human. The goal is not to transform the target into something less than human. Instead, the intention is to degrade the victim and exert dominance over them. This process is only effective if one acknowledges the other's humanity. As one psychologist noted,

> If I scream at someone that they're a 'pig' or 'vermin,' I wouldn't do that if I really thought they were a pig or vermin. What's the point? I scream this at them because I want to humiliate and shame them by making them think about something which they don't want to be.[46]

Referring to someone pejoratively as an animal would only produce the desired effect if social cognition were engaged, and the perpetrator was aware of the victim's humanity. Similarly, sexual humiliation, such as forced nudity, is very often seen in instances of psychological torture. Humiliation may arise from recognizing one's humanity and the desire to punish them. Techniques like these are popular in the so-called 'white torture' – the use of methods that leave no physical marks. Psychological torture (i.e., humiliation, mock executions, threats to harm family members or use of female interrogators if interaction with non-familial women is in violation of the victims' religious or cultural practices) can only be employed when perpetrators engage in social cognition and 'get into the minds' of their victims. This process is only possible when the target's humanity is acknowledged and thereby precludes dehumanization.

The theory that political violence is facilitated not by dehumanization but by the desire to punish fully sentient human beings for moral wrongdoing is supported by data on retributive justice. This can be observed in the data on third-party punishment decisions. One such study found that moral outrage drives the severity of punishment.[47] These researchers uncovered what they interpreted to be a strong association between dehumanization and moral outrage, as both provoked endorsements of more severe punishments for offenders than less morally outrageous crimes, and that participants were more likely to dehumanize individuals who commit crimes that induce moral outrage. The researchers noted that both moral outrage and dehumanization predict punishment independent of crime severity. It is possible that the ways in which the researchers quantified dehumanization might actually be indicators of moral outrage. After having been exposed to moral outrage and disgust inducing scenarios, participants' reactions may have been reflective of these emotions rather than dehumanization. Another study of third-party punishment found that crimes which elicit disgust were more harshly punished, regardless of the fact that this information was not relevant to sentencing.[48] These studies suggest that there is an association between disgust and moral outrage.

This is particularly observable in studies investigating public support for politically motivated torture surrounding terrorist activities. One reason for this is the assumption that targets are 'bad people' who will only respond to bad treatment.[49] Research indicates that punishment is often motivated by morality rather than the utilitarian results of the punishment, such as information acquisition.[50]

One study found a divide between Americans' professed motivation in support of political torture and their actual motivations.[51] Individuals who support torture often profess a utilitarian defense, despite substantial evidence among military and intelligence experts suggesting that torture is ineffective as a means of securing valuable information.[52] However, participants' behavior indicated that they were more motivated by the desire to inflict punishment, not by the efficacy of the interrogation in producing valuable information. Participants engaged in more severe methods of interrogation when the target was seen as "deserving" of punishment from a retributive standpoint.[53]

The above studies are consistent with the sentiment that "torturers perceive their actions as moral because their perceive their victims as evil."[54] These findings suggest that severe interrogation methods are perceived as an extension of punishment and thus individuals more likely to support such treatment for those they view as "deserving" of such punishment.[55] Again, "[...] *moral violence* emerges only when perpetrators see victims as capable of thinking, experiencing sensations and having moral emotions. In other words, when perpetrators perceive their victims as *human*."[56]

Theory three: a combination of the two theories

This second theory posits that dehumanization plays no role in moral violence; however, decades of theory suggests the opposite and concludes that dehumanization is an essential component in one's ability to inflict harm on a fellow human. Dehumanization, moral outrage and disgust appear to be inextricably linked. Perhaps political violence stems from some combination of these two dueling mechanisms/cognitive processes. It is possible that perpetrators believe that the target is morally deserving of the abuse, while also employing strategies to emotionally distance themselves. It is not uncommon for perpetrators of political violence to engage in tactics such as hooding, the intention of which is to simultaneously deindividuate the perpetrator (to obscure their identity) and dehumanize the victim, reducing the possibility for social cognition.[57]

It is possible that perpetrators of these crimes are utilizing cognitive task-switching mechanisms, allowing themselves to selectively humanize and dehumanize their victims, depending on the social context. As addressed previously, it is possible that dehumanization can be regulated to a degree within the same social context.[58] There is evidence that this might be true of politically motivated torture. First, unlike killing (especially mass killing), torture demands a more personal relationship with victims. One study of former government torturers and murders who worked during Brazil's military dictatorship found that torturers experience higher levels of psychological burnout than murderers, possibly because murders can more successfully dehumanize victims.[59] In contrast, as one former torturer noted, "the torturer must develop a personal dyadic psychological relationship with the victim."[60] This relationship emphasizes the engagement of social cognition. Similarly, it is crucial that torturers have a relationship with their victims, facilitated by social cognition that allows the torturer to evaluate if abuse is effective. If the perpetrator is engaging in this behavior for a political reason, such as the acquisition of information, it is necessary that the torturer be able to get into the victim's mind and assess what they might know. The perpetrator must evaluate the victim and decide which methods to use and at what intensity.[61] Such a process would require continuous updating as the perpetrator acquired additional cues about the efficacy of this process.

Despite the fact that "Torture always involves a personal relationship"[62] and might necessitate perpetrators engaging in behavior that recognizes victims' humanity, this does not mean that they are not also engaging in forms of dehumanization or deindividuation as a way of insulating themselves from the effects of their actions. As discussed in the introduction, dehumanization is a common response to situations that will foreseeably be emotionally taxing. This could be the case with something as emotionally demanding as perpetrating acts of violence. This is likely when considering how human brains are designed to experience vicarious pain when exposed to the suffering of others.[63] To some degree, the brain is built to spontaneously react as if observers are experiencing pain themselves.[64] This is an automatic response that would likely require trained voluntary inhibition.[65] In this way, dehumanization is likely to play a significant role in permitting individuals to distance themselves enough to perpetrate crimes, with intermittent instances of humanization.

Further research must be conducted to assess both of these theories. Both theories and their potential combination are relevant to war crimes trials because this research raises the question of intent. What is the role of the individual perpetrator and his or her authority figures? Were these behaviors unduly influenced by cognitive biases directed by another party? This debate could be relevant for both the defense and prosecution of war crimes trials. For the defense, it may be essential to investigate the role of situational factors and the sway that these had over basic cognitive processes of perception of facts and bias. Conversely, this research may be valuable for the prosecution, if perpetrators do not, in fact, engage in dehumanization to the degree previously believed, but rather deliberately choose to proceed in a manner that inflicts harm, with full awareness of their actions and its implications.

Psychological toll on perpetrators

There is evidence that suggests that extreme human rights abuses do not only affect victims. These actions can also take a toll on perpetrators, sometimes causing severe psychological trauma,[66] as those who perpetrate political violence learn to mediate the emotional repercussions of this process.

The types of people who perform political torture "well" are generally not sadists. An extensive investigation of former Brazilian policemen suggested that effective torturers were "rational, controlled, and cool" and that they possessed the ability to rationally evaluate which formula they wanted to utilize to elicit *controlled* suffering, ideally without risking permanent injuries or premature death.[67]

Sadists are not usually capable of this.[68] It is important to regulate one's emotions and maintain emotional control. Someone who cannot do this is not an effective torturer.[69] Reflecting on these men, one psychologist noted, "violence workers were not unusual or deviant in any way prior to practicing this new role, nor were there any persisting deviant tendencies or pathologies among any of them in the years following their work as torturers and executioners."[70] Again, this suggests that torturers are made, not born. This is a trained behavior, and one that demonstrates possession of mental faculties and awareness of the situation.

It is not uncommon for former perpetrators of political violence to experience severe psychological distress in the years following these encounters. Journalist Joshua E.S. Phillips examined the effects of torture and among his findings, he notes that soldiers "referenced their collective experience with detainee abuse as being especially painful and damaging."[71] Numerous sources have noted subsequent occurrences of substance abuse, post-traumatic stress disorder (PTSD), depression, anxiety, hypertension, insomnia, paranoia, anger management and even suicide.[72,73] Some evidence suggests that guilt is the primary determinant in predicting who will be psychologically impacted by their experience with torture.[74] One of the psychologists contracted by the Central Intelligence Agency (CIA) to devise their now notorious "enhanced interrogation techniques" even noted, "Those techniques are so harsh that it's emotionally distressing to the people who administer them."[75]

This evidence reaffirms that social cognition may play a prominent role during certain types of political violence. Intention, social cognition and evaluation are necessary to understand the mental state of the victim. Again, this suggests that absolute dehumanization may not occur. If perpetrators were truly able to fully disengage social cognition and view their victims as objects without the possession of feelings, emotions and thoughts – they might be less likely to exhibit symptoms of emotional exhaustion characteristic of humanization.

Partisanship and perceptions of reality

Group identity and political partisanship can also shape basic perceptions of reality.[76] It can impact judgments and memory. Partisan bias can even alter something as fundamental as mathematical aptitude.[77] This is problematic when group identity begins interfering with how individuals evaluate truth and facts. Thus, presenting the facts is not always as simple a task as lying or telling the truth. This is especially true of memory. One type of autobiographic memory is the *flashbulb memory*, which form in response to emotionally charged and/or surprising events, such as significant news stories. These types of memories are notoriously inconsistent over time, despite individuals having extreme confidence in their ability to accurately recall exact details surrounding the event in question.[78] This is not intentional or malicious. Memories are simply not a film reel that can be replayed at will with absolute consistency; it is a reconstruction of events susceptible to influence or labile during these processes. Additionally, memory is highly susceptible to political bias, as individuals are more likely to recall factual events differently, depending on one's political views. In one study of Americans, nearly half reported recalling an event that never happened: Republican participants reported that they recalled seeing Barack Obama meeting with the president of Iran, while Democratic participants remembered George W. Bush vacationing with a celebrity during Hurricane Katrina.[79] Neither of these events actually occurred.

Politics can shape interpretation of basic facts and reality. It can even alter basic visual perception. In another study, participants were shown a short video of police intervening in a political demonstration. Conservatives and liberals differed greatly on their interpretation of how violent the protestors were, depending on whether they viewed the protestors as being from their in-group or not, despite being exposed to the same exact footage.[80] This phenomenon has been studied for decades; an early social psychology study documented such inconsistencies in a 1954 football game between Princeton and Dartmouth students.[81] In the mid-1980s, researchers found that pro-Arab and pro-Israeli partisanship altered perceptions of media coverage of the Sabra and Shatila massacre.[82] Both groups reported the media being biased against their side. This is relevant because it sheds light on how political bias can shape and alter witness testimony and recollection of basic facts.

Final thoughts

This research is far from complete. Currently, there exists no decisive answer on the exact nature of dehumanization, how it manifests cognitively, its causes and its remedies. One must be conscientious of portraying research ethically, as science has been misappropriated at varying times throughout history in attempts to justify various inhumane policies. Although the data is converging and conflicting at times, it is hoped that this chapter can shed some light on how dehumanization may occur (or may not), which cognitive mechanisms permit its presence and which factors facilitate this process. While this in no way excuses the behavior of dehumanization, this research may prove useful in the prosecution or defense of human rights violations and may hopefully assist to explain how those who perpetrate these crimes are not monsters but rather average people capable of monstrous acts. Finally, it is hoped that this chapter might offer some insight on how to avoid these pitfalls in the future.

Notes

1 L.T. Harris and S.T. Fiske, 'Dehumanised Perception: A Psychological Means to Facilitate Atrocities, Torture, and Genocide?' *Zeitschrift für Psychologie/Journal of Psychology*, vol. 219, no. 3, 2011, pp. 175–181.
2 C.D. Cameron, L.T. Harris and K. Payne, 'The Emotional Cost of Humanity: Anticipated Exhaustion Motivates Dehumanization of Stigmatized Targets,' *Social Psychological and Personality Science*, vol. 7, no. 2, 2016, pp. 105–112.
3 Harris and Fiske, 'Dehumanised Perception.'

4 V.S.Y. Kwan and S.T. Fiske, 'Missing Links in Social Cognition: The Continuum from Nonhuman Agents to Dehumanized Humans,' *Social Cognition*, vol. 26, no. 2, 2008, pp. 125–128.
5 L.T. Harris and S.T. Fiske, 'Social Groups that Elicit Disgust are Differentially Processed in mPFC,' *Social Cognitive and Affective Neuroscience*, vol. 2, no. 1, 2007, pp. 45–51.
6 L.T. Harris and S.T. Fiske, 'Dehumanizing the Lowest of the Low Neuroimaging Responses to Extreme out-groups,' *Psychological Science*, vol. 17, no. 10, 2006, pp. 847–853.
7 E. Bruneau, N. Jacoby, N. Kteily and R. Saxe, 'Denying Humanity: The Distinct Neural Correlates of Blatant Dehumanization,' *Journal of Experimental Psychology: General*, vol. 147, no. 7, 2018, pp. 1078–1093.
8 K. Mathiak and R. Weber, 'Toward Brain Correlates of Natural Behavior: fMRI during Violent Video Games,' *Human Brain Mapping*, vol. 27, no. 12, 2006, pp. 948–956.
9 Harris and Fiske, 'Social Groups.'
10 N. Kteily, G. Hodson and E. Bruneau, 'They See Us As Less Than Human: Metadehumanization Predicts Intergroup Conflict via Reciprocal Dehumanization,' *Journal of Personality and Social Psychology*, vol. 110, no. 3, 2016, p. 343.
11 M. Cikara, J.J. Van Bavel, Z. Ingbretsen and T. Lau, 'Decoding "Us" and "Them": Neural Representations of Generalized Group Concepts,' *Journal of Experimental Psychological: General*, vol. 146, no. 5, 2017, pp. 621–631.
12 A.M. Sood, 'Motivated Cognition in Legal Judgment – An Analytic Review,' *The Annual Review of Law and Social Science*, vol. 9, no. 307, 2013.
13 Ibid.
14 E. Balcetis and D. Dunning, 'See What You Want to See: Motivational Influences on visual perception,' *Journal of Personality and Social Psychology*, vol. 91, no. 4, 2006, pp. 612–625.
15 B.K. Payne, 'Prejudice and Perception: The Role of Automatic and Controlled Processes in Misperceiving a Weapon,' *Journal of Personality and Social Psychology*, vol. 81, no. 2, 2001, pp. 181–192.
16 R.T. Azevedo, S.N. Garfinkel, H.D. Critchley and M. Tsakiris, 'Cardiac Afferent Activity Modulates the Expression of Racial Stereotypes,' *Nature Communications*, vol. 8, article no. 13854, 2017.
17 A. Bandura, B. Underwood and M.E. Fromson, 'Disinhibition of Aggression through Diffusion of Responsibility and Dehumanization of Victims,' *Journal of Research in Personality*, vol. 9, 1975, pp. 253–269.
18 Ibid.
19 A. Bandura, C. Barbaranelli, G.V. Caprara and C. Pastorelli, 'Mechanisms of Moral Disengagement in the Exercise of Moral Agency,' *Journal of Personality and Social Psychology*, vol. 71, no. 2, 1996, pp. 364–374.
20 S.M. Utych, 'How Dehumanization Influences Attitudes toward Immigrants,' *Political Research Quarterly*, vol. 71, no. 2, 2018, pp. 440–452.
21 S.M. Utych, 'Negative Affective Language in Politics,' *American Politics Research*, First Published 1 February 2017.
22 Ibid.
23 Utych, 'How Dehumanization Influences.'
24 P.A. Goff, J.L. Eberhardt, M.J. Williams and M.C. Jackson, 'Not Yet Human: Implicit Knowledge, Historical Dehumanization, and Contemporary Consequences,' *Journal of Personality and Social Psychology*, vol. 94, no. 2, 2008, p. 292.
25 Ibid.
26 Utych, 'How Dehumanization Influences.'
27 Ibid.

28 The Prosecutor v. Vojislav Šešelj, Appeal Judgment, Case No. MICT-16-99-A, 11 April 2018.
29 C.M. Lillie, B. Knapp, L.T. Harris and R.A. Wilson, 'This Is the Hour of Revenge: The Psychology of Propaganda and Mass Atrocities,' 2015. Online. Available HTTP: <https://ssrn.com/abstract=2580521> or <http://dx.doi.org/10.2139/ssrn.2580521> (accessed 11 June 2019).
30 N. Haslam, 'Dehumanization: An Integrative Review,' *Personality and Social Psychology Review*, vol. 10, no. 3, 2006, pp. 252–264.
31 G. Viki, L. Winchester, L. Titshall, T. Chisango, A. Pina and R. Russell, 'Beyond Secondary Emotions: The Infrahumanization of Out-Groups Using Human-Related and Animal-Related Words,' *Social Cognition*, vol. 24, no. 6, 2006, pp. 753–775.
32 J.P. Leyens, A. Rodriguez-Perez, R. Rodriguez-Torres, R. Gaunt, M.P. Paladino, J. Vaes and S. Demoulin, 'Psychological Essentialism and the Differential Attribution of Uniquely Human Emotions to Ingroups and Outgroups,' *European Journal of Social Psychology*, vol. 31, 2001, pp. 395–411.
33 N. Kteily, E. Bruneau, A. Waytz and S. Cotterill, 'The Ascent of Man: Theoretical and Empirical Evidence for Blatant Dehumanization,' *Journal of Personality and Social Psychology*, vol. 109, no. 5, 2015, pp. 901–931.
34 J.L. Martherus, A.G. Martinez, P.K. Piff and A.G. Theodoridis, 'Party Animals? Party Identity and Dehumanization,' 2018. Online. Available HTTP: <https://www.dropbox.com/s/1cq23ml0tuv3b4z/party-animals.pdf?dl=0> (accessed 11 June 2019).
35 T.S. Rai, P. Valdesolo and J. Graham, 'Dehumanization Increases Instrumental Violence, But not Moral Violence,' *Proceedings of the National Academy of Sciences of the United States of America*, vol. 114, no. 32, 2017, pp. 8511–8516.
36 T. Rai, P. Valdesolo and J. Graham, 'Our Enemies Are Human: That's Why We Want to Kill Them,' *Behavioral Scientist*, 18 August 2017.
37 Ibid.
38 A. Fiske, T. Rai and S. Pinker, *Virtuous Violence: Hurting and Killing to Create, Sustain, End, and Honor Social Relationships*, Cambridge: Cambridge University Press. 2014, p. 209.
39 K. Costello and G. Hodson, 'Exploring the Roots of Dehumanization: The Role of Animal-Human Similarity in Promoting Immigrant Humanization,' *Group Processes & Intergroup Relations*, vol. 13, no. 1, 2010, pp. 3–22.
40 M. Eastwood, 'Hitler's Notorious Jew Baiter: The Prosecution of Julius Streicher,' in P. Dojčinović (ed.), *Propaganda, War Crimes Trials and International Law: From Speakers' Corner to War Crimes*, Abingdon, New York, NY: Routledge, 2012, p. 209.
41 G.V. O'Brien, 'Indigestible Food, Conquering Hordes, and Waste Materials: Metaphors of Immigrants and the Early Immigration Restriction Debate in the United States,' *Metaphor and Symbol*, vol. 18, no. 1, 2003, pp. 33–47.
42 Utych, 'How Dehumanization Influences.'
43 Ibid.
44 E. Castano and R. Giner-Sorolla, 'Not Quite Human: Infrahumanization in Response to Collective Responsibility for Intergroup Killing,' *Journal of Personality and Social Psychology*, vol. 90, no. 5, 2006, pp. 804–818.
45 Lillie et al., 'This is the Hour of Revenge.'
46 D. Pizarro and T. Sommers, 'Very Bad Wizards,' *Dehumanization and Disintegration (with Paul Bloom)* [Audio Podcast], 26 December 2017. Online. Available HTTP: <https://verybadwizards.fireside.fm/130> (accessed 11 June 2019).
47 B. Bastion, T.F. Denson and N. Haslam, 'The Roles of Dehumanization and Moral Outrage in Retributive Justice,' *PloS One*, vol. 8, no. 4, 2013.
48 B.H. Capestany and L.T. Harris, 'Disgust and Biological Descriptions Bias Logical Reasoning during Legal Decision-Making,' *Social Neuroscience*, vol. 9, no. 3, 2014, pp. 265–277.

49 R. Janoff-Bulman, 'Erroneous Assumptions: Popular Belief in the Effectiveness of Torture Interrogation,' *Peace and Conflict: Journal of Peace Psychology*, vol. 13, no. 4, 2007, pp. 429–435.
50 K.M. Carlsmith and J.M. Darley, 'Psychological Aspects of Retributive Justice,' in M.P. Zanna (ed.), *Advances in Experimental Social Psychology*, San Diego, CA: Elsevier, vol. 40, 2008, pp. 193–236.
51 K.M. Carlsmith and A.M. Sood, 'The Fine Line between Interrogation and Retribution,' *Journal of Experimental Social Psychology*, vol. 45, no. 1, 2009, pp. 191–196.
52 Janoff-Bulman, 'Erroneous,' pp. 429–435.
53 A.M. Sood, 'Aggressive Interrogation and Retributive Justice: A Proposed Psychological Model,' in J. Hanson (ed.), *Ideology, Psychology, And Law*, Oxford: Oxford University Press, 2012, pp. 574–604.
54 Fiske et al., *Virtuous Violence.*
55 Carlsmith and Sood, 'The Fine Line.'
56 Rai et al., 'Our Enemies.'
57 P.G. Zimbardo, *The Lucifer Effect: Understanding How Good People Turn Evil*, New York, NY: Random House, 2007.
58 Mathiak and Weber, 'Toward Brain Correlates,' pp. 948–956.
59 M.K. Huggins, M. Haritos-Fatouros and P.G. Zimbardo, *Violence Workers: Police Torturers and Murderers Reconstruct Brazilian Atrocities*, Berkeley, CA: University of California Press, 2006, p. 215.
60 Ibid.
61 Zimbardo, *The Lucifer.*
62 Ibid., p. 289.
63 E.L. Terrighena, G. Lu, W.P. Yuen, T.M. Lee and K. Keuper, 'Effects of Vicarious Pain on Self-Pain Perception: Investigating the Role of Awareness,' *Journal of Pain Research*, vol. 10, 2017, pp. 1821–1830.
64 K.N. Ochsner, J. Zaki, J. Hanelin, D.H. Ludlow, K. Knierim, T. Ramachandran and S.C. Mackey, 'Your Pain or Mine? Common and Distinct Neural Systems Supporting the Perception of Pain in Self and Other,' *Social Cognitive and Affective Neuroscience*, vol. 3, no. 2, 2008, pp. 144–160.
65 S. O'Mara, *Why Torture Doesn't Work: The Neuroscience of Interrogation*, Cambridge, MA: Harvard University Press, 2015.
66 D. Grossman, *On Killing: The Psychological Cost of Learning to Kill in War and Society*, New York, NY: Little Brown, 2009.
67 Huggins et al., *Violence Workers*, p. 255.
68 Ibid., p. 166.
69 Ibid., p. 176.
70 P. Zimbardo, 'The Psychology of Power and Evil: All Power to the Person? To the Situation? To the System?' Online. Available HTTP: <https://www.academia.edu/4070633/The_Psychology_of_Power_and_Evil_All_Power_to_the_Person_To_the_Situation_To_the_System> (accessed 11 June 2019).
71 J.E.S. Phillips, *None of Us Were like This Before: American Soldiers and Torture*, London, New York, NY: Verso, 2010, p. 132.
72 Ibid.
73 O'Mara, *Why Torture.*
74 R. McNally, *Remembering Trauma*, Cambridge, MA: Belknap Press, 2003.
75 J. Mitchell, 'Man Who Interrogated Khalid Sheikh Mohammed Speaks Out,' 2014. Online. Available HTTP: <http://insider.foxnews.com/2014/12/15/exclusive-james-mitchell-man-who-interrogated-khalid-sheikh-mohammed-speaks-out-kelly> (accessed 11 June 2019).
76 J.J. Van Bavel and A. Pereira, 'The Partisan Brain: An Identity-Based Model of Political Belief,' *Trends in Cognitive Sciences*, vol. 22, no. 3, 2018.

77 D.M. Kahan, 'Ideology, Motivated Reasoning, and Cognitive Reflection: An Experimental Study,' *Judgment Decision Making*, vol. 8, no. 4, 2013, pp. 407–424.
78 W. Hirst and E.A. Phelps, 'Flashbulb Memories,' *Current Directions in Psychological Science*, vol. 25, no. 1, 2016, pp. 36–41.
79 S.J. Frenda, E.D. Knowles, W. Saletan and E.F. Loftus, 'False Memories of Fabricated Political Events,' *Journal of Experimental Social Psychology*, vol. 49, no. 2, 2013, pp. 280–286.
80 D.M. Kahan, D.A. Hoffman, D. Braman, D. Evans and J. Rachlinski, 'They Saw a Protest: Cognitive Illiberalism and the Speech-Conduct Distinction,' *Stanford Law Review*, vol. 64, 2012, p. 851.
81 A.H. Hastorf and H. Cantril, 'They Saw a Game; A Case Study,' *The Journal of Abnormal and Social Psychology*, vol. 49, no. 1, 1954, p. 129.
82 R.P. Vallone, L. Ross and M.R. Lepper, 'The Hostile Media Phenomenon: Biased Perception and Perceptions of Media Bias in Coverage of the Beirut Massacre,' *Journal of Personality and Social Psychology*, vol. 49, no. 3, 1985, p. 577.

Chapter 10

How dangerous propaganda works

Jordan Kiper

Introduction

In our current era of political polarization, it is not uncommon to hear that 'one person's news is another's propaganda.' This impression is mistaken. Unlike the reporters of a free press, propagandists do not attempt to persuade with factual claims but spread vitriolic rhetoric or disinformation to manipulate others in ways that ultimately maintain or alter a balance of power for the propagandist's advantage.[1] A fundamental characteristic of propaganda, regardless of its cultural manifestation, is the author's intention to manipulate others. The problem is identifying a propagandist's intentions, which is mired in epistemic challenges, since most propagandists rely on cultural idioms or coded language and deny their original intentions post hoc. It is understandable, then, that prosecutors in speech crime trials would prefer to focus less on the mind of the propagandist and more on the consequences of his or her words – that is, the 'imminent lawlessness' of the propaganda rather than the intentions behind it.[2]

Does this mean that propaganda is dangerous only when it results in lawlessness? Many judges in the United States have more or less said yes.[3] Basing propaganda's threat on consequence alone, however, is less supported in international criminal law, where speech crimes have received much attention over the last decade.[4] For many legal theorists, a propagandist's words become dangerous not because of any direct or linear effects they have on perpetrators but because of the way they function within a cultural context and reveal the violent intentions of the author and audience.[5] Though a subtle difference from cause-and-effect analysis, the core idea here is this: Audiences are not automatons, and propaganda rarely causes anyone to behave one way or another, but it does bear collective intentionality to change social relations, making violence against particular groups more acceptable, on which perpetrators then act.

The purpose of this chapter is to defend the above claim by drawing from three topics. The first is speech act theory.[6] Since John Austin's *How to Do Things with Words*, speech has been analyzed as having three aspects:

- Locution: what is said by a speaker.
- Illocution: what is intended by the speaker.
- Perlocution: what is experienced by the audience.[7]

Critically, a speaker's illocution indicates an intended change in the world with respect to an audience. For instance, an assertion, directive, commissive, expressive or declarative all indicate different speaker intentions and respective changes in social relations or the accepted social tenets of a community.[8] Equally as critical, a speech act cannot function without certain felicity conditions or contextual factors in place at the time of the utterance, which allow the speaker to achieve uptake. Uptake occurs when an audience understands the speaker's intended meaning and thus stands in a position to accept or reject it.

The second topic is social psychology or the scientific study of how persons influence and are influenced by others. Many of the discipline's most replicated studies examine how contextual social interactions alter people's cognition, emotions and behaviors, including circumstances that contribute to violence.[9] As such, social psychology is beneficial for understanding conditions in which persons are influenced by a speaker and are more likely to act on prejudices, if not perpetrate hostilities or aggression toward others.

The third topic is the body of propaganda of Vojislav Šešelj, a radical Serbian politician and notorious warmonger during the Yugoslav Wars.[10] Considering Šešelj's propaganda is a worthwhile case study, since the degree to which his words contributed to mass violence in the Yugoslav Wars remains an open question. The International Criminal Tribunal for the former Yugoslavia (ICTY) acquitted him of instigating persecution in 2016,[11] while the International Residual Mechanism for Criminal Tribunal's (IRMCT) Appeals Chamber (AC) overturned his acquittal in 2018.[12] Thus, a looming question is just how dangerous were Šešelj's words in the context of wartime Serbia?

Unless we are careful, questions like this one step unsteadily toward the presumption that propaganda has direct and linear causal effects on an audience – a presumption that many scholars, including myself, have argued is problematic.[13] When attempting to understand the dangers of propaganda, we ask an epistemic question: How do we know if an instance of propaganda is dangerous? We get into trouble if we then ask: Did the propaganda *cause* violence? For this question presumes that propaganda is, first, dangerous only if it directly results in violence, and, second, deterministically influences others. Both assumptions are problematic because a propagandist who attempts to incite mass violence, such as genocide, commits an inchoate offense, meaning the speech act is dangerous regardless of its consequence; and there is little evidence that propaganda has an indomitable influence on would-be perpetrators.

To illustrate, consider an analogous question raised by the Trial Chamber (TC) of Jean-Paul Akayesu at the International Criminal Tribunal for Rwanda (ICTR). They asked what proof is there for a 'possible causal link' between the statements of a propagandist and persons who engage in mass violence.[14] This begs the question that the relationship between propaganda and perpetrators is linear and easily demonstrable after the fact – an assumption that post hoc studies have shown is false. Post-conflict ethnographies reveal that propaganda's influence on perpetrators is subtle, indirect, distal, cumulative and circular.[15]

Moreover, after a decade of speech crime trials, demonstrating a 'possible causal link' with factual evidence has become more elusive than as once presumed, and revealed how faulty it is to believe that words have direct causal effects or that individuals perpetrate crimes like cogs in a machine.

I will not discuss from a legal standpoint how international courts should resolve the problem of proving when a propagandist causes violence. However, what I will say about propaganda may have some relevance for future cases from the vantage point of the cognitive and behavioral sciences. My goal is to show that by understanding how propaganda works, we can identify when it is dangerous.

Understanding dangerous propaganda

Propaganda is the systematic attempt to direct perception, cognition and behavior toward the intent of a propagandist; its most dangerous forms are those that intersect with hate media, which stigmatizes and demonizes an out-group.[16] An out-group is any recognizable civilian population considered 'other' relative to an in-group. Hate media occurs most frequently under a political regime with control over the marketplace of ideas.[17] Cross-culturally, hate media tends to use social expressions, disinformation (e.g., false news reports) and inflammatory speeches to glorify the in-group and justify mass violence against an out-group.[18] Mass violence is widely understood as the persecution of a recognizable civilian population, such as ethnic cleansing, or mass crimes, such as massacres, mass rape or genocide.[19]

Accordingly, dangerous propaganda (simply 'propaganda,' henceforth) occurs when a speaker (ab)uses mass media to foster hatred, support hostilities or encourage violence against an out-group.[20] As such, the speaker's communication can be analyzed as a speech act, where the content and manner of speech function to bring about a social change, as reflected in the speaker's intentions as well as the audience's uptake and subsequent actions. Additionally, the tripartite character of speech acts entails that propaganda is analyzable as having three aspects:

i A message *P* by speaker *S* at time *t*1 in context *c*.
ii The intention *I* of speaker *S* and uptake *U* of persons *R* in *c* at *t*1.
iii Actions *Q* of persons *R* at time *t*2 because of (i) and (ii).

The first is the *speech condition*, when a speaker with sociocultural or political authority and access to mass media conveys a distinct locution, namely, a message, whether spoken or written, to an audience. The message not only comprises the locution but accompanies *performatives* – speaking styles, symbolic representations or nonverbal communication – giving the message a surface meaning and an implied meaning, which persons with cultural competence would grasp.[21] In this case, *context* is the cultural environment of the speaker and audience, while *time* is the period in which the speech act is communicated.

The second aspect is the *mental condition* – the point at which the intentions of the speaker and audience come into contact. For the speech act to be successful, the speaker's illocution must parallel the audience's uptake, meaning the audience understands the speaker's intended social change. An unsuccessful speech act results in a misfire, where the audience is unreceptive, noncommittal, or confused.[22] A successful speech act results in a joint construal of meaning, where the audience demonstrates a relevant social behavior in the cultural context, indicating their rejection or acceptance of the speaker's utterance. Acceptance is further demonstrated by the speaker and audience sharing in emotions, acceptances, beliefs or expectations, otherwise known as collective intentionality.[23]

The final aspect of speech is its *consequence*. These perlocutionary effects should not be restricted to the immediate cause and effect of the speech act but should be thought of as occurring 'because of' (i) and (ii). This means that the speech's consequence includes both first-order effects, such as the speech's immediate psychological impact on the audience, and second-order effects on the audience's actions soon thereafter, such as behaviors that reflect back on the speech. As Austin observed, a speech act has social force not only because of its immediate psychological force but also because of the collective behaviors that result from the social changes induced by the speech act.[24]

This is a subtle point that requires reflection. Consider the speech act of declaring a couple married. Under the right felicity conditions, the result is not limited to the immediate psychological change in the couple. Rather, it includes an array of subsequent events, ranging from the commencing honeymoon to numerous socially sanctioned actions that occur because of the speech act. The same is true for what Searle calls 'institutional facts,' where an act of speech act can alter an entire community's behavior, whether it is immediate or long after the speech.[25] A declaration of war, for instance, when uttered by a recognized authority figure in the proper context can change the actions of a society, redirecting people from a peacetime to a wartime orientation.[26] Propaganda is similar. When a propagandist claims that an out-group is an existential threat and the in-group understands the speaker's intention to exclude the out-group, the consequences are not limited to the immediate context. Instead, they encompass the actions taken by the in-group at later times, provided they are done because of the speech act.

Yet how do we know when an in-group's behaviors are done because of propaganda? First, when actions resemble those advocated by a propagandist. For instance, years before the Rwandan genocide, the November 1991 edition of *Kangura*, a Hutu-extremist magazine edited by Hassan Ngeze, who was one of the accused in the ICTR's 'Media Case,' depicted a machete on its cover, with the caption: "Which weapons are we going to use to beat the cockroaches for good?"[27] Years later, Matthias Ruzindana, a Rwandan linguist at the ICTR, explained that, for Hutu extremists, 'cockroaches' was an epithet for Tutsis, who were portrayed in Hutu propaganda as threatening pests that needed to be exterminated.[28] Furthermore, *génocidaires* eventually used machetes to murder thousands of Tutsis as Ngeze intended, and thus reflected back on his propaganda. Second, perpetrator behavior resembles the propagandist's words. To illustrate, Predrag Dojčinović, a legal theorist and cognitive linguist, explains that an 'evidentiary feedback loop' often transpires with collective intentionality, such that the receiver of a speech act rationalizes the act promoted by the speaker using the speaker's own words. This occurs when persons from the in-group repeat language used by the propagandist to rationalize military aggression, dismiss concern for an out-group, or justify mass violence.[29] In other words, persons behaved in certain ways 'because of' the propaganda.

The speech condition: the context of Šešelj's speeches

Before focusing on the meaning or consequence of Šešelj's speeches, it is necessary to understand the context in which he gave them, namely, the rise of ultranationalism during the breakup of Yugoslavia. As a post-socialist political movement, Serbian ultranationalism centered on an irredentist ideology of uniting Serbs around an ethnoreligious identity: sharing an ethnic ancestry and supporting the reemerging nation and Orthodox Church.[30] The movement took shape in 1987, when Slobodan Milošević broke with socialists and declared his unequivocal support for Serbs in Kosovo and arguably began to wane after from 1991 to 2001, with the public ousting of Milošević. Throughout this period, Šešelj acted as a de facto ultranationalist propagandist and gave numerous inflammatory speeches that exploited three critical background conditions that appear to influence propaganda's effects on a population.[31]

Rising insecurities

The first background condition was socioeconomic insecurity. From 1980 to 1986, an economic crisis caused falling living standards for most Yugoslavs. Unemployment increased from 6 percent to 37 percent and coincided with a youth bulge, where persons under 25 experienced upward of 60 percent unemployment.[32] Economic distress, alongside perpetual bureaucratic gridlock, led to extensive social unrest, and eventually to a constitutional crisis between Serbian leaders and neighboring republics about the right to self-determination. While leaders in Slovenia, Croatia, Bosnia and Herzegovina, and Kosovo interpreted self-determination in Yugoslavia's 1971 Constitution as guaranteeing the right to independence, Serbian leaders disagreed and considered succession as unconstitutional.[33]

Numerous psychological studies demonstrate that as economic and social well-being plummet, so too does political trust.[34] In turn, political distrust engenders profound societal changes such as revivals, regime changes, or revolutions.[35] In

Serbia, political mistrust brought about a renaissance in ethnonationalism: the view that Serbian politics should no longer center on supporting so-called socialist brethren but defending Serbians exclusively. This view grew in popularity after Muslim Albanians and Croats demanded autonomy in Kosovo and Croatia, respectively.[36] For most Serbs, an autonomous, Muslim-controlled Kosovo meant losing their sacred heartland, while an independent Croatia raised fears about a return of fascism in the Balkans. Serbian ultranationalist exploited these fears to gain political support, comparing their opposition to Croatian fascism and Muslim extremism to the patriotism of Serbs at the 1389 Battle of Kosovo and rallying Serbs around a shared and threatened ethnonational identity.

Taken together, insecurities in the 1980s led to a revival in ethnonationalism, as evidenced by numerous religious or nationalistic rallies by the early 1990s, when many Serbs experienced visceral feelings of oneness with their ethnonation.[37] This is significant because psychological studies demonstrate that individuals whose personal identities are psychologically fused with their in-group, and feel threatened by an out-group, are more willing than others to engage in collective action for the in-group.[38] When this happens, a reciprocal existence is shared with one's in-group, such that one is strong whenever the in-group is strong, and likewise threatened if the in-group is threatened. As a result, a fused individual is often willing to sacrifice – even his or her life if not the lives of others – for the sake of the in-group. Hence, the threshold for Šešelj to drive 'fused' Serbs toward conflict would have been considerably lowered by the start of the Yugoslav Wars in 1991.

Control of the media

The second condition was giving speeches in a controlled media environment. From 1989 to 1990, Milošević undertook what he called an *anti-bureaucratic revolution*, encouraging a populist revolt with the goal of replacing non-Serbian officials in the Yugoslavian bureaucracy with Serbs. After sweeping across Serbia, Milošević's anti-bureaucratic revolution placed a majority of ultranationalists in office. Milošević then undertook three acts that secured his hold over Serbia until his arrest in 2001. He dismissed non-Serbs from the Yugoslav People's Army (JNA) and turned Yugoslavia's Secret police into his own personal army.[39] He then took control of Yugoslavia's national bank and transferred 2.5 billion Deutschmarks (equivalent to 1.5 billion dollars) into the pockets of his regime.[40] Finally, he purged thousands of journalists from Yugoslavia's media outlets and replaced them with Serbian ultranationalists.[41]

Consequentially, when Croatia and Bosnia and Herzegovina sought independence, the Milošević regime was able to propagate misinformation about neighboring republics. The Serbian media thus became inundated on a daily basis with false news reports and alleged conspiracies about non-Serbs, ranging from fabricated atrocity stories to an alleged Vatican-Tehran conspiracy to destroy the Serbian people.[42] Such misinformation reinforced a *big lie* that ultranationalists repeated throughout the wars – that Serbs must defend themselves and their lands because they could not survive among non-Serbs.

In terms of linguistic context, Milošević's controlled-media provided the right felicity conditions for Šešelj's inflammatory speeches. The daily barrage of misinformation about threatening neighbors would have prepared Serbian audiences to believe authority figures, such as Šešelj, who called on Serbs to defend the nation. Additionally, mere exposure to violent content, such as images of wartime victims in the daily news, would have increased support for aggressive self-defense.[43] Experimental studies demonstrate that exposure to violent images reinforce cognitive scripts for using aggression to manage social situations.[44] Cognitive neuroscience further demonstrates that exposure to violent media induces long-term potentiation (LTP) in neural pathways for desensitization.[45] The most common response, however, to threatening media is moral panic: a community-wide fear about an imminent evil that must be dealt with. According to criminologist John Scott, moral panic typically occurs in a social context where political entrepreneurs are attempting to influence the political marketplace of ideas by exaggerating societal threats.[46] Doing so allows them to gain public support and extract resources from the community to deal with the alleged threat. However, when the threat is associated with a recognizable outgroup, moral panic often engenders out-group violence, such as mobs or witch hunts, on which political entrepreneurs capitalize for personal gain, usually by extracting resources from a minority and using violence to intimidate political rivals.

This description bears an uncanny resemblance to the way Serbian ultranationalists used the media. Media sociologist Renaud de la Brosse, an expert witness in the ICTY's Milošević trial, has written that Serbian ultranationalists created a hyper-controlled media environment in the 1990s to disguise their warmongering as a necessary defense of the Serbian nation.[47] Under Milošević, Serbian journalists went so far as to air footage of innocent victims killed by Serbian forces, while claiming that they were Serbian victims killed by genocidal Croats or Muslims. Ultranationalists also used the media to obfuscate their own war profiteering and divert attention away from the ensuing mob-like culture enjoyed by Serbian warlords, while most of Serbia was going bankrupt.[48] In such an environment, Šešelj's speeches, which today appear bombastic threats about non-Serbs, would have been believable.

Manipulating preexisting culture

The third condition is manipulating preexisting cultural ideas, such as symbols, myths or folklore, to make radical ideas appear consistent, traditional and even patriotic. In effect, propagandists package new wine in old bottles; that is what Serbian ultranationalists did to justify their wartime efforts.

Ultranationalists twisted the Battle of Kosovo myth to advance a narrative about the nation itself being messianic and destined for rebirth, otherwise known as messianic nationalism.[49] This narrative included the ultranationalist claim that Serbs not only were defenders of Europe but were chosen by God, akin to the Hebrews. Ultranationalists manipulated the historical traumas suffered by Serbs, including Ottoman occupation and genocide under Croatian Ustasha in the Second World War, to advance the narrative of Serbian innocent victimhood. Summarizing this narrative, Serbian anthropologist Marko Živković says it is "an exaggerated, larger-than-life, megalomaniacal story."[50] It claims that Serbs became the 'heavenly people' after choosing the kingdom of heaven over an earthly kingdom at the Battle of Kosovo, but have since suffered worldly evils in their inevitable defense of what is good and right. Building on his narrative, ultranationalists portrayed Serbs as inherently innocent victims, while Muslims and Croats were the epitome of evil, as evidenced by historical events.

These narratives are highly relevant for understanding the possible effects of Šešelj's speeches. The psychology of mass violence finds that believing one's in-group is inherently innocent and a perpetual victim of persecution by an out-group, who serves as an historical enemy, often precedes the persecution of that very out-group. This phenomenon is known as 'accusation in a mirror' and is a common predecessor to atrocity.[51] For example, anthropologist Alex Hinton found that genocides are usually preceded by collective narratives of unresolved in-group grievances over historical injustices and generational fears about perennial victimization. Likewise, historian Mahmood Mamdani finds that victimhood narratives, if manipulated by leaders, engender a victim-turned-killer mentality, in which genuine out-group threats set off an agenda of radical self-defense.[52] Serbia faced a similar situation at the outset of the Yugoslav Wars, in which the breakup of Yugoslavia appeared to shatter the interethnic peace of the republic. When Serbian ultranationalists portrayed Serbia as surrounded by historic enemies but destined for rebirth, they likely manipulated many Serbs into feeling as perennial victims and justified in the aggressive self-defense of their nation.

The mental condition: Šešelj's intentions and audience uptake

Let us now consider Šešelj's dangerous intentions. To demonstrate this, my discussion will weave together several aspects of the legal case against Šešelj and the cultural authority he wielded as a leader of Chetnik paramilitary formations. In so doing, it will become evident that Šešelj's messages were intended to encourage Chetniks in particular to commit mass violence and that audiences registered his intentions with signs of uptake.

Šešelj's power and authority

In his own defense at the ICTY, Šešelj described his propaganda campaign as 'boosting morale,' even though he repeatedly stressed (1) the genocidal intent of Croats and Muslims, (2) the necessity of defending a Greater Serbia and (3) the need for a Serbian state.[53] For Šešelj, his speeches were delivered in places where the ethnic cleansing of non-Serbs occurred soon after, but he did not intend for violence or for his words to have influenced perpetrators. Remarkably, the TC agreed with this line of reasoning, which contributed to Šešelj's 2016 acquittal.

Nevertheless, in 2018, the IRMCT, found Šešelj guilty of instigating persecution in the form of ethnically cleansing Croats, based on a single speech he gave at an ultranationalist rally in the village of Hrtkovci, Vojvodina.[54] On 6 May 1992, hundreds of Serbian radicals and Chetniks converged on Hrtkovci, where Šešelj delivered an inflammatory speech. Drawing on Serbian fears and disinformation in Milošević's controlled media, Šešelj accused Croats of horrific crimes against Serbs, called for the expulsion of Croats from Serbia, and even read aloud the names of individual Croats who lived in Hrtkovci. In its judgment, the AC summarized the speech and its consequences as follows:

> Mr. Šešelj addressed his 'Serbian brothers and sisters,' declaring, among other things, that 'there was no room for Croats in Hrtkovci,' and that 'we will drive them to the border of Serbian territory, and they can walk on from there, if they do not leave before of their own accord.' He directly addressed Croats by telling them 'you have nowhere to return to' and ended his speech by stating: 'I firmly believe that you, Serbs from Hrtkovci and other villages around here, will also know how to preserve your harmony and unity, that you will promptly get rid of the remaining Croats in your village and the surrounding villages.' Following Mr. Šešelj's speech, the crowd chanted slogans such as 'Croats, go to Croatia,' and 'This is Serbia.'[55]

What the AC omitted was that Šešelj referred to local Croats as 'Ustasha,' and thus portrayed them Nazi perpetrators or sympathizers in persecuting Serbs. Within days of Šešelj's speech, 722 Croats fled Hrtkovci or were forced out by threats of violence from squads of Chetniks or by fraudulent housing transfers countenanced by local authorities. Given the parallel between these actions and Šešelj's inflammatory message, the AC concluded that they occurred because of Šešelj's speech, and thus he was responsible for instigating the crime of persecution.

It deserves mentioning that Šešelj's Hrtkovci speech was the only message for which he was convicted. Does this mean, then, that Šešelj's other speeches were not dangerous – or, as Šešelj himself claimed, were intended to boost morale, without any influence on perpetrators? If we consider Šešelj's overall propaganda campaign as it connected to Serbia's Chetnik subculture, it becomes evident that Šešelj intended to instigate far more violence than the AC was able to recognize.

The chief reason is that Šešelj was a powerful political figure with considerable influence over ultranationalists Serbs. By 1991, Šešelj was reputed for defending

Serbian nationalism throughout the 1980s, despite opposition from communist authorities. Most critically, Šešelj was the unequivocal leader of Serbia's ultranationalist front in 1989, when Momčilo Đujić, a former Orthodox priest and then highest-ranking living Chetnik *Vojvoda*, bestowed on Šešelj the title Chetnik Vojvoda or Duke, equivalent to Chief War Lord of the Serbs.[56]

Understanding the significance of Šešelj's official position requires some knowledge of Chetniks, a militant subculture of Serbia. From 1945 to 1989, the Chetniks – a self-proclaimed network of Serbian freedom fighters – were driven underground by Tito and fellow communist, who outlawed various forms of ultranationalism.[57] Before then, the Chetniks were a significant military force in the Balkans. Originating in the Balkan Wars, the Chetniks were guerilla forces who eventually formalized their political aspirations in the Second World War under Draža Mihailović, a Serbian general, who organized an armed resistance to defend Serbia from the Axis Powers. Their ultranationalist ideology, which would later rival Tito's communism, centered on three goals: (1) restore the Serbian Kingdom, (2) defend Serbian freedom and (3) terrorize Serbia's enemies.[58]

Since the movement's inception, *restoring the kingdom* has meant reinstating the Serbian monarchy and reclaiming what Chetniks perceive as Serbia's rightful homelands. These include a swathe of Balkan territories once held by Serbia's medieval kingdom, and granted to Serbia by the 1915 Treaty of London, a secretly signed treaty, when the Triple *Entente* promised Serbs an expanded territorial state for their alliance in the First World War.[59] In the 1990s, when Chetniks reemerged politically, Šešelj coined a specific phrase to signify this territory, which included South Croatia, the Dalmatian Coast, Bosnia and Herzegovina, and Montenegro. This phrase, which is notorious for its evocations among ultranationalists, is the *Karlobag-Ogulin-Karlovac-Virovitica* (KOKV) line. This linguistic expression demarcated, for Šešelj and ultranationalists, the territorial borders of an imagined Serbian state, otherwise known as 'Greater Serbia.'[60] The acquisition of this Serbian homeland – which became a goal of Serbian forces in the Yugoslav Wars – connects to the Chetnik notion of *freedom*, which has meant securing autonomy and protecting 'Serbian blood and Orthodox faith,' including resistance to any political or economic system that threatens Serbs.[61] From their inception in the Balkan wars, Chetniks used terror tactics, such as assassinations and ethnic cleansings, to terrorize their enemies into submission.

After being forced underground for nearly half a century, the Chetnik movement entered mainstream politics in the late 1980s, following Tito's death, the ensuing socioeconomic and political crises, and the impending collapse of communism in Eastern Europe. The surge in ultranationalism came when Serbian leaders, such as Šešelj, openly broke with communism, earning them an almost savior-like quality among Chetniks.[62] As Yugoslavia moved toward dissolution, Šešelj incorporated the Chetnik movement into the Serbian Radical Party (SRS), and joined forces with Milošević, the president-elect of Serbia and later head of the Federal Republic of Yugoslavia (FRY).[63] By 1990, Šešelj was thus one of the most powerful political figures in Serbia, especially among Chetniks, ultranationalists and the far right.

Šešelj's intentions as ultranationalist leader

How can we infer a speaker's intentions? Based on pragmatics, if multiple audiences interpret speaker *S* as having intended message *G*, then it is likely that S intended G.[64] Though circular, this notion is a valid ethnographic inference in practice because meaning is jointly construed between the speaker and audiences who share a linguistic common ground. Therefore, intentions are derivable from not only what the speaker utters (and claims to have meant post hoc) but also audience uptake and the broader actions of the speaker that indicate his or her goals, plans or desires.

When it comes to Šešelj, two activities underscore his intent to bring about violence, and reveal that his post hoc defense of intending to boost morale is specious. First, Šešelj acted as the *de facto* propagandist for Serbian ultranationalism throughout the 1990s. He traveled to Serbian populations in Serbia, Croatia and Bosnia and Herzegovina where he propagated disinformation about an impending Serbian genocide; instructed communities to defend themselves against Croatian and Muslim neighbors; and recruited thousands of Chetnik volunteers for war.[65] Though Šešelj claims to have instructed Chetniks to comply with humanitarian law, most did not. In fact, his own personal unit, known colloquially as 'Šešeljevci' or Šešelj's Men, operated alongside the Serbian Volunteer Guard (SDG), headed by the Serbian warlord Željko Ražnatović aka Arkan, JNA, Army of Republika Srpska (VRS), and other Serb-led forces.[66] Wherever these units went, they left a wake of pillaging, ethnic cleansings, mass rape and massacres. Although Šešelj insists Chetniks were not under his command after recruitment, it must be stressed that they were still under his authority as Chetnik Vojvoda, a traditional military title of the supreme commander, who directed Chetnik units.

Second, Šešelj knew about the perpetration of mass violence and said nothing to deter it. Documents introduced at his trial showed that he was regularly informed about Chetnik military activities. Further, nearly all of his recruits used tactics that blatantly disregarded the Geneva Conventions, and appeared beset on conquering territory along the KOKV line – and this was likely intentional. For Serbian media at the time praised the combination of Šešelj's recruitment and Milošević's military tactics. The Belgrade Communist newspaper *Borba* (Struggle), for instance, concluded that, based on such coordination, "Milošević believes he now has the historic opportunity to once and for all settle accounts with the Croats and do what Serbian politicians after World War I did not – rally all Serbs in one Serbian State."[67] It is difficult to imagine that Šešelj advocated for a Greater Serbia, recruited volunteers who violently pursued this goal, remained informed about their actions throughout the war, and yet did not understand the extent to which his volunteers engaged in war crimes.

Finally, evidence introduced by the ICTY indicated that many of Šešelj's recruits were ordered by unit commanders to engage in mass violence or lacked sound military hierarchies to report degenerative wartime conditions.[68] It is once again difficult to fathom how Šešelj could have lacked the foresight of mass crimes occurring. Sociologists of war have shown that mass violence is complex, rarely spontaneous, and typically designed by political elites to achieve their regime's goals.[69] Hence, Šešelj was too high-ranking among the Serbian elite to have not known about commanders ordering mass violence or should have had the foreseeability of criminal circumstances developing under the political and military chain of command.

Šešelj speaker-intention and audience uptake

Contrary to the legal case against him, Šešelj's intention to persecute non-Serbs, as reflected in his actions and speeches, was not isolated to Hrtkovci. For consider that Šešelj gave numerous speeches at ultranationalist rallies throughout the former Yugoslavia that resembled his Hrtkovci speech. Crucially, his speeches occurred at locations where months, weeks, and sometimes only days after he spoke, Serbian offenses launched attacks on civilian populations and, in many instances, committed war crimes or crimes against humanity. On these occasions, a cultural insider with knowledge of Chetnik subculture would have clearly discerned Šešelj's intentions and his audience's uptake.

For example, on 15 May 1991, just months before Serbia's war with Croatia, Šešelj traveled along what would become the Serbian frontline making inflammatory speeches and recruiting more combatants. At an ultranationalist rally in Borovo Selo, a Croatian village a few miles north of Vukovar, where a deadly siege and the infamous Ovčara massacre would take place (where hundreds of Croatian survivors of Vukovar were murdered), Šešelj gave a speech to gathered Chetniks, saying,

> We are sending a message to the new Ustasha head of state and Ustasha regime in Croatia: Serbian heads have rolled, struck down by the Ustasha hand in Serbian Krajina [...] We will avenge Serbian blood![70]

In response, Šešelj's audience, shouted back, "We will!" Šešelj went on to say, in a telling narrative that then reflected his intentions:

> As far as we are concerned, the Croats can leave Yugoslavia any time they want, but we are letting them know openly that they will not take a single inch of Serbian territory, not a piece of land on which there are Serb villages, demolished churches, pits in which Serbs were butchered, Serbian

> camps, Serbian killing fields, such as a Jasenovac. Should we permit that, we would be unworthy of our glorious ancestors and shamed before our descendants. The Croats may create their new state but only to the west of the Karlobag-Ogulin-Karlovac-Virovitica line. Everything to the east of that line is Serbia.[71]

Now, Šešelj may claim in his defense that he was boosting morale here. But that would not explain the ensuing call and response between himself and his audience. Šešelj went on to say,

> Tuđman and the new Ustasha government in Croatia have again put the criminal *kama* [a knife used by Ustasha in the Second World War to kill Serbs] under the throat of the Serbian people [...] We say to them we shall *take revenge* for each Serbian life and we shall also ask to pay up for past crimes. Also, for crimes in recent history. Nothing will remain unpunished and we will not allow the consequences of the occupation of the Serb lands and the Serb people.[72]
>
> (emphasis added)

At the end of Šešelj's speech, his mostly Chetnik audience began chanting "Revenge! Revenge! Revenge! (*Osveta! Osveta! Osveta!*)"

An outsider is likely to overlook numerous peripheral meanings in this speech. Most notable are Šešelj's equivocation between Franjo Tuđman, first democratically elected President of Croatian in 1990, and the Croatian people with the Ustasha, a military force reinstituted in Croatia under the Third Reich. The Ustasha are reviled today for enacting a practice to convert, ethnically cleanse, or annihilate Serbs and Jews from a Greater Croatia. While the Ustasha and Croats are by no means equivalent, the media under Milošević portrayed Tuđman's independent Croatia as a return to Ustasha-like fascism.[73] The Serbian media thus spread disinformation about Croats to debase them as modern-day Ustasha, and thereby heighten Serbian insecurities, notions of innocent-victimhood, and support for national rebirth. Building on these themes, Šešelj went one step further by advocating vengeance.

By knowing a bit about Chetnik culture, one can see why Šešelj's speech is a clear call to enact violence against Croats writ large. Like most of his speeches, Šešelj's Borovo Selo speech began by reiterating the threefold ideology of Chetniks and making claims to lands within the KOKV line. Such a trope signaled to his audience that his words should be interpreted within the frame of Chetnik ultranationalism. Šešelj then made his case for defending Serbian freedom by warning the crowd that Serbia was once again threatened by fascism in Croatia. He then rallied the attending Chetniks, telling the agitated crowd that they will "revenge Serbian blood." To which the crowd chanted "Revenge! Revenge! Revenge!"[74] This response is a sign of uptake. After all, Šešelj associates the Croatian threat with the defense of traditional Serbian lands and vengeance for

Serbian blood. Moreover, he insinuates that Chetniks would be shamed if they did not defend lands within the KOKV line and avenge Croatian victims, thus implying expulsion from Serbian territories or unilateral punishment for past crimes. When the audience chanted "revenge!" in response to Šešelj's speech, and Šešelj himself did not dispel it, it was a signal that he and the audience collectively intended mass violence against Croats.

The consequence: What happened because of Šešelj's speeches?

However, questionable Šešelj's knowledge and ultimate intentions remain, he held considerable influence over his followers. According to Balkan historian Yves Tomic, Šešelj was *the Vojvoda* – the unequivocal leader – for Chetniks, who revered and honored him.[75] Šešelj was also an unapologetic strongman with a great deal of charisma, and embodied an archetypal leadership quality, which many Serbs – and certainly Chetniks – have admired and followed. Taken together, Šešelj held much sway over his followers, a point emphasized by the ICTY prosecution, who described Šešelj in this way:

> We had insiders who talked about how powerful he [Vojislav Šešelj] was. How they looked up to him like he was a god. How his influence is evidenced by his popularity and the number of volunteers he was able to recruit, and the number of people who identified their group by using his name – the Šešeljevci.[76]

Possessing such influence is the most significant factor in getting others to perform actions that are otherwise considered immoral. Richard Wilson observes that Stanley Milgram's replicated shock-experiments show how most ordinary persons will abuse because of an authority figure's orders.[77] Given this, even if Šešelj hinted that followers should engage in mass violence – let alone encourage them to do so – they would have likely complied.

The parallel between Šešelj's speeches and the actions of his audiences reveal how influential he was as a propagandist. As an illustration, let us return to Šešelj's Borovo Selo speech and consider events that ensued soon thereafter in Vukovar, the first of many civilian populations sieged and terrorized by Serbian forces. Vukovar, a Croatian city a ten-minute drive south of Borovo Selo, was falsely portrayed by the Serbian media in 1991 as a stronghold for Croatian Ustasha.[78] Recall that during this time, Šešelj's Borovo Selo speech accused Croats of enacting fascism, thus encouraging Chetniks and Serbian ultranationalists that vengeance could be exercised against the Croatian city. As Serbian forces marched toward the city, the Serbian media and ultranationalist leaders depicted the Vukovar military operation as a *liberation* to stop, for instance, Ustasha from torturing Serbian children.[79] The truth was far different. A motley crew of Serbian forces, including the JNA and Serbian paramilitary forces, surrounded the civilian city and shelled it for 87 days. After the city fell, the alleged Ustasha stronghold could not be found, but a Serbian reporter still defended the siege, telling Reuters, an international news agency, that he witnessed the discovery of 41 Serbian children, who had been tortured to death by Croats. Reuters, in determining the facts of the story, discovered that it was a rumor, stemming from earlier disinformation propagated in Serbian media – demonstrating the echo chamber of ultranationalist propaganda.[80] Nevertheless, in Serbian media, the story was reported as factual, alongside other reports that Croats were sacrificing children and killing adults to harvest their organs on the black market.

At the same time, Serbian forces secretly transferred 261 prisoners from Vukovar to a nearby farm in Ovčara, where they were tortured, executed, and buried in a mass grave. Years later, testimony would come to light at the ICTY that Serbian combatants at Ovčara, some of them members of Šešelj's Chetnik paramilitary units, justified their actions as vengeance for the alleged Serbian victims of Ustaša crimes.[81] These actions not only parallel the vengeance that Šešelj called for at Borovo Selo but also underscore the dangers of vengeful speech alongside disinformation such as atrocity stories.

Revenge looks like a powerful psychological motivator and contributor to collective violence. Biologist Michael McCullough has found that hominins, including humans, likely evolved to respond to injustices or threats of repeat offense with revenge.[82] Based on game theoretical evidence and the archeological record, McCullough demonstrates that revenge is likely an adaptive strategy to prevent individual or group exploitation and thus threats to survival and fitness.[83] Likewise, Richard Wilson and colleagues conducted experiments among US and Serbian populations, disguising nine of Šešelj's speeches – which were originally coded and used as evidence by sociologist and propaganda expert witness Anthony Oberschall at Šešelj's ICTY trial – as primes about a fictional country and an out-group.[84] After exposure to one of the speeches, participants then made a series of political decisions, including supporting violence against the population targeted in the speech. Across populations, Wilson and colleagues found that Šešelj's speeches on revenge contributed to support for violence and lack of empathy for the out-group.[85] Hence, Šešelj's calls for violence at Borovo Selo, months before the siege of Vukovar, were probably highly persuasive for Chetnik followers.

To further demonstrate the influence of Šešelj's speech, there is direct evidence of perpetrators using Šešelj's own words to justify mass violence enacted on the Vukovar population. Specifically, Šešelj's notion of defending Serbia and thereby cleansing it of non-Serbs within his so-called KOKV line. That linguistic phrase was directly echoed by perpetrators videotaped later in the war. For instance, after the fall of Vukovar in 1991, a drunken Serbian paramilitary fighter was filmed saying, "War will be over when we have our limits – Karlobag, Karlovac, Ogulin, Virovitica. All place(s) where Serbian people live must be free, you know. We must clean up with the Croats."[86] Dojčinović claims that the shared mental concepts in Šešelj's speeches and perpetrator reports, such as the above paramilitary fighter's comments, are evidence of a 'mental fingerprint.'[87] That is, evidence that a perpetrator was influenced by a propagandist insofar as the perpetrator himself justifies his actions by repeating the language of a propagandist, which would not occur unless the language was influential.

Conclusion

A firm grasp of these three underlying concepts of speech are necessary if dangerous propaganda is to be understood. No study of language as a series of actions, and of the differences between the modes of speech that make action possible, is arguably more helpful than speech acts theory. By combining knowledge about speech acts and recent discoveries about the social motivations to accept or engage in mass violence, we can begin to understand when propaganda is most dangerous. I have tried to give a preliminary analysis of propaganda, including supporting evidence from the cognitive and behavioral sciences, that together allow us to identify when it is a social danger. I have argued that we cannot expect to judge accurately the dangers of propaganda by asking what immediately happened after (i) a message *P* by speaker *S* was uttered at time *t*1 in context *c*. We must go further by asking what were (ii) the intentions *I* of speak *S* and uptake *U* of persons *R* in *c* at *t*1 and what context-related cultural evidence is there for (iii) actions *Q* of persons *R* at time *t*2 because of (i) and (ii). To demonstrate this, I have drawn from my own ethnographic experience in the Balkans to analyze the propaganda of Vojislav Šešelj. It is my hope that the general formula I have provided can contribute to the work of other scholars interested in understanding or identifying forms of dangerous propaganda.

Notes

1 G. Jowett and V. O'Donnell, *Propaganda and Persuasion*, Seventh Edition, London: Sage, 2019, pp. 1–3.
2 This is the case for U.S. law, the precedent for which is based on Brandenburg v. Ohio, 395 U.S. 444 (1969). In international case law, the imminent lawlessness standard is based on Ferdinand Nahimana, Jean-Bosco Barayagwiza, Hassan Ngeze v. The Prosecutor, Judgment, Case No. ICTR-99-52-A, 28 November 2007.
3 In U.S. law, this was stated in Brandenburg (1969) and thereafter reinforced in Hess v. Indiana, 414 U.S. 105 (1973), N.A.A.C.P. v Claiborne Hardware Co., 485 U.S. 886 (1982), Texas v. Johnson, 491 U.S. 397 (1989), U.S. v. Lee, N.W.2d 250 (1993), and U.S. v. White, 401 U.S. 745 (2012).
4 See S. Benesch, 'The Ghost of Causation in International Speech Crime Cases,' pp. 254–268; P. Dojčinović, 'Word Scene Investigations: Toward a Cognitive Linguistic Approach to The Criminal Analysis of Open Source Evidence in War Crimes Cases,' pp. 71–117; A. Oberschall, 'Propaganda, Hate Speech and Mass Killings,' pp. 171–200, all in P. Dojčinović (ed.), *Propaganda, War Crimes Trials and International Law: From Speakers' Corner to War Crimes*, Abingdon, New York, NY: Routledge, 2012. J. Leader Maynard and S. Benesch, 'Dangerous Speech and Dangerous Ideology: An Integrated Model for Monitoring and Prevention,' *Genocide Studies and Prevention: An International Journal*, vol. 9, no. 3, 2016, pp. 70–95.

5 J. Kiper, 'Toward an Anthropology of War Propaganda,' *Political and Legal Anthropology Review*, vol. 38, no. 1, 2015, pp. 129–146. C. Mironko, 'The Effect of RTLM's Rhetoric of Ethnic Hatred in Rural Rwanda,' in A. Thompson (ed.), *The Media and the Rwandan Genocide*, London: Pluto Press, 2007, pp. 125–135. R.A. Wilson, *Incitement on Trial: Prosecuting International Speech Crimes*, Cambridge: Cambridge University Press, 2017. R.A. Wilson and J. Kiper, 'Brandenburg in an Era of Populism: Risk Analysis in the First Amendment, Law and Public Affairs' (in press).

6 J. Searle, *Speech Acts*, Cambridge: Cambridge University Press, 1969.

7 J.L. Austin, *How to Do Things with Words*, Cambridge, MA: Harvard University Press, 1962.

8 Austin, *How to Do*, pp. 150–163. See also J. Searle, *The Construction of Social Reality*, New York, NY: Free Press, 1995, pp. 190–191.

9 A few of the most prominent studies are as follows: A. Bandura, 'Moral Disengagement in the Perpetration of Inhumanities,' *Personality and Social Psychology Review*, vol. 3, no. 3, 1999, pp. 193–209. S. Milgram, *Obedience to Authority: An Experimental View*, New York, NY: Harper & Row, 1974. P. Zimbardo, *The Lucifer Effect: Understanding How Good People Turn Evil*, New York, NY: Random House, 2007.

10 For a review, see A. Oberschall, *Vojislav Šešelj's Nationalist Propaganda: Contents, Techniques, Aims and Impacts, 1990–1994*. Expert Report for the Office of the Prosecutor at the International Criminal Tribunal for the Former Yugoslavia, 2006. The Prosecutor v. Vojislav Šešelj, Case No. IT-03-67, exhibit no. P00005.

11 The Prosecutor v. Vojislav Šešelj, Trial Judgment, Case No. IT-03-67-T, 31 March 2016 [hereinafter Šešelj TJ].

12 In Prosecutor v. Vojislav Šešelj, Appeal Judgment, Case No. MICT-16-99-A, 11 April 2018, para. 1138 [hereinafter Šešelj AJ] states that the judgment itself refers only to Šešelj's hate speech in the town of Hrtkovci, Serbia. Furthermore, the AC explains in paras 1154–1155 the specifics of this crime, stating,

> Based on the foregoing, the Appeals Chamber finds Seselj responsible, pursuant to Article 1 of the Mechanism's Statute and Articles 5(d), 5(h), 5(i) and 7(1) of the ICTY Statute, for instigating deportation, persecution (forcible displacement), and other inhumane acts (forcible transfer) as crimes against humanity.
>
> para. 1155

13 Benesch, 'The Ghost,' pp. 257–259; Kiper, 'Toward an Anthropology,' pp. 129–131; Wilson, *Incitement*, pp. 144–146.

14 Prosecutor v Jean Paul Akayesu, Trial Judgment Case No. ICTR-96-4-T, 2 September 1998, para. 349 [hereinafter Akayesu TJ].

15 See, for example, A. Hinton, *Why Did They Kill? Cambodia in the Shadow of Genocide*, Berkeley, CA: University of California Press, 2005. M. Mamdani, *When Victims Become Killers: Colonialism, Nativism, and the Genocide in Rwanda*, Princeton, NJ: Princeton University Press, 2001. Mironko, 'The Effect of RTLM's Rhetoric.'

16 Jowett and O'Donnell, *Propaganda*, p. 7.

17 Leader Maynard and Benesch, *Dangerous Speech*, pp. 77–79.

18 T. Kamilindi, 'Journalism in a Time of Hate Media,' in A. Thompson (ed.), *The Media*, pp. 136–144.

19 Oberschall, 'Propaganda,' pp. 182–185.

20 Dojčinović, *Word Scene Investigations*, pp. 4–5; Wilson, *Incitement*, p. 4.

21 J.R. Searle, 'How performatives work,' *Linguistics and Philosophy*, vol. 12, no. 5, 1989, p. 552.

22 Austin, *How to Do*, pp. 24, 76, 114.

23 J.R. Searle, 'Collective intentions and actions,' in P. Cohen, J. Morgan, and M.E. Pollack (eds), *Intentions in Communication*, Cambridge: The MIT Press, 1990, p. 401.

24 Austin, *How to Do*, p. 117.

25 Searle, *Construction*, p. 43.
26 Searle, *How Performatives Work*, p. 549.
27 Wilson, *Incitement*, p. 255.
28 M. Kimani, 'RTLM: The Medium That Became A Tool for Mass Murder," in Thompson (ed.), *The Media*, pp. 119–122.
29 Dojčinović, *Word Scene Investigations*, pp. 95–96.
30 S. Ramet, *Thinking about Yugoslavia: Scholarly Debates about the Yugoslav Breakup and the Wars in Bosnia and Kosovo*, Cambridge: Cambridge University Press, 2005, p. 149.
31 See Benesch, 'The Ghost,' pp. 262–264; Wilson, *Incitement*, p. 263.
32 P.B. Mieczyslaw, *Regime Change in the Yugoslav Succession States: Divergent Paths Toward a New Europe*, Baltimore, MD: Johns Hopkins University Press, 2010, pp. 66–67.
33 D. Jović, *Yugoslavia: A State that Withered Away*, West Lafayette, IN: Purdue University Press, 2009, pp. 32, 145, 179.
34 See R.J. Dalton, *Democratic Challenges, Democratic Choices: The Erosion of Political Support in Advanced Industrial Democracies*, Oxford: Oxford University Press, 2004, p. 12.
35 P. Norris, *Critical Citizens: Global Support for Democratic Governance*, New York, NY: Oxford University Press, 1999, p. 26.
36 Jović, *Yugoslavia*, pp. 176–184.
37 P. Mojžes, 'Religion and the Yugoslav Wars (1991–1999),' in B. Radeljić and M. Topić (eds), *Religion in the Post-Yugoslav Context*, London: Lexington Books, 2015, pp. 1–16.
38 See R. Spears, 'Toward an Integrative Social Identity Model of Collective Action: A Quantitative Research Synthesis of Three Socio-Psychological Perspectives,' *Psychological Bulletin*, vol. 134, no. 4, 2008, p. 504.
39 M. Mann, *The Dark Side of Democracy: Explaining Ethnic Cleansing*, Cambridge: Cambridge University Press, 2004, p. 374.
40 J. Armatta, *Twilight of Impunity: The War Crimes Trial of Slobodan Milošević*, Durham, NC: Duke University Press, 2010, p. 128.
41 See I. Boljević, D. Odavić, V. Petrović, S. Rabrenović, B. Stanković, J.S. Janković, N. Vučo and D. Vukotić, *Reči i nedela: pozivanje ili podsticanje na ratne zločine medijima u Srbiji 1991–1992* (Words and Misdeeds: Calling for or Inciting War Crimes in the Serbian Media, 1991–1992), Beograd: Studija tužilaštva za ratne zločine Republike Srbije, 2011.
42 Ramet, *Thinking about Yugoslavia*, pp. 270–271.
43 See B. Bushman and C.A. Anderson, 'Comfortably Numb: Desensitizing Effects of Violent Media on Helping Others,' *Psychological Science*, vol. 20, no. 3, 2009, p. 273.
44 N. Carnagey, C.A. Anderson and B. Bartholow, 'Media Violence and Social Neuroscience,' *Current Directions in Psychological Science*, vol. 16, no. 4, 2007, pp. 180–181.
45 Ibid., pp. 180–181.
46 J. Scott, 'Moral Panic,' in J. Scott (ed.), *A Dictionary of Sociology*, New York, NY: Oxford University Press, 2014, p. 492.
47 R. de la Brosse, *Political Propaganda and the Plan to Create A 'State for All Serbs': Consequences of Using the Media for Ultra-Nationalist Ends*, Expert Report to the Office of the Prosecutor of the International Criminal Tribunal for the Former Yugoslavia, 2003.
48 Scott, 'Moral Panic.'
49 As cited in Ramet, *Thinking about Yugoslavia*, p. 149.
50 M. Živković, 'The Wish to Be a Jew: The Power of the Jewish Trope in the Yugoslav Conflict,' *Cahiers de l'URMIS*, vol. 15, no. 6, 2000, p. 249.
51 The basic idea of 'accusation in a mirror' is that propagandists 'impute to enemies exactly what they and their own party are planning to do.' A. Des Forges, *Leave*

None to Tell the Story: Genocide in Rwanda, New York, NY: Human Rights Watch, 1999, p. 66. See also Akayesu TJ, para. 99. The Prosecutor v. Ferdinand Nahimana, Jean-Bosco Barayagwiza, Hassan Ngeze, Judgment and Sentence, Case No. ICTR-99-52-T, 3 December 2003, para. 111.
52 Hinton, *Why Did They Kill?*.
53 Šešelj TJ, paras 56, 227, 230, 257, 275, 322, 331.
54 Šešelj AJ.
55 Ibid.
56 Prosecutor v. Šešelj, Case No. IT-03-67, Third Amended Indictment, 7 December 2007, para 3.
57 J. Tomasevich, *War and Revolution in Yugoslavia, 1941–1945: Occupation and Collaboration*, Stanford, CA: Stanford University Press, 1975, pp. 171–176.
58 Tomasevich, *War and Revolution*, pp. 256–261.
59 This issue was discussed at Šešelj's trial, where historian Yves Tomic demonstrated that the Treaty of London was unrelated to the territorial claims made by Šešelj, such as KOKV line, contrary to Šešelj's own rhetoric. See Prosecutor v. Šešelj, Case No. IT-03-67, trial transcript, 29 January 2008, pp. 2929–2940. Online. Available HTTP: <http://www.icty.org/x/cases/seselj/trans/en/080129ED.htm> (accessed 11 June 2019).
60 Dojčinović, *Word Scene Investigations*, p. 95.
61 Tomasevich, *War and Revolution*, pp. 256–261.
62 N. Cigar, *Genocide in Bosnia: The Policy of Ethnic Cleansing*, College Station, TX: Texas A&M Press, 1995, p. 201.
63 Ibid.
64 S. Croddy, 'Meaning and intention,' *Journal of Pragmatics*, vol. 12, no. 1, 1988, p. 1.
65 C. Bassiouni, 'Final Report on the United Nations Commission of Experts Established Pursuant to Security Council Resolution 780,' United Nations Security Council Report, December 28, 1994.
66 R. Lukić and A. Lynch, *Europe from the Balkans to the Urals: The Disintegration of Yugoslavia and the Soviet Union*, Oxford: Oxford University Press, 1996, p. 190.
67 Bassiouni, 'Final Report.'
68 For example, see The Prosecutor of the Tribunal against Goran Hadžić, First Amended Indictment, Case No. IT-04-75-I, 22 July 2011. See also Wilson, *Incitement*, p. 117.
69 See Mann, *The Dark Side of Democracy*.
70 Prosecutor v. Šešelj, Case No. IT-03-67, trial transcript, 7 November 2007, p. 1799. Online. Available HTTP: <http://www.icty.org/x/cases/seselj/trans/en/071107IT.htm> (accessed 11 June 2019).
71 Ibid., p. 1800.
72 Ibid., p. 1802.
73 Prosecutor v. Šešelj, Prosecution's Closing Brief, Case No. IT-03-67-T, 5 February 2012, paras 51, 122.
74 For 'revenge' rhetoric and its effects, see for example Prosecutor v. Šešelj, Case No. IT-03-67-T, Prosecution's Closing Brief, 5 February 2012, paras 32, 54, 185, 460.
75 As cited in Wilson, *Incitement*, p. 116.
76 Ibid.
77 Ibid., p. 227.
78 Boljević, *Reči i nedela*, pp. 388–393.
79 Ibid.
80 Ibid.
81 Online. Available HTTP: <http://www.icty.org/en/content/ljubica-došen> (accessed 12 May 2019).

82 See M. McCullough, *Beyond Revenge: The Evolution of the Forgiveness Instinct*, San Francisco, CA: Jossey-Bass, 2008.

83 Ibid., pp. 95–99.

84 C.M. Lillie, B. Knapp, L.T. Harris and R.A. Wilson, 'This Is the Hour of Revenge: The Psychology of Propaganda and Mass Atrocities,' 2015. Online. Available HTTP: <https://ssrn.com/abstract=2580521> (accessed 11 June 2019).

85 Ibid.

86 As cited in Wilson, *Incitement*, p. 274.

87 Dojčinović, *Word Scene Investigations*, pp. 95–96.

Chapter 11

Song as a propaganda tool in the genocide against the Tutsi in Rwanda

Évariste Ntakirutimana and Marie-Claire Uwamariya

Introduction

Music and lyrics are among the most persuasive forms of artistic expression used to communicate thoughts and emotions.[1] Ideologues, politicians, activists and musicians have historically utilized music and songs to capture people's attention for various purposes, including national or ethnic ideologies.[2]

In Rwanda, *Abanyuramatwi*, a choir composed of Hutu singers after the 1959 Social Revolution,[3] praised the first Hutu leaders, Dominique Mbonyumutwa and Grégoire Kayibanda in their music.[4] Mbonyumutwa and Kayibanda were influential historical figures that led the people of Rwanda from the monarchy regime to the First Republic in 1961.[5] Their favorite and best-known songs were *Jya mbere Rwanda* (Rwanda: Go Forward), *Isafari ya demokarasi* (Journey to democracy), *Ganza Rwanda urabikwiye* (Reign high Rwanda, you deserve it) and *Turatsinze* (We have won). These songs feature many prominent references to the political ideology from the Social Revolution of 1959.[6]

Abanyuramatwi praised the heroism of the first president of the Republic and glorified the bravery of the Hutu majority who were considered to be dominated and oppressed by the Tutsi minority. The choir also glorified the *Mouvement Démocratique Républicain* (MDR: Democratic Republican Movement) *Parmehutu*, which was recognized as the party for Hutu emancipation.

Similarly, during the Second Republic (1973–94), there were groups that praised the power of President Juvenal Habyarimana,[7] who was depicted as a providential guide, and his one-party political system defined by the *Mouvement Révolutionnaire National pour le Développement* (MRND: National Revolutionary Movement for Development). There existed a plethora of orchestras such as the *Impala Popular Band*, *Abamararungu* and the Simon Bikindi's *Irindiro Ballet* which praised the former president.[8]

All of these groups were made up of singers who used their music primarily to recall Rwandan history. The themes of their songs revolved around the acts of the Tutsi who dominated and oppressed the Hutu during the past period of monarchy and colonization. These groups were also engaged in propaganda by reviving the circumstances that led to the 1959 Social Revolution. Their songs were used as tools to demonstrate that the Hutu had won and were now emancipated from their oppressors, conveying a message of heroism and, above all, the hatred toward the oppressors, the Tutsi. These groups were among the most recognized musicians in Rwanda during the Second Republic. Several decades later, through his songs, Simon Bikindi became one of the key figures in developing hatred against the Tutsi and may have directly and indirectly contributed to the spreading of genocidal ideas in Rwandan society. This chapter aims to determine the exact nature of Simon Bikindi's songs within the context of the Rwandan genocide.

Methodology

This section explains the origin and nature of the linguistic data and how the data was collected and analyzed.

Simon Bikindi had a repertoire of about 25 songs, some of which were used for wedding ceremonies. However, we will focus on three of them, namely, *Akabyutso*, *Intabaza* and *Twasezereye ingoma ya cyami*, for analysis. These songs were chosen to reflect the songs examined by the International Criminal Tribunal for Rwanda (ICTR) during the trial of Simon Bikindi.[9] Bikindi was indicted and charged with four counts of genocide and two counts of crimes against humanity.[10]

Susan Benesch and Carol Pauli[11] put forth different criteria for an inciting message in their respective works. Benesch's criteria include (a) the nature of the message and the audience understanding, (b) speaker authority and audience capacity, (c) recent violence, (d) survival of marketplace of ideas, (e) dehumanization and audience conditioning, and (f) prior similar messages, while Pauli has the following criteria: (a) media environment, (b) political context, (c) audience characteristics, (d) authority of the message source, (e) content of the message, (f) channel of communication and (g) overt acts.[12]

In this chapter, in addition to an analysis of Benesch and Pauli's respective approaches, a lexicological approach will be applied to show whether or not a message is an inciting message. This methodological approach examines messages by selecting the key words or terms used in order to explain them along with the context.[13] To paraphrase Ferdinand de Saussure, the father of modern linguistics, words *per se* don't have meanings, they have value and use.[14] This framework shows the teleological effect of the songwriter, whereby the intention of the author will also be investigated. All elements included in Benesch and Pauli's models will be clarified with the application of sociolinguistic analysis.

We will also demonstrate that these three songs, written and performed by Bikindi, encouraged the hate of Hutu against Tutsi and incited the perpetration of the genocide in 1994. Propaganda is defined here broadly as information, ideas, opinions or images spread in order to influence people's point of view or behavior.[15] As native Kinyarwanda speakers, and for reasons of the most accurate analysis, we use the original text in Kinyarwanda, accompanied by an English translation provided by the ICTR language section, *mutatis mutandis*.[16]

The trial of Simon Bikindi

The prosecution alleged that Simon Bikindi knowingly and intentionally encouraged people to commit genocide.[17] He was accused of collaborating with the government and military leaders and Radio-Télévision Libre des Mille Collines (RTLM)[18] personnel to organize and incite people to commit genocide. He was further charged with recruiting members of *Interahamwe* (youth wing of the MRND party), overseeing their training, and personally ordering them to kill. He was also accused of acts of sexual violence, as well as personal participation in the killings of several people. Uniquely and specifically, however, "Simon Bikindi was charged with persecution on the basis that he intentionally composed songs that provoked anti-Tutsi discrimination."[19]

In 2008, the ICTR Chamber ruled that even though Simon Bikindi composed the songs with the specific intent of encouraging ethnic hatred, he did not control what RTLM aired.[20] With that decision, the related counts (conspiracy to commit genocide, genocide, complicity in genocide and murder and persecution as crimes against humanity) were summarily dismissed. The ICTR convicted Bikindi of direct and public incitement to commit genocide and sentenced him to 15 years imprisonment.[21] Bikindi was released in 2016.[22] He died on 15 December 2018 in Benin, where he lived quietly, tending a small farm. This chapter aims to contribute to justice inasmuch as it can determine the genuine nature of the songs' messages in Kinyarwanda and their impact on Rwandan society.

Simon Bikindi, biography and creation

Simon Bikindi was born on 28 September 1954 in a former Rwerere Commune, Gisenyi Prefecture. Between 1990 and 1994, he was a well-known singer-songwriter of popular music and director of *Irindiro*, a performance ballet. Bikindi was also a staff member in the Ministry of Youth and Sports, and a member of the MRND political party.

Simon Bikindi was perceived as a talented singer-songwriter and poet. His songs were aired by RTLM, an "extremist Hutu radio station that broadcast Tutsi hate rhetoric and calls for violence during the genocide."[23] The songs were particularly popular because of their recognizable rhythm and the use of a traditional instrument in Rwanda, the cithara. The rhythm and use of the cithara also contributed to Simon Bikindi's increasing and widespread popularity. The following table inventories and categorizes Simon Bikindi's songs.

The first column comprises the songs that deal with Rwandan politics and history and praise the bravery of the Hutu people and their leaders. The second column contains songs about the 1990–94 war, and the lyrics indicate that freedom must be attained by fighting in order to safeguard the benefits from the Rwandan revolution (1959) and independence (1962). These songs were also meant to boost the morale of the army, especially the combatants. The last column lists the songs related to weddings or marriage. The three areas are historically and culturally important for Rwandan people depending on the situation implied.

There are other songs that were composed when Bikindi was in exile in République Démocratique du Congo (RDC), former Zaïre, starting from July 1994. The best-known song was composed in Mugunga, an important refugee camp in the Former Zaire, and was called 'Imboroza.' We don't know much about this song, but as it was composed in a refugee camp and refers to 'something that makes people cry,' we can presume it refers to the Rwandan Patriotic Front (RPF)[24] that defeated the former Rwanda army and led to the displacement of people into refugee camps like this one. Bikindi started singing when he was young. In the course of his early career, he sang several other songs, such as "Marigarita" (*Marguerite*). The lyrics to these two songs from other periods of Bikindi's life are not currently able to be found, so the analysis will focus on the relevant songs from Table 11.1.

Table 11.1 Simon Bikindi's songs

Politics or and Rwandan History	*Liberation war (1990–94)*	*Wedding or marriage*
Twasezereye ingoma ya cyami (we bade farewell to the monarchy)	Ingabo z'u Rwanda (Rwanda Army/ Rwanda militaries)	Umwari warezwe neza (well-educated girl)
Akabyutso (awakening)	Ingabo ni izirurwanira (militaries are those who fight for Rwanda)	Uwo tungana (who has the same age as I)
Intabaza (the alert)	Ni mwe mwariraye (it is you who spend the night fighting)	Umwumba (that bring pleasure, good time)
Nanga agasuzuguro (I hate disdain, disrespect)	Imparirwakunesha (those used to defeat the enemy)	Murakenyere muraberewe (put your good clothes and look good)
Mbwira abumva (I speak to those who understand)	Ni nde watubasha? (who can defeat us?)	Roza (rosa)
Karahanyuze (that has run its course; that has seen its day)	Tuzakomeza kururwanirira (we will still be fighting for Rwanda)	Ugereyo amahoro meza (arrive there in good peace)
Nanga abahutu (I hate the Hutu)	Tuzakurwanirira Rwanda (we will fight for you Rwanda)	Oya ngwino urare (oh, please came and spend the night)
Kirikiri (onomatopoeia that imitates a kind of rythmical dance)	Mwaraharwanye, ngabo z'u Rwanda (you really fougth, Rwanda militaries	Imboroza (that makes people cry)
–	Ramping rapide (prompt crawl)	–
8	9	8

More recently, after his release from prison in 2016, Bikindi composed a song to honor Mrs. Victoire Ingabire Umuhoza, a political opponent of the current Rwandan Government. Mrs. Umuhoza was sentenced in 2012 by the High Court of Kigali for "conspiracy against the country through terrorism and war" and "genocide denial" and was released in 2018, after President Paul Kagame granted her, and two thousand other prisoners, early release.[25] The song is titled "Umuhoza Ingabire Victoria Intwari Mutunguruzwa Rumenerangabo" and its lyrics praise Umuhoza's bravery.

The collection of popular songs catalogued above indicates that Bikindi was, indeed, a well-known artist with a status that could enable him to exercise significant influence over the Rwandan society. The following section focuses on three specific songs in order to show that they may have provoked anti-Tutsi discrimination. It must be noted that these songs are comparably identical to a number of RTLM broadcasts, *Kangura*[26] writings, and the evidence presented in the ICTR's so-called 'Media Case.'[27]

Simon Bikindi's message: cry havoc and let slip the dogs of war

This section is devoted to the analysis of the message conveyed by Simon Bikindi to his audience, the Rwandan people. The three songs that form the corpus of the study are as follows:

- *Twasezereye ingoma ya Cyami* (We bade farewell to the monarchy or we said goodbye to the monarchy).
- *Akabyutso* or *Nanga abahutu* (I hate the Hutu or The Awakening).
- *Intabaza* or *Bene Sebahinzi* (The descendants of Sebahinzi or The Alert).

These three songs propose a particular version of the history of Rwanda in general and of the Hutu specifically. This version of history emphasizes the Hutu initiative and leadership in abolishing the monarchy in 1959. The songs serve to remind the listener that the Hutu were long marginalized by the previous systems of power. Not only is this message a simple reminder, but context tells us it is also a form of encouragement to mobilize the Hutu against the Tutsi. Moreover, the songs' lyrics are filled with emotional language which aggravates feelings of resentment for the Hutu listener. Through the use of such language, these three songs convey a form of sociopolitical propaganda.

1 Message of Twasezereye Ingoma Ya Cyami *(We bade farewell to the monarchy)*

Simon Bikindi composed this song in order to participate in an artistic festival competition at the Rwandan Government's commemoration of the 25th anniversary of national independence on 1 July 1987. The song is composed of a refrain and six couplets.

1.1 Refrain: The refrain comprises the following keywords

Twasezereye	We said goodbye
Ingoma mbi ya cyami	The bad monarchy regime
Ingoma gikolonize	Colonialism
Demokarasi itwizihiye	The bonds of democracy
Twishimire ubwigenge	Let us rejoice for independence

Simon Bikindi refers to the colonial period to remind the Hutu of the suffering caused by the previous feudal (1959) and colonial regimes (1896–1962)[28] He encourages all the Hutu to safeguard the gains from the 1959 Rwandan Revolution and the 1962 Independence.[29] These words imply that action needs to be taken, or else the Hutu will be dominated and mistreated by the Tutsi as they were doing during the pre-independence period.[30]

1.2 Couplets 1–2: These couplets comprise the following keywords

Terera amaso inyuma	Turn your eyes back
Ibuka ikiboko ibuka ishiku	Remember the whip, remember the forced labor
Iminsi y'akazi kadahemberwa	Remember the days of unremunerated labor
Wishimire ubwigenge	Let us rejoice for independence

Ibuka, which appears five times, means to remember the past of suffering.

Ibuka imitaga wiririwaga ugenda	Remember tough days of marching
Ibuka amajoro menshi urara rubunda	Remember the nights spent uncovered
Amaturo y'umutware cg umwami	Bringing offering to the chief or the king
Kwigomwa amaturo abawe bayakeneye	Giving up things that your family needs
Gushengurwa n'umutwaro nta shimwe	So worn down, without being thankful
Twishimire ubwigenge	Let us rejoice for independence

In these couplets, the word ***Ibuka*** (remember or recall) is highlighted. Bikindi also mentions specific forms of oppression Hutu faced during this period: ***ikiboko*** (whip), ***ishiku*** (forced labor), ***akazi kadahemberwa*** (unremunerated work), ***kugenda imitaga*** (days of marching), and so on. By using these words, Simon Bikindi invites the Hutu to keep in their minds these past discomforts.

Ndi Rudahungumuruho	I am one who does not run away from difficulties
Ndi urukinabarenza	I am one who admires/imitates the wise
Ndi nyiringongo mwene Nyagahinga	I am a talented fighter from Nyagahinga
Ndi Umuhungu urengera ingabo	I am a boy who protects the army
Ndi Rusakaranamisakura	I am one who brings out the arrows

Ndi Umugemashuro wa Kirenga	I am a famous warrior from Kirenga
Ndi imbabaza abafozi	I am the one who makes archers suffer

Ndi (I am) can be understood as an identification reference to the composer-singer. By using the word **Ndi** (I am), the composer-singer characterizes himself as the song's protagonist – a hero sent to liberate the Hutu.

This refrain is a good introduction to the forms of speech produced by Simon Bikindi that express his joy and satisfaction with the freedom that Rwandans found after years of slavery during the monarchy and the colonial regimes.

The lyrics emphasize both anger with the previous systems of governance in Rwanda and the heroic revolt of the Hutu people. These lyrics especially call attention to the actions of Hutu heroes Mbonyumutwa[31] and Kayibanda[32] who fought to recover freedom for the Hutu people.

1.3 Couplets 3–4: Bikindi thanks the important persons who freed the majority

Ndi muto sinabibonye	I am very young and did not witness all this
Narabibwiwe ndanabisoma	It was told to me and I read about it
Nshimira Imana yandinze umuruho	And then on understanding it, I praised the Creator
Nishimira ubwigenge by'umwihariko	And for this particular reason, I rejoice for Independence
Ndashima byimazeyo	I am thankful with all my heart
Abarwanashyaka batubohoye	For those militants who liberated us
Kayibanda, Mbonyumutwa	Kayibanda, Mbonyumutwa
Izindi ntwari bari kumwe	And the other heroes/brave ones who were with them
Dukesha ubwigenge	Those from whom we received this Independence

The lyrics show that the protagonist is grateful to God and to the Hutu leaders Kayibanda and Mbonyumutwa, as well as other heroes who fought for independence. By thanking God, through a framework of reference understood by his historically and culturally conditioned audience, Bikindi refers indirectly to the regimes of feudalism and colonialism. The lyrics suggest that Bikindi wants the Hutu people to be vigilant in order to avoid mistreatment suffered during the previous regimes.

1.4 Couplet 5: Praise to President Habyarimana

Intwari Habyarimana	Habyarimana the hero
Tuguhaye impundu	We cheer for you, pride of the youth
Komeza uyobore	Continue to lead valiantly

Bikindi praises Habyarimana who built on the work of previous Hutu heroes. These lyrics praise the heroes and hold them in high esteem which demonstrates to the listener that people in the current state should try and emulate their actions. The last couplet recalls the past 25 years of independence and invokes all age groups of Hutu people.

Urubyiruko rw 'u Rwanda	Young people of Rwanda
Yemwe bakobwa	You girls
Yemwe bahungu	You boys
Rubyiruko rw 'u Rwanda	Young people of Rwanda
Abagago b'ibikwerere	Grown-up men
Abagore b'amajigija	Grown-up women
Abasaza n'abakecuru	Old men and old women
Abangavu n'ingimbi	Teenage girls and boys

Through his lyrics, Bikindi sends a message to all members across generations of Rwandan society to keep in mind the role of independence, and the history that characterized the pre-independence period. Through lyrics that glorify the past and implicitly call people to action, Bikindi may have fueled hate against the Tutsi. The term ***Ubwigenge*** (independence) is mentioned three times and repeated more than any other word, which gives it special significance.

Due to the length of the second and third songs (4 and 6 pages, respectively), we will adopt a macroscopic approach by analyzing points with similar meanings. The full versions of the songs and their texts *in extenso* could be found on YouTube[33] or at the ICTR archives.[34]

2 *Message of* Akabyutso or Nanga Abahutu *(I hate the Hutu or The Awakening)*

The song *Akabyutso* or *Nanga Abahutu* (I hate the Hutu or The Awakening) was composed in 1993. According to *Nanga Abahutu*, Simon Bikindi was influenced by various sources in the writing of this song and in the creation of its strong messages of hatred. One of the strongest sources of influence for Bikindi were the 'Ten Commandments,'[35] a propagandistic manifesto addressed to the Hutu and proposed as rules that would help them to free themselves from the oppression of the Tutsi during the feudal period, as APROSOMA (Association for Social Promotion of the Masses)[36] told them on 27 September 1959 at a political rally in Ngoma, Astrida.[37] This political rally was convoked to achieve Hutu unity in order to resist the Tutsi government's agenda. It was baptized 'The celebration of the liberation of the Bahutu.' At that rally, Joseph Habyarimana Gitera, a Hutu activist, outlined ten principles that should rule the relationship between the Hutu and the Tutsi. Evoking the Ten Commandments of the Bible, they subsequently became the 'Ten Commandments of the Hutu.'

This composition was also inspired by an article in the newspaper *Kinyamateka*,[38] *Mbwirabumva*, *Nanga Abaparmehutu baryana*, (I hate Parmehutu party members who tear each other apart), which appeared on the front page of the Catholic Weekly, signed by the pseudonym 'Mbwiruwumva.' The words and themes of this article are very similar to the words and themes found in Bikindi's lyrics, so it appears that Bikindi may have composed his lyrics with inspiration from this source. The hatred expressed and specific ironic undertones found in both further emphasize this connection.

2.1 *Hatred toward the 'perverted Hutu'*

Bikindi's lyrics also criticize the 'perverted Hutu' through the identification of what he considers to be traitorous behaviors. Bikindi's lyrics declare his 'hatred' of the 'perverted Hutu' who fall into the following five categories:

- Those who have forsaken their Hutu identity (*Ba bandi bagirira isoni ubwoko bwabo).*
- Those who look down on other Hutu (*Ba bandi basuzugura abandi bahutu*).
- Those who are greedy, who merely live off of *ubuhake*,[39] clientelism and bribes (doled out by Tutsi), and those who would go so far as to kill other Hutu. They are killers-for-hire (*Ba bandi b'ibisahiranda bakunda guhakirizwa babeshwaho n'ubuhake bakakira utuntu tudafite umumaro bahawe n'abatutsi kugira ngo bice abandi bahutu. Abo ni abahutu kabuhariwe*).
- Those who are so naive that they get involved in a war (alongside Inkotanyi[40] Tutsi) of which they are ignorant; they are considered fools *(Ba bandi bashukwa bakifatanya n'abatutsi mu ntambara badasobanukiwe bakagereranywa n'abasazi).*
- Those who when a Hutu makes a mistake do not correct him by taking him aside and contribute to the greater good, namely, ensuring the sustainability of Hutu unity (*Ba bandi igihe umuhutu akoze ikosa batamuhanira mu gisenge ngo bamushyire ku ruhande bakora neza ngo bashimangire ubumwe bw'abahutu*).[41]

2.2 *Appeal to the union of the Hutu*

This part of the song's lyrics express criticism of Hutu people who might hate other Hutu. The voice of Simon Bikindi assumes and performs an advisory role in this song. As examined previously, Bikindi uses a number of strategies through the lyrics of this song to unify the Hutu people against a common enemy. His tactics, so far, have included the demonization of a common enemy (the Tutsi) and the demonization of the 'perverted Hutu' to create suspicion and also to engender a stronger union among those who exert the values deemed important in his lyrics. In this song, however, another tactic is used to garner a similar effect. In this piece, he calls for unity among the Hutu and encourages Hutu to cooperate and not focus their hate at each other. This is a departure from his steep criticism of the 'perverted Hutu.' Instead, the protagonist advocates for cooperation among Hutu to work toward a greater good. Together with the last stanza, the lyrics suggest that Hutu should correct each other when one of them strays from values intrinsic to the Hutu as a group and ultimately strive for unity and not to hate members of their own group. Combining the message of hatred with a call for unity is particularly powerful given the political climate and further fuels ethnic hatred.

PART I: REFRAIN I: 1–14: PROVOCATION

The refrain starts with the phrase *Ngire nte* and ends with the phrase *Njyewe nanga abahutu* (*bis*). *Ngire nte?* (What am I going to do?). The latter is a question that highlights the internal struggle of the narrator. Bikindi's lyrics here are directed toward the group of Hutu people who are embarrassed because of the past behavior of their brothers and sisters. Bikindi speaks as an advisor who regrets the actions of the previous generation. To illustrate his point, he speaks to all Hutu people who question their own destiny.

Ngirengirente yari umwana muto uteye nyina agahinda	What am I going to do I was a small child who causes sorrow for his/her mother
Agatera se Uruhagararo	Who causes worry for his/her father

These words invite the listener to the mindset of a child, a child who causes sorrow, a child with a bad temper. Through these lyrics, the narrator draws a comparison between a child's mindset and the mindset of the new independent Hutu in the republic. The mindset of the child causes worries for the parents of the child, and similarly, the Hutu in the new republic are endangering their motherland Rwanda. In this comparison, the 'father' of the independent Hutu is the political leader and the father of the nation, Juvenal Habyarimana, who was provoked and scorned by Hutu traitors, the troublemaking children. This manner of expressing regret is aimed at the conscience of the Hutu. This is a lyrical tactic to raise the awareness of all the Hutu around their common discontent, in order to unify them and help them change their adverse attitudes to fighting for absolute Hutu control.

Intumva yabyaye intumbwe	Those who can't understand give birth to the foolish
Umutisiga abyara umusazi	The idiot gives birth to a crazy person
Igihuru kibyaye igihunyira	The bush gives birth to an owl

These lyrics also suggest that the Hutu are undermining themselves. The lyrics convey that actions taken by the Hutu in the current time period stem from foolishness and irrationality, and these actions plunge their country into darkness. In its contextualized symbolism, these words can be understood as a provocation directed at the Hutu to change their actions.

Ukuri guca mu ziko ntigushye	The truth passes through fire without burning up

These words pose a challenge to Bikindi's Hutu brothers and sisters; he does not fear declaring the 'truth,' even if this truth hurts them. This lyric seems to claim that if the Hutu understood that they have to be united and struggle against all the enemies of freedom, then they would know the 'truth.' Before this can happen, the Hutu need to stop detesting themselves. This self-hatred is why the song's narrator 'hates' them.

Mbwira abunva	I speak to those who understand
Ndarire Imana	I had a revelation from God
Mbambure imanzi	I am reviving the old heroes

Bikindi presents himself through these lyrics as a prophet who comes to reveal the will of God and recalls the heroism of the Hutu ancestor-heroes. He uses this positioning as a prophet to convey the message of deliverance. The 'hatred' is reinforced in the following verse:

Njyewe nanga abahutu (bis)	Me, I despise Hutu

These words also emphasize Bikindi's anger with the Hutu who do not understand his message.

PART 2: COUPLET 1: 15–42: KIND OF DETESTABLE HUTU

Njyewe nanga ibihutu	I despise those bad Hutu
Kandi nanga ibyihuture	I despise those Hutu who are ashamed of their identity

These words reveal how the singer disdains a particular kind of Hutu, the kind of Hutu who denies their identity, similar to his criticism of the 'perverted Hutu' in a previously analyzed song. He levels insults at them using the words ***Ibihutu*** (Bad Hutu, pejorative term) and ***ibyihuture*** (Hutu who changed identity and became Tutsi), both strong pejorative forms of expression. The word ***abahutu*** is used eight times as emphasis.

PART 3: REFRAIN 2: 43–57: CALL OUT TO THE HUTU

The singer repeats some words of the first refrain, building his lyrical argument for why he 'hates' the Hutu.

Ngwino wumve (bis)	Come to hear
Mbwira abumva (bis)	I speak to those who understand

This is an invitation to meet the singer in a place unknown, a place where the song is delivered to his audience. Bikindi does not speak to the 'bad Hutu' who would not understand but speaks to an 'enlightened' Hutu who recognizes what he sees. These lyrics shame those who do not understand in an effort to convince the listener that what Bikindi says is right and they would be foolish not to believe his message.

PART 4: COUPLET 2: 58–73: HATEFUL OF THE HUTU

The following words, depicting Hutu in pejorative and hateful terms, may, for example, contain communications with an element of actionability:

Njyewe nanga ibihutu (thrice)	I hate those bad Hutu
Bigendera inzira ubugari	Who walk a path only because it is wide
Ibihutu bidashishoza	Who are undiscerning
Bitareba	Unable to see
Biteranya, bitemana, bikegura bikarwana bitazi imvano yayo	Who are easily manipulated, who tear themselves apart and fight in a war they don't even understand
Bikamarana	They are annihilating one another
Urunva Atari ishyano koko!	This is truly a tragedy!
Njyewe nanga umuhutu	I despise a Hutu
Umuhutu uhabwa igiceri	A Hutu who receives a coin
Akica umuhutu	To kill a Hutu

Bikindi denounces the behavior of 'bad Hutu' and labels them as killers and corrupt. These lyrics claim that the 'bad Hutu' are unable to discern between fighting among themselves and fighting a united battle for true Hutu independence. These lyrics liken 'bad Hutu' to criminals and traitors and suggest that if a Hutu is not a part of what Bikindi sees as the right battle, they are worthy of being despised. In this respect, and given the political and cultural context in which these lyrics were presented, Bikindi's words may have been a contributing factor in mobilizing and inciting the 'bad Hutu' to take part in the genocide in 1994.

PART 5: REFRAIN 3: 74–82: A TRUE ORACLE

The following words repeat the ideas that we have commented on already:

Igihuru kibyara igihunyira	The bush gives birth to an owl
Ukuri guca mu ziko ntigushye	The truth passes through fire without burning
Mbwira abumva	I speak to those who understand
Ndarire Imana	I had a revelation from God

One interpretation of this stanza is that Bikindi felt that he needed to disclose the real nature of the Hutu people so that he might protect them from what he believed would destroy them – not fighting for the 'true cause.' These lyrics serve as an invitation to dialogue among the Hutu, but the lyrics are compelling enough to also be interpreted as a harsh warning to the Hutu. Utilizing language of divine revelation and fear, the lyrics suggest to the Hutu that they should be wise and abstain from vice which may destroy their community. By invoking God, Bikindi underscores the importance of this message.

PART 6: COUPLET 3: 83–122: THE FORGETFUL OF THE HUTU

This small couplet describes the 'forgetful Hutu.' The 'forgetful Hutu' do not remember the suffering that the Tutsi perpetrated against their heroes and ancestors. Bikindi recalls the past suffering of the Hutu at the hands of the Tutsi. The description of the suffering of the Hutu aims to provoke an emotional response in the Hutu listener. We find evidence of this process in the following lines:

Njyewe nanga abahutu	I hate the Hutu
Ba bahutu batibuka Nzira ya Muramira	Those who do not remember Nzira ya Muramira[42]
Ngo bibuke urwo yapfuye	That they remember how he was killed
Bibuke icyamwishe	That they remember why he died
Njyewe nanga abahutu	I hate the Hutu
Ba bahutu batibuka Mashira ya Sabugabo	Those Hutu who do not remember Mashira ya Sabugabo[43]

This passage gives two examples of Hutu kings (Nzira ya Muramira and Mashira ya Sabugabo) who were killed by the Tutsi. These killings are brought up to suggest that past atrocities and spite be remembered by the Hutu in the present. Further, it implies that the Hutu should be compelled to avenge their heroes. Called on by the lyrics to remember emotionally charged events from the past and act on them in the present is a dangerous precedent. When the lyrics suggest avenging, the link to incitement of violence becomes clearer.

This couplet contains familiar symbols for the Hutu that recall the places where the Hutu (men and women) suffered and were killed. Bikindi wants the Hutu to remember this. This is yet another tactic to provoke resentment and encourage the Hutu to act on this resentment.

Bibuke urwo yapfuye	That they remember how he was killed
Bibuke icyamwishe	That they remember what killed him
Njyewe nanga abahutu	I hate the Hutu
Ba bahutu batibuka Nyagakecuru mu Bisi bya Huye.	Huye/Those Hutu who do not remember Nyagakecuru killed in Bisi bya Huye[44]
Ba bahutu batibuka Rukara, Basebya na Ndungutse	Those Hutu who do not remember Rukara, Basebya and Ndungutse[45]

PART 7: REFRAIN 4: 123–131

This is a repetition of the first refrain with provocative language targeted at the Hutu.

PART 8: COUPLET 4: 132–175: INCONSTANT AND HYPOCRITICAL HUTU

In this couplet, we observe the same framework encouraging hate based on criticism of the Hutu and implying the need for Hutu unity and ideological homogeneity.

Njyewe nanga abahutu	I hate the Hutu
Badashyira mu gisenge	Who do not have any personal discipline
Undi muhutu wabakoshereje	Another Hutu who is wrong
Ariko ubumwe bukomeze	That unity might continue
Njyewe nanga ibihutu	I hate those bad Hutu
Bigendera inzira ubugari	Who walk a path only because it is wide
Nk'ibihuna	They can't see
Ibihutu bidashishoza	The bad Hutu who are undiscerning

These words depict the situation of corrupt Hutu who are unwilling or unable to see that they need to help their own people. The lyrics also suggest that failure to be discerning and to recognize the need to help their own people will lead to the destruction of the Hutu people. This is a dramatic claim and one that suggests any Hutu not directly involved in helping is contributing to the demise of the Hutu. This framework, describing an inconsistent and hypocritical Hutu attitude, may have encouraged Hutu to participate in violent acts in 1994 by suggesting that failure to act for the 'true cause' and interests of all the Hutu would make someone a bad and undiscerning Hutu.

Finally, in the song *Nanga Abahutu* (I hate the Hutu) or *Akabyutso* (The Awakening), Bikindi proposes through his lyrics that the Hutu are detestable and that their behavior is unreasonable and that they plot against themselves and collaborate with their enemies. The lyrics serve to alarm the Hutu listener – hearing repeatedly that inaction will lead to the demise of the Hutu people serves as a warning and a call to action. The frequency of certain emotionally charged and alarming works used in this song highlights that a 'hate framework' is employed by Bikindi through his lyrics to elicit certain actions:

PART 9: REFRAIN 5: 175–185

This is a repetition of the first refrain with provocative language targeted at the Hutu.

Table 11.2 Key words of Nanga Abahutu

Words	*Translation*	*Times*
Kwanga	To hate	31
Abahutu	The Hutu	44
Kwibuka	To remember	17

3 Message of Bene Sebahinzi (The descendants of Sebahinzi or The Alert)

The song *Bene Sebahinzi* or *Intabaza* (The descendants of Sebahinzi or The Alert) is the longest song for analysis. It has 31 lengthy parts and lasts 20:32 minutes. The narrator relates the specific story of the Hutu and calls it *Bene Sebahinzi* or *Intabaza*, 'the sons of the Farmer' or 'The Alert.' The content can be summarized as follows:

1 The crisis is explained by highlighting the catastrophic situation in the whole country in the present time of the song.
2 The cause of the crisis is an enemy from outside who is disguising himself. This disguise alludes to the Tutsi who have allies from a foreign country, Uganda. This allusion to the Tutsi is concretely demonstrated by the terms used by Simon Bikindi in the song. Those terms are ***Interanyabagabo*** (one who causes discord among men), ***inshira*** *(the venomous snake),* ***intasi*** *(one who is spy),* ***inyambarabishahu*** *(one who dresses up the testicles: reference to the royal drum* ***Karinga*** *that used to be decorated with Hutu testicles killed during fight),* ***mwima/Mushirarungu*** *(royal avenue/where people are happy),* ***inka*** *(cow)* ***ingoma*** *(the drum as the symbol of monarchy).*
3 The search for a solution to the crisis according to the lyrics is to form a Hutu front, ***impuzamugambi*** (persons who are united by accomplishing their aim), to be awake or vigilant, to fight against the Tutsi and to promote ***rubanda nyamwinshi*** (the majority of the population who are Hutu).

In our analysis, portions of the song with similar messages are grouped together.

3.1 Part I: Refrain: Catastrophic situation or crisis in Rwanda

This refrain, which is the beginning of the song, describes what Bikindi perceives to be the crisis in Rwanda:

Inka zaméze impengeri ku mutemeri	Cows' udders are diseased[46]
Isake zitakibika. inkokokazi zitagiteraaa	The roosters are no longer crowing, the hens are no longer laying eggs
Nyambarabishahu yongeye guhabwa umurishyo	That Inyambarabishahu [one who dresses up in male genitals] was being drummed again
Interanyabagabo yabagezemo	Interanyabagabo, the one who causes discord among men has come among you
Inshimutamugabo umwe wanganye na mwene Bishingwe yahashinze ibirindiro	The one who steals men, the one who is enemy of the son of Bishingwe, has settled in the area
None uduhunda tugiye guhenera ijuru	And the rear tips of the spears are now pointed toward the sky ...

Ababyeyi bagiye gucura imiborogo	The parents will be crying in sorrow
Abana basigaye ari imfubyi gusa	The children will become orphans
Bene so bararuriye. Tabara	Your brothers and sisters are eating Rwanda. Rescue us

This refrain places the Hutu people in a context of grave apprehension. It gives examples of the misery caused by the lack of action by the Hutu illustrating a grave state of affairs if action is not taken. The lyrics also pose a clear threat of war and destruction which is particularly evident in the lyrics, "The one who steals men, the one who is enemy of the son of Bishingwe, has settled in the area" and also, "The parents will be crying in sorrow/The children will become orphans." This declaration by Bikindi can be read as an intentional and purposeful alert to the Hutu to be cognizant of the imminent danger brought about by the Tutsi. Bikindi's lyrics condemn the implied aggressiveness of the Tutsi, and through this declaration, he prompts the Hutu to action and possibly even revolt.

3.2 Part 2: 2–4: All the country in trouble

This song enumerates the threatened places on Rwandan territory implying that danger looms everywhere. The lyrics emphasize that fear and the unhappiness are pervasive in the country. Here are some of the former territories named in the song: Ndorwa, Mayaga, Mutara, Buriza, Bwanacyambwe, Buganza, Bugesera, Gisaka, Budaha, Buyenzi mu Bufundu, Nduga, Bukonya, Bugoyi, Akanage, Bwishaza, Rusenyi, Nyantango and Kinyaga. All of these places taken together form a set of symbolic representations: the East, the West, the North, the South and the center of Rwanda. The enumeration of all of these places serves to demonstrate the totality of danger and destruction. It shows that this danger does not exist only in a corner of the country but extends throughout, thus taking on an omnipresent quality. The omnipresence of danger can serve as a call to action because these lyrics suggest that conflict is inescapable.

3.3 Part 3: 5–15: Resort to the soothsayer

As the narrator deals with Biryabayoboke,[47] who is interacting with Mutabazi,[48] who is called to come and rescue the sons of Sebahinzi, the solution to the problems the narrator describes is expected to come from an expert diviner.

MAKING DIVINATION FOR ALL GROUPS OF RWANDAN PEOPLE

In the song, the diviner performs his craft and makes predictions. The diviner performed divination and made predictions among the Babanda, Bega, Bazigaba, Buguyane and Bagesera, the Rwandan clans.

MAKING DIVINATION TO SEVERAL HEROES FROM THE DIFFERENT AREAS IN RWANDA

As the song progresses, the diviner also performs his procedures for several heroes from the different areas in Rwanda with the following conclusions:

- Mashira the Hutu, son of Sabugabo over there in Nyanza, I predicted to him that the girl who was given to him in marriage was not only a wife but a spy who would plan his murder.
- Nyaruzi son of Haramanga in Mukindo near Makwaza.
- Benginzage [alias] Nyagakecuru over there in the Huye range, I told her that her goat keepers were rather seeking her head. The next day she was, indeed, murdered.
- Gisurere in Suti from Banega over there in Bunyambiriri.
- Ndagano, the kinglet of the Bukunzi and of the Busozo.
- Nzira the Hutu, son of Muramira, telling him that Ruganzu did not enter his house as a servant but as an enemy spy who had infiltrated through his army. He did not listen to my advice and the following day all his people were exterminated by the same Ruganzu.
- Basebya, son of Nyirantwari in Ndorwa, I told them that they had been betrayed, that they would be killed and that Rukara would be hanged. A while later, that happened: He was hanged.
- The famous Joseph Gitera.
- Mbonyumutwa while the country was on the edge of the abyss. The alarm rang in Byimana and the war drum was heard in Kanyanza in Ndiza.

The divine predictions given in the lyrics show that those who do not listen are punished in terrible ways. It seems, based on the divinations in the lyrics, that the only way to avoid the terrible fates suffered by those who failed to listen is to listen to the divine presage. As noted earlier, Bikindi situates himself as a diviner in his songs, so the implication follows that failing to take action, as he suggests, would result in horrible suffering.

SOLUTION TO THE CRISIS

The narrator further expresses the heroic will, which is to achieve the victory of the Hutu people identified as 'Bene Sebahinzi.' He declares, "Mutabazi oroshya nguhe intsinzi," which can be translated as "Mutabazi, calm down and listen, for I will tell you the cause and the solution to these problems."

CAUSE OF THE CRISIS

In his advice, we meet the origin of the crisis: the bad spirit attacking "from abroad." The narrator relates these words of the diviner:

Dore imvano	Look here is the cause
Ibi byago byose murimo biterwa n'uriya muzimu uturutse ishyanga	All these problems are due to the spirit that attacks from abroad
Uyu muzimu ko afite amayeri menshi	This spirit that has so many tricks

According to a Rwandan traditional belief, all crises and all misfortunes are usually caused by 'bad people' who are used and influenced by the 'bad spirit.' These 'bad people' use various tricks; they are sorcerers who collaborate with the 'bad spirits.' These kinds of people are also referred to as persons who bring bad omens.

3.4 *Part 4:16–30: Metamorphosis of the Tutsi and ten solutions to the crisis*

The narrator illustrates the metamorphosis through the symbol of a snake shedding its skin to transform itself:

> *Mutabazi ntarumwa n'inshira kandi ntasamwa n'umuzimu utera aturutse ishyanga*
>
> Mutabazi cannot be struck by the spitting cobra, and he is not possessed by the spirit that attacks from a foreign place.

The snake represents the Tutsi and also refers to the movement of the RPF, rhetorically and politically taken as a dangerous snake. Comparing the Tutsi to a snake has obvious connotations of evil and conniving; Bikindi knew this and utilized this metaphor to further demonize the Tutsi to the Hutu listener.

This metaphor introduces an analogy between animals, spirits and people. The entire Tutsi people is compared to a possessed person going through various transformations, including nonhuman appearances. We find this particular figure in the following lines:

Dore nguyu yigize umugore	See the spirit is appearing as a woman
Dore nguriya kandi abaye umukobwa	See it also appearing as a girl
Dore kandi abaye ikirura	See it also appearing as a wolf
Dore nguyu yigize umuhinzi	See it also appearing as a farmer
Dore nguwo ruswa ayisesekaje mu bisahiranda	See it there spreading bribes among the greedy and the corruptible
Dore nguwo yabaye muramu wa ntibibuka	See it there appearing as brother-in-law of one who forgets
Dore kandi abaye umukwe wa Mbonabihita	And see it appearing as the son-in -aw of one who is careless

Dore nguriya mwene Sebahinzi ashukisha inka	See it here, bribing a child of Sebahinzi by offering cows
Turamutsinda tunamuhadike	We will defeat it and keep it from returning

All of these images illustrate that Rwanda's diverse population live a life of deception and hypocrisy, and as pharisees. The 'bad spirits' have two faces, or *ikirumirahabiri* (those who bite from both ends). In all of these lyrical examples, the pattern of continuous animosity which has characterized the Hutu and the Tutsi relationship during the past is recalled. This piece of the song further emphasizes the omnipresence of danger, as nearly every person or animal can also be a bad spirit. These lyrics suggest that the Tutsi have already invaded all aspects of life, which implies that immediate action may be necessary to counter the already pervasive bad spirits.

TEN SOLUTIONS TO THE CRISIS

The narrator states that the Hutu would end up victorious. We find this in the following statement:

Dore intsinzi, fata ingoma uyishyire ku mureko	Here is the victory, take the drum to the highest peak
Uhamagare bene Sebahinzi bose baze mbahe intsinzi, bahamagare	Call all the children of the father of the farmers together, for I shall give them the solution

The following piece of the song recalls the suffering endured by the Hutu during the monarchy and the colonial period:

Ubuhake, ubucakara, ikiboko, shiku, n'umujishi byari byarazambaguje rubanda. Ibyo byatawe ruhenu kera	Slavery, the whip, the laborious farming and the carrying of the king and dignitaries exhausted the common people

These lines remind the listener that the Hutu slave had a difficult past. Through these lyrics the narrator invites the Hutu to remember that suffering. The majority people, the Hutu, are then invited to stay alert, as explained in the following lines:

Rubanda nyamwinshi murabe maso, kandi bene Sebahinzi nimwibuke iryo shyano ryo gahera ishyanga kandi ritazagaruka mu Rwanda!	You people in the majority, stay awake! And children of the father of farmers are untitled! So that those curses may remain outside and never return to Rwanda!

The narrator then recognizes that the country comprises three distinct groups who all have a stake in the future of their country. It is expressed in these lyrics:

Nibaze bene Sebahinzi. Yaba umuhutu, umutwa cyangwa umututsi, nta n'umwe ugomba kwibeshya cyangwa ngo anarote mu nzozi ko yafata bubutegetsi akoresheje intwaro. Bene Sebahinzi rero nimusabe amatora yategurwa ... Nihatorwa umuhutu, twemere atuyobore, nihatorwa umututsi, twemere atuyobore, nihatorwa umutwa, twemere atuyobore. U Rwanda ni urwacu uko turi batatu twese nta n'umwe usumba undi	May they come! None of the children of father of farmers, neither Hutu nor Twa nor Tutsi should do wrong or have an inconceivable dream of taking over the government through the force of arms. Therefore, children of the father of farmers call for elections. If a Hutu is elected, let us accept that person to lead! If a Tutsi is elected, let us accept that person to lead! If a Twa is elected, let us accept that person to lead! This Rwanda is for all three of us. No one is greater than another

This suggests that the diviner has communicated his message to all Rwandans. If they follow his advice, they will find the solution to their never-ending problems:

Kuragura byo urabizi rwose	Your divination is most true

In short, the ten solutions are put forward through the following recommendations:

1	To make a Hutu front	*Gukora ubumwe bw'amahutu*
2	The majority of the population	*Rubanda nyamwinshi*
3	To be awakened	*Kuba maso*
4	To promote first all the interests of the majority	*Kurengera mbere ya byose inyungu za rubanda nyamwinshi*
5	To save and to keep well the gains of the 1959 Revolution	*Kurengera no gufata neza inyungu zimpinduka (revolisiyo yo muri 1959)*
6	To fight against Inkotanyi because they are the source of the many political parties created in order to destroy MRND and because they train the Hutu to be killed	*Kurwanya inkotanyi kubera ko arizo nkomoko y'amashyaka menshi ya politiki yakozwe kugira ngo asenye MRND kandi bakaba bakurura iyicwa ry'abahutu*
7	To throw away the corruption by cows and the drum which means a return of the Tutsi to political power	*Kwamaganira kure ruswa y'inka no kuzibira inzira zose zishobora kongera gusubiza umututsi ku butegetsi muri politiki*
8	To be united in order to have the same objective which will help the Hutu to make progress	*Kwiyunga kugira tugire intego imwe izafasha abahutu kugera ku majyambere*
9	To join in large numbers the Rwandan armed forces	*Kwinjiza no kongera ku bwinshi ingabo z'Igihugu*
10	To call for election immediately in a democratic way because that is the way to victory and the solution for the majority	*Gusaba amatora vuba na bwangu mu nzira ya Demokarasi kubera ko ari yo nzira nyayo yo kubona intsinzi ya rubanda nyamwinshi*

3.5 Part 5: 31: Verification of the result of the divination

This part marks the end of the song and the new refrain. It verifies the result of the previous divinations. Bikindi proclaims,

Mbwira abumva!	I speak to those who understand
Wumvise intabaza? (bis)	Did you listen to the alert?
Wumvise akabyutso?	Did you listen to the awakening?
Mbabarira umbwire (bis)	Forgive me, tell me
Niba ibyo nakubwiye bwumvise	If you have understood what I told to you
Erega nakumvise (thrice)	Yes, I have understood you
Ndagushimiye cyane (four times)	I am grateful
Niba ibyo nakubwiye wumvise	If you have understood what I told to you
Jya uzirikana cyane ariya magambo	Keep well those words
Ari mu gitondo, ku manywa, nimugoroba	In the morning, during the day, and in the evening
Mbe mbwira abumva mwana wa data!	Then I speak to those who understand, child of my father!

The song ends with agreement between the narrator and the diviner.

The three songs *Twasezereye ingoma ya cyami* (We said goodbye to the monarchy), *Akabyutso* or *Nanga Abahutu* (The Awakening) and *Intabaza* or *Bene Sebahinzi* (The descendants of Sebahinzi or The alert), as understood by the Rwandan audience in Kinyarwanda, can be described directly given the specific cultural and historical context. The lyrics of these three songs reflect the ideas of their composer and singer Simon Bikindi, and his underlying intentions, particularly in regard to the Tutsi. The songs convey an appeal to the Hutu to subscribe to the stereotypes and caricatures of the past regarding the relations between the Hutu and the Tutsi. It can be proposed that these three songs were composed in order to manipulate, instruct and eventually prompt the Hutu to action. The impact of these songs on the 1994 genocide was reinforced by one of Bikindi's main objectives, which was to unify and mobilize the Hutu in order to save the Republic and the gains of the 1959 Social Revolution, allegedly endangered by their enemy, the Tutsi. Bikindi's songs became an instrument of incitement for the mass atrocity crimes perpetrated in 1994.

Table 11.3 Key words of Bene Sebahinzi

Words	*Translation*	*Times*
Bene Sebahinzi	the Sons of the farmers' fathers	27
Kuragura	To diviner	22
Mutabazi	Who is called to come and rescue	14
Rubanda nyamwinshi	The people in the majority	7
Kumarana	Killing one another, destroying each other's houses, are looting one another	6
Mbwirabumva	I speak to those who understand	6

Conclusion

This chapter aims to determine the content-based nature and role of Simon Bikindi's three songs in inciting the Hutu perpetrators to kill the Tutsi during the Rwandan genocide. The impact of these songs on the genocidal acts, as argued by the prosecution in the ICTR case against Simon Bikindi, was underestimated and eventually dismissed in its entirety by the judges. The authors of this chapter believe that the lexicological analysis, as interpreted and understood by the native speakers, reveals the true nature of the messages conveyed by Bikindi through the three specific songs.

In *Twasezereye*, Simon Bikindi recalls the precolonial period and the colonial period in order to remind the Hutu of the suffering caused during the feudal monarchy and colonization. He thereby encouraged the Hutu through his lyrics to safeguard, by all means, the gains from the 1959 Rwandan Revolution and the 1962 Independence.

In *Nanga Abahutu*, Simon Bikindi denounces the Hutu whose behavior, as collaborators of the Tutsi enemy, is deemed to be unacceptable. Bikindi's message awoke the Hutu who were not cooperative and incited them to fight against their common enemy, the Tutsi. This song can be seen as the most powerful of the three songs selected for the purposes of this analysis. The excessive use of the word *kwanga* (hate), for example, is noteworthy within the contextual circumstances of incitement to genocide in 1994.

Regarding *Bene Sebahinzi*, the longest among the three songs, Bikindi used a particular form of dramatization. He declared that the country was in grave danger that could not be avoided without resorting to advice from a soothsayer. This represents a traditional practice when a disaster was imminent or occurring in the given cultural and historical context. Simon Bikindi thus went to consult a soothsayer and came up with the ten solutions mentioned in section 3.4. The ten solutions consequently reveal the intentional component of Bikindi's song: to build an active and effective Hutu front against the Tutsi.

The key question, however, is whether the message conveyed by Simon Bikindi encouraged hatred against the Tutsi and whether its content had direct or indirect impact on the perpetration of the crime of genocide in 1994. Numerous social science studies and related ICTR jurisprudence show that the three songs analyzed in this chapter were aired by Radio Rwanda and RTLM and that comments encouraging hatred against the Tutsi were made by journalists.[49] In addition to that, it is also known that on the roadblocks and during the attacks, many people used Bikindi's songs to boost morale. It can thus be stated that through the medium of his songs, Bikindi awoke and alerted the Hutu, reinforcing the Hutu front whose main objective was to eliminate the Tutsi and their accomplices. This indicates that Bikindi's songs fueled and encouraged hatred of the Hutu perpetrators directed toward the annihilation of the Tutsi. It should be emphasized, however, that the genocide in Rwanda was a result of many facts and factors that cannot be listed exhaustively. All things considered, Simon Bikindi's songs can certainly be recognized as a significant contributing factor to the incitement of genocide committed against the Tutsi in Rwanda in 1994.

Notes

1 A. Richard and T. Renee (ed.), *The Routledge Companion to Music Cognition*, Abington, PA, New York, NY: Routledge, 2017.
2 J. Garratt, *Music and Politics: A Critical Introduction*, Cambridge: Cambridge University Press, 2018, and J. Street, *Music and Politics*, Cambridge: Cambridge University Press, Polity Press, 2012.
3 J-P. Chretien and M. Kabanda, *Rwanda Racisme et Genocide: L'ideologie hamitique*, Paris: Belin, 2013, pp. 107–139.
4 Gregoire Kayibanda is the first president of Rwanda. He brought the Hutu majority to power after advocating for Rwanda's independence in 1962. He reigned from 1962 to 1973. Dominique Mbonyumutwa is a Rwandan politician who served on an interim basis as the first president of Rwanda from January to October 1961, after the abolition of Rwandan monarchy.
5 Chretien and Kabanda, *Rwanda*, pp. 141–154.
6 J.-M. Vianney Higiro, 'Rwandan Private Media on the Eve of the Genocide,' in A. Thompson (ed.), *The Media and the Rwandan Genocide*, London: Pluto Press 2007, p. 88.
7 Juvenal Habyarimana is the second president of Rwanda. He replaced Gregoire Kayibanda by a military putsch in July, 1973. He reigned from 5 July 1973 to 6 April 1994.
8 *Irindiro* is a folk-dance company founded in 1980 and led by Simon Bikindi.
9 *Topical analysis of the Songs Twasezereye: We bade farewell; Nanga abahutu or Akabyutso: I hate the Hutu or The Awakening; and Bene Sebahinzi or lntabaza: The descendants of Sebahinzi or The Alert* by Simon Bikindi, exhibit no. 73(E), admitted 13 February 2007, tendered by Prosecutor, Joint Expert Report of Gamaliel Mbonimana and Jean de Dieu Karangwa, The Prosecutor v. Simon Bikindi, Case No. ICTR-01-72-T [hereinafter Mbonimana and Karangwa JER].
10 The Prosecutor Against Simon Bikindi, Case No. ICTR-2001-72-I, 15 June 2005.
11 G.S. Gordon, 'Music and Genocide: Harmonizing Coherence, Freedom and Nonviolence in Incitement Law,' *Santa Clara Law Review*, vol. 50, no. 3, 2010, pp. 625–630.
12 See also G.S. Gordon, *Atrocity Speech Law: Foundation, Fragmentation, Fruition*, New York, NY: Oxford University Press, 2016, pp. 278–279, and R.A. Wilson, *Incitement on Trial: Prosecuting International Speech Crimes*, Cambridge: Cambridge University Press, 2017, pp. 49–56.
13 See D. Geeraerts, *Theories of Lexical Semantics*, Oxford: Oxford University Press, 2010.
14 F. de Saussure, *Course in General Linguistics*, translated by R. Harris, London: Bloomsbury, 2013.
15 G.S. Jowett, V. O'Donnell, *Propaganda and Persuasion*, Fourth Edition, London: Sage, 2006, p. 7.
16 Mbonimana and Karangwa JER.
17 The Prosecutor Against Simon Bikindi, Case, No. ICTR-2001-72-I, 15 June 2005.
18 Thompson, *The Media*. For more, see J.-P. Chretien, 'RTLM: Propaganda: The Democratic Alibi,' pp. 55–61; M. Kimani, 'RTLM: The Medium that Became a Tool for Mass Murder,' pp. 110–124, in A. Thompson (ed.), *The Media and the Rwandan Genocide*, London: Pluto Press, 2007; C. Mironko, 'The Effect of RTLM's Rhetoric

of Ethnic Hatred in Rural Rwanda,' in A. Thompson (ed.), *The Media and the Rwandan Genocide*, London: Pluto Press, 2007, pp. 125–135. See also The Prosecutor v. Ferdinand Nahimana, Jean-Bosco Barayagwiza and Hassan Ngeze, Appeal Judgment, Case No. ICTR-99-52-T, 3 December 2003, paras 342–619 [hereinafter Nahimana et al. TJ].

19 J.T. McCoy, '*Mbwirabumva* (I Speak to Those Who Understand): Three Songs by Simon Bikindi and the War and Genocide in Rwanda,' Florida State University Libraries, Tallahassee, FL, 2013.

20 J. Semujanga et J.L. Galabert (eds), *Faire face au négationnisme du génocide des Tutsi*, Paris: Editions Izuba, 2013, p. 154.

21 Simon Bikindi v. The Prosecutor, Case, No. ICTR-01-72-A, 18 March 2010.

22 J.E.K. Parker, *Acoustic Jurisprudence: Listening to the Trial of Simon Bikindi*, Oxford: Oxford University Press, 2015, p. 55.

23 Gordon, 'Music,' p. 613.

24 RPF members and combatants, also known as 'RPF-Inkotanyi,' a Kinyarwanda term for RPF accomplices/enemy.

25 Online. Available HTTP: <https://guardian.ng/news/world/rwandan-opposition-leader-freed-from-jail/> (accessed 28 January 2019).

26 *Kangura*, bimonthly newspaper, established in May 1990. For more, see M. Kabanda, 'Kangura: The Triumph of Propaganda,' pp. 62–72, and 'The Verdict: Summary Judgment from the Media Trial,' pp. 277–307, in A. Thompson (ed.), *The Media and the Rwandan Genocide*, London: Pluto Press, 2007.

27 The Prosecutor v. Ferdinand Nahimana, Jean-Bosco Barayagwiza, Hassan Ngeze, Case No. ICTR-99-52-A, 28 November 2007. Gordon, 'Music,' p. 613.

28 C. Vidal, 'La désinformation en histoire: Données historiques sur les relations entre hutu, tutsi et twa durant la période précoloniale,' *Dialogue*, no. 200, Bruxelles: Imprimerie Litt, 1997, pp. 11–20.

29 Online. Available HTTP: <http://www.mdrwi.org/livres/succession%20%20regimes%20politiques.htm> (accessed 28 January 2019).

30 Online. Available HTTP: <https://fr.wikipedia.org/wiki/Histoire_du_Rwanda#%C3%89poque_coloniale> (accessed 28 January 2019).

31 A. Twagilimana, *Historical Dictionary of Rwanda*, Second Edition, London: Rowman & Littlefield, 2016, p. 145.

32 Ibid., p. 133.

33 Online. Available HTTP: <http://www.youtube.com/results?reload=9&search_query=bikindi+simon+songs+youtube> (accessed 28 January 2019).

34 Online. Available HTTP: <http://www.unictr.org/sites/unictr.org/files/case-documents/.../031203.pdf> (accessed 28 January 2019).

35 D. Saxon, 'Propaganda as a Crime Under International Humanitarian Law: Theories and Strategies for Prosecutors,' in P. Dojčinović (ed.), *Propaganda, War Crimes Trials and International Law: From Speakers' Corner to War Crimes*, Abingdon, New York, NY: Routledge, 2012, pp. 118–141.

36 Twagilimana, *Historical Dictionary*, pp. 25–26.

37 Online. Available HTTP: <http://www.google.com/search?source=hp&ei=gdjaW6bhIcWjsAGd8qDACw&q=Political+rally+in+Ngoma%2C+Astrida&oq=Political+rally+in+Ngoma%2C+Astrida&gs_l=psy-ab.12..33i160k1.1504.26042.0.29968.38.32.2.1.1.0.841.4640.3-3j6j0j1.10.0....0...1c.1.64.psy-ab..25.13.4721.0..0j35i39k1j0i131k1j0i20i263k1j0i203k1j0i13k1j0i13i30k1j33i22i29i30k1.0.G8OqgWYtN7c> (accessed 28 January 2019).

38 *Kinyamateka*, no. 8, February 1965, pp. 1–2. *Kinyamateka*, a monthly newspaper in Kinyarwanda, affiliated with the Roman Catholic Church, was created in 1933 and greatly expanded in 1955, with circulation rising from 5,000 to 20,000, after

Grégoire Kayibanda, future president of Rwanda, became its editor. The newspaper then served as a vehicle for the ideas behind the Social Revolution, repeatedly arguing that the 'Hutu majority' must have political representation. See also J.J. Carney, *Rwanda before the Genocide: Catholic Politics and Ethnic Discourse in the Late Colonial Era*, New York, NY: Oxford University Press, 2014, p. 185.

39 *Ubuhake* is a kind of clientship in which the Hutu were entitled to use Tutsi's cattle in exchange for services.

40 RPF members and combatants (basic meaning).

41 See the song *Akabyutso* or *Nanga Abahutu* (I hate the Hutu or Awakening).

42 Nzira ya Muramira was the king of Bugara (kingdom in Kivu, former Zaire) whose army was famous.

43 Mashira ya Sabugabo was the king of Nduga (one of the Rwanda kingdoms) whose daughter was very beautiful and attractive.

44 Nyagakecuru was a famous historical woman who conquered Huye Mountain in Butare (South of Rwanda) and established her dominion.

45 Rukara, Basebya and Ndungutse were historical men, heroes known for their disrespect toward authorities and famous persons.

46 Reference to rashes that appear on the udders perhaps due to a disease such as a herpes virus that can rapidly spread throughout a herd of dairy cattle and prevent proper lactation.

47 Forged and connotative name that means 'only the faithful eat it.' It refers to a diviner who ordinarily eats client offerings.

48 Mutabazi is also a connotative name that means 'liberator.' This person came to the diviner seeking Hutu salvation.

49 See The Prosecutor v. Georges Ruggiu, Judgement and Sentence, Case No. ICTR-97-32-I, 1 June 2000, and Nahimana et al. TJ, 3 December 2003.

Chapter 12

Speaking the unspoken

Syrian propaganda, incitement and mass violence in response to the 2011 protests

Saskia Baas

Introduction

Entering its ninth year, the war in Syria has killed an estimated 400,000 people, while an unprecedented number of 13 million Syrians – over half of Syria's pre-war population – have been displaced from their homes. While international humanitarian law has been blatantly violated by all parties to the conflict, some of the most brutal acts of violence have been perpetrated by the Syrian government. This includes the forcible disappearance of tens of thousands of Syrians, the use of chemical weapons against civilian populations and the indiscriminate bombing of civilian targets in Aleppo and Eastern Ghouta, among others. The UN Commission of Inquiry on Syria has consistently condemned the Syrian government's use of violence against civilians. In their recent report on the siege and recapture of Eastern Ghouta, the government's war tactics are described as "barbaric and medieval," amounting to war crimes and crimes against humanity.[1]

The Syrian government's use of mass violence against civilian populations started immediately after the emergence of peaceful protests in Syria in the spring of 2011. Since then, the government's response has been consistently marked by large-scale and indiscriminate military violence against civilians, mass detention and torture, enforced disappearances and summary executions with victims often including young children.[2] The sieges of Daraa and Homs in the spring and summer of 2011 should be seen as preludes to the kind of slaughter more recently perpetrated in Aleppo and Ghouta.

For the Assad regime – which constitutes the rule of an Alawite religious minority over a Sunni Muslim majority – the violent response to the 2011 civil protest movement served its agenda of sectarian survival from the very beginning. As protests spread in the wake of the Arab Spring, the regime was able to guarantee the loyalty of Syria's religious minorities by spreading fear of a Sunni takeover of the state. It used government and privately owned media under its control to spread this fear, but this did not result in the type of overt hate speech that marked ethnic and sectarian violence in Rwanda and Bosnia and Herzegovina. In fact, to outside observers, the regime's official narrative on the protests may seem devoid of clear sectarian references. The immediacy with which the Assad regime resorted to sectarian incitement when the first protests broke out in 2011 can only be observed within a broader understanding of sectarian dynamics and governance in Syria. More specifically, the messages sent by the regime must be contextualized within the lexicon of Assadist propaganda and the taboos that this lexicon poses on public speech.

This chapter aims to demonstrate the Assad regime's resort to sectarian incitement in response to the outbreak of popular protests in Syria in 2011. To this end, the chapter will first provide a brief background to the emergence and survival of Alawite rule in Syria. Then, the chapter moves on to discuss the features of Assadist propaganda prior to the 2011 uprising and the inner workings of the state media apparatus that produced this propaganda. The remaining sections analyze the Syrian state media narrative concerning the Arab Spring and the peaceful protests that took place in Syria in 2011. The analysis provided in these sections draws on the author's archive of 728 news broadcasts, press releases and editorials produced by Syrian state media outlets between 1 January and 31 July 2011. This collection was obtained through the archive of the BBC media monitoring service: a service that gathers and translates local news sources. In addition to this archive of primary media content, the chapter builds on author interviews with nine Syrian journalists who occupied key positions in state-controlled media institutions in Syria during the 2011 events and who had fled the country. These interviews served to understand the day-to-day practices in the Syrian news media and the particular rules and policies that were imposed during the uprising. Furthermore, to understand how the regime's messages were interpreted from the perspective of Syrian minorities, the author conducted seven interviews with Syrians from a minority background. All interviews were completed during fieldwork in Beirut (Lebanon) in January 2015, in Gaziantep (Turkey) in January and July 2016, and in Istanbul (Turkey) in January 2016.[3]

The Alawites in Syria and the origins of minority rule

Prior to the Syrian war and the mass displacement it has caused, the Alawite minority constituted 10 percent of the Syrian population, while Sunni Arabs formed the population's majority at 65 percent.[4] Other minorities included the Kurds (15 percent), Christians (5 percent), Druze (3 percent) and Ismai'lis (1 percent).[5] Although the Alawite community thus constitutes a minority of the Syrian population, the country has been ruled by the Assad family – belonging to the Alawite community – since the installation of Hafez al-Assad as president in 1971. The Assad dictatorship has survived through heavy reliance on repression by its Alawite-dominated security apparatus. While it is impossible to provide a full overview of Syrian history that does justice to all of its complexities and nuances within the limits of this chapter, a brief overview of key historical developments will be provided to help understand the emergence and nature of Alawite minority rule under the Assads.

First of all, it is important to understand that the question of whether Alawites can be considered Muslims has been a major source of contestation that has defined their relation with the Sunni majority throughout Syria's history.[6] Alawites were considered non-Muslim heretics for centuries and were generally viewed with contempt by Syria's Sunni community. Centuries of marginalization during Mamluk and Ottoman rule had pushed the Alawites to Syria's rural coastal areas and into the lowest strata of Syrian society by the time Syria and Lebanon were placed under French mandate in 1920.[7]

The French mandate period (1920–43) saw the gradual acknowledgment of Alawites by the Muslim community as a branch of Shi'ite Islam, through a series of official religious proclamations (*fatwa's*).[8] This period also saw the introduction of policies that improved Alawites' access to education and their overall standard of living. Another important development during this period was the gradual Alawite domination of the armed forces.[9] By the end of the French mandate, the Alawites were strongly overrepresented in the armed forces, where they constituted 65 percent of the non-commissioned officers while constituting only around 10 percent of Syria's population. This enabled their rise to power during the 1960s.

The turbulent 1940s and 1950s saw the Alawites' political emancipation through the ranks of the Ba'ath party. As an Arab nationalist ideology that incorporated aspects of socialism, Ba'ath ideology was popular among the impoverished rural communities.[10] Its glorification of Arab culture, the promise of unity among Arabs and its secular foundation made the ideology particularly appealing among minorities.[11] Alawites became increasingly active in its Lattakia branch, located in the Alawite coastal heartland. Here, Hafez al-Assad became politically active during his secondary school years, after which he enrolled in the military academy where he was selected for the air force. He quickly climbed through the ranks and eventually became minister of defense after the Ba'ath party took over power through a military coup in 1963. He secured the support he needed within the army to take over the presidency in a bloodless coup in 1970,[12] which installed the Assad family's rule of Syria that has lasted until the present day.

Repression under the Assads

Hafez Al-Assad remained president until his death in 2000, ruling the country for almost 30 years, after which his son and current-day president Bashar Al-Assad took over. Both dictators relied on a combination of repression, bargaining, patronage and myth-making to sustain their position.[13] Religious minorities – Christian, Druze, Isma'ilis – shared fears of majority rule with the ruling Alawite minority and generally accepted the regime. The constituency of the Muslim Brotherhood, banned since the installation of Ba'ath rule, formed the most significant threat to the Assads and contested the secular orientation of the regime. To bring the Sunni majority into the regime's coalition, Hafez broke with the secularist fundaments of Ba'ath ideology and created a 'state religion': a moderate version of Islam that was actively promoted, sponsored and institutionalized by the regime.[14]

To quell any residual dissent, the regime relied on a large and highly repressive security apparatus, which was dominated by Alawites. The *mukhabarat* – the colloquial word for the intelligence services – became fully ingrained in Syrians' everyday life. A huge network of secret informers – working as taxi drivers, waiters, bus station employees, street vendors and other well-positioned jobs – ensured that everyone was constantly being watched without knowing who exactly was watching them. State institutions, university campuses, youth groups and other public spaces became fully infiltrated.[15] The regime's far-reaching powers to investigate, arrest and prosecute suspected dissidents resulted in a large number of political detainees who were often held without charges or trial.[16] Arbitrary arrests, torture and summary executions were common.[17] The continuous fear of the omnipresent intelligence and the extreme consequences of dissent created a society where expressing loyalty to the regime became a matter of survival.[18]

The lexicon of Assadist propaganda

State propaganda was designed to legitimize both Ba'ath one-party rule and the system of minority rule that placed Alawites, and the Assad family in particular, in control of politics and society. The regime's narrative was forced onto society through the state media, which was under full control of the regime and closely linked to its intelligence apparatus.[19] Its lexicon relied heavily on the Ba'ath ideology's main pillars: Arab nationalism and socialism. These elements were complemented with a narrative affirming that the Assads – and Alawites more generally – were in fact Muslims. Four interconnected myths were created and sustained through propaganda.

First, the myth of a united Syrian society was created in which no internal conflict and no internal differences existed. This was achieved by appealing to Arab nationalism, and Syrians were habitually depicted first and foremost as Arabs, emphasizing Arab language and culture as a unifying force within Syria and across the Arab world.[20] Not only was Arab identity emphasized, it was also the only identity that existed, as the lexicon did not allow references to tribal, sectarian and religious differences that existed within society. Propaganda forged a reality in which Alawites, or other Muslim sects, simply did not exist, as the sheer reference to such concepts was prohibited.

Second, state propaganda emphasized imagery of the Assads as devout Muslims. But because any reference to sectarian distinctions, that is, different schools of thought within Islam, would break the myth of unity, a "homogenized version of Islam" was constructed to which the Assads adhere in public appearances.[21] [22] The news media contributes to the president's public image as a practicing Muslim by reporting on his attendance of prayers and religious celebrations, for example during the month of Ramadan.[23]

The leadership of the Assads is thus partially legitimized through propaganda that creates the image of an undivided Arab society with a uniform religion, which is devoutly practiced by the president himself. The presumed legitimacy of the Assads' rule culminates in a third myth, that of the Syrian people's voluntary submission to their leadership. Propaganda carries images and messages in which the Syrian people praise their leader in orchestrated public spectacles of worship, such as rallies and ceremonies. Newspapers carry messages of ordinary citizens pledging loyalty to their leader and the phrase *Baya'nak* ('we pledged alliance to you') constituted a prominent place in the regime's lexicon.[24] The myth of popular consent to the Assads' rule was further emphasized through media broadcasts of elections and periodical referenda on the continuation of the Assads' presidency, where Assad would typically receive over 99 percent of the vote.[25]

Finally, the fourth myth communicated though propaganda as a means to bolster the regime's reputation is that of a constant struggle against Syria's enemies. State propaganda constructed the image of a conspiracy being devised by Zionism and Western imperialism. The Assads' foreign policies in the face of these threats are presented as demonstrating 'steadfast resistance' (*samud*), where no compromise to the defense of national interest is made.[26] Emphasis on the threats created by Syria's proclaimed enemies also works to necessitate national unity and legitimizes the regime's heavy reliance on its security apparatus and glorification of the armed forces.

In general, Syrian society was represented in the media as a homogenous mass, united in their admiration of their leader. Any form of conflict-laden language was avoided,[27] except when directed toward acknowledged enemies. Consequently, the image of society transmitted through the media was in complete contradiction with daily experiences, in which sectarian differences featured prominently. Syrian writer Mohamed Dibo[28] describes this paradox as follows:

> sectarianism [formed] a presence that was constantly felt, while the prohibition of any discussion of sectarianism was absolute. The accusation of 'causing sectarian division' was laid down against all kinds of political opposition groups and was used in the prosecution and imprisonment of large numbers of individuals; thus facilitating the regime's monopoly over the issue. People had to find different ways to navigate around this deadly elephant in the room.

As a result of the taboo on sectarian differences, Syrians developed indirect ways to assess a person's sectarian affiliation through family names, location of origin or their accent in Arabic.[29] With such extreme differences between day-to-day life in Syria and the mythical society portrayed through state media, propagandists did not likely aim to *convince* audiences of the regime's legitimacy. Rather than aiming to alter people's thoughts, state propaganda's primary function was to provide a language through which citizens expressed their loyalty to the regime.[30]

The Syrian state media and the machinery of propaganda

Throughout Hafez al-Assad's rule, private media outlets were forbidden by law and only three government-owned newspapers existed: *Al-Ba'ath*, *Al-Thawra* and *Tishreen*, in addition to the state-owned TV and radio channels. The content of these selected outlets was subject to a rigid system of prepublication censorship. When Bashar inherited the presidency after his father's death in 2000, private media were allowed in Syria for the first time, but severe restrictions remained.[31] Private outlets generally could not cover news or politics, which remained the privilege of the state-owned media outlets in addition to a few publishers and broadcasters in the hands of individuals with close ties to the regime.[32]

The proliferation of satellite TV and the Internet in the 2000s infringed more effectively on Assad's monopoly on information and required the introduction of different forms of control. By 2009, 74 percent of Syrian households had access to satellite TV which enabled them to watch news broadcasts that were not controlled by the government, such as those of popular pan-Arab news stations Al-Jazeera and Al-Arabiya.[33] These stations' reporting on Syrian issues did not respect the taboos and red lines that existed for Syrian broadcasters, leading to critical reporting on the Syrian-Israeli negotiations, uncensored appearances of Syrian exiled oppositionists including those affiliated to the Muslim Brotherhood and open questioning of the legitimacy of Bashar's inheritance of power when his father died.[34]

The regime's control over information also became challenged by the increased access to the Internet in Syria. The decade prior to the start of the Syrian uprising saw considerable growth in Internet usage: in March 2011, an estimated number of around 4 million Syrians used the Internet, constituting roughly 17 percent of the population.[35] Although Facebook, YouTube and a range of websites were officially blocked, circumvention of this blockade through foreign proxy servers was a common phenomenon.[36] The regime maintained its control over the Internet through the Syrian Telecommunications Establishment (STE) and the Syrian Information Organization (SIO), which used software to spot banned words. Website managers were required to maintain a record of their visitors and cybercafes were frequently raided by the police or intelligence. Internet users who broke the rules were at risk of being questioned, arrested and jailed. Common charges included "the spread of false information with the aim of harming the state" and "weakening national sentiment."[37]

The making of news: the practice of journalism in a Totalitarian Press

As mentioned earlier, only a few media outlets were authorized to broadcast or publish news, and these outlets were either state-owned or owned by individuals from within the regime's inner circle. The key press outlets at the start of the Arab Spring in 2011 were the three state-owned newspapers – Tishreen,

Al-Thawra and Al-Ba'ath – and one privately owned newspaper Al-Watan. The latter outlet was privately owned by Rami Makhlouf, Bashar al-Assad's maternal cousin. The main TV channels that broadcast news were the state-owned Syria TV and Al-Ikhbariyah, in addition to the privately owned Addounia TV.[38]

The Syrian media sector offered prestigious, highly paid jobs, and finding a job in the media depended on having the right connections. Syrian journalists interviewed by the author explained that Alawites were in a privileged position for getting jobs in the media as well as for promotions within media organizations. As a result, the vast majority of media employees were Alawites.[39] Departments involved in the production of news, entrusted with the sensitive task of reporting on political affairs, consisted of particularly high numbers of Alawite staff and were full with *mukhabarat*.[40]

News content produced by journalists had to be developed around the four myths of regime propaganda that are outlined above. The production of content related to the army, the security, foreign affairs and the Assad family and its inner circle was off limits to journalists.[41] Journalists merely transmitted these issues through the regime's messages, which they gathered via several state-directed guidance channels, the most important one being the state press agency – the Syrian Arab News Agency (SANA) and a media unit in the presidential palace. For any political news, journalists simply lightly edited SANA press releases to make them more accessible for viewers and readers.[42]

Compliance of media professionals with the rules of state propaganda was ensured through a variety of control mechanisms. Direct censorship was one such mechanism and was implemented in Syria through Articles 9 and 10 of the press law.[43] But authorities also relied on more subtle techniques: Trusted regime loyalists occupied the key editorial positions within news outlets, and these figures were in positions to decide on promotions if a journalist performs well.[44] They also had the ability to impose disciplinary measures if a journalist crossed the line, ranging from demotion to a full suspension from the profession. Their connections to the *mukhabarat* could lead to more severe consequences – abduction, extrajudicial imprisonment and torture – and the threat of such consequences worked to keep journalists in line.

The pressure on media professionals to comply with the rules was high, but the red lines journalists had to respect were not written down explicitly in official guidelines or directives. Media professionals explained that they informed themselves of the official discourse by closely monitoring public statements made by state officials.[45] Officials from the ministry of information would also typically call meetings with news editors to inform them of the government's stance on particular issues.[46]

The unfolding of the Arab Spring

Since the 1970s, Syrians have thus lived in a repressive one-party system, in which a clique of Alawites controlled politics and society through its extensive security apparatus. Members of this power elite had unrivalled access to state resources and found opportunities for self-enrichment through their privileged status. Coupled with the overt corruption of the power elite, the widening socioeconomic gap between those in or close to power and those outside increased resentment among large segments of the population. However, the Alawite minority remained loyal to the presidential family, despite large segments also living in poverty: Fear of repression or persecution under a majority rule kept them behind the incumbent presidency and created shared interests with other religious minorities. An uprising of the Muslim Brotherhood between 1979 and 1982 indicates that the fear of a majority uprising was at least partially grounded in reality.

Within this context, the events unfolding throughout the Arab world in the early months of 2011 must have been grounds for concern among Syria's ruling clique. Starting with the self-immolation of Mohamed Bouazizi in Tunisia in December 2010, mass protests quickly spread across the Arab world during the weeks that followed. In January 2011, the Tunisian Ben Ali regime fell, and popular protests spread to Egypt, overthrowing President Mubarak in early February. That same month, protests started in Libya where state repression rapidly escalated the situation into a civil war. The protests in the Arab world made headlines in the international media and dominated day-to-day reporting of news stations across the globe. Arab satellite stations Al Jazeera and Al Arabiya were following the developments by the minute with live broadcasts of major events and protests.

Before the first mass protests happened in Syria in March 2011, the Syrian regime's propaganda apparatus struggled to frame the protest movements in other Arab countries. Dictators were being overthrown across the region, and the legitimacy of repressive self-enriching authoritarian regimes was being openly contested by protestors. With these images pouring into Syrian living rooms every day through Al Jazeera, the regime's struggle to frame these protests in a favorable way is instructive for understanding the regime's framing of protests spreading in Syria later on. According to the interviewed journalists, the script that was developed for reporting on the protests in Libya was transferred to the Syrian context when protests broke out there.[47]

As mentioned, political news stories were not made by journalists working in the news media but rather disseminated to them by institutions controlled by the regime – the news agency SANA and the media unit inside the presidential palace were the main sources for dissemination of the official narrative and transmission of red lines. Throughout the Tunisian revolution and the spread of mass demonstrations to Egypt, SANA did not issue press releases on events going on in the Arab world. SANA's first press release providing an official account of the Arab Spring was only issued on 5 February and dealt with the Egyptian demonstrations under the headline "Demonstrations in Egypt continue for the 12th day."[48] On 2 and 3 February, press releases had already reported on the situation in Egypt indirectly, discussing the evacuation of Syrian students from Egypt to Syria in the context of what is referred to as "the ongoing events."[49] This silence regarding the demonstrations in Tunisia and Egypt most likely reflects the regime's search for an appropriate frame and the lack of specific guidelines for reporting, as recollected by a former media employee who worked at a private station at the time:

> When the Tunisian president was toppled, the newsroom editor made a report about it and he asked [the manager] what the red lines were. The reply was: 'it's a people's revolution,' At 1pm the news was broadcast and then the newsroom manager came and screamed at everyone. The statement from the newsroom manager was to make no reports about the Arab Spring, not negative, not positive.[50]

The lack of information provided to Syrians by the state's official channels did not mean Syrian audiences were not informed about the demonstrations; satellite stations were dominated by images and commentary concerning the events in Tunisia and Egypt, and information was accessible through the Internet, despite the restrictions on Internet usage. Rather, the silence in the Syrian state media meant that a clear code for speaking about these events in public was not made available through news messages. Such a narrative was, however, starting to develop through editorial commentaries and opinion columns in state newspapers. Through this platform otherwise used by key regime loyalists to provide their interpretation of current events, the uprisings in Tunisia and Egypt started gaining prominence, particularly after the fall of Ben Ali on 14 January. An increasingly consistent frame was used for the discussion of the Tunisian revolution in its aftermath and the Egyptian demonstrations as they were escalating in the second half of January 2011. This frame linked the Tunisian and Egyptian uprisings to the disappointment of Tunisian and Egyptian people in the pro-Western orientation of their governments and their lack of commitment to the plight of the Palestinians. As such, the revolutions were presented as an expression of Arab nationalism: citizens of the Arab world demanding true Arab leadership.[51]

An important publication in this respect is an editorial by Buthaina Shabaan, Assad's media advisor, in Tishreen on 31 January. At this point in time, mass protests were ongoing in Egypt, which Shabaan framed as "renaissance of the Arabs and its struggle against colonialism." The frustration that led to the demonstrations, however, is explained as a frustration of Arab youth over the Western-Zionist-inflicted suffering of Arabs in Palestine and Iraq.[52] The inaction of Arab leaders in the face of this threat is portrayed in stark contrast with the Assad regime's steadfast resistance against these known external enemies. This frame was soon adopted by the news media. As a state TV employee describes, "In the TV there was an order that the media should show Syria as a different situation from other Arab countries."[53]

Escalation of protests in Libya

In the direct aftermath of Ben-Ali's departure, calls for protests were being made by several Syrian groups through the Internet. On account of heavy security surveillance, the calls for protests did not lead to demonstrations throughout the month of February. Events in Libya quickly escalated during the second half of February 2011. On the 'Day of Rage' on 17 February, dozens of peaceful protestors were shot by the security forces, and these bloody images were all over the news. But the frame that was developed for the Egyptian revolution would not work for the Libyan case: Gaddafi was a longtime ally of the Assad regime and known for his anti-Western and anti-Israeli stance. An employee at a news program recalls that new guidelines were developed for the Libyan revolution, which were later extended to apply to the Syrian protests:

> With the Libyan revolution, things changed. I made the first report, following the guidance of the Egyptian revolution. The censorship rejected my report. They said this will have different guidelines: this is a conspiracy. I asked about the killings of the demonstrators. They said, 'there are no killings.' This policy continued with the Syrian revolution.[54]

This eventually led to the surfacing of a coherent narrative on the opinion pages of Syria's main newspapers, representing the events in Libya as being orchestrated to create a pretext for foreign intervention. The narrative assumes that the revolutions in Tunisia and Egypt were genuine, but that the West – and the United States more specifically – had now developed a strategy to capitalize on these events in the case of Libya. While violence escalated in Libya during February and March 2011, protests also started spreading in Syria. Events in Syria escalated rapidly, with the government army besieging the southern city of Daraa by the end of April to crush protests. The Syrian media quickly became focused on covering these internal developments.

Spreading protests, government crackdown and an emerging propaganda strategy

Calls for protests in Syria already spread during the aftermath of Hosni Mubarak's downfall in the second half of February 2011. But this did not immediately lead to mass protests in Syria: A protest in Damascus on 17 February attracted no more than around 1,500 demonstrators, and the crowd was quickly dispersed by the police.[55] The push for more sizable protests came from the southern city of Daraa, where a group of teenage boys was arrested for painting anti-regime graffiti on the walls of their school. The boys were interrogated and taken to the security branches where they were held for interrogation and torture for weeks, prompting the boys' relatives and neighbors to protest for their release: a protest that continued to grow in size in the course of the following days.[56] Simultaneously, protests spread in other Syrian cities, and demonstrations took place in Damascus, Al Hasaka, Hama and Deir Ezzor on 15 March, constituting the undeniable start of a revolution in Syria.[57] From then on, protests quickly became a regular event across Syria, and the security forces responded with violence. The brutal killing of protestors by the security forces made the protest movement grow in size, prompting the government to lay a full siege on the city of Daraa by the end of April and on the city of Homs a month later. In just two months' time, hundreds of protestors were killed, while thousands of people had been arbitrarily arrested and held in detention where they were being brutally tortured every day.[58]

While the protests were spreading in the course of March 2011, the Syrian media initially did not report on the demonstrations and continued regular broadcasting as if nothing was happening. Journalists interviewed for this research explained that they received instructions to continue work as usual, as long as there were no clear guidelines on how to report on the issue.[59] The first reports from the Syrian state media started appearing after mass protests had occurred in Daraa after Friday prayers on 18 March and its violent aftermath had made international headlines. As security forces opened fire on the protestors, the situation escalated severely in the days that followed. Eyewitnesses appeared on Al Jazeera and Al Arabiya to relate their experiences, and a security forces attack on protestors at Daraa's main mosque on 23 March resulted in a major bloodshed. In the following days and weeks, state media reports on the protests became frequent and started showing the contours of a coherent narrative. Public statements from Buthaina Shabaan – Assad's media advisor – and President Bashar al-Assad himself, addressing the People's Assembly on 30 March in a televised speech, further consolidated this narrative. Importantly, neither media reports nor government officials denied that protests were taking place, but they did downplay their size and impact. The narrative pushed by the regime relayed two core messages: (1) The government was leading a genuine reform process to address citizens' concerns, and (2) the protests formed a cover for a foreign 'conspiracy.' However, while the supposed conspiracy that had caused unrest in Libya had been portrayed as linked to U.S. imperialism, the events in Daraa were portrayed as stemming from an *Islamist* conspiracy, with Gulf countries and Turkey as its foreign drivers.

In the wake of escalations in Daraa, Shabaan's press statement on 24 March referred to the establishment of a government-led committee to investigate the events through an upcoming broader reform process to address citizens' concerns. With regard to the protests themselves and the people involved she stated, "What took place in Daraa was not a peaceful demonstration, but rather an armed movement. [Financed and armed from outside, the] purpose of this [movement] is to foment sectarian sedition in Syria and the region."[60]

Two former Syrian journalists recalled the press statement by Buthaina Shabaan and indicated how, between the lines, it revealed the regime's line with regard to the protests:

> [After] the attack on [Al-Omari] mosque [in Daraa] it was announced on TV that armed terrorists were attacking the government. There was a lot of chaos at the TV office [...] On Thursday night Buthaina Shabaan held a press conference. She said that there were armed militia in Al-Omari Mosque and that they were [serving] a foreign agenda, referring to Turkey and Saudi

> Arabia. She announced that the upcoming period would see the development of a party law and a media law and that they would increase the salaries of civil servants. This was a clear message: everyone in a demonstration is a terrorist and is fighting against the Alawites. And that they will give money to 'solve' any demands made by people. When they refer to foreign involvement, Turkey or Saudi,[61] the hidden message is that they are Islamists.[62]
>
> Very quickly after the first protests in Daraa, Buthaina Shaaban gave an important speech. She is known to be a strong sectarianist. There had been protests in Daraa and people had been killed. We were expecting a speech saying something about investigating the incidents or something like that. Instead, she said something like 'All Syrians are united, across our differences. We will not allow foreign forces to create problems between us.' This stood out because they never say anything about 'our differences': this is unheard of coming from the regime.[63]

In a speech to the General Assembly on 30 March, President Assad conveyed the same message in his first public statement regarding the events unfolding in Syria: He listed a number of political and economic reforms that various government committees had initiated to address the calls for reforms. In addition, the President provided his reading of the protests in Syria, emphasizing that the protests were instigated by a foreign conspiracy that threatens to destroy Syria. It is remarkable that the president explicitly referred to 'sects,' while this is – as explained above – a taboo in public speech:

> It is no secret to you that Syria is today facing a great conspiracy, the strings of which spread from far away countries and close countries, with some strings in the homeland. [...] They began with instigation. Instigation began many weeks before the unrest in Syria. They began [their] incitement using satellite channels and the Internet but achieved nothing. After that they moved on to fabrication. They forged information, voice, images, video, and everything. They then played on sectarianism, using incitement and sending SMS messages warning each sect of attacks by other sects. [...] They would tell people: Be careful, the other sect is now out in the street. They managed to get people out to the streets. [...] They then used weapons. They began killing people indiscriminately so that there would be blood. [...] Those were the methods. As for the structure, [...] it is an organized structure. There are support groups with members in different governorates and abroad.

While the statements of Shabaan and Assad may not seem explicitly sectarian in nature, the statements have to be interpreted against the backdrop of the unwritten rules of public speech in Syria. These rules prohibit any explicit reference to sectarian and religious differences between the Syrian people. It is thus significant that two key regime officials make explicit reference to sects and sectarianism in their first public statements on the protests in Syria. Furthermore, it is important to note that while state officials and state media used relatively covert terms to refer to a foreign-incited Sunni uprising, these messages were accompanied by much more explicit messages spread through regime-loyal private media outlets. For example, neither state officials nor state media channels could directly implicate Saudi Arabia or Turkey, as this would clearly carry diplomatic implications. This was therefore left to the private media, as a former employee of a newspaper explains:

> The media started to show King Abdallah in advertisements drinking wine. This was on private channels, so that if the Saudi [government] would object, Bashar [Al Assad] could say that it's not his media. Also, they started to attack Qatar and Turkey in Al Dunya tv. But not [only] via news, rather in talk shows with people from the regime giving commentaries.

The two speeches revealed the script for reporting on the demonstrations in Syria, and this script was perfectly understood by media professionals. Employees in the regime-controlled media started producing stories that reflected the official reading of events, as two former journalists at state media outlets explained:

> They [started] writing stories mentioning that the protesters worked with Al Qaeda and that many were from Saudi Arabia. Bashar became the idol who was protecting the minorities. They were showing videos of Islamists killing people: this became the daily work in the Syrian TV.[64]
>
> Since the beginning of the revolution, Haitham Satayeh [Ba'ath Party], Buthaina Shabaan and the Omran al Zoubi [Minister of Information] used to come to us in our offices. They visited the newspaper and told us to try and make the revolution to be seen as Islamic uprising. [...] We were lying [...] We made the revolution seem Islamist. We wrote about the bombings, saying that terrorists did it, even though I knew it was coming from the security forces. For my section [of the newspaper], I would send my journalists to cover [the] demonstrations. I would task them to meet with the mayor, meet with the imam and make clear that they should speak what the regime was saying.[65]

Journalists knew they had no choice but to follow these scripts. They were constantly being watched and "tested" by regime loyalists and *mukhabarat* on the work floor:

> When the revolution was going on [my colleagues] started to insult people who were not with the regime. They would say things like 'this stupid revolution' and they pushed me to say that as well. [They were] calling [the demonstrators] 'terrorists,' They pushed me to say that too, but I can't say that. They push you to show loyalty. All the time, I was afraid. I tried to

> avoid going to work and when I went, I didn't talk to anyone and go home again quickly.[66]
>
> You just wear your smile to work. Loyalists in the watch room were saying 'burn Deraa.' There were patrols and watchmen everywhere [and] I was being watched.[67]
>
> The atmosphere was becoming like, if you write the truth, they will kill you. They would even kill you if you brought medicine to an injured person.[68]

By the end of March 2011, the script for reporting on the protests as a Sunni uprising that resulted from an Islamist conspiracy had been transmitted to the regime's propaganda apparatus. Knowing their lives would be in danger if they wrote the truth, media professionals spread this script in their daily reporting.

Coding and decoding sectarian motives: 'the Sunnis are coming'

The situation in Daraa escalated further, and by the end of April 2011, the Syrian army besieged the city, sent tanks and installed snipers to shoot at the protestors. Hundreds of people were killed and arrested, while popular protests continued to spread in other major cities including Homs and Hama, which were similarly besieged. At the same time, protests spread across the country, and the government's violent response continued to make international headlines. International pressure mounted on the Assad regime to resign, and the first signs of a move to armed opposition appeared in June 2011 with a mutiny of a Syrian army unit in Jisr al-Shughur. In July, defected officers of the Syrian army established the 'Free Syrian Army' with the explicit goal to overthrow the Assad regime. Throughout these developments, the international media reported on the demonstrations and bloodshed in Syria on a daily basis.

One of the core tasks of the government-controlled media therefore became to create media content to discredit the reporting of these international channels. The pan-Arab channels were a prime target, as they had served Syrian audiences for years prior to the Arab Spring. State-owned and private pro-government media outlets started running stories and talk shows in which the credibility of Al Jazeera, Al Arabiya and other satellite channels was questioned. Their criticism focused on the reliance of these channels on eyewitness reports, claiming that these eyewitnesses were actors who were being paid. Moreover, commentators showed 'evidence' of how images and videos of the demonstrations and clashes were being manipulated. Syrian pro-government news channel Al-Ikhbariyah al-Suriyah, for instance, repeatedly broadcast an 'analysis' of a video clip of a female protestor being taken away by a policeman on 28 March. When replayed in slow motion, the 'analysis' showed that the event had been deliberately staged for the camera.[69] Some of the most extreme 'conspiracy reports' were aired on the privately owned but pro-regime Al-Dunya TV. This channel produced a special program that revealed the 'media conspiracy' called 'The Misleading Media.' In September 2011, this program aired episodes in which it was claimed that Al Jazeera had built replicas of Syrian cities in Qatar, where actors were enacting large-scale demonstrations and clashes with the security forces.[70]

There are numerous examples of reporting that supported the regime's narrative that the protests were merely a cover for Islamist terrorists. On 26 April, the Syrian TV aired a 'confession' of a supposed terrorist from Daraa, Mustafa Bin Yousef Khalifa Aiyash, who claimed that he was paid 50,000 Syrian pounds to organize demonstrations and call for *jihad*. He further described the availability of sophisticated weapons among the group.[71] Another such televised 'confession' relays the account of a supposed terrorist, who claimed that he was,

> instructed by other members of terrorist groups to record footage of the security personnel murdered by the armed groups and buried in a mass grave, and that the video was to be sent to satellite channels and published under the pretense that the bodies belong to citizens killed by security forces.[72]

SANA press releases structurally depicted the protests and clashes in Syria as 'incidents' caused by 'terrorists,' 'infiltrators,' 'gunmen' and 'criminals,'[73] and the Syrian state TV's more elaborate reports built on this terminology. An important way in which reporting re-enforced fears of a violent Sunni takeover was by depicting 'terrorists' and 'infiltrators' as originating from Sunni areas. News reports about armed gangs and terrorists that mention their area of origin refer to specific neighborhoods or towns known to be the home of Sunni communities. An example is the following report, which depicts perpetrators as originating from Al-Hulah plain, which forms a Sunni enclave in the middle of an Alawite-dominated area. They purportedly carried out attacks in the village of Aqrab (mixed Sunni and Alawite) and Misyaf (mixed Alawite, Christian and Ishmai'li):

> [Unidentified correspondent video report] Groups of saboteurs coming from Al-Hulah plain in Homs have burned down the buildings of the city's council, the water bill payment centre, and the [Al-Ba'th] Party branch in the village of Aqrab, 35 kilometres west of Hama City centre. They carried out acts of riots, which resulted in harming the citizens, beating them with sticks and batons, and throwing stones at them, as well as setting official institutions and departments ablaze.
>
> [Unidentified citizen] Yesterday evening, a group of saboteurs came [...] to the village's entrance leading to Hama and the western entrance leading to Misyaf. They burned tires and blocked the roads.[74]

While the violence and unrest were categorically depicted as the result of an Islamist scheme, the state media simultaneously reported extensively on the reform measures the government had introduced to address citizens' concerns, such as the appointment of a new cabinet, economic reforms and the various committees drafting proposals to reform the Political Parties Act.[75] In addition, reports of citizens and prominent figures expressing their love and loyalty to the president were a common feature.[76]

On 20 June 2011, President Bashar al-Assad addressed the nation in a televised speech from Damascus University. While his previous speeches had contained covert references to the armed Islamist 'conspiracy' behind the uprising, inciting fear of the Sunni majority among Syria's religious minorities, this speech made the regime's reading of the revolution as an Islamist scheme fully explicit:

> The most dangerous [component of the conspiracy] is represented by those who have extremist and *takfiri* [holding other Muslims to be infidels] thought. We have tested and known this thought for decades when it tried to infiltrate into Syria, but Syria managed to get rid of it through the awareness and wisdom of its people.[77] Today, we do not feel that this kind of thinking is different from what we have seen in decades. It is the same. Only the tools, methods, and faces have changed. It sits in dark alleys and appears whenever it has the opportunity and whenever it finds a mask to wear. It kills in the name of religion, destroys in the name of reform, and spreads chaos in the name of freedom. [...] [The conspirators] have evoked a hateful sectarian rhetoric, which neither belongs to us nor we belong to it. [They] attacked civilians, the police, and military men by attacking military posts and positions or through assassinations. [...] In Jisr al-Shughur they perpetrated abominable massacres, the images of which we saw in the news media. [...] What is important is that they possessed advanced weapons, which were not there in the past, as well as advanced communication equipment.[78]

In his speech, the president compares the 'conspirators' to 'germs': "They proliferate every moment and everywhere. They cannot be eradicated but we can strengthen the immunity of our bodies against them."

The above speech forms a full articulation of the regime's strategy of sectarian incitement. As mentioned above, the explicit references to sectarianism are a major break from the regular taboos that guide public speech in Syria in which the existence of sects and sectarianism is categorically denied. Furthermore, the messages sent by the president and by the regime's media apparatus were decoded by Syrian minorities as containing clear references to Syria's Sunni majority and directly evoked fears of coming under a Sunni rule, which was associated with being enslaved and killed. Four interviewees belonging to religious minorities provide examples of how the messages were interpreted as such:

> From the early days of the revolution, the regime framed it as a Sunni attempt to take over the country. They did not say this explicitly, but as a minority, we understood it from their messages: a group of terrorists in

Homs [...] armed gangs in Daraa [...] These are all Sunni areas. It means: watch out, the Sunni will try to take over. Most people believed it and were afraid.[79]

I am a minority, [and seen as supporting the revolution] so my Alawite colleagues used to tell me "Is this what you want? The Sunni from Daraa to take over?"[80]

In my area [Alawite area of Baniyas] people believe in the state TV. But some of them also watched Al Jazeera and Al Arabiya. And there were some doubts. Some people may know that the regime is lying, but they also fear what may happen and they fear the Sunnis. This fear controlled them. People didn't necessarily side with the regime because they believe the regime, but because of fear. Problems between Sunni and Alawites have been going on for long. In the Alawi memory, Sunnis used to kill them and take their children. The regime was telling people "if the Sunni rule this country, they will kill you. They will enslave you."[81]

When the problems started in 2011 [this was] because [of] the *Akhuan Muslimeen* [Muslim Brotherhood]. They were planning the war. They tried it before, when my president Hafiz was there. They tried to start a war in Hama.[82] The military went there, because the Akhuan Muslimeen put bombs in buses. But they were stopped by the army. [...] Even before the war started in 2011, they had a plan to make this war. They were working in secret, they were hiding their activities. If they meet you on the street, they will smile at you, but meanwhile they were planning to make a war with us. [...] They are dangerous. They used to kill Christians and Alawites. [...] Then they started to work together in Deraa. They want to make all of Syria Islamic.[83]

Conclusion

The above analysis indicates that from the onset of civilian protests in Syria during March 2011, the Syrian regime designed and implemented a propaganda strategy intended to incite fear of Sunni domination among religious minorities. Messaging in speeches and statements by regime officials, including the president himself, was in tandem with reporting by the state-controlled media, both state and privately owned. These factors jointly contributed to a seamlessly coherent narrative through which religious minorities were being warned of a conspiracy by the Sunni majority to take over the country, instigated by Sunni-dominated countries such as Saudi Arabia and Turkey. The regime's narrative simultaneously denied and legitimized the excessive violence it used against the protestors in the streets and in the torture facilities of its security branches. Denial served as a cover toward the outside world, while legitimization ensured cooperation of minorities in the state-led slaughter.

Collectively, the sources used for this research provide the first building blocks toward a full historical account of the crimes committed by the Syrian regime against its own population over the past eight years. But the account provided here also has its limitations, and more research is needed to complete the picture. First of all, this analysis draws on an archive of media messages that is limited to written outputs and transcripts of TV broadcasts. While this offers a broad range of materials to analyze, the emotive content of TV and radio broadcasts was not captured. Second, the archive was limited to traditional news media and does not contain social media content. In terms of the insight gathered through interviews with former journalists, the number of interviewees is limited. It was difficult to locate former media employees and to win their trust to speak openly about their experiences. This obstacle was even greater when interviewing members of minorities and regime supporters. Despite being small in number, these interviews do provide key insights into the interpretation of media messages during the Syrian crisis. While the above thus forms a starting point for understanding the Syrian regime's use of propaganda in response to the 2011 protests, future research could expand this understanding by focusing on the use of social media and the minorities' consumption of media. Other important avenues for scholarly research are the further development and shifts in propaganda during subsequent years of the conflict.

Notes

1 Independent International Commission of Inquiry on the Syrian Arab Republic, 'The Siege and Recapture of Eastern Ghouta,' Conference Room Paper, 20 June 2018. Online. Available HTTP: <https://www.ohchr.org/EN/HRBodies/HRC/IICISyria/Pages/IndependentInternationalCommission.aspx> (accessed 12 June 2019).

2 'Syria: Crimes Against Humanity in Daraa: Killings, Torture in a Locked-Down City under Siege,' New York, NY: Human Rights Watch (HRW), 2011a. Online. Available HTTP: <https://www.hrw.org/news/2011/06/01/syria-crimes-against-humanity-daraa> (accessed 12 June 2019). 'We Live as in War: Crackdown on Protesters in the Governorate of Homs,' New York, NY: Human Rights Watch, 2011b. Online. Available HTTP: <https://www.hrw.org/report/2011/11/11/we-live-war/crackdown-protesters-governorate-homs-syria> (accessed 12 June 2019).

3 Interviews were conducted in English or in Arabic with translation assistance of a person identified as a trusted person by the interviewee. With one exception, it was explained to all interviewees that the interview served the author's research aims of understanding the role of the Syrian media during the uprising. The one exception to this rule is an active supporter of the Assad regime who was interviewed in Beirut without full disclosure of the purpose of the research. Rather, the interview was presented as part of the author's research that aimed for a general understanding of the situation in Syria. All interviewees were guaranteed anonymity. No names will be provided in this chapter, nor will other details about the interviewees be provided that could lead to their identification.

4 The massive displacement, killing and disappearance of predominantly Sunni Syrians has altered the sectarian balance: With Syria's population having been reduced from 23 million to around 15 million, Alawites now constitute around 15 percent of Syria's

total population, while Sunni Arabs make up roughly 47 percent. F. Balanche, 'Sectarianism in Syria's Civil War,' The Washington Institute for Near East Policy, 2018.

5 Balanche, 'Sectarianism.' N. van Dam, *The Struggle for Power in Syria: Politics and Society under Asad and the Ba'th Party*, New York, NY: I.B. Tauris, 2011.

6 P.S. Khoury, 'Syrian Political Culture: A Historical Perspective,' in R.T. Antoun and D. Quataert (eds), *Syria: Society, Culture, and Polity*, Albany, NY: State University of New York Press, 1991. Y. Talhamy, 'The Fatwas and the Nusayri/Alawis of Syria,' *Middle Eastern Studies*, vol. 46, no. 2, 2010, pp. 175–194.

7 M.A. Faksh, 'The Alawi Community of Syria: A New Dominant Political Force,' *Middle Eastern Studies*, vol. 20, no. 2, 1984, pp. 133–153.

8 P. Seale, *Assad of Syria. The Struggle for the Middle East*, London: I.B. Tauris & Co Ltd, 1988. D. Pipes, 'The Alawi Capture of Power in Syria,' *Middle Eastern Studies*, vol. 25, no. 4, 1989, pp. 429–450.

9 van Dam, *The Struggle*. O. Haklai, 'A Minority Rule over a Hostile Majority: The Case of Syria,' *Nationalism and Ethnic Politics*, vol. 6, no. 3, 2007, pp. 19–50.

10 Seale, *Assad*, p. 26.

11 S.J. King, *The New Authoritarianism in the Middle East and North Africa*, Bloomington, IN: Indiana University Press, 2009, p. 39.

12 Seale, *Assad*, pp. 162–165.

13 King, *The New Authoritarianism*. R. Hinnebusch, 'Class and State in Ba'thist Syria,' in Antoun and Quataert (eds), *Syria*. L. Wedeen, *Ambiguities of Domination. Politics, Rhetoric, and Symbols in Contemporary Syria*, Chicago, IL: University of Chicago Press, 1999.

14 T. Pierret, *Religion and State in Syria: The Sunni Ulama from Coup to Revolution*, Cambridge: Cambridge University Press, 2013, p. 21.

15 A. Rathmell, 'Syria's Intelligence Services: Origins and Development,' *The Journal of Conflict Studies*, vol. 16, no. 2, 1996.

16 *Middle East Watch, Human Rights in Syria*, New York, NY: Human Rights Watch, 1990, p. 44.

17 Amnesty International, *Syria, Briefing Paper no. 16*, Nottingham: Amnesty International, 1979, pp. 7–9.

18 S. Haugbolle, 'Imprisonment, Truth Telling and Historical Memory in Syria,' *Mediterranean Politics*, vol. 13, no. 2, 2008, p. 264. Wedeen, *Ambiguities*.

19 W. Rugh, *Arab Mass Media: Newspapers, Radio, and Television in Arab Politics: Newspapers, Radio, and Television in Arab Politics*, Westport, CT: Praeger Publishers, 2004. BBC Media Action, 'Syria: Country Case Study,' 2012. Online. Available HTTP: <http://downloads.bbc.co.uk/mediaaction/pdf/syria.pdf> (accessed 12 June 2009). *A Wasted Decade: Human Rights in Syria during Bashar al-Asad's First Ten Years in Power*, New York, NY: Human Rights Watch, 2010. Seale, *Assad*.

20 Wedeen, *Ambiguities*. U. Freitag, 'In Search of 'Historical Correctness': The Ba'th Party in Syria,' *Middle Eastern Studies*, vol. 35, no. 1, 1999, pp. 1–16.

21 L.T. Goldsmith, *Cycle of Fear: Syria's Alawites in War and Peace*, London: C. Hurst & Co Publishers, 2015.

22 Syrian school syllabi, for example, make no mention of the different (Sunni, Shi'a) branches of Islam.

23 M. Kedar, *Asad in Search of Legitimacy: Message and Rhetoric in the Syrian Press under Hafiz and Bashar*, Brighton: Sussex University Press, 2005, pp. 30–31, 89–90.

24 Wedeen, *Ambiguities*.

25 Kedar, *Asad in Search*, pp. 44–45.

26 Ibid., p. 166. Haugbolle, 'Imprisonment,' p. 264.

27 Wedeen, *Ambiguities*.

28 M. Dibo, Mohammed, 'Assad's Secular Sectarianism,' 2014. Online. Available HTTP: <https://www.opendemocracy.net/en/north-africa-west-asia/assads-secular-sectarianism/> (accessed 12 June 2009).
29 Goldsmith, *Cycle*, p. 117.
30 Wedeen, *Ambiguities*, p. 6.
31 BBC Media Action, 'Syria.' L. Caldwell, 'Privileging the Private: Media Development in Syria, Arab Media and Society,' 2010. Online. Available HTTP: <http://www.arabmediasociety.com/> (accessed 12 June 2009).
32 BBC Media Action, 'Syria,' p. 7. Institute for War and Peace Reporting (IWPR) Syria Media Map, 2013, p. 17. Online. Available HTTP: <https://iwpr.net/printed-materials/syria-media-map> (accessed 12 June 2009). Interview with a former Syrian journalist at a state-owned newspaper, 15 January 2016, Istanbul.
33 BBC Media Action, 'Syria,' p. 5.
34 N. Ghadbian, 'Contesting the State Media Monopoly: Syria on Al-Jazira Television,' *MERIA Journal*, vol. 5, no. 2, June 2001, pp. 79–81.
35 Reporters Sans Frontières (RSF), 'Internet Enemies: Middle East/North Africa – Syria,' 2011.
36 R.F. Worth, 'Web Tastes Freedom inside Syria, and It's Bitter,' *New York Times*, 29 September 2010.
37 RSF, 'Internet Enemies.' HRW, 'A Wasted Decade,' 2010.
38 Addounia TV is reportedly owned by a group of businessmen with close ties to the regime.
39 Interviews with former Syrian journalists, 23 January 2016 in Gaziantep, 13 January 2016 in Istanbul and 12 January 2016 in Istanbul.
40 Interviews with former Syrian TV employee, 12 January 2016 in Istanbul.
41 Interview with former Syrian journalist, 13 January 2016 in Istanbul.
42 Interview with former Syrian journalist, 13 January 2016 in Istanbul and 5 July 2016 in Gaziantep.
43 Rugh, *Arab*, pp. 37–38. BBC Media Action, 'Syria,' p. 6.
44 Rugh, *Arab*, pp. 29–39.
45 Interview with former Syrian journalist, 13 January 2016 in Istanbul and 5 July 2016 in Gaziantep.
46 Rugh, *Arab*, pp. 39–40.
47 Interviews with former Syrian news journalists, 5 July 2016 in Gaziantep and 13 January 2016 in Istanbul.
48 SANA Press Release, 5 February 2011.
49 'Higher Education Council Provides Facilitations for the Return of Syrian Students Delegated to Egypt,' *SANA*, 2 February 2011, and 'Syrian Flights to Transport Syrians and Non-Syrian out of Cairo Continue,' *SANA*, 3 February 2011.
50 Interview with former Syrian journalist, 5 July 2016 in Gaziantep.
51 Two important examples include 'A Hard Lesson,' editorial in Al-Watan by Chief Editor Waddah Abd-Rabbuh, 16 January 2011, and 'Tunisia's Revolution … From the Authoritarian State to the National State,' editorial in al-Bath by Chief Editor Muhammad Kanaysi on 23 January 2011.
52 'The Voice of the Masses,' by Buthaynah Sha'ban in Tishreen, 31 January 2011.
53 Interview with former Syrian TV employee, 13 January 2016 in Istanbul. This instruction is confirmed by other interviewees.
54 Interview with former Syrian journalist, 5 July 2016 in Gaziantep.
55 W. Sawah and S. Kawakibi, 'Activism in Syria: Between Nonviolence and Armed Resistance,' in L. Khatib and L. Lust (eds), *Taking to the Streets: The Transformation of Arab Activism*, Baltimore, MD: John Hopkins University, 2014, p. 161. E. Hokayem,

Syria's Uprising and the Fracturing of the Levant, Abingdon, New York, NY: Routledge, 2013, p. 42.

56 HRW, 2011.

57 Sawah and Kawakibi, 'Activism.'

58 HRW, 2011.

59 Interviews with former Syrian journalists, 12 and 16 January 2016 in Istanbul, 23 January 2016 in Gaziantep and 5 July in Gaziantep.

60 Full transcript of the press statement could not be retrieved, partial transcript found in 'Daraa events not peaceful protest but "armed movement" – Syrian president's aide,' text of report by Lebanese Hezbollah Al-Manar TV on 24 March 2011.

61 It is important to note that neither state officials nor state media channels directly implicated Saudi Arabia or Turkey, as this would clearly carry diplomatic implications. This was left to the private media.

62 Interview with former Syrian TV employee, 16 January 2016 in Istanbul.

63 Interview with former Syrian journalist, 29 January 2015 in Beirut.

64 Interview with former Syrian TV employee, 23 January 2016 in Gaziantep.

65 Interview with former Syrian newspaper journalist, 15 January 2016 in Istanbul.

66 Interview with former Syrian TV employee, 12 January 2016 in Istanbul.

67 Interview with former Syrian news journalist, 5 July 2016 in Gaziantep.

68 Interview with former Syrian news journalist, 21 January 2016 Gaziantep.

69 Media Feature: Syria questions credibility of foreign reporting, Media feature by BBC Monitoring, 29 March 2011.

70 Author's archive of media content contains videos of two separate episodes of the Dunya TV program on 9 September and 19 September 2011 where this "evidence" is relayed.

71 'Confession of Detained Terrorist Cell Member,' *Syria TV*, 26 April 2011

72 "'Terrorists in Syria' Confess to Working with Biased Media," *Syria TV*, 20 June 2011.

73 SANA Press Releases, March–June 2011.

74 "'Group of saboteurs' vandalizing public property arrested in Hamah."

75 SANA Press Releases, March–June 2011.

76 These included reports of rallies in support of the president and the government's reform process, for example Syria TV reports "'Dozens of thousands' of Syrians reportedly hold rally supporting government," 18 June 2011. ''Another example is a SANA Press Release 'Rallies in Most Provinces Voice Rejection of Foreign Interference in Syrian Affairs,' 9 July 2011.

77 Reference to the Muslim Brotherhood uprising in the 1979–82 period.

78 Syrian president addresses nation on current crisis, national dialogue. Text of report by Syrian TV, 20 June 2011.

79 Interview with a Syrian belonging to the Druze minority, 19 January 2015 in Beirut.

80 Interview with a Syrian belonging to the Ismaeli minority, 13 January 2016 in Istanbul.

81 Interview with a Syrian from the Alawite minority, 11 January 2015 in Beirut.

82 Reference to the Muslim Brotherhood uprising in 1979–82, which had its epicenter in the city of Hama.

83 Interview with a Syrian from the Alawite minority, 12 January 2015 in Beirut.

Bibliography

A Wasted Decade: Human Rights in Syria during Bashar al-Asad's First Ten Years in Power, New York: Human Rights Watch, 2010.

'Abd-al-Kahir ibn Tahir al-Baghdadi, A.-M., *Moslem Schisms and Sects (al-Fark bain al-firak) Being the History of the Various Philosophic Systems Developed in Islam*, translated from the Arabic with Introduction and Notes by A.S. Halkin, Tel Aviv: Palestine Publishing, 1935.

Adang, C. et al. (eds), *Accusations of Unbelief in Islam: A Diachronic Perspective on Takfir*, Leiden: Brill, 2016.

Addis, A., 'International Propaganda and Developing Countries,' *Vanderbilt Journal of Transnational Law*, vol. 21, 1988.

Akyol, M., 'A Medieval Antidote to ISIS,' *New York Times*, December 21, 2015.

Allard K. Lowenstein International Human Rights Clinic, *Persecution of the Rohingya Muslims: Is Genocide Occurring in Rakhine State? A Legal Analysis*, New Haven, CT: Yale Law School for Fortify Rights, 2015.

Alexander, R., *Bosnian, Croatian, Serbian: A Grammar with Sociolinguistic Commentary*, Madison: University of Wisconsin Press, 2006.

Al-Ibrahim, B., 'ISIS, Wahhabism and Takfir,' *Contemporary Arab Affairs*, vol. 8, no. 3, 2015.

'Allies and Aliens: A Mission in Critical Thinking,' *Media Smarts*, 2005. Online. Available HTTP: <http://mediasmarts.ca/game/allies-and-aliens-mission-critical-thinking> (accessed 26 August 2019).

al-Salam Faraj, A., *al-Farida al-gha'iba*, Amman, n.d., in J.J.G. Jansen (ed.), *The Neglected Duty: The Creed of Sadat's Assassins and Islamic Resurgence in the Middle East*, London: Macmillan Publishing, 1986.

al-'Ubaydi, M. et al., *The Group That Calls Itself a State: Understanding the Evolution and Challenges of the Islamic State*, The Combatting Terrorism Centre at West Point, December 2014.

Ambos, K., *Der Allgemeine Teil des Völkerstrafrechts: Ansätze einer Dogmatisierung*, Second Edition, Berlin: Duncker and Humblot, 2004.

Ananth, V., 'WhatsApp Races against Time to Fix Fake News Mess Ahead of 2019 General Elections,' *The Economic Times*, 24 July 2018.

Anders, G., 'Testifying about 'Uncivilized Events': Problematic Representations of Africa in the Trial Against Charles Taylor,' *Leiden Journal of International Law*, vol. 24, no. 4, 2011.

Anderson, B., *Imagined Communities: Reflections on the Origin and Spread of Nationalism*, Revised Edition, London: Verso, 1998.

Anđelić, N., *Bosnia-Herzegovina: The End of a Legacy*, London: Frank Cass, 2003.

Anscombe, G.E.M., *Intention*, Cambridge, MA: Harvard University Press, 2000.

Antkowiak, T.M., 'Remedial Approaches to Human Rights Violations: The Inter-American Court of Human Rights and Beyond,' *Columbia Journal of Transnational Law*, vol. 46, no. 2, 2008.

Antoun, R.T. and Quataert, D. (eds), *Syria: Society, Culture, and Polity*, Albany, NY: State University of New York Press, 1991.

Arakelova, V., 'Sufi Saints in the Yezidi Tradition I: Qawlē H'usēyīni H'alāj,' *Iran & the Caucasus*, vol. 5, 2001.

Armatta, J., *Twilight of Impunity: The War Crimes Trial of Slobodan Milošević*, Durham, NC: Duke University Press, 2010.

Armijo, E., 'Meet the New Governors, Same as the Old Governors,' New York, NY: Knight First Amendment Institute, Columbia University, 2019.

Arnautović, S., *Izbori u Bosni i Hercegovini; Analiza izbornog procesa*, Sarajevo: Promo-cult, 1996.

'Āsim Al-Maqdisī, A.M., *Millat Ibrāhīm: The Religion of Ibrāhīm*, Second Edition, London: Al-Tibyān Publications, n.d.

Austin, J.L., *How to Do Things with Words*, Cambridge, MA: Harvard University Press, 1962.

Azevedo, R.T. et al., 'Cardiac Afferent Activity Modulates the Expression of Racial Stereotypes,' *Nature Communications*, vol. 8, article no. 13854, 2017.

Baars, B.J. and Gage, N.M., *Cognition, Brain, and Consciousness: Introduction Cognitive Neuroscience*, Second Edition, Amsterdam: Elsevier, 2010.

Badar, M.E., *The Concept of Mens Rea in International Criminal Law: The Case for a Unified Approach*, Oxford, Portland: Hart Publishing, 2013.

Badar, M.E. et al., 'The Radical Application of the Islamic Concept of Takfir,' *Arab Law Quarterly*, vol. 31, 2017.

Balanche, F., *Sectarianism in Syria's Civil War*, Washington, DC: The Washington Institute for Near East Policy, 2018.

Balcetis, E. and Dunning, D., 'See What You Want to See: Motivational Influences on Visual Perception,' *Journal of Personality and Social Psychology*, vol. 91, no. 4, 2006.

Bambauer, D.E., 'Shopping Badly: Cognitive Biases, Communications, and the Fallacy of the Marketplace of Ideas,' *University of Colorado Law Review*, vol. 77, 2006.

Bandura, A. et al., 'Disinhibition of Aggression through Diffusion of Responsibility and Dehumanization of Victims,' *Journal of Research in Personality*, vol. 9, 1975.

Bandura, A. et al., 'Mechanisms of Moral Disengagement in the Exercise of Moral Agency,' *Journal of Personality and Social Psychology*, vol. 71, no. 2, 1996.

Bandura, A., 'Moral Disengagement in the Perpetration of Inhumanities,' *Personality and Social Psychology Review*, vol. 3, no. 3, 1999.

Bantekas, I. and Nash, S., *International Criminal Law*, London: Routledge-Cavendish, 2007.

Basci, E., 'Yazidis: A Community Scattered in between Geographies and Its Current Immigration Experience,' *International Journal of Humanities and Cultural Studies*, vol. 3, no. 2, 2016.

Basic Principles and Guidelines on the Right to a Remedy and Reparation for Victims of Gross Violations of International Human Rights Law and Serious Violations of International Humanitarian Law, U.N. Doc. A/RES/60/147, 21 March 2006.

Bassiouni, C., 'Final Report on the United Nations Commission of Experts Established Pursuant to Security Council Resolution 780,' United Nations Security Council Report, 28 December 1994.

Basso, K.H. and Selby, H.A. (eds), *Meaning in Anthropology*, Albuquerque, NM: University of New Mexico Press, 1976.

Bastion, B. et al., 'The Roles of Dehumanization and Moral Outrage in Retributive Justice,' *PloS One*, vol. 8, no. 4, 2013.

Behrens, P. and Henham, R. (eds), *Elements of Genocide*, London, New York, NY: Routledge, 2013.

Benesch, S., 'Vile Crime or Inalienable Right: Defining Incitement to Genocide,' *Virginia Journal of International Law*, vol. 48, no. 3, 2008.

Bergsmo, M. et al. (eds), *Historical Origins of International Criminal Law: Volume* 1, Oslo: Torkel Opsahl Academic ePublisher, 2014.

Bin Qasim, A. (ed.), *Ad'durar As'samiyah fi Al-Ajwibah An'najdiyah*, vol. 10, Buraydah: Alqassem Publishers, 1996.

Boljević, I. et al., *Reči i nedela: pozivanje ili podsticanje na ratne zločine medijima u Srbiji 1991–1992* (Words and Misdeeds: Calling for or Inciting War Crimes in the Serbian Media, 1991–1992), Beograd: Studija tužilaštva za ratne zločine Republike Srbije, 2011.

Böse, M. et al. (eds), *Justice without Borders: Essays in Honour of Wolfgang Schomburg*, Leiden: Brill Publishers, 2018.

Bourdieu, P., *Distinction: A Social Critique of the Judgment of Taste*, translated by R. Nice, Cambridge, MA: Harvard University Press (first published 1979), 1984.

Brown, A., 'What Is so Special about Online (as Compared to Offline) Hate Speech?' *Ethnicities*, vol. 18, no. 3, 2018.

Browning, C., *Ordinary Men: Reserve Police Battalion 101 and the Final Solution in Poland*, New York, NY: Harper Collins (first published 1992), 1998.

Brubaker, R., *Nationalism Reframed: Nationhood and the National Question in the New Europe*, Cambridge: Cambridge University Press, 1996.

Brubaker, R., *Ethnicity without Groups*, Cambridge, NY: Harvard University Press, 2006.

Bruneau, E. et al., 'Denying Humanity: The Distinct Neural Correlates of Blatant Dehumanization,' *Journal of Experimental Psychology: General*, vol. 147, no. 7, 2018.

Bulatović, Lj., *Radovan*, Belgrade: Evro, 2002.

Bunzel, C., *From Paper State to Caliphate: The Ideology of the Islamic State*, The Brookings Project on U.S Relations with the Islamic World, Washington, DC: The Brookings Institution, 2015.

Bushman, B. and Anderson, C.A., 'Comfortably Numb: Desensitizing Effects of Violent Media on Helping Others,' *Psychological Science*, vol. 20, no. 3, 2009.

Buyse, E., 'Words of Violence: "Fear Speech," or How Violent Conflict Escalation Relates to the Freedom of Expression,' *Human Rights Quarterly*, vol. 36, no. 4, November 2014.

Cameron, C.D. et al., 'The Emotional Cost of Humanity: Anticipated Exhaustion Motivates Dehumanization of Stigmatized Targets,' *Social Psychological and Personality Science*, vol. 7, no. 2, 2016.

Canna, S. (ed.), *Countering Violent Extremism: Scientific Methods and Strategies*, Dayton, OH: Air Force Research Laboratory, 2011.

Capestany, B.H. and Harris, L.T., 'Disgust and biological descriptions bias logical reasoning during legal decision-making,' *Social Neuroscience*, vol. 9, no. 3, 2014.

Carlsmith, K.M. and Sood, A.M., 'The Fine Line between Interrogation and Retribution,' *Journal of Experimental Social Psychology*, vol. 45, no. 1, 2009.

Carnagey, N. et al., 'Media Violence and Social Neuroscience,' *Current Directions in Psychological Science*, vol. 16, no. 4, 2007.

Carney, J.J., *Rwanda before the Genocide: Catholic Politics and Ethnic Discourse in the Late Colonial Era*, New York, NY: Oxford University Press, 2014.

Carney, T., 'Being (im)polite: A Forensic Linguistic Approach to Interpreting a Hate Speech Case,' *Language Politics in Africa*, vol. 45, no. 3, 2014.

Cassese, A., *International Criminal Law*, Second Edition, Oxford: Oxford University Press, 2008.

Cassese, A. and Gaeta, P., *International Criminal Law*, Third Edition, Oxford: Oxford University Press, 2013.

Castano, E. and Giner-Sorolla, R., 'Not Quite Human: Infrahumanization in Response to Collective Responsibility for Intergroup Killing,' *Journal of Personality and Social Psychology*, vol. 90, no. 5, 2006.

Chaaban, J., 'Youth and Development in the Arab Countries: The Need for a Different Approach,' *Middle Eastern Studies*, vol. 45, no. 1, 2009.

Child, J. and Ormerod, D., *Smith, Hogan and Ormerod's Essentials of Criminal Law*, Oxford: Oxford University Press, 2017.

Chretien, J.-P. and Kabanda, M., *Rwanda Racisme et Genocide: L'ideologie hamitique*, Paris: Belin, 2013.

Cikara, M. et al., 'Decoding "Us" and "Them": Neural Representations of Generalized Group Concepts,' *Journal of Experimental Psychological: General*, vol. 146, no. 5, 2017.

St. Clair, A. N., *The Image of the Turk in Europe*, New York, NY: Metropolitan Museum of Art, 1973.

Clarke, K., *Fictions of Justice: The International Criminal Court and the Challenge of Legal Pluralism in Sub-Saharan Africa*, Cambridge: Cambridge University Press, 2009.

Cohen, P. et al. (eds), *Intentions in Communication*, Cambridge, MA: The MIT Press, 1990.

Cohen, R., 'Regulating Hate Speech: Nothing Customary about It,' *Chicago Journal of International Law*, vol. 15, no. 1, 2014.

Combs, N.A., *Fact-Finding without Facts: The Uncertain Evidentiary Foundations of International Criminal Convictions*, Cambridge: Cambridge University Press, 2010.

Control Council Law No. 10, art. II(2)(a) and (b), reprinted in T. Taylor, *Final Report to the Secretary of the Army on the Nuremberg War Crimes Trials under Control Council Law No. 10*, Washington, DC: U.S. Government Printing Office, 1949.

Convention (II) with Respect to the Laws and Customs of War on Land and Its Annex: Regulations Concerning the Laws and Customs of War on Land, The Hague, 29 July 1899.

Convention (IV) Respecting the Laws and Customs of War on Land and Its Annex: Regulations Concerning the Laws and Customs of War on Land, The Hague, 18 October 1907.

Convention (II) for the Amelioration of the Condition of Wounded, Sick and Shipwrecked Members of Armed Forces at Sea, Geneva, 12 August 1949.

Convention (III) Relative to the Treatment of Prisoners of War, Geneva, 12 August 1949.

Convention (IV) Relative to the Protection of Civilian Persons in Time of War, Geneva, 12 August 1949.

Costello, K. and Hodson, G., 'Exploring the Roots of Dehumanization: The Role of Animal-Human Similarity in Promoting Immigrant Humanization,' *Group Processes & Intergroup Relations*, vol. 13, no. 1, 2010.

Crapanzano, V., *Serving the Word: Literalism in America from the Pulpit to the Bench*, New York, NY: New Press, 2000.

Croddy, S., 'Meaning and Intention,' *Journal of Pragmatics*, vol. 12, no. 1, 1988.

Crone, P. and Zimmermann, F., *The Epistle of Salim Ibn Dhakwan*, Oxford: Oxford University Press, 2001.

Cryer, R. et al. (eds), *An Introduction to International Criminal Law and Procedure*, Third Edition, Cambridge: Cambridge University Press, 2014.

Çelebi, E., *Seyahatname*, translated by T.T. Kuran and N. Akbaş, Istanbul: Üçdal Neşriyat, 1986.

Dabiq, no. 1–15, 2014–2016.

Dalton, R.J., *Democratic Challenges, Democratic Choices: The Erosion of Political Support in Advanced Industrial Democracies*, Oxford: Oxford University Press, 2004.

van Dam, N., *The Struggle for Power in Syria: Politics and Society under Asad and the Ba'th Party*, New York, NY: I.B. Tauris, 2011.

Dammen McAuliffe, J. (ed.), *Encyclopaedia of the Qur'an*, vol. 2, Leiden: Brill, 2001.

Dancygier, B., *The Language of Stories: A Cognitive Approach*, Cambridge: Cambridge University Press, 2012.

Davidson, D., *Essays on Actions and Events*, New York: Oxford University Press, 2001.

Davidson, T. et al., 'Automated Hate Speech Detection and the Problem of Offensive Language,' *Proceedings of the Eleventh International AAAI Conference on Web and Social Media*, Montréal, Canada, 2017.

Degerald, M., 'How Daesh Talks about the World: Central Points of Daesh Discourse,' 10 March 2016, Online. Available HTTP: <https://historyxisis.wordpress.com/tag/sahwat/> (accessed 5 June 2019).

Dekmejian, R.H., *Islam in Revolution: Fundamentalism in the Arab World*, Second Edition, Syracuse, NY: Syracuse University Press, 1995.

Dembour, M.-B. and Kelly, T., *Paths to International Justice: Social and Legal Perspectives*, Cambridge: Cambridge University Press, 2007.

Des Forges, A., *Leave None to Tell the Story: Genocide in Rwanda*, New York, NY: Human Rights Watch, 1999.

Dinstein, Y., *The Defence of 'Obedience to Superior Orders' in International Law*, Oxford: Oxford University Press, 2012.

Dojčinović, P., *The Metaphors of Causation or A Conflict of Concepts in International Criminal Justice*, Research Paper, 7 March 2008, Online. Available HTTP: https://papers.ssrn.com/sol3/papers.cfm?abstract_id=2850854 (accessed 15 June 2019).

Dojčinović, P. (ed.), *Propaganda, War Crimes Trials and International Law: From Speakers' Corner to War Crimes*, Abingdon, New York, NY: Routledge, 2012.

Dojčinović, P., 'The Chameleon of Mens Rea and the Shifting Guises of Culture-Specific Genocidal Intent in International Criminal Proceedings,' *Journal of Human Rights*, vol. 15, no. 4, 2016.

Dojčinović, P., 'A Mouthful of Crimes: Facing the Challenges of Culture-Specific Propaganda as Evidence in International War Crimes Trials,' Princeton University, 12 May 2017.

Donia, R.J., *Sarajevo: A Biography*, London: Hurst and Co. and Ann Arbor, MI: University of Michigan Press, 2006.

Donia, R.J. (ed.), *From the Republika Srpska Assembly, 1991–1996: Excerpts from Delegates' Speeches as Body of Evidence for the International Criminal Tribunal at The Hague*, Sarajevo, Tuzla: University Press, 2012.

Donia, R.J., *Radovan Karadžić: Architect of the Bosnian Genocide*, New York, NY: Cambridge University Press, 2015.

Drennan, S., 'Constructing Takfir,' *Combating Terrorism Centre at West Point*, vol. 1, no. 7, July 2008.

Dressler, J. and Garvey, S.P., *Cases and Materials on Criminal Law*, Sixth Edition, St. Paul, MN: West Academic Publishing, 2012.

El-Badawy, E. et al., 'Inside the Jihadi Mind: Understanding Ideology and Propaganda,' Centre on Religion and Geopolitics, October 2015.

Elias-Bursać, E., *Translating Evidence and Interpreting Testimony at a War Crimes Tribunal: Working in a Tug-of-War*, London: Palgrave Macmillan, 2015.

Ellul, J., *Propaganda – The Formation of Men's Attitudes*, New York, NY: Vintage, 1973.

Eltringham, N., 'Illuminating the Broader Context': Anthropological and Historical Knowledge at the International Criminal Tribunal for Rwanda,' *Journal of the Royal Anthropological Institute*, vol. 19, no. 2, 2013.

Esposito, J. (ed.), *The Oxford Encyclopedia of the Modern Islamic World*, vol. 5, Oxford: Oxford University Press, 2009.

Esposito, J.L. and El-Din Shahin, E. (eds), *The Oxford Handbook of Islam and Politics*, Oxford: Oxford University Press, 2013.

European Parliament, Joint Motion, 'Resolution on the Systematic Mass Murder of Religious Minorities by the so-called ISIS/Daesh,' 3 February 2016, 2016/2529 (RSP).

Facebook, 'Credible Violence,' *Community Standards.*

Facebook, 'Hate Speech,' *Community Standards.*

Faksh, M.A., 'The Alawi Community of Syria: A New Dominant Political Force,' *Middle Eastern Studies*, vol. 20, no. 2, 1984.

Fiske, A. et al., *Virtuous Violence: Hurting and Killing to Create, Sustain, End, and Honor Social Relationships*, Cambridge: Cambridge University Press. 2014.

Freitag, U., 'In Search of "Historical Correctness": The Ba'th Party in Syria,' *Middle Eastern Studies*, vol. 35, no. 1, 1999.

Frenda, S.J. et al., 'False Memories of Fabricated Political Events,' *Journal of Experimental Social Psychology*, vol. 49, no. 2, 2013.

Freud, S., *Massenpsychologie und Ich-Analyse*, Seventh Edition, Frankfurt am Main: Fischer Verlag, 2005.

Friedenberg, J. and Silverman, G. (eds), *Cognitive Science: An Introduction to the Study of Mind*, London: Sage Publications, 2006.

Gamer, B.A. (ed.), *Black's Law Dictionary*, Ninth Edition, St. Paul, MN: West, a Thompson Business, 2009.

Garland, B. (ed.), *Neuroscience and the Law: Brain, Mind, and the Scales of Justice*, New York, NY, Washington, DC: Dana Press, 2004.

Garratt, J., *Music and Politics: A Critical Introduction*, Cambridge: Cambridge University Press, 2018.

Geeraerts, D., *Theories of Lexical Semantics*, Oxford: Oxford University Press, 2010.

Geertz, C., *Local Knowledge: Further Essays in Interpretive Anthropology*, New York, NY: Basic Books, 1983.

Gellner, E., *Nations and Nationalism*, Ithaca, NY: Cornell University Press, 1983.

Geneva Convention for the Amelioration of the Condition of the Wounded and Sick in Armed Forces in the Field, 12 August 1949.

Ghadbian, N., 'Contesting the State Media Monopoly: Syria on Al-Jazira Television,' *MERIA Journal*, vol. 5, no. 2, June 2001.

Gilbert, G. et al. (eds), *The Delivery of Human Rights: Essays in Honour of Professor Sir Nigel Rodley*, New York, NY: Routledge, 2012.

Goff, P.A. et al., 'Not Yet Human: Implicit Knowledge, Historical Dehumanization, and Contemporary Consequences,' *Journal of personality and social psychology*, vol. 94, no. 2, 2008.

Goffman, E., *Frame Analysis: An Essay on the Organization of Experience*, Cambridge, MA: Harvard University Press, 1974.

Gökçen, A., *Osmanlı ve İngiliz arşiv belgelerinde Yezidiler*, Istanbul: Bilgi University, 2012.

Gölbaşı, E., *The Yezidis and the Ottoman State: Modern Power, Military Conscription, and Conversion Policies, 1830–1909* (Unpublished Master's Dissertation), Istanbul: Bogazici University, 2008.

Goldsmith, L.T., *Cycle of Fear: Syria's Alawites in War and Peace*, London: C. Hurst & Co Publishers, 2015.

Gordon, G.S., 'Music and Genocide: Harmonizing Coherence, Freedom and Nonviolence in Incitement Law,' *Santa Clara Law Review*, vol. 50, no. 3, 2010.

Gordon, G.S., *Atrocity Speech Law: Foundation, Fragmentation, Fruition*, New York, NY: Oxford University Press, 2017.

Grandits, H., *Multikonfesionalna Hercegovina: vlast i lojalnost u kasnoosmanskom društvu*, Sarajevo: Institut za istoriju, 2014.

Gråtrud, H., 'Islamic State *Nasheeds* as Messaging Tools,' *Studies in Conflict and Terrorism*, vol. 39, no. 12, 2016.

Grdešić, M., 'Serbia's Anti-Bureaucratic Revolution as Manipulation? A Cultural Alternative to the Elite-Centric Approach,' *Comparative Studies in Society and History*, vol. 58, no. 3, 2016.

Grossman, D., *On Killing: The Psychological Cost of Learning to Kill in War and Society*, New York, NY: Little Brown, 2009.

Group of authors, *The Hartford Guidelines on Speech Crimes in International Criminal Law*, The Hague: Peace and Justice Initiative, 2018.

Hajdarpašić, E., *Whose Bosnia? Nationalism and Political Imagination in the Balkans, 1840–1914*, Ithaca, NY: Cornell University Press, 2015.

Haklai, O., 'A Minority Rule over a Hostile Majority: The Case of Syria,' *Nationalism and Ethnic Politics*, vol. 6, no. 3, 2007.

Hanson, J. (ed.), *Ideology, Psychology, and Law*, Oxford: Oxford University Press, 2012.

Harmful Content: The Role of Internet Platform Companies in Fighting Terrorist Incitement and Politically Motivated Disinformation, New York, NY: NYU Stern Center for Business and Human Rights, 2017.

Hare, I. and Weinstein, J. (eds), *Extreme Speech and Democracy*, Oxford: Oxford University Press, 2010.

Harris, L.T. and Fiske, S.T., 'Dehumanizing the Lowest of the Low Neuroimaging Responses to Extreme Out-Groups,' *Psychological Science*, vol. 17, no. 10, 2006.

Harris, L.T. and Fiske, S.T., 'Social Groups that Elicit Disgust are Differentially Processed in mPFC,' *Social Cognitive and Affective Neuroscience*, vol. 2, no. 1, 2007.

Harris, L.T. and Fiske, S.T., 'Dehumanised Perception: A Psychological Means to Facilitate Atrocities, Torture, and Genocide?' *Zeitschrift für Psychologie/Journal of Psychology*, vol. 219, no. 3, 2011.

Hart, H.L.A. and Honoré, T., *Causation in the Law*, Second Edition, Oxford: Clarendon (first published 1959) 1985.

Haslam, N., 'Dehumanization: An Integrative Review,' *Personality and Social Psychology Review*, vol. 10, no. 3, 2006.

Hastorf, A.H. and Cantril, H., 'They Saw a Game; A Case Study,' *The Journal of Abnormal and Social Psychology*, vol. 49, no. 1, 1954.

Haugbolle, S., 'Imprisonment, Truth Telling and Historical Memory in Syria,' *Mediterranean Politics*, vol. 13, no. 2, 2008.

Hayward, J.S., *Fatwa on Terrorism and Suicide Bombings*, London: Minhaj-ul- Qur'ān International, 2010.

Heberer, P. and Matthäus, J. (eds), *Atrocities on Trial: Historical Perspectives on the Politics of Prosecuting War Crimes*, Lincoln, NE, London: University of Nebraska Press, 2008.

Heller, K.J., *The Nuremberg Military Tribunals and the Origins of International Criminal Law*, Oxford: Oxford University Press, 2011.

Hemon, A., *The Book of My Lives*, New York, NY: Picador, 2013.

Hinnant, L., 'The ISIS Radio Station Targeting European Recruits Sounds Like NPR,' *Business Insider*, 1 June 2015.

Hinton, A., *Why Did They Kill? Cambodia in the Shadow of Genocide*, Berkeley, CA: University of California Press, 2005.

Hirst, W. and Phelps, E.A., 'Flashbulb Memories,' *Current Directions in Psychological Science*, vol. 25, no. 1, 2016.

Hobsbawm, E.J. and Ranger, T. (eds), *The Invention of Tradition*, Cambridge: Cambridge University Press, 1983.

Hogan, P.C., *Ulysses and the Poetics of Cognition*, New York, NY, London: Routledge, 2014.

Hokayem, E., *Syria's Uprising and the Fracturing of the Levant*, Abingdon, New York, NY: Routledge, 2013.

Holbrook, D., *The Al-Qaeda Doctrine: The Framing and Evolution of the Leadership's Public Discourse*, London: Bloomsbury Publishing, 2014.

Hovland, C.I. et al., *Communication and Persuasion: Psychological Studies of Opinion Change*, New Haven, CT: Yale University Press, 1953.

'How ISIS Games Twitter,' *The Atlantic*, 16 June 2014.

Huggins, M.K. et al., *Violence Workers: Police Torturers and Murderers Reconstruct Brazilian Atrocities*, Berkeley, CA: University of California Press, 2006.

Humphrey, N., *The Mind Made Flesh: Frontiers of Psychology and Evolution*, Oxford: Oxford University Press, 2013.

Huntington, S.P., *The Clash of Civilizations and the Remaking of World Order*, New York, NY: Simon and Schuster, 1996.

Ibn Salih al-Mahmood, A.-R., *Man-made Laws vs. Shari'ah*, Riyadh: International Islamic Publishing House, 2003.

Imamović, M., *Pravni položaj i unutrašnjo-politički razvitak Bosne i Hercegovine od 1878. do 1914*, Second Edition, Sarajevo: Bosanski kulturni centar, 1997.

Independent International Commission of Inquiry on the Syrian Arab Republic, 'The Siege and Recapture of Eastern Ghouta,' Conference Room Paper, 20 June 2018.

Ingram, H.J., 'The Strategic Logic of Islamic State Information Operations,' *Australian Journal of International Affairs*, vol. 69, no. 6, 2015.

Ingram, H.J., 'An Analysis of *Inspire* and *Dabiq*: Lessons from AQAP and Islamic State's Propaganda War,' *Studies in Conflict and Terrorism*, vol. 40, no. 5, 2016.

Ingram, H.J., *Learning from ISIS's Virtual Propaganda War for Western Muslims: A Comparison of Inspire and Dabiq*, The Hague: International Centre for Counter Terrorism, 2017.

International Law and Human Rights Clinic, *Invisible Threats: Mitigating the Risk of Violence from Coded Hate Speech Against Human Rights Defenders in Guatemala*, 2019.

International Military Tribunal, Nuremberg, Trial of the Major War Criminals Before the International Military Tribunal, 14 November 1945–1 October 1946, vol. 1, Nuremberg, Germany 1947.

Ismail, R., *Saudi Clerics and Shi'a Islam*, Oxford: Oxford University Press, 2016.

Izutsu, T., *The Concept of Belief in Islamic Theology: A Semantic Analysis of Iman and Islam*, Santa Clarita, CA: Books for Libraries, 1980.

Jaconelli, J., 'Incitement: A Study in Language Crime,' *Criminal Law and Philosophy*, vol. 12, no. 2, 2018.

Jančić, J., *Srpski General Ratko Mladić*, Novi Sad: Matica Srpska, 1996.

Janoff-Bulman, R., 'Erroneous Assumptions: Popular Belief in the Effectiveness of Torture Interrogation,' *Peace and Conflict: Journal of Peace Psychology*, vol. 13, no. 4, 2007.

Jansen, J.J.G., *The Neglected Duty: The Creed of Sadat's Assassins and Islamic Resurgence in the Middle East*, London: Macmillan Publishing, 1986.

Jarrett, C., 'AI Could Make Trolls Think Twice before Retweeting Offensive Content,' *VentureBeat*, 4 February 2018.

Jasanoff, S., *Science at the Bar: Law, Science, and Technology in America*, Cambridge, MA: Harvard University Press, 1995.

Joscelyn, T., 'Islamic State Rescinds One of Its Most Problematic Religious Rulings,' *FDD's Long War Journal*, 20 September 2017.

Joscelyn, T., 'Islamic State Radio Tries to Quell Controversy over takfir,' *FDD's Long War Journal*, 26 September 2017.

Jović, D., *Yugoslavia: A State that Withered Away*, West Lafayette, IN: Purdue University Press, 2009.

Jowett, G.S. and O'Donnell, V., *Propaganda and Persuasion*, Fifth Edition, London: Sage, 2012.

Kahan, D.M., 'Ideology, Motivated Reasoning, and Cognitive Reflection: An Experimental Study,' *Judgment Decision Making*, vol. 8, no. 4, 2013.

Kahan, D.M. et al., 'They Saw a Protest: Cognitive Illiberalism and the Speech-Conduct Distinction,' *Stanford Law Review*, vol. 64, 2012.

Kamatali, J-M., 'Following Orders in Rwanda,' *New York Times*, 5 April 2014.

Kassim, A., 'Defining and Understanding the Religious Philosophy of jihādī-Salafism and the Ideology of Boko Haram,' *Politics, Religion & Ideology*, vol. 16, no. 2–3, 2015.

Kaye, D., *Report of the Special Rapporteur on the Promotion and Protection of the Right to Freedom of Opinion and Expression*, U.N. Doc. A/HRC/38/35, 6 April 2018.

Kearney, J. D. and Merrill, T.W., 'The Influence of Amicus Briefs on the Supreme Court,' *University of Pennsylvania Law Review*, vol. 148, no. 3, 2000.

Kearney, M.G., *The Prohibition of Propaganda for War in International Law*, New York, NY: Oxford University Press, 2007.

Kedar, M., *Asad in Search of Legitimacy: Message and Rhetoric in the Syrian Press under Hafiz and Bashar*, Brighton: Sussex University Press, 2005.

Kelsall, T., *Culture under Cross-Examination: International Justice and the Special Court for Sierra Leone*, Cambridge: Cambridge University Press, 2009.

Kepel, G., *Muslim Extremism in Egypt: Prophet and Pharaoh*, London: Al Saqi Books, 1985.

Khatib, L. and Lust, L. (eds), *Taking to the Streets: The Transformation of Arab Activism*, Baltimore, MD: John Hopkins University, 2014.

Khushalani, Y., *The Dignity and Honour of Women as Basic and Fundamental Human Rights*, The Hague: Martinus Nijhoff Publishers, 1982.

Kiper, J., 'Toward an Anthropology of War Propaganda,' *Political and Legal Anthropology Review*, vol. 38, no. 1, 2015.

King, S.J., *The New Authoritarianism in the Middle East and North Africa*, Bloomington, IN: Indiana University Press, 2009.

Kinyamateka, no. 8, February 1965.

Kogen, L., *Testing a Media Intervention in Kenya: Vioja Mahakamani, Dangerous Speech and the Benesch Guidelines*, Philadelphia, PA: Center for Global Communication Studies, 2013.

Kretzmer, D. and Klein, E. (eds), *The Concept of Human Dignity in Human Rights Discourse*, Alphen aan den Rijn: Kluwer Law International, 2002.

Kteily, N. et al., 'The Ascent of Man: Theoretical and Empirical Evidence for Blatant Dehumanization,' *Journal of Personality and Social Psychology*, vol. 109, no. 5, 2015.

Kteily, N. et al., 'They See Us as Less than Human: Metadehumanization Predicts Intergroup Conflict via Reciprocal Dehumanization,' *Journal of Personality and Social Psychology*, vol. 110, no. 3, 2016.

Kushner, B., *The Thought War: Japanese Imperial Propaganda*, Honolulu: University of Hawai'i Press, 2006.

Kwan, V.S.Y. and. Fiske, S.T., 'Missing Links in Social Cognition: The Continuum from Nonhuman Agents to Dehumanized Humans,' *Social Cognition*, vol. 26, no. 2, 2008.

Lahoud, N. and Pieslak, J., 'Music of the Islamic State,' *Survival: Global Politics and Strategy*, vol. 60, no. 1, 2018.

Land, M.K., 'Speech Duties,' *The American Journal of International Law Unbound*, vol. 112, 2018.

Lapidot-Lefler, N. and Barak, A., 'Effects of Anonymity, Invisibility, and Lack of Eye-Contact on Toxic Online Disinhibition,' *Computers in Human Behavior*, vol. 28, no. 2, 2011.

Leader Maynard, J. and Benesch, S., 'Dangerous Speech and Dangerous Ideology: An Integrated Model for Monitoring and Prevention,' *Genocide Studies and Prevention: An International Journal*, vol. 9, no. 3, 2016.

Le Bon, G., *Psychologie des Foules*, Paris: Quadrige/Presses Universitaires de France, 1963.

Lee, N., 'Convert or Die: Forced Religious Conversions and the Convention on the Prevention and Punishment of the Crime of Genocide,' *Georgetown Journal of International Law*, vol. 47, no. 606, 2015–2016.

Lemkin, R., *Acts Constituting a General (Transnational) Danger Considered as Offences Against the Law of Nations*, 1933.

Lemkin, R., *Axis Rule in Occupied Europe*, Concord, NH: The Rumford Press, 1944.

Lewis, B., *Islam in History: Ideas, People, and Events in the Middle East*, Chicago, IL: Open Court Publishing, 2001.

Leyens, J.P. et al., 'Psychological Essentialism and the Differential Attribution of Uniquely Human Emotions to Ingroups and Outgroups,' *European Journal of Social Psychology*, vol. 31, 2001.

Lieber, F., *Instructions for the Government of Armies in the United States in the Field*, Washington, DC: Government Printing Office, 1898.

Lillie, C.M., Knapp, B., Harris, L.T. and Wilson, R.A., 'This Is the Hour of Revenge: The Psychology of Propaganda and Mass Atrocities,' 2015. Online. Available HTTP: https://ssrn.com/abstract=2580521 (accessed 11 June 2019).

London Charter of the International Military Tribunal, 8 August 1945.

Lukić, R. and Lynch, A., *Europe from the Balkans to the Urals: The Disintegration of Yugoslavia and the Soviet Union*, Oxford: Oxford University Press, 1996.

Lupo, S., *History of the Mafia*, translated by A. Shugaar, New York, NY: Columbia University Press, 2009.

Lynch, A., *Thought Contagion: How Belief Spreads Through Society*, New York, NY: Basic Books, 2006.

Magazine Monitor, 'Who, What, Why: Who are the Yazidis?' *BBC News*, 8 August 2014.

Maher, S., *Salafi-Jihadism, The History of an Idea*, London: Hurst & Company, 2016.

Maheshwari, N. and Kumar, V.V. (eds), *Military Psychology: Concepts, Trends and Interventions*, New Delhi: Sage Publication India, 2016.

Mamdani, M., *When Victims Become Killers: Colonialism, Nativism, and the Genocide in Rwanda*, Princeton, NJ: Princeton University Press, 2001.

Mann, M., *The Dark Side of Democracy: Explaining Ethnic Cleansing*, Cambridge: Cambridge University Press, 2004.

Margalit, A., *The Decent Society*, translated by N. Goldblum, Cambridge, MA: Harvard University Press, 1996.

Martherus, J.L., Martinez, A.G., Piff, P.K. and Theodoridis, A.G., 'Party Animals? Party Identity and Dehumanization,' 2018. Online. Available HTTP: <https://www.dropbox.com/s/1cq23ml0tuv3b4z/party-animals.pdf?dl=0> (accessed 11 June 2019).

Martin, R.C. (ed.), *Encyclopedia of Islam and the Muslim World*, London: Macmillan, 2004.

Marwick, A.E., 'Why Do People Share Fake News? A Sociotechnical Model of Media Effects,' *Georgetown Law Technology Review*, vol. 2, 2018.

Mathiak, K and Weber, R., 'Toward Brain Correlates of Natural Behavior: fMRI during Violent Video Games,' *Human Brain Mapping*, vol. 27, no. 12, 2006.

Matias, J.N., 'Posting Rules in Online Discussions Prevents Problems & Increases Participation,' *Civil Servant*, 8 October 2016. Online. Available HTTP: <https://civilservant.io/moderation_experiment_r_science_rule_posting.html> (accessed 27 August 2019).

McCoy, J.T., '*Mbwirabumva* (I Speak to Those Who Understand): Three Songs by Simon Bikindi and the War and Genocide in Rwanda,' Florida State University Libraries, Tallahassee, FL, 2013.

McCullough, M., *Beyond Revenge: The Evolution of the Forgiveness Instinct*, San Francisco, CA: Jossey-Bass, 2008.

McGoldrick, D. et al. (eds), *The Permanent International Criminal Court: Legal and Policy Issues*, London: Hart Publishing, 2004.

McNally, R., *Remembering Trauma*, Cambridge, MA: Belknap Press, 2003.

Meijer, R. (ed.), *Global Salafism: Islam's New Religious Movement*, New York, NY: Columbia University Press, 2009.

Mercier, H. and Sperber, D., *The Enigma of Reason*, Cambridge, MA: Harvard University Press, 2017.

Michot, Y., *Muslims under Non-Muslim Rule*, Oxford: Interface Publications, 2006.

Middle East Watch, Human Rights in Syria, New York, NY: Human Rights Watch, 1990.

Mieczyslaw, P.B., *Regime Change in the Yugoslav Succession States: Divergent Paths Toward a New Europe*, Baltimore, MD: The John Hopkins University Press, 2010.

Milanović, M., 'The Sorry Acquittal of Vojislav Šešelj,' *EJIL: Talk! Blog of the European Journal of International Law*, 4 April 2016. Online. Available HTTP: <https://www.ejiltalk.org/the-sorry-acquittal-of-vojislav-seselj/> (accessed 27 August 2019).

Milgram, S., *Obedience to Authority: An Experimental View*, New York, NY: Harper & Row, 1974.

Mitchell, R.P., *The Society of the Muslim Brothers*, Oxford: Oxford University Press, 1993.

Moghadam, A., 'The Salafi-Jihad as a Religious Ideology,' *Combating Terrorism Centre at West Point*, vol. 1, no. 3, February 2008.

Montgomery Watt, W., *Islamic Political Thought*, Edinburgh: Edinburgh University Press, 1968.

Moore, J.W. et al., 'Attribution of Intentional Causation Influences the Perception of Observed Movements: Behavioral Evidence and Neural Correlates,' *Frontiers in Psychology*, vol. 4, no. 23, 2013.

Mozur, P., 'A Genocide Incited on Facebook, With Posts from Myanmar's Military,' *New York Times*, 15 October 2018.

Mullaney, A., 'Wiping Out an Entire Religion: How ISIS will Inevitably Eliminate an Ancient Culture Unless the United States Employs Military and Diplomatic Intervention,' *Suffolk Transnational Law Review*, vol. 39, no. 1, 2016.

Mullins, C., *The Leipzig Trials: An Account of the War Criminals' Trials and a Study of German Mentality*, London: Forgotten Books, 1921.

Nesser, N., 'Abū Qatāda and Palestine,' *Welt des Islams*, vol. 53, no. 3–4, 2013.

Neuman, G.L., 'Bi-Level Remedies for Human Rights Violations,' *Harvard International Law Journal*, vol. 55, no. 3, 2014.

Niezen, N. and Sapignoli, M. (eds), *Palaces of Hope: The Anthropology of the United Nations*, Cambridge: Cambridge University Press, 2017.

Norris, N., *Critical Citizens: Global Support for Democratic Governance*, New York, NY: Oxford University Press, 1999.

O'Brien, G.V., 'Indigestible Food, Conquering Hordes, and Waste Materials: Metaphors of Immigrants and the Early Immigration Restriction Debate in the United States,' *Metaphor and Symbol*, vol. 18, no. 1, 2003.

Ochsner, K.N. et al., 'Your Pain or Mine? Common and Distinct Neural Systems Supporting the Perception of Pain in Self and Other,' *Social Cognitive and Affective Neuroscience*, vol. 3, no. 2, 2008.

O'Connor, C. and Weatherhall, J.O., *The Misinformation Age: How False Beliefs Spread*, New Haven, CT, London: Yale University Press, 2019.

O'Mara, S., *Why Torture Doesn't Work: The Neuroscience of Interrogation*, Cambridge, MA: Harvard University Press, 2015.

Online Hate Index, *Center for Technology & Society*, 4–19, 2018.

Orentlicher, D.F., 'Criminalising Hate Speech in the Crucible of the Trial: *Prosecutor v. Nahimana*,' *American University International Law Review*, vol. 21, no. 4, 2006.

Parker, J.E.K., *Acoustic Jurisprudence: Listening to the Trial of Simon Bikindi*, Oxford: Oxford University Press, 2015.

Payne, B.K., 'Prejudice and Perception: The Role of Automatic and Controlled Processes in Misperceiving a Weapon,' *Journal of Personality and Social Psychology*, vol. 81, no. 2, 2001.

Phillips, J.E.S., *None of Us Were Like This Before: American Soldiers and Torture*, London, New York, NY: Verso, 2010.

Pierret, T., *Religion and State in Syria: The Sunni Ulama from Coup to Revolution*, Cambridge: Cambridge University Press, 2013.

Pieslak, J., *Radicalism and Music: An Introduction to the Music Cultures of al-Qa'ida, Racist Skinheads, Christian-Affiliated Radicals, and Eco-Animal Rights Militants*, Middletown, CT: Wesleyan University Press, 2015.

Pieslak, J. and Lahoud, N., 'The *Anashid* of the Islamic State: Influence, History, Text, and Sound,' *Studies in Conflict and Terrorism*, 23 April 2018. Online. Available HTTP: <https://www.tandfonline.com/doi/full/10.1080/1057610X.2018.1457420> (accessed 27 August 2019).

Pipes, D., 'The Alawi Capture of Power in Syria,' *Middle Eastern Studies*, vol. 25, no. 4, 1989.

POSSIBLE Agency, 'WeCounterHate: How to Identify Hate Speech,' 2018. Online. Available HTTP: <https://perma.cc/24YN-VA5Y> (accessed 9 June 2019).

Pratkanis, A. and Aronson, E., *Age of Propaganda: The Everyday Use and Abuse of Persuasion*, Revised Edition New York, NY: W.H. Freeman and Company, 2001.

Protocol Additional to the Geneva Conventions of 12 August 1949, and Relating to the Protection of Victims of International Armed Conflicts (Protocol I), 8 June 1977.

Protocol Additional to the Geneva Conventions of 12 August 1949, and Relating to the Protection of Victims of Non-International Armed Conflicts (Protocol II), 8 June 1977.

Radeljić, B. and Topić, M. (eds), *Religion in the Post-Yugoslav Context*, London: Lexington Books, 2015.

Rahim, F. et al., 'ISIS Takes to Airwaves, Transmits Fatwas in Jalalabad, Afghanistan,' *NBC News*, 19 December 2015.

Rai, T.S. et al., 'Dehumanization Increases Instrumental Violence, but Not Moral Violence,' *Proceedings of the National Academy of Sciences of the United States of America*, vol. 114, no. 32, 2017.

Rai, T. et al., 'Our enemies are human: that's why we want to kill them,' *Behavioral Scientist*, 18 August 2017.

Ramet, S., *Thinking about Yugoslavia: Scholarly Debates about the Yugoslav Breakup and the Wars in Bosnia and Kosovo*, Cambridge: Cambridge University Press, 2005.

Ramsay, G., *Jihadi Culture on the World Wide Web*, London: Bloomsbury Publishing, 2013.

Rapoport, Y. and Ahmed, S., *Ibn Taymiyya and His Times*, Karachi: Oxford University Press, 2010.

Rathmell, A., 'Syria's Intelligence Services: Origins and Development,' *The Journal of Conflict Studies*, vol. 16, no. 2, 1996.

Rečnik srpskohrvatskoga književnog jezika, Novi Sad, Zagreb: Matica Srpska, Matica Hrvatska, 1967.

'Removing Myanmar Military Officials from Facebook,' *Facebook Newsroom*, 28 August 2018.

Report of the Committee on the Elimination of Racial Discrimination: Sixty-Fourth Session (23 February–12 March 2004), Sixty-Fifth Session (2–20 August 2004), General Assembly, Official Records, Fifty-Ninth Session, Supplement No. 18 (A/59/18), New York, NY: United Nations Publications, 2004.

Report of the Detailed Findings of the Independent International Fact-Finding Mission on Myanmar, U.N. Doc. A/HRC/39/CRP.2, 17 September 2018.

Report of the Working Group on Enforced or Involuntary Disappearances, U.N. Doc. E/CN.4/1998/43, 12 January 1998.
Reporters Sans Frontières (RSF), 'Internet Enemies: Middle East/North Africa – Syria,' 2011.
'Responding to Online Hate,' *Media Awareness Network*, 2012. Online. Available HTTP: <https://mediasmarts.ca/sites/mediasmarts/files/guides/responding_online_hate_guide.pdf> (accessed 9 June 2019).
Richard, A. and Renee, T. (eds), *The Routledge Companion to Music Cognition*, New York, NY, Abington, PA: Routledge, 2017.
Robin, C., *Fear: The History of a Political Idea*, Oxford, New York, NY: Oxford University Press, 2004.
Romney, K., 'ISIS Destruction of Ancient Sites Hits Mostly Muslim Targets,' *National Geographic*, 2 July 2015.
Roose, K., 'Facebook Banned Infowars. Now What?' *New York Times*, 10 August 2018.
Roy, O., *Den Globaliserende Islam*, Copenhagen: Vandkunsten, 2004.
Rugh, W., *Arab Mass Media: Newspapers, Radio, and Television in Arab Politics: Newspapers, Radio, and Television in Arab Politics*, Westport, CT: Praeger Publishers, 2004.
Rumiyah, no. 1, September 2016.
Rumiyah, no. 7, March 2017.
Rumiyah, no. 9, May 2017.
Rumiyah, no. 10, June 2017.
Said, B., 'Hymns (*Nasheeds*): A Contribution to the Study of the Jihadist Culture,' *Studies in Conflict & Terrorism*, vol. 35, no. 12, 2012.
Saks, M.J. and Faigman, D.L., 'Expert Evidence after Daubert,' *Annual Review of Law and Social Science*, vol. 1, 2005.
Sapolsky, R., *Behave: The Biology of Humans at Our Best and Worst*, London: Vintage, 2017.
Saramago, J., *The History of the Siege of Lisbon*, translated by G. Pontiero, New York, NY: Harcourt Brace, 1996.
Saussure, F. de, *Course in General Linguistics*, translated by R. Harris, London: Bloomsbury, 2013.
Schabas, W.A., 'Hate Speech in Rwanda: The Road to Genocide,' *McGill Law Journal*, vol. 46, no. 141, 2000.
Schabas, W.A., 'The Jelisić Case and the Mens Rea of the Crime of Genocide,' *Leiden Journal of International Law*, vol. 14, no. 1, 2001.
Schabas, W.A., *Genocide in International Law: The Crime of Crimes*, 2nd Edition, Cambridge: Cambridge University Press, 2009.
Schabas, W.A., *The Trial of the Kaiser*, Oxford: Oxford University Press, 2018.
Scheffer, D., *All the Missing Souls: A Personal History of the War Crimes Tribunals*, Princeton, NJ: Princeton University Press, 2012.
Scott, J. (ed.), *A Dictionary of Sociology*, New York, NY: Oxford University Press, 2014.
Scottish Catholic Observer, 'Pope Condemns the ISIS Slaughter of 30 Christians,' 24 April 2015.
Seale, P., *Assad of Syria. The Struggle for the Middle East*, London: I.B. Tauris & Co Ltd, 1988.
Searle, J.R., *Speech Acts: An Essay in the Philosophy of Language*, Cambridge: Cambridge University Press, 1969.
Searle, J.R., 'The Intentionality of Intention and Action,' *Cognitive Science*, vol. 4, no. 1, 1980.

Searle, J.R., 'How Performatives Work,' *Linguistics and Philosophy*, vol. 12, no. 5, 1989.

Searle, J.R., *Mind, Language and Society: Philosophy in the Real World*, London: Phoenix, 1999.

Searle, J.R., *Making the Social World: The Structure of Human Civilization*, New York, NY: Oxford University Press, 2010.

Semujanga, J. and Galabert, J.L. (eds), *Faire face au négationnisme du génocide des Tutsi*, Paris: Editions Izuba, 2013.

Shah, S. and Brown, R., 'Programming for Peace: Sisi Ni Amani Kenya and the 2013 Election,' *ICTs, Statebuilding and Peacebuilding in Africa*, 2014.

Shea, N., 'Falling for ISIS Propaganda about Christians,' 21 July 2016. Online. Available HTTP: <https://www.the-american-interest.com/2016/07/21/falling-for-isis-propaganda-about-christians/> (accessed 5 June 2019).

Shelton, D., *Remedies in International Human Rights Law*, First Edition, Oxford: Oxford University Press, 1999.

Škaljić, A., *Turcizmi u srpsko-hrvatskom jeziku* (Turcisms in Serbo-Croatian Language), Sarajevo: Svjetlost, 1973.

van Sliedregt, E., *Individual Criminal Responsibility in International Law*, Oxford: Oxford University Press, 2009.

van Sliedregt, E., *International Criminal Law*, Oxford: Oxford University Press, 2012.

Sloman, S. and Fernbach, P., *The Knowledge Illusion: Why We Never Think Alone*, New York, NY: Riverhead Books, 2017.

'Social Media and Conflict in South Sudan: A Lexicon of Hate Speech Terms,' *Peace Tech Lab*, vol. 2–18, 2016.

Solis, G.D., *The Law of Armed Conflict: International Humanitarian Law in War*, Cambridge: Cambridge University Press, 2016.

Sood, A.M., 'Motivated Cognition in Legal Judgment – An Analytic Review,' *The Annual Review of Law and Social Science*, vol. 9, no. 307, 2013.

Spears, R., 'Toward an Integrative Social Identity Model of Collective Action: A Quantitative Research Synthesis of Three Socio-Psychological Perspectives,' *Psychological Bulletin*, vol. 134, no. 4, 2008.

Stahn, C., *A Critical Introduction to International Criminal Law*, Cambridge: Cambridge University Press, 2019.

Starr, S.B., 'Rethinking "Effective Remedies": Remedial Deterrence in International Courts,' *New York University Law Review*, vol. 83, 2008.

Staub, E., *The Roots of Evil*, Cambridge: Cambridge University Press, 1989.

Stern, J. and Berger, J.M., *ISIS: The State of Terror*, London: William Collins, 2015.

Sternberg, R.J. and Sternberg, K., *The Nature of Hate*, New York, NY: Cambridge University Press, 2008.

Stockwell, P., *Cognitive Poetics: An Introduction*, London, New York: Routledge, 2002.

Stratenwerth, G. and Wohlers, W., *Schweizerisches Strafgesetzbuch: Handkommentar*, Bern: Stämpfli, 2007.

Street, J., *Music and Politics*, Cambridge: Cambridge University Press, Polity Press, 2012.

Strossen, N., *Hate: Why We Should Resist It with Free Speech, Not Censorship*, New York, NY: Oxford University Press, 2018.

Stroud's Judicial Dictionary of Words and Phrases, J.S. James, Barrister-at-Law, vol. 3, I-O, London: Sweet & Maxwell Limited, 1986.

Su, S., 'New Test with Related Articles,' *Facebook Newsroom*, 25 April 2017.

Suler, J., 'The Online Disinhibition Effect,' *CyberPsychology & Behavior*, vol. 7, no. 3, 2004.

Sun, R. (ed.), *Grounding Social Sciences in Cognitive Sciences*, Cambridge: The MIT Press, 2012.

Syed, N., 'Real Talk About Fake News: Towards a Better Theory for Platform Governance,' *Yale Law Journal Forum*, vol. 127, 9 October 2017.

'Syria: Crimes Against Humanity in Daraa: Killings, Torture in a Locked-Down City under Siege,' New York, NY: Human Rights Watch, 2011.

Talhamy, T., 'The Fatwas and the Nusayri/Alawis of Syria,' *Middle Eastern Studies*, vol. 46, no. 2, 2010.

Taub, A. and Fisher, M., 'Facebook Fueled Anti-Refugee Attacks in Germany, New Research Suggests,' *New York Times*, 21 August 2018.

Taylor, P.M., *Munitions of the Mind – A History of Propaganda from the Ancient World to the Present Day*, Manchester, New York, NY: Manchester University Press, 2003.

Terrighena, E.L. et al., 'Effects of Vicarious Pain on Self-Pain Perception: Investigating the Role of Awareness,' *Journal of Pain Research*, vol. 10, 2017.

Thaler, R. and Sunstein, C., *Nudge: Improving Decisions about Health, Wealth, and Happiness*, New York, NY: Yale University Press, 2009.

Thies, C. (ed.), *Der Wert der Menschenwürde*, Paderborn: Ferdinand Schöningh Verlag, 2009.

Thompson, A. (ed.), *The Media and the Rwandan Genocide*, London: Pluto Press, 2007.

Thompson, M., *Forging War*, London: Article 19, 1994.

Timmermann, W.K., *Incitement in International Law*, London, New York, NY: Routledge 2015.

Timmermann, W.K., 'Inciting Speech in the Former Yugoslavia: The Šešelj Trial Chamber Judgment,' *Journal of International Criminal Justice*, vol. 15, no. 1, 2017.

Tomasevich, J., *War and Revolution in Yugoslavia, 1941–1945: Occupation and Collaboration*, Stanford, CA: Stanford University Press, 1975.

Tritton, A.S., *Muslim Theology*, London: Royal Asiatic Society, 1947.

Turner, M., *The Literary Mind*, New York, NY, Oxford: Oxford University Press, 1996.

Twagilimana, A., *Historical Dictionary of Rwanda*, Second Edition, London: Rowman & Littlefield, 2016.

UNHRC, 32nd Session, Human Rights Situation that Require the Council's attention, 'They Came to Destroy: ISIS Crimes against the Yazidis,' U.N. Doc. A/HRC/32/CRP.2, 15 June 2016.

United Nations Convention on the Prevention and Punishment of the Crime of Genocide (1948).

Utych, S.M., 'Negative Affective Language in Politics,' *American Politics Research*, First Published 1 February 2017.

Utych, S.M., 'How Dehumanization Influences Attitudes toward Immigrants,' *Political Research Quarterly*, vol. 71, no. 2, 2018.

Valeska, D., 'The Expansive Right to an Effective Remedy: Common Developments at the Human Rights Committee and the Inter-American Court,' *British Journal of American Legal Studies*, vol. 3, no. 1, 2014.

Vallone, R. P. et al., 'The Hostile Media Phenomenon: Biased Perception and Perceptions of Media Bias in Coverage of the Beirut Massacre,' *Journal of Personality and Social Psychology*, vol. 49, no. 3, 1985.

Van Bavel, J.J. and Pereira, A., 'The Partisan Brain: An Identity-Based Model of Political Belief,' *Trends in Cognitive Sciences*, vol. 22, no. 3, 2018.

Van Schaack, B., 'Engendering Genocide: The Akayesu Case before the ICTR,' 2008.

Varela, F.J. et al., *The Embodied Mind: Cognitive Science and Human Experience*, Cambridge, MA: The MIT Press, 1993.

Vidal, C., 'La désinformation en histoire: Données historiques sur les relations entre hutu, tutsi et twa durant la période précoloniale,' *Dialogue*, no. 200, Bruxelles: Imprimerie Litt, September–October 1997.

Viki, G. et al., 'Beyond Secondary Emotions: The Infrahumanization of Out-Groups Using Human-Related and Animal-Related Words,' *Social Cognition*, vol. 24, no. 6, 2006.

Violations of the Laws and Customs of War: Report of Majority and Dissenting Reports of American and Japanese Members of the Commission on Responsibilities, Conference of Paris, 1919, reprinted in *American Journal of International Law*, vol. 14, no. 1–2, 1920.

Wagemakers, J., *A Quietist Jihadi: The Ideology and Influence of Abu Muhammad al-Maqdisi*, Cambridge: Cambridge University Press, 2012.

Waldron, J., *The Harm in Hate Speech*, Cambridge, MA: Harvard University Press, 2012.

Walker, K., 'Four Ways Google Will Help to Tackle Extremism,' *Financial Times*, 18 June 2017.

Waller, J., *Becoming Evil. How Ordinary People Commit Genocide and Mass Killing*, Cambridge: Cambridge University Press, 2002.

We Live as in War: Crackdown on Protesters in the Governorate of Homs, New York, NY: Human Rights Watch, 2011.

Wignell, P. et al., 'A Mixed Methods Empirical Examination of Changes in Emphasis and Style in the Extremist Magazines Dabiq and Rumiyah,' *Perspectives on Terrorism*, vol. 11, no. 2, 2017.

Wiktorowicz, Q., 'The New Global Threat: Transnational Salafis and Jihad,' *Middle East Policy*, vol. 8, no. 4, 2001.

Wiktorowicz, Q., 'Anatomy of the Salafi Movement,' *Studies in Conflict and Terrorism*, vol. 29, no. 3, 2006.

Wilson, R.A., *Writing History in International Criminal Trials*, Cambridge: Cambridge University Press, 2011.

Wilson, R.A., *Incitement on Trial: Prosecuting International Speech Crimes*, Cambridge: Cambridge University Press, 2017.

Wilson, R.A., 'The Hartford Guidelines on Speech Crimes in International Criminal Law,' *EJILTalk!* 31 August 2018.

Wilson, R.A. and Kiper, J., 'Brandenburg in an Era of Populism: Risk Analysis in the First Amendment, Law and Public Affairs' (forthcoming in *University of Pennsylvania Journal of Law & Public Affairs*).

Winter, C., 'The Virtual "Caliphate": Understanding Islamic State's Propaganda Strategy,' *Quilliam Foundation*, July 2015.

Wittgenstein, L., *Philosophical Investigations*, Third Edition, translated by G.E.M. Anscombe, London: Pearson, 1973.

Wolff, L., *The Singing Turk: Ottoman Power and Operatic Emotions on the European Stage from the Siege of Vienna to the Age of Napoleon*, Palo Alto, CA: Stanford University Press, 2016.

Wood, G., 'What ISIS Really Wants,' *The Atlantic*, March 2015.

Woolford, A., 'The Ontological Destruction of Canadian Aboriginal Peoples,' *Genocide Studies and Prevention*, vol. 4, no. 1, 2009.

Worth, R.F., 'Web Tastes Freedom Inside Syria, and It's Bitter,' *New York Times*, 29 September 2010.

York, J. and Kayyali, D., 'Facebook's Real Name Policy Can Cause Real-World Harm for the LGBTQ Community,' *Electronic Frontier Foundation*, 2014. Online. Available HTTP: <https://www.eff.org/deeplinks/2014/09/facebooks-real-name-policy-can-cause-real-world-harm-lgbtq-community> (accessed 27 August 2019).

Zahar, A., 'The ICTR's 'Media' Judgement and the Reinvention of Direct and Public Incitement to Commit Genocide,' *Criminal Law Forum*, vol. 16, 2005.

Zanna, M.P. (ed.), *Advances in Experimental Social Psychology*, vol. 40, San Diego, CA: Elsevier, 2008.

Zarkov, D. and Glasius, M. (eds), *Narratives of Justice In and Out of the Courtroom: Former Yugoslavia and Beyond*, Heidelberg: Springer, 2014.

Zarzūr, 'A. (ed.), *Ibn Taymiyyah, Muqaddima fī uṣūl al-tafsīr*, Kuwait: Dār al-Qur'ān al-Karīm, 1971.

Zeki, S. and Romaya, J.P., 'Neural Correlates of Hate,' *PLoS One*, vol. 3, no. 10, October 2008.

Zimbardo, P.G., *The Lucifer Effect: Understanding How Good People Turn Evil*, New York, NY: Random House, 2007.

Živković, M., 'The Wish to Be a Jew: The Power of the Jewish Trope in the Yugoslav Conflict,' *Cahiers de l'URMIS*, vol. 15, no. 6, 2000.

Index

Note: **Bold** page numbers refer to tables, *italic* page numbers refer to figures and page numbers followed by 'n' denote endnotes.